MW00785594

Sino-Russian Relations in the 21st Century

Jo Inge Bekkevold · Bobo Lo
Editors

Sino-Russian Relations in the 21st Century

Editors
Jo Inge Bekkevold
Centre for Asian Security Studies
Norwegian Institute for Defence Studies
Oslo, Norway

Bobo Lo
Institut français des relations internationales
Brighton, UK

ISBN 978-3-319-92515-8 ISBN 978-3-319-92516-5 (eBook)
https://doi.org/10.1007/978-3-319-92516-5

Library of Congress Control Number: 2018943641

Cover image: © MicroStockHub
Cover design: Tjaša Krivec

Printed on acid-free paper

This Palgrave Macmillan imprint is published by the registered company Springer International Publishing AG part of Springer Nature
The registered company address is: Gewerbestrasse 11, 6330 Cham, Switzerland

Acknowledgements

The inception of this volume was the "New perspectives on Sino-Russian relations" conference organized at the Norwegian Institute for Defence Studies (IFS) in Oslo in September 2014, in the aftermath of the Ukraine crisis. The analyses presented in this volume have since evolved in tandem with developments in Sino-Russian relations over the last few years. We want to express our sincere thanks to the participants at the conference, the contributors in the book, and the anonymous reviewers for their comments that have helped us sharpen our arguments along the way to preparing the final manuscript.

The original conference and this book would not have been possible without generous financial support from the Norwegian Research Council through its NORUSS research programme on The High North/Arctic and Russia, and the support of the Fridtjof Nansen Institute as well as the Norwegian Institute for Defence Studies. Finally, Sarah Roughley and her staff at Palgrave Macmillan deserve special thanks for their patience and in believing in the project and guiding it through the publication process.

Oslo, Norway — Jo Inge Bekkevold
Brighton, UK — Bobo Lo

Contents

Notes on Contributors

Robin Allers is Senior Fellow at the Norwegian Institute for Defence Studies (IFS). He has studied at the Institute d'Études Politiques (Sciences Po) in Paris and at the University of Hamburg where he earned his Ph.D. in History. Before joining IFS in 2009, Allers worked at the History Department of the University of Oslo. His teaching and research interests include NATO, EU as an international security actor, EU-NATO relations, and German and Norwegian security policy. Recent publications include "The framework nation: can Germany lead on security?", *International Affairs* (2016) and "Modern deterrence? NATO's Enhanced Forward Presence on the eastern flank", in K. Friis, *NATO and Collective Defence in the 21st century* (2017).

Jo Inge Bekkevold is Head of Centre for Asian Security Studies at the Norwegian Institute for Defence Studies (IFS). His research focuses on China's rise and Asian security issues. His recent publications include *International Order at Sea: How it is Challenged. How it is Maintained* with Geoffrey Till (Palgrave Macmillan, 2016), *China in the Era of Xi Jinping: Domestic and Foreign Policy Challenges* with Robert S. Ross (Georgetown University Press, 2016), and *Security, Strategy and Military Change in the 21st Century: Cross-Regional Perspectives* with Ian Bowers and Michael Raska (Routledge, 2015). Bekkevold is a former career diplomat.

Stephen Blank has since 2013 been a Senior Fellow at the American Foreign Policy Council in Washington. From 1989–2013 he was a

Professor of Russian National Security Studies at the Strategic Studies Institute of the U.S. Army War College in Pennsylvania. Dr. Blank has been *Professor of National Security Affairs* at the Strategic Studies Institute since 1989. In 1998–2001 he was *Douglas MacArthur Professor of Research* at the War College. He has published widely on Soviet/Russian, U.S., Asian and European military and foreign policies. Dr. Blank's M.A. and Ph.D. are in Russian History from the University of Chicago.

Alexander Cooley is Director of Columbia University's Harriman Institute and the Claire Tow Professor of Political Science at Barnard College in New York. His books include *Great Games, Local Rules: The New Great Power Contest in Central Asia* (Oxford University Press, 2012) and *Dictators without Borders: Power and Money in Central Asia* (Yale University Press, 2017).

Alexander Gabuev is a senior fellow and the chair of the Russia in the Asia-Pacific Program at the Carnegie Moscow Center. His research is focused on Russia's policy toward East and Southeast Asia, political and ideological trends in China, and China's relations with its neighbors—especially those in Central Asia. Prior to joining Carnegie, Gabuev was a member of the editorial board of Kommersant publishing house and served as deputy editor in chief of *Kommersant-Vlast*, one of Russia's most influential newsweeklies. Gabuev has previously worked as a non-resident visiting research fellow at the European Council on Foreign Relations (ECFR) and taught courses on Chinese energy policy and political culture at Moscow State University. Gabuev is a Munich Young Leader of Munich International Security Conference and a member of Council on Foreign and Defense Policy (Russia).

Bjørn Elias Mikalsen Grønning is a Research Fellow at the Norwegian Institute for Defence Studies. He has published on Japan's security, defense and alliance policy, Japan's foreign policy relations with the U.S., China, Russia, the Philippines and Vietnam, missile defense and maritime security. Grønning has served as a visiting research fellow at Keio University and as a specially appointed researcher at Osaka University. His doctoral dissertation examined Japan's security policy response to the contemporary power shift in China's favor.

Christopher Weidacher Hsiung is a Research Fellow at the Norwegian Institute for Defence Studies and Ph.D.-candidate in political science at Oslo University. Hsiung has previously held positions at the Swedish Embassy in Beijing, the Swedish Trade Office in Taipei, at the European University Centre at Peking University, and as a researcher at the Fridtjof Nansen Institute (FNI). In 2014 he was a visiting scholar at the School of International Studies at Peking University. Hsiung has also studied Chinese language in Beijing, Wuhan and Taipei.

Mingjiang Li is an Associate Professor at the S. Rajaratnam School of International Studies, Nanyang Technological University, Singapore. He is also the Coordinator of the China Programme at RSIS. He received his Ph.D. in Political Science from Boston University. His main research interests include China-ASEAN relations, Sino-U.S. relations, Asia Pacific security, and domestic sources of Chinese foreign policy. He is the author (including editor and co-editor) of 14 books. He has published papers in various peer-reviewed journals including *Asian Security, the Journal of Strategic Studies*, *Global Governance*, *Cold War History*, *Journal of Contemporary China*, *The Chinese Journal of International Politics*, *The Chinese Journal of Political Science*, *China: An International Journal*, *China Security*, *Harvard Asia Quarterly*, *Security Challenges*, and *The International Spectator*. Dr. Li frequently participates in various track-two events on East Asian regional security.

Bobo Lo is an Associate Research Fellow with the Russia/NIS Center at the French Institute of International Relations (IFRI), and a Non-Resident Fellow with the Lowy Institute, Sydney, Australia. Dr. Lo writes extensively on Russian foreign policy. His most recent book, *A Wary Embrace: What the China-Russia Relationship Means for the World*, was published by Penguin Random House Australia in April 2017. Lo's *Russia and the New World Disorder* (Brookings and Chatham House, 2015) was previously described by *The Economist* as 'the best attempt yet to explain Russia's unhappy relationship with the rest of the world.' Shorter recent writings include 'Chutzpah and realism: Vladimir Putin and the making of Russian foreign policy, *Russie.NEI.Visions* (forthcoming May 2018); 'An accident waiting to happen: Trump, Putin, and the US-Russia relationship', Lowy Institute Analysis, October 2017; and 'New order for old triangles? The Russia-China-India matrix', *Russie.NEI.Visions*, April 2017.

Angela Poh is a Ph.D. candidate at the S. Rajaratnam School of International Studies, Nanyang Technological University, Singapore. Her research focuses on international sanctions, Chinese foreign policy and Asia-Pacific security. Her articles have been featured in journals such as *The Washington Quarterly* and *Asian Security*. She has also contributed chapters to edited book volumes and commentaries to various international news outlets. She obtained her B.A., summa cum laude, from Marymount Manhattan College in New York and her M.Sc. (Distinction) from the University of Oxford, where she studied as a Clarendon Scholar. She was also a Senior Visiting Student at Peking University School of International Studies from 2015 to 2016.

Tom Røseth is Assistant Professor at the Defence Command and Staff College, Norwegian Defence University College. His main research areas are Russo-Chinese relations, Arctic security policies and Russian foreign policy. Røseth has previously been a Fellow at the Norwegian Institute for Defence Studies, and worked for several years with security policy issues in the Norwegian Defence Establishment. He wrote his Ph.D. on Russia's response to China's rise.

Paul N. Schwartz is a Senior Fellow with the Russia and Eurasia Program at the Center for Strategic and International Studies in Washington, D.C. where he specializes in Russian military affairs. He has written extensively on recent military developments in Russia including its ongoing military modernization efforts, its latest weapons programs, recent campaigns in Ukraine and Syria, and the evolution of its military R&D programs and its defense industry. He has focused especially on Sino-Russian defense cooperation, and has written a number of articles and reports on the topic.

Morena Skalamera is a fellow conducting research on the geopolitics of energy at Harvard University's Belfer center. Her Ph.D. dissertation dealt with European-Russian energy cooperation. Skalamera has also written several articles in the realm of politics as related to the EU-Russia and Russia-China energy security relations.

Bin Yu is Professor of Political Science at Wittenberg University, Ohio, USA. Yu is also senior fellow of the Shanghai Association of American Studies and Senior Fellow at Russian Studies Center of the East China Normal University in Shanghai. He is the author and co-author of six books, and more than 150 book chapters/articles in professional journals, and many op-ed pieces in the media. Since 1999, Yu has provided quarterly assessment of China, Russia and Central Asia for the Center for Strategic and International Studies (CSIS) in Washington D.C. He earned his Ph.D. at Stanford University.

Abbreviations

A2/AD	Anti-access/area-denial
ABM	Anti-Ballistic Missile (Treaty)
ADB	Asian Development Bank
AIIB	Asian Investment and Infrastructure Bank
AL-31	Saturn AL-31 Russian aircraft turbofan engine
APEC	Asia-Pacific Economic Cooperation
ASEAN	Association of Southeast Asian Nations
BCM	Billion Cubic Meters
BP	British Petroleum
BRI	Belt and Road Initiative
BRIC	Group of Brazil, Russia, India and China
BRICS	Group of Brazil, Russia, India, China and South Africa
CAGP	Central Asia-China gas pipeline
CASS	Chinese Academy of Social Sciences
CEO	Chief Executive Officer
CFSP	Common Foreign and Security Policy (EU)
CHNL	Centre for High North Logistics
CIC	China Investment Corporation
CICA	Conference on Interaction and Confidence-Building Measures in Asia
CIS	Commonwealth of Independent States
CNOOC	China National Offshore Oil Corporation
CNPC	China National Petroleum Corporation
COSCO	China Ocean Shipping Company
COSL	China Oilfield Services Ltd

CPSP	Comprehensive partnership of strategic cooperation (between China and Russia)
CSCE	Conference for Security and Cooperation in Europe
CSDP	Common Security and Defence Policy (EU)
CSTO	Collective Security Treaty Organization
CTBT	Comprehensive Nuclear Test Ban Treaty
D-30	Soloviev D-30 Russian aircraft turbofan engine
DF-31AG	Dong Feng 31 (Chinese mobile ICBM)
DPRK	Democratic People's Republic of Korea (North Korea)
E3 + 3	EU Three + 3 (See P5 + 1)
EC	European Community
EEU	Eurasian Economic Union
EEZ	Exclusive Economic Zones
ESPO	East Siberia-Pacific Ocean
EU	European Union
EurAsEC	Eurasian Economic Community
F-22	Lockheed Martin F-22 Raptor (fifth-generation fighter aircraft)
F-35	Lockheed Martin F-35 Lightning II (fifth-generation combat aircraft)
FDI	Foreign Direct Investment
FTA	Free Trade Agreement
G-7	Group of Seven (Canada, France, Germany, Italy, Japan, the United Kingdom and the United States)
G-8	Group of Eight (G-7 + Russia)
G-20	Group of Twenty
GDP	Gross Domestic Product
GICNT	Global Initiative to Combat Nuclear Terrorism
HADR	Humanitarian Assistance and Disaster Relief
ICBM	Inter-continental Ballistic Missile
IL-76	Ilyushin Il-76 (Russian transport aircraft)
IMF	International Monetary Fund
INF	Intermediate-Range Nuclear Forces Treaty
IPO	Initial Public Offering
IRBM	Intermediate Range Ballistic Missile
IS	Islamic State
ISIS	Islamic State of Iraq and Syria (Islamic State of Iraq and al-Sham
IT	Information Technology
J-11B	Shenyang J-11B (Chinese fighter aircraft)
JASDF	Japan Air Self-Defence Forces
JCPOA	Joint Comprehensive Plan of Action (on Iran's nuclear program)

JGSDF	Japan Ground Self-Defence Forces
JMSDF	Japan Maritime Self-Defence Forces
JSDF	Japan Self-Defence Forces
K2	Karshi-Khanabad (military base in Uzbekistan)
LNG	Liquefied Natural Gas
MD	Missile Defense
MENA	Middle East North Africa
MFA	Ministry of Foreign Affairs
Mi-17	Russian transport and combat helicopter
MOD	Ministry of Defence
MOFCOM	Chinese Ministry of Commerce
MOU	Memorandum of Understanding
MTCR	Missile Technology Control Regime
NATO	North Atlantic Treaty Organization
NDB	New Development Bank (formerly BRICS Development Bank)
NDRC	National Development and Reform Commission (China)
NFU	No First Use (Nuclear Weapons Doctrine)
NGO	Non-Governmental Organization
NOCs	National Oil and Gas Companies
NPT	Treaty on the Non-Proliferation of Nuclear Weapons
NSG	Nuclear Suppliers Group
NSR	Northern Sea Route
NSS	National Security Strategy
NWO	New World Order" (Declared by US President George H. W. Bush in 1990)
OBOR	One Belt One Road (Belt and Road Initiative)
ODA	Official Development Assistance
OECD	Organisation for Economic Co-operation and Development
ONGC	Indian Oil and Natural Gas Corporation
OPEC	Organization of the Petroleum Exporting Countries
OSCE	Organization for Security and Co-operation in Europe
P5	Permanent Five (the permanent members of the United Nations Security Council)
P5+1	Permanent Five plus Germany (P5 and Germany joint diplomatic efforts with Iran with regard to its nuclear program)
PESCO	Permanent structured cooperation (EU)
PLA	People's Liberation Army
PLAAF	People's Liberation Army Air Force
PLAN	People's Liberation Army Navy
PPP	Purchasing Power Parity
PRC	People's Republic of China

PYD	Syrian Kurdish Democratic Union Party
RATS	Regional Anti-Terrorism Structure
RFE	Russian Far East
ROK	Republic of Korea (South Korea)
S-400	Russian mobile surface-to-air missile system
SCO	Shanghai Cooperation Organization
SLOC	Sea lines of communication
SOE	State Owned Enterprise
SREB	Silk Road Economic Belt
SRF	Silk Road Fund (China)
Su-27 Flanker	Russian fighter jet
SU-30MK2	Russian multi-role fighter aircraft
Sukhoi Su-35	Russian multi-purpose fighter
THAAD	Terminal High Altitude Area Defense (missile defense system)
TNK-BP	Tyumenskaya Neftyanaya Kompaniya (Tyumen Oil Company)—British Petroleum
TPP	Trans-Pacific Partnership
UN	United Nations
UNCLOS	United Nations Convention on the Law of the Sea
US	United States
USD	United States Dollar
USGS	United States Geological Survey
USSR	Union of Soviet Socialist Republics (Soviet Union)
WB	World Bank
WTO	World Trade Organization
WWI	World War I (First World War)
WWII	World War II (Second World War)
YJ-12	Yingji-12 (Chinese anti-ship cruise missile)
YJ-18	Yingji-18 (Chinese anti-ship and land attack cruise missile)
ZTE	ZTE Corporation (Chinese telecommunications and information technology company)

List of Figures

CHAPTER 1

Introduction

Bobo Lo

It is hard to imagine a warmer political relationship in recent times than that of Russian president Vladimir Putin and Chinese president Xi Jinping. The two not only see each other more frequently than any other pair of international leaders, but their meetings are a publicist's dream, supplementing warm affirmations of friendship with a stream of bilateral agreements. The Putin–Xi dynamic, and Sino-Russian partnership, suggest a world where common interests, mutual trust, and shared purpose are more than just slogans.[1]

This is also a relationship between two of the world's leading powers. In just three decades China has transformed itself from a regional backwater in East Asia into a global actor whose heft is exceeded only by the United States. While Russia's claims to great power status are more debatable, its actions can have global resonance, as we have seen over Ukraine and Syria. The significance of Sino-Russian interaction has been further highlighted against the backdrop of an international environment more turbulent than at any time in the last three decades.

For some observers, the 'strategic partnership' between Beijing and Moscow represents the most serious challenge to the world order.[2] For others, it offers a practical template for a more effective and equitable

B. Lo (✉)
Brighton, UK

J. I. Bekkevold and B. Lo (eds.), *Sino-Russian Relations in the 21st Century*, https://doi.org/10.1007/978-3-319-92516-5_1

global system. Either way, Sino-Russian engagement asks real questions about constructs that have long been taken for granted: the nature and structure of global governance; the universality of norms and values; the role of international institutions; understandings of sovereignty; the meaning and application of power; and interpretations of security, globalization, and regionalism.

There is, however, a danger of being caught up in all the hype. Should we take the professions of likemindedness in Beijing and Moscow at face value? Does the substance of their partnership match up to its ambitious rhetoric? We may indeed be witnessing the evolution of a new type of relationship, one that transcends historical suspicion and much of the conventional wisdom of international relations.[3] But it is legitimate to ask whether the edifice of Sino-Russian partnership is more fragile than it looks, sustained by the suspension of disbelief and sublimation of tensions for the sake of short-term geopolitical goals.

We have, after all, been down this path before. During the Sino-Soviet 'unbreakable friendship' of the 1950s, the two countries maintained a strategic and ideological alliance against the United States and its allies. However, this lasted barely a decade, before relations lapsed into a 30-year period of cold, and occasionally hot, confrontation. We are told that things are different today, that Sino-Russian partnership rests on much more secure foundations. This may be true, but if so it raises real questions about how the two sides arrived at this point. What has changed to create a new reality, both in the relationship itself and its broader international context? And how resilient is this new paradigm?

The collection of essays in this volume sets out to answer these questions by examining recent developments across the whole spectrum of the relationship—from the macro level of grand strategy and geopolitics down to bilateral interaction in specific areas, such as energy, military ties, Central Asia, the Middle East, and the Arctic. The picture that emerges is complex and often contradictory. On the one hand, the Sino-Russian relationship boasts major achievements, and is certainly more effective than many. On the other hand, significant differences and uncertainties remain, notwithstanding determined efforts by both sides to address these. The result is an interaction characterized by ambiguity and fluidity, in which little is decided and much remains possible.

Two Lines of Argument

The open-ended possibilities of the Sino-Russian relationship are reflected in the debate over its current condition and future prospects. In essence, there are two schools of thought, which might loosely be described as 'believers' and 'skeptics'. This division, of course, is imperfect. Even the most bullish view of the relationship would recognize the existence of disagreements and tensions within it. Conversely, most skeptics would admit that there are areas where Beijing and Moscow cooperate quite effectively and to their mutual satisfaction. The difference in evaluation is often one of emphasis, and there are gradations of view within each category. Inevitably, too, assessments are susceptible to the impact of external factors—be it the global financial crash of 2008, Moscow's annexation of Crimea, fluctuating oil prices, political instability in the United States and Europe, or the contrasting fortunes of the Russian and Chinese economies. No relationship operates in a vacuum or develops in strictly linear fashion.

Accentuating the Positive

The main thesis of the believers is that the overall direction of travel in the relationship is one of strategic, economic, and normative convergence. This is reflected not only in the proclamations of leaders, but also in measurable outcomes. In the UN Security Council, for example, Russia and China have worked closely and successfully to counter Western actions aimed at unseating the Assad regime in Syria. Elsewhere, their cooperation has given impetus to emerging international institutions, such as the BRICS (Brazil, Russia, India, China, South Africa) framework, the SCO (Shanghai Cooperation Organization), and the AIIB (Asian Infrastructure Investment Bank). And bilaterally, the two countries have stepped up their interaction, especially following the sharp deterioration of Russia-West relations post-Crimea. They have concluded major energy agreements; their troops participate regularly in large joint military exercises; and high-level arms sales have resumed after a hiatus of several years.

No less importantly for this narrative, the two sides have transcended a difficult past. The territorial issue—and the question of China's 'lost one and a half million square kilometers'—has been resolved.[4] Chinese 'illegal migration', which had been a major source of tension in the

1990s, is off the agenda.[5] And Sino-Russian engagement in Central Asia is characterized more by cooperation than competition, defying the predictions of many Western commentators.

None of this is to suggest that partnership is without its problems. The point, however, is that both sides understand that their core interests are served by ever closer cooperation. Russia needs China as a geopolitical counterweight to the United States; a primary market for its energy and commodity exports; a buyer of high-tech weaponry; and as its principal partner in building a new world order. Beijing values the partnership for similar and compatible reasons: to constrain US 'hegemonic' power; to strengthen China's strategic position in the Asia-Pacific in the face of American and Japanese attempts at containment; and to manage a highly unstable security environment in Eurasia. In the face of these imperatives, such problems as there are in the relationship, such as the unbalanced nature of bilateral trade, are minor and soluble.

The Counter-Narrative

Where the believer sees achievement and opportunity, the skeptical view focuses on continuing contradictions in the relationship. While it acknowledges that this has expanded considerably over the past two decades, it identifies two major problems. The first is that the results of Sino-Russian cooperation are much less impressive than advertised; there is a marked disjunction between rhetoric and substance—whether it is in relation to the BRICS, a common commitment to a new world order, or energy and infrastructural development.

Second, much of the progress in the relationship is brittle. Despite strenuous efforts to minimize tensions, these remain significant and long-term. There is no denying the increasing asymmetry between the two sides, in terms of their individual national development and within the bilateral relationship. China has emerged as the second global superpower, while Russia suffers from slow growth (1.5% in 2017), political atrophy, and social anaesthetization.[6] Beijing, not Moscow, sets the terms of their interaction—expanding Chinese influence across Eurasia; resisting Moscow's lead in confronting the United States; and determining the extent and nature of bilateral energy ties. Well might the Kremlin look to China to alleviate the consequences of the crisis in Russia-West relations. But Chinese leaders have been careful not to align themselves too closely with Putin.

There is little expectation among skeptics of an early crisis in the relationship. Beijing and Moscow evidently recognize that their interests are best served by maximizing the positives and underplaying any disagreements. This is especially so in the current international environment, which resembles more a new world disorder than order.[7] Nevertheless, structural weaknesses in the relationship show little sign of being rectified. Quite the contrary: since early 2014 the balance of power and influence has tilted further toward China, one of the unintended outcomes of Putin's Ukrainian adventure. As Beijing pursues a more ambitious, increasingly globalist foreign policy, the long-time 'division of labor' between Chinese economic primacy and Russian political leadership in Eurasia is being eroded.[8] The public image of closeness and shared interests will become more difficult to sustain in the face of widening inequalities and competing priorities. Instead of strategic convergence, we could see a gradual accumulation of tensions and an increasingly problematic interaction.

The Big Questions

The main lines of the debate have been apparent for much of the post-Cold War era. What has changed is the wider context of the relationship. In recent years, a striking contrast has emerged between the comparative normality of expanding Sino-Russian cooperation, and the growing unpredictability of outside events. In these circumstances, some observers argue, the self-declared 'strategic partnership' has attained a new level. With many of the old certainties having evaporated, Moscow and Beijing are turning to each other more than ever for support and reassurance. And instead of being an outlier, their relationship has become central to the international system, one of the few pillars of stability in an otherwise chaotic world.[9]

The logic of this argument is plausible. What could be more natural than two authoritarian regimes, whose suspicion of the United States and of international disorder is well-documented, working together to promote a common vision of stability, security, and prosperity? The case for convergence is all the more compelling given that China and Russia are two of the world's leading powers, share a 4200 km border, and abhor Western liberal internationalism.

Yet rationality is a subjective—and selective—phenomenon. Just because convergence 'makes sense' does not mean that it is actually happening. Other factors can come into play to bring about a different calculus (and outcomes). It is vital, then, to disentangle the reality of Sino-Russian interaction from its rhetoric and sometimes specious logic. And this means addressing a number of key questions.

Views of the International System

Perhaps the most important of these is how the respective leaderships in Beijing and Moscow view the international system. It has become axiomatic that they are of one mind, and indeed there is much to support this claim. Both are highly critical of American unilateralism and hegemonism; oppose Western moral interventionism and democracy promotion; and call for a new world order in which the emerging powers of the non-West enjoy greater influence and status. Moreover, as noted earlier, they have backed up this talk with concrete actions—such as close policy coordination in the UN Security Council, and expanding the activities of the BRICS and the SCO.

However, it is one thing to agree that the US-led international system is unsatisfactory in many respects; it is quite another to reach a consensus on what to do about it. Should the current system be scrapped altogether, as many in Moscow wish, or merely reformed? And how would a new or reformed world order look? Standard formulations such as the 'democratization of international relations' are scarcely enlightening, for they can mean anything—and nothing. Similarly, the notion of a 'multipolar world order' or 'polycentric system' poses more questions than it answers. The Kremlin is inclined to see the world in triangular terms, dominated by the interaction between America, China, and Russia, in which the latter plays the part of a global 'swing' power.[10] But influential voices in Beijing regard the United States as the only true counterpart to a rising China, and still the global leader[11]; doubt the utility and reliability of Russia as a geopolitical ally; and espouse the virtues of multilateralism rather than great power multipolarity. How are such contrasting perspectives to be reconciled? And, if differences do remain, can they be managed so as to maintain the generally positive trajectory of the relationship?

The Bilateral Relationship in Chinese and Russian Foreign Policy

This leads to another critical question: the role and relative importance of each country in the other's foreign policy. Over the past decade, the Sino-Russian partnership has become much more significant to both parties, as well as for international society in general. Yet the picture remains unclear. In many respects, China is the centerpiece of Putin's foreign policy—the key to an emerging world order, the chief instrument for counterbalancing the geopolitical and normative influence of the United States, the centerpiece of its 'turn to the East', and a means of reinforcing the legitimacy of the Putin regime on the basis of authoritarian solidarity. Yet despite this, the world-view of the Russian elite remains overwhelmingly Westerncentric. The United States continues to be the primary point of strategic reference, the European Union is still Russia's largest trading partner by far,[12] and the generic 'West' exerts considerably greater influence on Russian society than an illusory 'China model' or 'Asian values'.

The dichotomy is even starker when it comes to Russia's place in Chinese views of the world. On the one hand, Beijing sets great store by a good relationship with Moscow. Despite misgivings about Russian behavior over Crimea and the consequent crisis with the West, the Chinese leadership has largely kept these to itself, and prioritized the expansion of bilateral cooperation. On the other hand, partnership with Russia is a second-order preoccupation compared to domestic modernization, relations with the United States, developments in East Asia, or even trade and investment ties with Europe. This, in turn, raises the question of how committed China is to active cooperation with Russia, or whether its priority is more to keep Moscow onside so that it does not obstruct or undermine Chinese goals elsewhere. Tellingly, one of the enduring themes in Beijing's discourse on the relationship is defensive: emphasizing the importance of securing China's 'strategic rear' in the north (Russia) and west (Central Asia), and maintaining strategic flexibility.

The Challenges of Asymmetry

The question of the relative importance of the relationship leads to another recurrent motif: the growing imbalance between a fast rising power and one that is declining in many respects. In 2017, China's GDP was more than eight times larger than Russia's, and the gap is likely to widen. Events have conspired to accentuate the asymmetries of power. The Ukraine crisis, in particular, has shown that China is the closest thing Russia has to a friend, and that Putin has far greater need for Xi than the other way around. At a time when Russia's geopolitical options are constrained, China retains abundant strategic choice, courted by suitors from the West and non-West alike.

To date, Beijing and Moscow have fudged the issue of inequality, mainly by claiming a de facto division of labor and capabilities—Chinese economic primacy alongside Russian political and security ('hard power') leadership. But such has been the spectacular expansion of Chinese influence across post-Soviet Eurasia that one wonders how long this artificial distinction can be sustained. Economic power of the magnitude exerted by Beijing has inescapable geopolitical and security consequences, and will test the long-term resilience of Sino-Russian partnership. Farther afield, the globalization of Chinese foreign policy has implications for Russia, particularly if Xi's vision of China 'moving closer to center stage' in world affairs is realized.[13]

In theory, it should not matter whether a relationship is asymmetrical or 'unbalanced' if both sides benefit from cooperation.[14] Who cares then who is the 'senior' or 'junior' partner (or 'elder' or 'younger' brother[15])? Russian attitudes toward China have also matured in recent years. The 'threat' of a Chinese demographic invasion has receded, while few believe that the sale of weapons to the People's Liberation Army (PLA) endangers national security.[16] On the contrary, the United States is seen to pose a greater existential and normative menace.

Yet this is not to say that the Putin elite has adjusted to Russia being a junior partner of China. The imbalance of power within the relationship remains a source of anxiety to some in Moscow, who worry about over-dependence on China.[17] They are concerned, justifiably, that this will allow Beijing to dictate the terms of their bilateral engagement—whether in the energy sector, the Russian Far East, or post-Soviet Eurasia. The feeling of strategic dependence has been heightened by the crisis between Russia and the West, and the reluctance of the Chinese to step into the vacuum left by the fall in European trade and investment. It may be that Russian anxieties will be alleviated only by a corresponding and definitive deterioration in China's relations with the West.[18]

There is also a critical psychological dimension to asymmetry. Over the past decade, Putin has staked his legitimacy on the idea of a resurgent Russia second to none. This applies mainly vis-à-vis the United States, but is also relevant to China. Indeed, the stigma of a neocolonial dependency is all the greater given that Russians have historically harbored a sense of superiority toward their southern neighbor.

And while they have moved on in important respects, old attitudes have not disappeared. It grates that the economic relationship, with the obvious exception of arms exports, closely resembles China's ties with developing countries in Africa and Latin America—natural resource exports in return for manufacturing imports.

Bridging the Gap Between Rhetoric and Reality

These hang-ups have undermined cooperation in the past. The protracted negotiations over major energy deals testify to the 'drag' effect of non-commercial factors, on top of the usual differences over pricing. A wary conservatism also helps account for the slowness of cooperation in Central Asia, where Russian anxiety over Chinese influence has, until recently, restricted the development of regional structures such as the SCO. There are signs of a more flexible and welcoming stance since 2014, but it remains to be seen whether this is a product of particular circumstances—namely, the crisis in Moscow's relations with the West—or whether its signals a structural shift in Russian thinking.

Chinese attitudes toward Russia are even more difficult to track. Beijing talks up Russia's stature in the world ('greatness') and Putin's policies. He himself scores very well with the Chinese public, who admire him as a strong leader willing and able to put the United States in its place. But it is important to distinguish between admiration for Putin the man, and more critical views of Russia as a stagnant polity and non-modernizing economy. It is commonly asserted that the support Beijing and Moscow give each other reinforces the legitimacy and stability of their respective regimes. But the evidence to back up such claims is sketchy. While some in Beijing criticized the West for provoking the initial crisis with Russia over Ukraine, there is concern that Moscow's actions since then have further destabilized the international order. In short, as with many other aspects of the relationship, Chinese views of Putin's Russia are marked by ambiguities and contradictions. It is by no means clear whether positive feelings toward Putin will translate into a broader and lasting likemindedness.

Reconciling Chinese and Russian Interests

Much will depend on the synergies between Chinese and Russian interests—in energy and military cooperation, Central Asia and the Middle

East, the Arctic and Northeast Asia (including the Russian Far East). On the face of things, there is considerable scope for progress across the board. In energy, for example, Russia is the world's leading oil and gas exporter, and China the largest importer. Both countries have an obvious interest in managing conflicts in central Eurasia and the Asia-Pacific. Russia is in sore need of foreign direct investment, while China has dramatically stepped up its overseas economic activities in recent years. In Northeast Asia, Beijing and Moscow are keen to limit the exercise of American power, while also containing North Korean excesses. And in the Arctic, there are possibilities—albeit in the longer term—for cooperation in connection with the Northern Sea Route (NSR) and the development of Russia's natural resources in the far north.

Yet for every plus there is a downside, real or potential. Thus, in energy China and Russia have a complementary relationship, which they wish to develop. But they naturally aim to do so in the most advantageous way for themselves, notwithstanding talk of 'win-win' outcomes. Energy security for one side is not necessarily the same for the other. Each aspires to dominate the Asian (and global) energy market: Russia through its control of pipelines and sale of resources, China by exploiting low oil and gas prices and diversifying supply. Each uses the other as leverage with other partners, meaning that their own cooperation is necessarily complicated by external and often non-economic considerations. These are not necessarily deal-killers, but they challenge optimistic forecasts about the linear growth of energy ties.

Similarly, in Central Asia the perceived benefits of Sino-Russian cooperation are counterbalanced by the heightened risk of tensions between them. Cooperation, yes, but on whose terms? Beijing and Moscow have tried to finesse this question by denying the existence of any potential conflict and instead proclaiming consensus. Thus, during Xi's visit to Moscow in May 2015, they agreed that China's Silk Road Economic Belt (SREB)—part of its overall Belt and Road Initiative (BRI)—and Putin's Eurasian Economic Union (EEU) were complementary projects. But the proof lies not in such motherhood statements, but in actions on the ground. So far, the scorecard reads unimpressively. In the first two years of the agreement, Beijing received some 40 infrastructural project proposals, all of which it rejected as unviable.[19]

This raises larger questions about Sino-Russian interaction. If China's strategic as well as economic footprint in Eurasia continues to grow at its present rate, how will the Kremlin react? Will it reconcile itself to the apparently inevitable, or will it take vigorous measures to reassert its once dominant influence in the region? There is much talk about a Greater Eurasia, in which China and Russia effectively co-manage a vast strategic space extending from Central Europe to East Asia.[20] But so far this vision appears aspirational at best, a somewhat desperate attempt by Moscow to sustain the EEU, manage Chinese influence, and talk up Russia's credentials as a game-maker. What if Greater Eurasia suffers the same fate as previous attempts at Moscow-led integration? Would the Putin regime then still believe that uniting against the United States was more important than containing Chinese influence?

There are few clear answers at this stage. But perhaps that is the point—there are plenty of opportunities in the Sino-Russian relationship, but also significant limitations and risks. Potential does not equate to achievement. And public declarations of unity do not necessarily reflect consensus, but may simply paper over the cracks.

Strategic Shocks and the Strategic Partnership

One of the biggest challenges the Sino-Russian relationship faces over the next decade is to sustain cooperation in the face of strategic shocks. Sometimes these may give impetus to closer convergence, as in the case of the global financial crisis and the Russian annexation of Crimea. But there are also factors that could inhibit partnership or give rise to serious tensions between Moscow and Beijing. In 2015–2016, the combination of recession in Russia and the slowing of the Chinese economy had a damaging impact on bilateral trade and investment.[21] Similarly, the slump in global energy prices during that period delayed progress in implementing key agreements. If prices stay low over the next few years (as many forecast), one of the pillars of Sino-Russian cooperation will be severely weakened.

Ongoing instability in the heart of Eurasia also opens up plenty of possibilities, both for enhanced cooperation and more intense competition. Moscow and Beijing may make common cause in regional security management—against Islamist radicalism or grassroots democratic movements. But their interests could come into conflict in the event of an unstable political succession in, say, Kazakhstan.[22] The separation of political and economic interests, increasingly tenuous today, may become non-existent in a few years' time. And, as already noted, a globally assertive Chinese foreign policy could change the whole dynamic of their interaction.

The single most important variable could be the state of the US–China relationship. If Washington and Beijing are able to reach a long-term strategic accommodation, the gains of the Sino-Russian partnership over the past two decades may turn out to be increasingly limited and somewhat fragile. Conversely, if the current cycle of US–China tensions degenerates into open rivalry, the pressures for strategic and normative convergence between the Kremlin and Zhongnanhai could become irresistible. Washington's decision to identify *both* China and Russia as geopolitical foes,[23] and Donald Trump's public desire for a trade war with China,[24] are likely to prove highly counter-productive, giving impetus to a bona fide authoritarian alliance between Moscow and Beijing.

The Many Dimensions of Sino-Russian Relations

This volume is divided into four parts. It begins with an examination of the role and influence of grand strategy in Sino-Russian relations—how Russia fits into Beijing's evolving thinking about the world, and the place of China in Putin's 'polycentric system of international relations'. **Li Mingjiang** and **Angela Poh** emphasize that a common desire in Moscow and Beijing to challenge US hegemony has brought them closer despite lingering problems of mistrust and asymmetry. The steady institutionalization of ties, bilateral and multilateral, has moved their relationship from an 'axis of convenience' to a fully fledged strategic partnership.

Alexander Gabuev highlights the impact on Sino-Russian partnership of the conflict in Ukraine and the consequent crisis in Russia's relations with the United States and Europe. With no prospect of a return to 'business as usual' with the West, Moscow has gravitated toward Beijing—and far more quickly and comprehensively than anyone anticipated. And although Russia has become the junior partner in a relationship characterized by 'asymmetric interdependence', it now recognizes this as both unavoidable and manageable.

The second part of the book explores a number of bilateral and regional aspects of Sino-Russian engagement. **Morena Skalamera** focuses on the pivotal energy relationship, in particular the mega-deals in oil and gas concluded in 2013–2014. She argues that even before the Ukraine crisis Moscow was already 'looking East', as much for economic as geopolitical and security reasons, while Beijing was keen to diversify its energy imports. As in other areas of the relationship, China increasingly calls the shots. Yet this has not precluded constructive engagement.

One of the boom areas of Sino-Russian partnership has been military cooperation, where there has been an upsurge in sales of hi-tech weaponry as well as ever more ambitious joint military exercises. **Paul Schwartz** views such developments as evidence of a growing alignment between Russia and China, based on increased trust and a common desire to counter Western strategic pressure. Although a true military alliance remains improbable, international circumstances suggest that this alignment will remain for the foreseeable future.

Sino-Russian interaction in Central Asia has become an increasingly significant part of their larger relationship, with both positive and negative aspects. Both sides have talked up their cooperation, yet such rhetoric masks significant contradictions. In his chapter, **Alexander Cooley** speaks of 'public cooperation and private rivalry'. He differs from several other contributors to this volume by arguing that Beijing 'does not share Moscow's fundamental counter-hegemonic disposition toward the West.' This disjunction reinforces a growing asymmetry in Central Asia, with Russia's acute need for a non-Western geostrategic partnership enabling China to set the terms of their engagement.

Jo Inge Bekkevold's chapter considers a hitherto neglected area of Sino-Russian relations, the Middle East. He identifies a major strategic shift whereby the once hegemonic position of the United States is giving to a new great power triangle in the region. He agrees that Russia and China have more in common with each other than with the United States, but observes nevertheless that their goals and tools of influence differ substantially. This, he notes, could become a source of tension between them.

The change in Russian attitudes toward China is reflected in their increasingly positive engagement in the Arctic, the subject of **Christopher Hsiung** and **Tom Roseth**'s chapter. Whereas Moscow had previously been reluctant to accept China as a legitimate player there, it now recognizes the vital importance of Chinese investment, especially in energy ventures such as the Yamal LNG project. The ongoing crisis in Russia-West relations could give further momentum to Sino-Russian cooperation in the Arctic, as elsewhere, although significant challenges remain.

Part III explores some of the larger international issues, such as Chinese and Russian attitudes to global order and governance.

Bin Yu highlights the distinctive approaches of Beijing and Moscow, which arise out of contrasting historical legacies, comparative advantages (Russia's military power; China's economic strengths), and different experiences with the US-led international system. One theme that emerges very clearly, however, is that Washington's actions—'punishing Russia and hedging China'—have brought them closer together, while simultaneously weakening the West.

Stephen Blank's chapter examines the global triangular dynamic between the United States, Russia, and China. He highlights the growing asymmetry of the Sino-Russian partnership, and concludes that it is resulting in a de facto alliance based on ideological and strategic convergence. He warns against American complacency, and argues that the closeness of ties between Moscow and Beijing, together with Washington's failings, have real implications for the United States and for international security.

Bjorn Gronning looks at the impact of Sino-Russian partnership on Japanese policy. He notes Japan's vulnerability to coordinated military pressure from Beijing and Moscow, and its particular stake in the preservation of the US-led global order. He highlights two apparently contradictory perceptions in Tokyo: first, the view that the growth of Sino-Russian ties reflects a tactical rather than strategic convergence; and, second, the belief that China's rise makes it necessary for Japan to consider autonomous strategic engagement with Russia, even in the face of US objections.

Similarly, **Robin Allers** analyzes recent trends in European responses to China and Russia individually and to the Sino-Russian relationship. He argues that European policy 'has to be understood within the larger context of great power relations,' and US strategic choices in particular. He notes the general tendency to underestimate Europe as a political and security actor, and asserts that it can and should play a key role in defending a liberal rules-based international order.

In the concluding section of the book, **Jo Inge Bekkevold** highlights some of the principal themes covered in this volume, notably the growing convergence of interests and perceptions between Moscow and Beijing, and the widening imbalance of power in their relationship. He considers the implications of Sino-Russian partnership for twenty-first century international relations, and suggests some scenarios for how [the Sino-Russian relationship] might evolve over the next decade and beyond.

Notes

1. Huang (2018).
2. See, for example Chase et al. (2017). The latest US National Security Strategy (December 2017) does not specifically mention Sino-Russian partnership, but asserts that 'China and Russia challenge American power, influence, and interests, attempting to erode American security and prosperity', White House (2017), p. 2.
3. Fu (2016), p. 97.
4. As a result of the 'unequal treaties' of Aigun (1858), Peking (1860), and Tarbagatai (1864), China ceded much of the present-day Russian Far East. It lost further territory in Central Asia in the 1880s. In 2004, the two sides reached a final border settlement, ratified the following year by China's National People's Congress and the Russian Duma. The formal transfer of territory took place in July 2008.
5. Lukin (2018), p. 19.
6. Kolesnikov (2018).
7. Lo (2015).
8. Ibid., pp. 149–150. Russian and Chinese scholars acknowledge the increasingly anachronistic nature of this 'division of labor'—remarks by Timofei Bordachev and Yang Cheng at a conference on 'Shaping Eurasia: What Convergence between China's Silk Road and the Eurasian Union?', French Institute of International Affairs, Paris, 15 September 2016.
9. Karaganov (2016a).
10. Lo (2017), pp. 80–81, Karaganov (2016a), Trenin (2017).
11. Wang (2015), Wang (2017), Yan (2015).
12. In 2017, the EU accounted for 42.2% of Russia's external trade, compared to China's share of 14.9%—all this despite three years of EU sanctions and Russian counter-sanctions, see European Commission (2018).
13. Xi Jinping report to the 19th Congress of the Chinese Communist Party, 18 October 2017, Xi (2017).
14. This is a key argument of Marcin Kaczmarski's book, *Russia-China Relations in the Post-Crisis International Order*.
15. The formulation 'elder brother/younger brother' was used to describe the Sino-Soviet relationship in the 1950s.
16. Gabuev (2016), p. 23.
17. Gabuev observed in late 2015 that 'China is now the Number One source of anxiety for Russia's high-ranking officials, state capitalists, and oligarchs', Gabuev (2015).
18. See Kaczmarski (2018).
19. Gabuev (2017).
20. Karaganov (2016b), Bordachev (2017).

21. Bilateral trade, which had reached USD 95 billion in 2014, fell to USD 64 billion in 2015 and increased only barely to USD 66 billion in 2016. Conversely, in 2017 Russian economic recovery, higher oil prices, and renewed political and economic confidence in China, provided favorable conditions for a boost in bilateral trade—up to USD 84 billion.
22. Kazakhstan President Nursultan Nazarbaev will be 78 in July 2018.
23. The US National Defense Strategy (January 2018) states: 'The central challenge to US prosperity is *the reemergence of long-term, strategic competition* [original italics] by ... revisionist powers. It is increasingly clear that China and Russia want to shape a world consistent with their authoritarian model ...', Department of Defense (2018).
24. Diamond (2018).

Literature

Bordachev, Timofei. 2017. Energetic Russia and the Greater Eurasia Community. Valdai Club, December 28. http://valdaiclub.com/a/highlights/main-results-of-2017-energetic-russia/.

Chase, Michael S., Evan S. Medeiros, J. Stapleton Roy, Eugene B. Rumer, Robert Sutter, and Richard Weitz. 2017. *Russia-China Relations: Assessing Common Ground and Strategic Fault Lines*, NBR Special Report #66, July. The National Bureau of Asian Research, Seattle, Washington, DC. http://www.nbr.org/publications/specialreport/pdf/free/09152017/SR66_Russia-ChinaRelations_July2017.pdf.

Department of Defense. 2018. 2018 National Defense Strategy of the United States: Sharpening the American Military's Competitive Edge. Available at https://www.defense.gov/Portals/1/Documents/pubs/2018-National-Defense-Strategy-Summary.pdf.

Diamond, Jeremy. 2018. Trump Hits China with Tariffs, Heightening Concerns of Global Trade War. *CNN*, March 23. https://edition.cnn.com/2018/03/22/politics/donald-trump-china-tariffs-trade-war/index.html.

European Commission. 2018. European Union, Trade in Goods with Russia. Directorate-General for Trade. http://trade.ec.europa.eu/doclib/docs/2006/september/tradoc_113440.pdf. Accessed 7 June 2018.

Fu, Ying. 2016. How China Sees Russia. *Foreign Affairs*, January/February. https://www.foreignaffairs.com/articles/china/2015-12-14/how-china-sees-russia.

Gabuev, Alexander. 2015. A Reality Check for Russia's China Pivot. Carnegie Moscow Center, September 29. Available at http://carnegie.ru/2015/09/29/reality-check-for-russia-s-china-pivot/iiar.

Gabuev, Alexander. 2016. Friends with Benefits? Russian-Chinese Relations after the Ukraine Crisis. Carnegie Moscow Center, June 29. Available at http://carnegie.ru/2016/06/29/friends-with-benefits-russian-chinese-relations-after-ukraine-crisis-pub-63953.

Gabuev, Alexander. 2017. Belt and Road to Where? Carnegie Moscow Center, December 8. https://carnegie.ru/2017/12/08/belt-and-road-to-where-pub-74957.

Huang, Kristin. 2018. Why Vladimir Putin's and Xi Jinping's Mutual Admiration Society Looks Like It's Here to Stay. *South China Morning Post*, March 19. http://www.scmp.com/news/china/diplomacy-defence/article/2137905/why-vladimir-putin-and-xi-jinpings-mutual-admiration.

Kaczmarski, Marcin. 2015. *Russia-China Relations in the Post-crisis International Order*. London and New York: Routledge.

Kaczmarski, Marcin. 2018. The Decreasing Asymmetry in Russia–China Relations. Finnish Institute of International Affairs Comment No. 6, February. https://storage.googleapis.com/upi-live/2018/02/comment6_russia-china.pdf.

Karaganov, Sergei. 2016a. Global Challenges and Russia's Foreign Policy. *Russia in Global Affairs*, November 20. http://eng.globalaffairs.ru/pubcol/Global-Challenges-and-Russias-Foreign-Policy-18468.

Karaganov, Sergei. 2016b. From East to West, or Greater Eurasia. *Russia in Global Affairs*, October 25. http://eng.globalaffairs.ru/pubcol/From-East-to-West-or-Greater-Eurasia-18440.

Kolesnikov, Andrei. 2018. A Mandate for Stagnation: After Russia's Presidential Election. Carnegie Moscow Center, March 22. https://carnegie.ru/commentary/75859.

Lo, Bobo. 2015. *Russia and the New World Disorder*. Washington, DC: Brookings and Chatham House.

Lo, Bobo. 2017. *A Wary Embrace: What the China–Russia Relationship Means for the World*. Sydney: Penguin Random House.

Lukin, Alexander. 2018. A Russian perspective on the Sino-Russian rapprochement. *Asia Policy* 13 (1, January): 19–25.

Trenin, Dmitri. 2017. Russia's Evolving Grand Eurasia Strategy: Will It Work? Carnegie Moscow Center, July 20. http://carnegie.ru/2017/07/20/russia-s-evolving-grand-eurasia-strategy-will-it-work-pub-71588.

Wang, Jisi. 2015. The "Two Orders" and the Future of China–US Relations. *ChinaFile*, July 9. https://www.chinafile.com/reporting-opinion/two-way-street/two-orders-and-future-china-us-relations.

Wang, Jisi. 2017. Sino-US Ties Can Avoid Thucydides Trap. *Global Times*, November 11. http://www.globaltimes.cn/content/1074642.shtml.

White House. 2017. *National Security Strategy of the United States*, Washington, DC, December. https://www.whitehouse.gov/wp-content/uploads/2017/12/NSS-Final-12-18-2017-0905.pdf.

Xi, Jinping. 2017. Report to the 19th Congress of the Chinese Communist Party, October 18. Available at http://www.xinhuanet.com/english/download/Xi_Jinping's_report_at_19th_CPC_National_Congress.pdf.

Yan, Xuetong. 2015. Why a Bipolar World Is More Likely Than a Unipolar or Multipolar One. *The World Post*, June 22. http://www.huffingtonpost.com/yan-xuetong/bipolar-world-likely_b_7104590.html.

PART I

Grand Strategies

CHAPTER 2

The Indispensable Partner: Russia in China's Grand Strategy

Mingjiang Li and Angela Poh

In 2008, Bobo Lo characterised the China–Russia relationship as an 'axis of convenience', and suggested that cooperation between the two countries was driven by 'expediency and opportunism' rather than by genuine like-mindedness.[1] Challenging such a perspective, China's former Vice Foreign Minister, Fu Ying, wrote in a *Foreign Affairs* article some years later that 'the Chinese-Russian relationship is a stable strategic partnership and by no means a marriage of convenience: it is complex, sturdy, and deeply rooted'.[2] In this chapter, we argue that while their engagement has remained 'largely pragmatic and unsentimental',[3] China and Russia's common desire to challenge US hegemony and create a multipolar international system has driven them to strengthen their bilateral ties despite lingering mutual mistrust. Moreover, the various bilateral and multilateral cooperation mechanisms established by both countries since the end of the Cold War have provided a solid foundation for them

M. Li (✉) · A. Poh
S. Rajaratnam School of International Studies (RSIS), Nanyang Technological University, Singapore, Singapore
e-mail: ismjli@ntu.edu.sg

A. Poh
e-mail: MPOH001@e.ntu.edu.sg

J. I. Bekkevold and B. Lo (eds.), *Sino-Russian Relations in the 21st Century*, https://doi.org/10.1007/978-3-319-92516-5_2

to move beyond an 'axis of convenience' towards a genuine 'comprehensive strategic partnership of coordination'.[4]

Focusing largely on the Chinese perspective, this chapter proceeds in three sections. First, we analyse China's vision of the role Russia plays in its broader international strategy. Second, we examine developments in the post-Cold War relationship, and argue that Sino-Russian relations have deepened over time, especially under President Xi Jinping. Finally, we discuss how the relationship could evolve in the near future.

Defining China's Grand Strategy

We need first to define what we mean by China's 'grand strategy'. Many analysts have focused on Beijing's long-term goals. In a controversial work, Michael Pillsbury posits that instead of merely defending its core interests or wishing to become as powerful as the US, China aims to achieve global economic, cultural and military dominance.[5] Other observers are more nuanced in their assessments of China's ambitions. Michael Swaine, for instance, argues that China has developed a 'calculative grand strategy' aimed at achieving three inter-related objectives: (i) preserving domestic order and well-being; (ii) defending against external threats to national sovereignty; and (iii) ensuring maximum geopolitical influence in the Asia-Pacific region and beyond. To support these objectives, it has pursued market-led economic growth; cultivated positive relations with all states, particularly the major powers; exercised restraint in the use of force; and expanded its involvement in regional and global affairs.[6]

According to Avery Goldstein, Beijing has adopted various policy tools in support of its goals, including reassurance, great power diplomacy and partnership-building.[7] June Dreyer contends that China's grand strategy exhibits both threatening and peaceful intentions, as illustrated by its military modernisation and growing activism in the resolution of international problems.[8] Such a grand strategy is essentially a compromise between 'soft' diplomacy to create an environment conducive to China's domestic development, and 'hard' coercion underpinned by prudent military modernisation to protect China's national interests.[9] Zhao Minghao argues that China's grand strategy reflects an 'internal-external rebalancing'. Internally, the country relies on bold reforms to achieve rapid economic growth. Externally, China aims to enhance its position as a global power and maximise its national security. To achieve the latter, China has sought to develop an international coalition with the developing world, particularly the BRICS (Brazil, Russia, India, China, South Africa) countries.[10] Rosemary Foot suggests that China's grand strategy is a combination of accommodation with the existing US-dominated global order and a 'hedging' policy to better protect China's interests.[11]

A small group of scholars have questioned whether a Chinese grand strategy exists at all. Stig Stenslie posits that while Chinese leaders may have engaged in strategic thinking about great power goals, they have yet to develop a coherent grand strategy. Instead, they are pragmatic, inward-looking and constantly engaged in 'short-term fire-fighting'.[12] Mark Frazier argues that even if the Chinese leaders had any grand strategy, competing interests within the Chinese body politic would make it very difficult to implement.[13]

Chinese Perspectives on Grand Strategy

China's leaders have long promoted 'peaceful development' as the country's grand strategy, and this has been echoed by the Chinese academic community. Some overseas Chinese scholars, too, maintain that Beijing's long-term strategic goal is to 'catch up with developed countries in building a prosperous and strong modern country (*fuqiang de xiandai guojia*), with a high degree of internal harmony'.[14] Consequently, Chinese foreign policy is designed to help maintain national security and regime stability, secure access to natural resources for domestic economic development and boost its international influence.[15]

Other analysts argue, however, that China is keen to become a global power. Ye Zicheng links this aspiration to the resolution of various internal challenges and the careful handling of China's principal bilateral relationships.[16] The prominent scholar, Yan Xuetong, asserts that China should attempt to establish an alternative world order. This would be based on a China-led morality, instead of the military and economic strength that is at the core of the existing US hegemonic system.[17]

Since the 18th National Congress of the Communist Party of China in 2012, Xi Jinping has consistently promoted the 'China Dream', otherwise known as the 'great rejuvenation of the Chinese nation', as an overarching political ideology. This trend has been enshrined following the 19th Party Congress in 2017, which saw the hyper-concentration of power in Xi's hands, and the institutionalisation of 'Xi Jinping Thought on Socialism with Chinese Characteristics for a New Era'. Such concepts reflect the political elite's long-cherished dream of rejuvenating the Middle Kingdom, and restoring China's pre-eminent position in the world—morphing from a backward, isolated country into one that is rich, powerful (*fuguo qiangjun*), and glorious.[18] The domestic and foreign policies pursued by the leadership, including towards Russia, are intended to help realise this 'dream'.

Russia's Place in Chinese Grand Strategy

The Chinese leadership has high hopes for Russia in three different aspects: (i) shared positions on the international order; (ii) countering US hegemony, particularly in the Asia-Pacific region; and (iii) ensuring stability in Central Asia.

The International Order

While Russia remains a weaker power compared to the United States, the European Union and Japan, its strategic significance to China should not be underestimated given that its views on the post-Cold War international order are the closest to Beijing's. Despite substantial economic cooperation with the West, China and Russia perceive the United States and Europe as unfairly stigmatising and pressurising them for political gain. As a result, they have often relied on each other for support, especially on issues relating to multipolarity, sovereignty, non-intervention and human rights.

As early as April 1997, during Chinese president Jiang Zemin's visit to Russia, the two countries issued a joint statement in support of a multipolar world and the establishment of a new international order,[19] a stance that was to be reiterated on many subsequent occasions. More recently, in 2016 Vladimir Putin and Xi Jinping signed a joint statement vowing to 'strengthen global strategic stability' and to support the principle of non-intervention. They condemned the attempts by some countries, namely the United States, to interfere 'in the internal affairs of other states with the aim of forging a change of legitimate governments'.[20] This common view of the international order has given real impetus to their efforts to enhance the strategic partnership.

The Asia-Pacific

China is keen to enlist Russia's support in mitigating American influence in the Asia-Pacific region and beyond. It views the expansion of NATO's security role in Eastern Europe and Washington's efforts to consolidate its security alliances and partnerships in East Asia as a 'dual containment' of China and Russia.[21] China's former ambassador to Russia, Liu Guchang, argues that the US and its allies have become more provocative in East Asia, challenging China and seeking to undermine its relations with neighbouring countries. The deepening of Sino-Russian collaboration, in Liu's view, would help China deal with these challenges, and counter unilateralist and hegemonic tendencies in international affairs.[22]

Chinese decision makers and analysts believe that regular military exercises with Russia play an especially valuable role in this context. The Joint Sea-2014 naval exercise, for instance, took place amidst rising tensions between China and Japan over the Diaoyu/Senkaku islands. Beijing may have hoped that the proximity of the exercises to the islands might help to exert pressure on Tokyo. But it is questionable whether such calculus is justified. Russia has so far refrained from taking China's side in its maritime disputes with Japan and other countries in the region, and pursued its own interests instead. Thus, warm relations with Beijing did not stop it from fulfilling a contract to deliver six Kilo-class submarines to Vietnam—a move with clear implications for China's security interests in the South China Sea.

Moscow has been more helpful on the 'history issue'. In a May 2014 joint statement, China and Russia proclaimed that they opposed any act of historical revisionism that could threaten the post-WWII order.[23] They also co-organised various activities to commemorate the seventieth anniversary of Japan's capitulation in WWII. Beijing has indicated, too, its interest in working with Moscow to build a new security mechanism in Northeast Asia, in opposition to the US–Japan alliance.[24] In June 2016, Xi and Putin issued a joint statement expressing 'concern over the [US's] unilateral deployment of anti-missile systems all over the world', notably the Aegis Ashore ballistic missile defense system in Europe, and the Terminal High Altitude Area Defense (THAAD) in Northeast Asia.[25] More broadly, Beijing and Moscow have called for a new regional security architecture in the Asia-Pacific, based on 'mutual trust, mutual benefit, equality and collaboration'.[26] This would be open, transparent, equal and inclusive—and therefore a better model than the existing US-centred hub-and-spokes system.[27]

Central Asia

China sees Russia as a useful partner in maintaining stability in Central Asia—a region vital for peace and stability in its western province of Xinjiang.[28] Ever since the disintegration of the Soviet Union, Central Asia has been an area of geopolitical contention. Consequently, Beijing and Moscow must strengthen their strategic collaboration in the region, both in order to contain major power rivalry and to address daunting socio-economic and political challenges in the five Central Asian republics.[29] The US withdrawal of troops from Afghanistan in 2014 poses further challenges to Central Asian security, underlining the importance of Sino-Russian security cooperation in the region.[30]

At the same time, Beijing is sensitive to Russian concerns about China's growing presence in Central Asia—a region Moscow regards as its sphere of influence. Xi has taken care to reassure Putin that China's Belt and Road Initiative (BRI) does not reflect a desire to assert dominance.[31] In May 2015, Moscow and Beijing agreed to combine Putin's Eurasian Economic Union (EEU) project with China's Silk Road Economic Belt (SREB), and the two sides have since broadened the idea of regional cooperation to embrace the concept of a Greater Eurasia. Beijing's caution stems partly from its past experience with Moscow. Russian objections had earlier blocked Chinese efforts to develop the economic component of the Shanghai Corporation Organization (SCO), for example through the establishment of a Free Trade Agreement (FTA) and SCO Development Bank. It remains to be seen whether Beijing can continue to manage Russian sensitivities given the continuing rapid growth of Chinese influence in Central Asia.

Developments in the Sino-Russian Relationship After the Cold War

We argue that the Sino-Russian relationship has gone through three different phases from the end of the Cold War to the present day: (1) positive but cautious (1991–2000); (2) 'axis of convenience', with important foundations established (2001–2011); and (3) extensive cooperation across a wide range of areas, moving towards a qualitative change in relations (2012–2017).

Phase I: 1991–2000

Beijing established formal diplomatic ties with the newly independent Russia in 1991 soon after the collapse of the Soviet Union. In 1992, the foundation for bilateral relations was established during Yeltsin's first visit to China, when the two countries issued a joint statement on friendly state-to-state relations. Bilateral ties were consolidated following Jiang Zemin's visit to Russia in September 1994, with the commitment to a 'constructive partnership of good neighbourliness, friendship and mutually beneficial cooperation'. Yeltsin's visit to China in April 1996 saw Beijing and Moscow upgrade their relationship to a 'partnership of strategic coordination based on equality and benefit and oriented towards the 21st century'.[32] In the same year, they established the 'Shanghai Five' grouping, which later became the SCO.

China and Russia also set up mechanisms on cooperation in economics, science and technology. The institutionalisation of bilateral exchanges, especially at the presidential and prime ministerial levels, became a key feature of the strategic partnership. To enhance security cooperation, the respective defence ministers signed an agreement in 1993 on the mutual non-use of nuclear weapons, and in 1996–1997 they concluded further agreements on military confidence-building measures. Bilateral trade, however, remained modest, amounted to a mere USD 5.7 billion in 1999,[33] and being largely restricted to cheap manufactured goods.

Sino-Russian relations during this period can be characterised as positive but cautious. Beijing and Moscow had emerged from their respective domestic crises (Tiananmen and the disintegration of the former Soviet Union) and were keen to build positive ties, particularly to counter Washington's dominant influence. However, negative historical memories—most notably over the Tsarist annexation of large areas of the Qing empire in the nineteenth century, and the Sino-Soviet split after 1960—continued to pose challenges to the relationship.

Phase II: 2001–2011

Sino-Russian relations reached another milestone in July 2001 with the 20-year Treaty of Good-Neighbourliness, Friendship, and Cooperation, which laid the legal foundation for the long-term development of their 'strategic partnership of collaboration'. The next decade witnessed new levels of cooperation in many areas of the relationship—coordination on global issues, trade and investment, energy, military and security affairs, Central Asia, and culture and human contacts. This progress established the foundation for the strategic partnership that Beijing and Moscow today.

Beijing and Moscow instituted a number of measures to develop economic ties. In August 2008, China's State Council announced a policy to use the yuan for foreign trade in China's northeastern border regions on an experimental basis. Both sides committed themselves to gradually substituting their own currencies for the US dollar in bilateral transactions. By the end of 2010, the Russian ruble became the second most traded currency in China's foreign trade settlements after the Malaysian ringgit. In addition, the two governments approved plans for investment development and cooperation between China's northeast and Russia's Far East and Eastern Siberian regions.

China and Russia benefited from the upgrade of the 'Shanghai Five' to the SCO in 2001, as well as from improved security conditions in Central Asia. During Putin's 2004 visit to China, they finally settled the 4300 kilometre-long common border—a vital step in deepening strategic trust between them.

Societal links also grew significantly from the mid-2000s. The Sino-Russian People-to-People Cooperation Council played a leading role in organising various major events, such as 'the Year of China' and 'the Year of Russia' in 2006–2007 and 'the Chinese Language Year' and 'the Russian Language Year' in 2009–2010. Many of these exchanges sought to address issues relating to education, culture, medicine, sports, tourism, media, archives and youth. Russia started hosting over a dozen of Confucius Institutes or Confucius Classrooms, and nearly 100 tertiary institutions in Russia offered Chinese language courses. From 2006, Russians were also among China's top three visitors by volume, with approximately 2.5 million Russians travelling to China in 2011.[34]

Shared strategic and economic interests between China and Russia enabled the two countries to put aside mutual mistrust, and to engage in extensive cooperation in many areas. The top leadership in both countries made serious efforts to develop bilateral projects, while underplaying any differences. Granted, the Sino-Russian relationship from 2001 to 2011 was still very much an 'axis of convenience',[35] driven primarily by the desire of both countries to maximise their influence vis-à-vis the US and its allies. As Bobo Lo points out, there were significant 'uncertaint[ies] over the long-term future of the Russian Far East; Moscow's anxieties about China's economic capabilities; incipient rivalry in Central Asia; competing visions of strategic architecture in East Asia; and different perceptions of the world and China's and Russia's roles in it'.[36] Despite significant improvements, trade, economic and security ties between both countries also remained limited during this period. Nevertheless, this phase saw the laying of important structural foundations that enabled the relationship to improve rapidly, and to flourish during the Xi-Putin era.

Phase III: 2012–2017

China–Russia relations entered a new phase after Xi Jinping became China's paramount leader in 2012. Unlike his predecessors, he has made fulfilment of the China Dream the grand strategic goal. There has been a heightened emphasis on the three aspects mentioned in the preceding section: (i) reinforcing China's ideological stance on the international order; (ii) countering US hegemony, particularly in the Asia-Pacific region; and (iii) ensuring stability in Central Asia. As a result, Russia has become an even more important international partner for China. The strong foundations of bilateral cooperation established during the earlier phases of the relationship have also allowed Beijing and Moscow to raise it to new levels.

In March 2013, Xi chose Russia for his first presidential visit, a mere eight days after his formal appointment as China's president. Putin reciprocated the gesture by inviting Xi as the first foreign head of state to visit Russia's military command centre, a move that Chinese analysts interpreted as a sign of deepening strategic trust.[37] Xi, like Putin, appeared keen to signal to Washington that China and Russia were able to work together in counter-balancing American influence. During Xi's visit, the two leaders vowed to upgrade the strategic partnership, and to make this a priority in their respective foreign policies. Their joint statement implicitly targeted the United States by declaring that China and Russia 'oppose[d] any country or a bloc of countries unilaterally and without limit strengthening antimissile capabilities, harming strategic stability and international security'.[38]

Xi has been especially keen to establish strong personal ties with Putin and show that Beijing's affinity with Moscow goes beyond material interests. Since he became president, Moscow has become his most frequently visited capital city, and he has met with Putin on more than 20 occasions.[39] They attended each other's military parades held to mark the 70th anniversary of the end of World War II. And Xi even attended a private birthday party for Putin during the 2013 APEC summit in Bali, Indonesia, where the two leaders discussed their fathers' experiences in the second world war 'over vodka and sandwiches'.[40] The personal affinity between these two leaders has facilitated the smooth and rapid development of Sino-Russian relations.

Political, economic and societal engagement between China and Russia has expanded considerably since Xi's first state visit to Moscow. This is particularly evident in three areas: (i) military cooperation; (ii) trade and energy; and (iii) cooperation between regional governments.

Military cooperation: Since 2012, Beijing and Moscow have intensified military-to-military contacts, engaged in ever more ambitious joint exercises, and increased the volume of arms transfers. There were seven high-level meetings in 2016 alone. On the sidelines of the Hangzhou G20 summit in September 2016, Xi reaffirmed China's commitment to enhance military cooperation with Russia.[41] The People's Liberation Army (PLA) and Russian armed forces have conducted exercises, both bilaterally and under the auspices of the SCO. Since 2012, these have increased in complexity, geographical reach, coordination and capabilities. There is also a new focus on missile defence, reflecting their support for each other's security interests and common displeasure with the expansion of US antimissile capabilities.

While the PLA has relied heavily on arms purchases from Russia since the 1990s, Moscow's agreement in 2014 to sell Su-35S jet fighters, the S-400 surface-to-air missile system, and advanced ship-to-ship missiles to China marks a new stage, especially significant when viewed in the context of China's ongoing military modernisation. The Su-35S fighter is believed to be capable of countering the American F-22, while the S-400 missiles could significantly boost China's missile defence capabilities vis-à-vis the United States in the event of a cross-strait or maritime conflict in the East China or South China Seas.[42]

Trade and energy: Building on the efforts of the earlier phases, Sino-Russian trade reached USD 88.2 billion by 2012, compared to USD 38.9 billion in 2009. At the 2014 Conference on Interaction and Confidence-Building Measures in Asia (CICA), the two countries pledged to increase trade to USD 100 billion by 2015 and USD 200 billion by 2020,[43] and to expand the use of the Chinese yuan and

Russian ruble in bilateral trade, investment and loans.[44] Cooperation has also been upgraded to include high-technology and capital-intensive areas, such as nuclear energy, aviation, space, information technology and shipbuilding. There have been detailed discussions of joint projects on long-distance wide-body aircraft, heavy-lift transport helicopters, satellite navigation systems, and manned space flight and deep space exploration.[45]

China and Russia have natural synergies in the energy sector, and have strengthened cooperation in this area. Previously, this had been constrained by the discourse in Russia about the 'China threat' and 'Chinese economic expansionism', and the consequent fear of overdependence on China as a monopsonic customer.[46] Yet even before 2012 there were several major projects in play. In 2004, China and Russia reached an oil supply agreement whereby Russia provides around 10 million tonnes of oil annually by rail. In 2009, the two countries concluded the 'loans-for-oil' agreement, under which China provided loans amounting to USD 25 billion in return for Russia supplying 15 million tonnes of oil per annum over a period of 20 years (2011–2030).

Sino-Russian energy cooperation is set to grow further as China becomes more dependent on foreign oil and gas. According to the International Energy Agency, its foreign oil dependence rate will reach 80% by 2035. Currently, 52% of Chinese oil imports come from the Middle East (mainly Saudi Arabia, Iran, Iraq, and Oman), 23% from Africa, 10% from former Soviet States (Russia and Kazakhstan), 7.2% from South America (mainly Venezuela and Brazil) and 2.3% from the Asia-Pacific region. Critically, 80% of China's oil imports pass through the Malacca Strait, and volatile conditions in the Middle East may cause it to reduce its reliance on this region. In these circumstances, oil cooperation with Russia has become key to China's energy security.[47] Moscow, for its part, is keen to signal to the West that the economic sanctions imposed on it following the annexation of Crimea are futile given that it has the China option.

For many years, Sino-Russian gas cooperation stagnated because of disagreements over price, Chinese equity ownership, and pipeline routes. But in May 2014, Beijing and Moscow finally reached an agreement to deliver an annual 38 billion cubic metres of Russian natural gas over 30 years, a deal then worth an estimated USD 400 billion.[48] This followed soon after the 2013 Rosneft–CNPC (China National Petroleum Corporation) oil supply agreement, in which Rosneft undertook to deliver 360 million tonnes of oil over 25 years (valued at USD 270 billion). As a result, Russia's oil exports to China jumped to 52.5 million tonnes in 2016, making it the largest supplier of Chinese oil needs (ahead of Saudi Arabia). Meanwhile, Moscow became much more flexible on the question of Chinese equity ownership in Russian upstream ventures. This was reflected most notably in the Yamal Liquefied Natural Gas (LNG) project, where China holds a 29.9% stake.[49] China and Russia also agreed to further cooperation in the nuclear power industry, following the successful construction of the first unit of the Tianwan nuclear power plant in 2017.[50]

Interregional cooperation: There has been a spike of interest in cross-border and other sub-national cooperation schemes. At the 2014 CICA summit, Putin and Xi declared their intention to accelerate the development of cross-border infrastructure, including a bridge across the Amur River.[51] At the St Petersburg International Economic Forum, Chinese Vice President Li Yuanchao called for joint efforts to implement Russia's Far East development plan and China's Northeast Area Revitalisation programme, with the ultimate goal of building an integrated economic region. Putin and Xi's agreement in May 2015 to integrate the EEU with the SREB provided added incentives for local governments to intensify cross-border cooperation.

Chinese analysts are optimistic about the prospect of an integrated Far East economic region. They believe that the USD 400 billion gas deal has paved the way for cooperation in many other areas, including agriculture, mineral resources, infrastructure, manufacturing industry, finance, logistics and tourism. One Chinese policy proposal mentions the possibility of setting up a Far East Development Bank, supported by the USD 2 billion Russia–China Investment Fund established in 2012 by two government-backed investment vehicles, the Russian Direct Investment Fund and China Investment Corporation (CIC).[52]

Beijing and Moscow are especially hopeful about the possibilities in agriculture and food security. According to Chinese estimates, there are about 5.2 million hectares of fertile agricultural land in Russia's Far East region close to China's Heilongjiang province. This provides many opportunities for cooperation between Heilongjiang and neighbouring regions in the Russian Far East (RFE). According to a Chinese local official, over 100 Chinese companies have made investments in the agricultural sector in the RFE, farming a total of 480,000 hectares by 2014, four times that of 2005s figures.[53]

More broadly, Heilongjiang has sought to construct production chains with Russian border regions in areas such as aircraft and automobile manufacturing, food processing and mineral resource development. It has proposed extending preferential loans to support infrastructural projects in Russia in exchange for Russian mineral resources.[54] The municipal government of Harbin, capital of Heilongjiang, plans to take advantage of the national strategy of developing the border regions to build the city into a regional hub for Sino-Russian cooperation. To this purpose, it has started to establish a free trade area,[55] organised a number of trade fairs, and encouraged cross-border tourism.[56]

Conclusion

The impressive development of the Sino-Russian partnership has been driven not only by common material interests, but also by convergent views on the international order. China and Russia hope to counter US hegemony as well as mitigate Western pressure on their respective foreign policies. This combination of the pragmatic and the ideological suggests that their relationship has moved beyond an 'axis of convenience' to a fully-fledged strategic partnership. Liu Guchang notes that strategic trust between them has reached unprecedented levels, while Qu Xing, president of the China Institute for International Studies, lauds their partnership as a model of major power relations.[57] Certainly, challenges remain—lingering mutual suspicion, the continued 'China threat' or 'Chinese expansionism' discourse in Russia, the disjunction between relatively modest economic cooperation and booming political ties, uncertainties in Russian foreign policy, red tape, and so on. Both sides recognise, too, that the growing economic disparity between them is resulting in an increasingly asymmetrical relationship—something that has become especially apparent since the conflict in Ukraine heightened Russia's China-dependence.

Nevertheless, the rapid increase in cooperation across many areas has brought genuine substance to the rhetoric of a 'comprehensive strategic partnership of coordination'. While it remains to be seen whether this will indeed result in a qualitative change to the relationship, China and Russia look poised to enhance and solidify their strategic partnership in the near future. This has acquired real resilience, driven as much by endogenous factors as by external circumstances. Both sides identify real incentives in developing cooperation in multiple areas, and the US factor to sustaining the relationship is no longer as influential as it used to be. With sufficient political will and stable domestic conditions in both countries, there is enormous potential for Sino-Russian relations to evolve into a highly effective and lasting strategic partnership.

Notes

1. Lo (2008), p. 3.
2. Fu (2016), p. 96.
3. Lo (2017), p. xvii.
4. Ministry of Foreign Affairs of the People's Republic of China (2017).
5. Pillsbury (2015).
6. Swaine (2000), Swaine and Tellis (2000).
7. Goldstein (2001).
8. Dreyer (2007).
9. Goldstein (2005).
10. Zhao (2015).
11. Foot (2006).
12. Stenslie (2014).
13. Frazier (2010).
14. Liu and Hao (2014).
15. Ibid.
16. Ye (2011).
17. Yan (2011).
18. The China Dream and 'Xi Jinping thought' confirm the trend, apparent for some years now, that the leadership has definitively abandoned Deng Xiaoping's precept of maintaining a low profile.
19. United Nations (1997).
20. Xinhua (2016), Ministry of Foreign Affairs of the Russia Federation (2016).
21. Zuo (2001).
22. Yu (2014).
23. Ministry of Foreign Affairs of the People's Republic of China (2014).
24. Wang (2013).
25. Xinhua (2016).
26. Embassy of the People's Republic of China in Moscow (2010).
27. Ibid.
28. On China and Russia's cooperation in the SCO and Central Asia, see also chapter by Alexander Cooley in this edited volume.
29. Ma (2009).
30. Guo (2014).
31. Zhao (2014), pp. 96–109.

32. Ministry of Foreign Affairs of the People's Republic of China.
33. Lo (2008), p. 84.
34. China National Tourism Administration (2011).
35. Lo (2008).
36. Ibid., p. 177.
37. Qing and Zhang (2013).
38. Herszenhorn and Buckley (2013).
39. Meick (2017), p. 5.
40. The Economist (2017).
41. Meick (2017), p. 19.
42. Liu (2014).
43. Shuang and Zhou (2014).
44. Ibid.
45. Yuan (2014).
46. Cui (2014).
47. Lin (2014).
48. Twenty-First Century Economic News (2014).
49. Ibid.
50. Ibid.
51. Construction of the bridge started in December 2016.
52. Yang (2014).
53. Wang (2014).
54. Song (2014).
55. Wan (2014)
56. Qu (2014).
57. Yu (2014).

Literature

China National Tourism Administration. 2011. *2011 nian 1-12 yue fen lai hua lv you ru jing ren shu* [Data on Foreign Tourists in China During Jan–Dec 2011]. Available at http://www.cnta.gov.cn/Zwgk/lysj/201506/t20150610_18706.shtml.

Cui, Weihong. 2014. zhong e ou zai zhongya de nengyuan jing he guanxi [Competition and Cooperation Among China, Russia, and Europe in Central Asia]. *guoji guanxi yanjiu* [International Relations Studies] 2: 64–73.

Dreyer, June T. 2007. China's Power and Will: The PRC's Military Strength and Grand Strategy. *Orbis* 51 (4): 651–664.

Embassy of the People's Republic of China in Moscow. 2010. The Joint Statement of the Russian Federation and the Republic of China About a More Intensive Multilateral Cooperation, Partnership, and Strategic Coordination Between Russia and China, Beijing, September 28. Available at http://ru.china-embassy.org/rus/zgxw/t757139.htm.

Foot, Rosemary. 2006. Chinese Strategies in a US-Hegemonic Global Order: Accommodating and Hedging. *International Affairs* 82 (1): 77–94.

Frazier, Mark W. 2010. China's Domestic Policy Fragmentation and "Grand" Strategy in Global Politics. *Asia Policy* 10 (July): 87–101.

Fu, Ying. 2016. How China Sees Russia: Beijing and Moscow Are Close, but Not Allies. *Foreign Affairs* 95 (Jan/Feb): 96–105.

Goldstein, Avery. 2001. The Diplomatic Face of China's Grand Strategy: A Rising Power's Emerging Choice. *The China Quarterly* 168 (December): 835–864.

Goldstein, Avery. 2005. *Rising to the Challenge: China's Grand Strategy and International Security*. Stanford, CA: Stanford University Press.

Guo, Qiong. 2014. xin xingshi xia zhong e jiaqiang zai zhongya hezuo de liyi fenxi [An Analysis on the Interests of Sino-Russia Enhancing Cooperation in Central Asia in the New Context]. *ya fei zongheng* [Asian and African Affairs] 2: 73–82.

Herszenhorn, David M., and Chris Buckley. 2013. China's New Leader, Visiting Russia, Promotes Nation's Economic and Military Ties. *The New York Times*, March 22. Available at http://www.nytimes.com/2013/03/23/world/asia/xi-jinping-visits-russia-on-first-trip-abroad.html?mcubz=0.

Lin, Boqiang. 2014. shijie nengyuan xin geju xia de zhong e hezuo [Sino-Russian Cooperation in the New World Energy Structure]. *shanghai zhengquan bao* [Shanghai Security News], July 3.

Liu, Weihua, and Yufan Hao. 2014. Australia in China's Grand Strategy. *Asian Survey* 54 (2): 367–394.

Liu, Yupeng. 2014. e mei: zhong e jiu chushou su-35 dacheng yizhi [Russian Media: China and Russia Agree on Su-35 Fighters Sale]. *zhongguo guofang bao* [China Defense News], June 3.

Lo, Bobo. 2008. *Axis of Convenience: Moscow, Beijing and the New Geopolitics*. London and Washington, DC: Chatham House and Brookings Institution Press.

Lo, Bobo. 2017. *A Wary Embrace: What the China–Russia Relationship Means for the World*. Sydney and Melbourne: Penguin Books.

Ma, Fengshu. 2009. zhongya diqu anquan yu zhong e zhanlue xiezuo [Regional Security in Central Asia and Sino-Russian Strategic Collaboration]. *dangdai shijie shehuizhuyi weinti* [Issues of Contemporary World Socialism] 3: 48–58.

Meick, Ethan. 2017. China–Russia Military-to-Military Relations: Moving Towards a Higher Level of Cooperation. *U.S.–China Economic and Security Review Commission*, Staff Research Report, March 20.

Ministry of Foreign Affairs of the People's Republic of China. China and Russia: Partnership of Strategic Coordination. Available at http://www.fmprc.gov.cn/mfa_eng/ziliao_665539/3602_665543/3604_665547/t18028.shtml.

Ministry of Foreign Affairs of the People's Republic of China. 2014. Xi Jinping Holds Talks with President Vladimir Putin of Russia, Stressing to Expand and Deepen Practical Cooperation, Promoting China–Russia Comprehensive Strategic Partnership of Coordination to Higher Level, May 20. Available at http://www.fmprc.gov.cn/mfa_eng/topics_665678/yzxhxzyxrcshydscfh/t1158516.shtml.

Ministry of Foreign Affairs of the Russia Federation. 2016. The Declaration of the Russian Federation and the People's Republic of China on the Promotion of International Law, June 25. Available at http://www.mid.ru/en_GB/foreign_policy/news/-/asset_publisher/cKNonkJE02Bw/content/id/2331698.

Ministry of Foreign Affairs of the People's Republic of China. 2017. Xi Jinping Holds Talks with President Vladimir Putin of Russia: The Two Heads of States Agree to Make Joint Efforts to Continuously Deepen China–Russia Comprehensive Strategic Partnership of Coordination, July 4. Available at http://www.fmprc.gov.cn/mfa_eng/zxxx_662805/t1475872.shtml.

Pillsbury, Michael. 2015. *The Hundred-Year Marathon: China's Secret Strategy to Replace America as the Global Superpower*. New York: Henry Holt.

Qing, Huang, and Zhang Ping. 2013. zhong e guanxi ershi nian: wenbu fazhan de zhanlue xiezuo [Twenty Years of Sino-Russian Relations: The Steady Growth of Strategic Collaboration]. *eluosi xuekan* [Journal of Russian Studies] 15 (3): 25–33.

Qu, Jing. 2014. shou jie zhong e bolanhui ji di ershiwu jie "ha qia hui" luomu [The First Sino-Russian Expo and the 25th Harbin Trade Fair Concludes]. *heilongjiang ribao* [Heilongjiang Daily], July 5.

Shuang, Ming, and Zhou Ailin. 2014. zhong e benbi jiesuan zai tisu, jingmao hezuo yinglai nuanchun [China and Russia Accelerate Settlement with Their Own Currencies; Economic and Trade Cooperation to Experience Good Opportunities]. *diyi caijing ribao* [First Financial and Economic News], May 22.

Song, Kui. 2014. dazo zhong e kuajing chanyelian [Creating Cross-Border Industrial Chains Between China and Russia]. *heilongjiang jingji bao* [Heilongjiang Economic News], April 10.

Stenslie, Stig. 2014. Questioning the Reality of China's Grand Strategy. *China: An International Journal* 12 (2): 161–178.

Swaine, Michael. 2000. Does China Have a Grand Strategy? *Current History* 99 (639): 274–279.

Swaine, Michael, and Ashley J. Tellis. 2000. *Interpreting China's Grand Strategy: Past, Present and Future*. Santa Monica: RAND Corporation.

The Economist. 2017. Unlikely Partners: Xi Jinping and Vladimir Putin Behave Like the Best of Buddies. *The Economist*, July 27. Available at https://www.economist.com/news/china/21725611-suspicion-between-russia-and-china-runs-deep-xi-jinping-and-vladimir-putin-behave-best.

Twenty-First Century Economic News. 2014. zhong e gong qi xieyi, zhuli zhongguo nengyuan gongji duoyuanhua [Sino-Russian Gas Deal Good for the Diversification of China's Energy Supply]. *ershiyi shiji jingji baodao* [21st-Century Economic News], May 23.

United Nations. 1997. Russian–Chinese Joint Declaration on a Multipolar World and the Establishment of a New International Order. *United Nations General Assembly*, A/52/153 S/1997/384, April 23. http://www.un.org/documents/ga/docs/52/plenary/a52-153.htm.

Wan, Jia. 2014. harbin tansuo jianli zhong e zimaoqu [Harbin Explores the Possibility of Building a Sino-Russian Free Trade Area]. *guoji shang bao* [International Business News], March 19.

Wang, Haiyun. 2013. zhong e ying zai wending dongbeiya anquan zhixu shang jiaqiang zhanlue xiezuo [China and Russia Should Strengthen Collaboration on Stabilising the Security Order in Northeast Asia]. *eluosi xuekan* [Journal of Russian Studies] 3 (1): 5–9.

Wang, Ying. 2014. fang Heilongjiang sheng dui e nongye chanye xiehui huizhang li demin [An Interview with Li Demin, President of the Heilongjiang–Russian Association for the Agricultural Sector]. *Heilongjiang jingji bao* [Heilongjiang Economic News], July 2.

Xinhua. 2016. China, Russia Sign Joint Statement on Strengthening Global Strategic Stability. *Xinhua News*, June 26. Available at http://news.xinhuanet.com/english/2016-06/26/c_135466187.htm.

Yan, Xuetong. 2011. *Ancient Chinese Thought, Modern Chinese Power*, ed. Daniel Bell, Zhe Sun and trans. Edmund Ryden. Princeton, NJ: Princeton University Press.

Yang, Bosen. 2014. gongjian yuandong jingjiqu huo cheng zhong e hezuo shenji xin silu [Jointly Building the Far East Economic Region May Become an Alternative for the Upgrading of Sino-Russian Cooperation]. *zhongguo shehui kexue bao* [China Social Science Bulletin], June 11.

Ye, Zicheng. 2011. *Inside China's Grad Strategy: The Perspective from the People's Republic*, ed. and trans. Steven I. Levin and Guoli Liu. Lexington: The University Press of Kentucky.

Yu, Zhao, et al. 2014. pujin fanghua: zhong e guanxi zai xian "dingceng sheji" zuoyong [Putin's China Visit: The Role of "Top-Down Design" in Sino-Russian Relations]. *Xinhua News*, May 20. Available at http://news.xinhuanet.com/world/2014-05/20/c_126520478.htm.

Yuan Chang. 2014. dazao zhong e hezuo shengjiban [Upgrade the Sino-Russian Cooperation]. *guangming ribao* [Guangming Daily], July 28.

Zhao, Huasheng. 2014. qianping zhong e mei san da zhanlue zai zhongya de gongchu [The Co-existence of Chinese, Russian, and American Grand Strategies in Central Asia], *guoji guancha* [International Observation] 1: 96–109.

Zhao, Minghao. 2015. "March Westwards" and a New Look on China's Grand Strategy. *Mediterranean Quarterly* 26 (1): 97–116.

Zuo, Fengrong. 2001. zouxiang ershiyi shiji de zhong e zhanlue xiezuo huoban guanxi [Walking Towards a 21st-Century Sino-Russian Strategic Partnership of Collaboration]. *shijie jingji yu zhengzhi* [World Economics and Politics] 8: 53–55.

CHAPTER 3

Unwanted but Inevitable: Russia's Deepening Partnership with China Post-Ukraine

Alexander Gabuev

Introduction

"Have you all woken up yet? I'm not asking those of you from the Far East, of course, but the Muscovites." the Russian President Dmitry Medvedev asked on July 2, 2010, opening a meeting that was intended to chart a twenty-first-century course for Russia's engagement with an increasingly dynamic Asia-Pacific region.[1] The meeting, gathering many government heavyweights, took place in Khabarovsk four time zones east of Moscow, so Medvedev didn't resist the temptation to poke fun at his jet-lagged colleagues. But the President's words were aimed at a wider audience than just the sleep-deprived group of powerful people attending this meeting. In fact, the whole country needed to wake up to a new reality—the Pacific century, in which the growing middle class of Asian nations would be the engine of the global economy.

A. Gabuev (✉)
Moscow Center of the Carnegie Endowment for International Peace, Moscow, Russia
e-mail: AGabuev@carnegie.ru

J. I. Bekkevold and B. Lo (eds.), *Sino-Russian Relations in the 21st Century*, https://doi.org/10.1007/978-3-319-92516-5_3

At the heart of a new Pacific century lay the rise of China, Russia's most powerful and important neighbor, with whom it shares a 4200 km border. Khabarovsk, in which the strategy meeting was taking place, was founded in 1858 in the territories annexed by Russia from the Qing Empire after the signing of the Aigun Treaty. Back then the Romanov Empire was one of several Western colonial powers tearing apart a China stuck in the past due to the conservatism of its Manchu rulers. In this period, known in China as the "century of humiliation," Russia held the upper hand in its relationship with its giant neighbor. Following the establishment of the People's Republic of China in 1949, with Moscow's massive help, the USSR was the "elder brother" to the young communist state, helping it to leapfrog into industrialized modernity. Up until the end of the twentieth century, the Russian elite and the Russian people maintained a patronizing attitude towards China, and looked down upon their Eastern neighbor as a giant country with far too many poor people.

This cultural stereotype, combined with Russia's obsession with the West following the collapse of the USSR and a general lack of knowledge resulting in ethnic phobias, had prevented Moscow from developing any strategy on China, or with any other Asian powerhouse. Russia's policy in the Asia-Pacific had been incoherent, reactive and not informed by any grand vision of Russia's future role in the region. With its centralized system of economic and political power, Russia had looked predominantly Westward, as the Kremlin tried to cement Moscow's ties with the European Union, while at the same going through emotional cycles in its relationship with the United States, the world's only superpower. The wealthiest and most powerful people in Russia were busy building their relationships to Europe, buying property on the French Riviera or in London's Belgravia, sending kids to English boarding schools, and bringing their companies to London and New York for IPOs. For nearly two decades after the end of the Cold War, China was not a country that would galvanize anybody's imagination in post-Soviet Russia.

The rude awakening came in 2009, following the collapse of Lehman Brothers and the global credit crunch. With the global financial crisis, the Russian elite discovered that the almighty West it had come to admire so much proved to be in trouble, triggering a global economic crisis and plunging the world, including the United States and the Eurozone, into a severe recession that which made the financial crisis of 1997–1998 pale in comparison. By contrast, China's economy continued to grow as if nothing had happened, or at least so it seemed from Moscow. In 2009 Hong Kong overtook London as the top global IPO destination. Executives of "China Inc." started to travel the world with a shopping cart, offering "loan for commodities" schemes to cash-strapped countries rich in natural resources. Moscow humbly became one of the many participants in that scheme when Russia in October 2009 finally agreed to build the first direct oil pipeline to China in order to help troubled Transneft and Rosneft, the oil pipeline monopoly and the largest state-owned oil company, respectively.

This was the context against which Dmitry Medvedev had gathered his ministers in Khabarovsk to start a serious conversation about the future strategy of Russia's engagement with the Asia-Pacific, and in particular with China. Medvedev's speech exposed significant scars resulting from Russia's recent economic shock. And of course, the meeting and its purpose was fully supported and blessed by Prime Minister Vladimir Putin, at the time still the most powerful person in the country.

Following President's Medvedev's instructions, by the beginning of 2011 the Russian government had produced a strategy document outlining the main measures to boost Russia's economic and political influence in the Asia-Pacific region. The classified document was the first attempt by the Russian authorities to produce something resembling a strategic assessment of long-term trends in Asian economies and geopolitics. The document also contained some concrete steps for Moscow's policy and economic outreach in this region in order to turn Asia's dynamism into an engine for growth for the whole Russian economy, and in particular for the resource-rich but sparsely populated Eastern Siberia and the Russian Far East. These Russian regions are geographically part of Asia, but weren't successfully integrated into Asian supply chains. The document was a mixture of bold and well-informed suggestions with ill-founded assumptions about Russia's technological superiority over many Asian countries.[2] In line with Medvedev's obsession with cutting-edge technologies and modernization, the strategy discussed Russia's future technological cooperation with Asia, but unrealistically portrayed Russia as a source of high-tech exports to the region. Nevertheless, despite the document's shortcomings, it was the first comprehensive strategy document that set out the course of Russia's engagement with China and other Asian powers.

When Vladimir Putin returned to the Kremlin in 2012 it was expected that Moscow's pivot to Asia would be an important part of his presidency, and that it would be implemented in a gradual and well-calculated fashion. However, the crisis over Ukraine and the annexation of Crimea and Western sanctions against Russia have turned the tables. These events had a profound impact on Russia's foreign, domestic, and economic policies, including its relationship with China. Instead of rolling out its China and Asia policies step-by-step, Moscow suddenly had to undergo a crash course in building closer ties to Beijing. Russia's pivot to Asia is happening as we speak, but it is unfolding both more rapidly and in a totally different direction than any of the Russian policy-makers attending the morning strategy meeting back in 2010 could have imagined. Instead of becoming an Asian-Pacific powerhouse in its own right, Russia is increasingly finding itself in a position of being Beijing's junior partner, with few alternative choices available. The growing nexus between the two largest continental powers in Eurasia has many implications for the international security order, but first and foremost it is boosting China's capabilities as a global player. This state of affairs, although it reflects many trends in Sino-Russian relations that predate the war in Ukraine, was never preordained and is a direct result of the radical change of direction that Russia took in early 2014.

Russia's View of China Before 2009: A Strategic Card Gaming the West

Russia and China had been moving closer to each other for a long time already before the war in Ukraine and the global economic crisis of 2008. Three structural and fundamental factors explain the converging trend in the Sino-Russian relationship, and why Moscow increasingly views Beijing as an important partner. These three factors are the importance of stability on Russia's eastern flank, economic compatibility, and developments in the international system.

Stability on the Eastern Flank

For a large part of Russian history, the current 4200 km long border with China has been a source of significant tension and mistrust. The border is the product of Tsarist Russia's expansion into what Qing rulers claimed to be their territory, or at least part of its sphere of influence. Ultimately Moscow pushed Beijing out and established itself as a Far Eastern power as a result of the Aigun Treaty (1858) and the

Beijing Treaty (1860). During the Cold War, after the worsening of relations between Moscow and Beijing following Joseph Stalin's death and the Soviet Communist Party's 20th Congress, the border witnessed a high degree of military tension. At least two serious military incidents took place in 1969, and at the high point of Sino-Soviet confrontation in the 1960s and 1970s both nations invested significant resources preparing for invasion.[3] Moscow and Beijing amassed thousands of troops along the border, and doomsday scenarios envisaged the use of tactical nuclear weapons for deterrence. Military expenditures to contain each other imposed a heavy financial burden on both sides, channeling scarce national resources away from economic modernization. Against this background, as soon as an opportunity to normalize relations presented itself, both the Soviet and Chinese leaderships jumped at it. What started as a significant drawdown in military deployments and capabilities along both sides of the border, and establishment of some confidence-building measures, soon led to a revival of cross-border trade in the 1990s and, ultimately, a diplomatic process towards solving the territorial dispute. In 2001, the two sides signed the friendship treaty, and in 2004 the border deal was reached with delimitation completed in 2007.

In expediting a border agreement with Russia, China was trying to reduce unpredictability and uncertainty along its longest land border, as well as to set a positive example for its other neighboring countries. Stability on the Russian border enabled China to divert resources to other important areas of national strategy, including the transformation of the People's Liberation Army into a modern combat machine with a blue-water navy that would help China to become a global maritime power and compete with the United States for influence in the Asia-Pacific. Russia shared similar motivations—as the country didn't have the resources to keep a significant military presence in the Far East. Moreover, Moscow had a sober view about the changing balance of power between Russia and China, and was aware that time was on Beijing's side. Hence, the Kremlin ultimately decided that the downsides of minor territorial concessions to China would be far less than an open territorial dispute with the Asian giant.

Since 2004, the border agreement has arguably been the most important stabilizing factor in Sino-Russian relations. In the view of Russia, the bottom line defining ties to China is a non-conflictual relationship, an attitude shared by China. If Russia and China were adversaries, it would have potentially catastrophic implications for both nations.

Economic Cooperation and Compatibility

The second fundamental factor driving Russia closer towards China is the growing economic compatibility between these two countries. Despite a relatively large and diverse economy, in its economic relationship with the outside world Russia is primarily a raw materials exporter. However, despite its rich endowment of various natural resources, Russia lacks the capital to explore them, and also has a relatively poor record in building the infrastructure needed to bring these commodities to the international market. China, on the other hand, has increasing demands for raw materials coupled with an abundance of capital to invest overseas, and has world-class experience in building infrastructure. Since China became net importer of crude oil in 1993, its dependence on supplies of hydrocarbons and other natural resources from overseas has increased rapidly in tandem with the growth of the Chinese economy. In short, Russia and China have very compatible economies. Russia has in the East another market for its commodities just next door which could play the same role as Europe used to play in Russia's economic development. And for China, Russia could potentially be another source of hydrocarbons, metals, food and other commodities that could contribute to a further diversification of supplies and increase China's energy and food security.

This underlying logic in their respective economies became more evident to Russia in 2003, as the oil price started to inflate the prices of other commodities. Around that time Russia launched its first large energy projects with China. Yukos owner Mikhail Khodorkovsky planned to build an oil pipeline to China, but the project did not materialize because of his imprisonment and the appropriation of Yukos' assets by the Russian state. However, the China National Petroleum Corporation (CNPC) provided a loan to Rosneft that enabled the latter to buy Yuganskneftegaz, the crown jewel in Khodorkovsky's empire, in exchange for a contract for oil supplies to China. These transactions put in place a foundation for future energy cooperation between the two countries, but for reasons I will discuss later, the full potential of energy cooperation would be realized only several years later.

Support on the International Arena

Last but not least, the third important factor driving Russia closer to China was international politics. Throughout the 1990s, Russia's relationship with the West had been ambiguous and contradictory. After the collapse of the Soviet Union, it hoped to be fully integrated into the transatlantic family. However, towards the end of the 1990s Russia's relationship with Europe and the United States was in a downward spiral. Western criticism of the war in Chechnya, NATO expansion and the U.S.-led air campaign against Russia's traditional ally Serbia despite Moscow's protests, were all perceived very negatively by the Russian elite. During the same period, China viewed renewed U.S.–Japan defense cooperation with growing concern. It was during Boris Yeltsin's visit to China in 1999 that he, standing alongside his Chinese colleague Jiang Zemin, famously declared that U.S. President Bill Clinton shouldn't forget that Russia was a nuclear power, and that China and Russia would have a say over global affairs in a multipolar world.[4] Some analysts have pointed to this moment, or at least this period, as the turning point in Russia's relations with the West and China.[5] Following Al-Qaeda's 9/11 terrorist attack against the U.S., the new Russian leader Vladimir Putin made another attempt to reach out to the West. Despite his KGB background, Putin was during his first term arguably a pro-Western Russian leader, who was even arguing for Russia's integration into NATO. However, towards the end of 2004 his illusions about strategic partnership with the West had evaporated. The U.S. invasion of Iraq, another round of NATO expansion, and, most importantly, the West's support for color revolutions in Georgia and Ukraine (viewed in the Kremlin as Western intelligence plots), turned Putin's Russia into a non-Western power. Russia's increasingly anti-Western stance coincided with a shift in its domestic politics, as it gradually turned more authoritarian.

In China, Putin found a partner who shared his suspicions of Western democracy promotion. From 2004, Putin's Russia increasingly looked to China for support of its quest for a multipolar world order. Neither country defined what they actually meant by such an order, but this common goal, at least at the rhetorical level, helped them to maintain a symbolic unity while avoiding discussions about their differences. In fact, during this period China was also trying to engage the West and avoid direct conflict, in line with Deng Xiaoping's 'keeping a low profile' formula (*taoguang yanghui*). Putin's Russia was readier than China to adopt a confrontational stance against the United States, and was much more vocal in the UN Security Council in defending Iran against sanctions or protecting non-democratic regimes like Zimbabwe or Myanmar. Beijing never failed to exploit this more aggressive Russian foreign policy, quietly siding with Russia when it exercised its veto, while at the same time pursuing its interests in a pragmatic manner. Although the partnership between Beijing and Moscow on the international arena was still tactical rather than strategic, their common suspicions towards the West and authoritarian trends in both countries formed an important basis for cooperation.

Explaining Russia's Foot-Dragging in Shaping a China Strategy

In retrospect, 2004 appears to be a pivotal year in Sino-Russian relations. This was the year when all three fundamental factors—border stability, economic compatibility, and international affairs—were driving Moscow and Beijing closer together. The border issue was finally solved, building a foundation of trust that had earlier been absent in their bilateral relations. Commodity prices started to climb along with China's soaring demands, making the mutual compatibility of the two economies more obvious for the leaders of both countries. Finally, the U.S. invasion of Iraq and the color revolutions in the post-Soviet space increased China and Russia's common suspicion of the West and their eagerness to increase cooperation in the international arena. However, it would take another decade before these factors would profoundly shape and change the nature of the Sino-Russian relationship. The main reasons explaining the gradual development of the relationship even after 2004, and why it would take several years before Russia drafted a China strategy, are to be found on the Russian side of the equation.

The most important factor was the lack of interest in the Russian elite in things Asian, and in China in particular. After the dissolution of the Soviet Union and well into the 1990s, there was a profound belief in Russia's destiny to become a member of the Euro-Atlantic family. At the time, integration with the West was the major driving force behind Moscow's foreign policy. Despite setbacks like the war in Chechnya and the NATO air campaign against the Milosevic regime, the Kremlin saw partnership with the West as the ultimate goal for Russia, a logic Vladimir Putin also followed during his first term in power. The large bulk of the Russian population resides closer to Europe than to Asia, and it is therefore natural that Russia's infrastructural as well as cultural links to Europe are more developed than links to Asia. Centuries of a Euro-oriented Russian culture also contributed to a lack of interest and even neglect in the Russian political and economic elite towards Asia. While Europe was viewed as source of social and political progress coupled with modern technology, Asia and China in particular were viewed as poor, backward and inferior.

Russian oligarchs, members of the ruling elite and Russian corporates brought their assets to Europe to establish a permanent presence there. Geographical and cultural proximity, as well as high living standards and Europe's receptiveness to Russian money (however dubious), have made it the primary overseas destination for the Russian elite. It should come as no surprise that corporate strategies have followed the interests of their owners. Russian companies, private and state-owned alike, have rushed to London and Frankfurt for cheap loans and IPOs, and mostly looked to Europe or the United States when searching for markets and business partners. All these factors help to explain why the Russian top leadership until 2008 had little interest in establishing a presence in the Asia-Pacific or tapping into the vast opportunities provided by China's economic growth.

Russia's China policy not only suffered from a lack of strategic interest in China among government and corporate players, but the collapse of the Soviet Union also delivered a huge blow to the Russian China-watching community.[6] From being members of the middle class living on lavish government funds dedicated to study of a major Cold War adversary, government officials and academic experts dealing with China quickly became a group of virtually abandoned intellectuals struggling to make ends meet as the state stopped its funding. Many of the best and brightest in the field soon migrated elsewhere and quit China-watching entirely. Those who stayed didn't have the resources to develop their knowledge of China, since their employers had no money to buy new books or support research trips. Russian Sinologists were simply unable to understand and keep up with the profound changes unfolding in the People's Republic of China following Deng Xiaoping's bold reforms. This sorry state of affairs of course resulted in Moscow's decreased ability to navigate ties with Beijing, and has continuing repercussions for Russia's China policies.

One immediate result of the neglect of Russia's China-watching expertise was a notable rise of Sinophobia in Russian society and even among elites. Without strong public voices who could distinguish between fact and fiction with regard to developments in China and provide realistic assessments of what China's rise meant for Russia's future, the rapid emergence of a new superpower next door was seen mostly in a negative light. A particular source of Moscow's concerns about the rise of China was the demographic imbalance between the resource-rich but scarcely populated Siberia, and China's Northeast. The mix of an acute sense of insecurity, lack of knowledge, and centuries of psychological superiority felt towards people of Asian descent gave rise to the wildest suspicions about China's strategic intentions towards Russia. Sinophobia thus became one of the major obstacles on the Russian side to unlocking the full potential of bilateral cooperation with China.

The result of all this was that until the global financial crisis of 2008–2009, China only played the role of a bargaining chip in Russia's often troubled relations with the West. The most visible example of this was Russia's energy diplomacy with the European Union. In the middle of the 2000s, the Kremlin discovered that Europe's dependency on Russian natural gas could be used as political leverage against neighboring countries and European states. The first "gas wars" Russia conducted against Belarus and Ukraine severely undermined its credibility as a reliable gas supplier to Europe. Many European customers didn't want to sign new long-term contracts with Gazprom, and were increasingly looking for alternatives like LNG or routes bypassing Russia that could provide Europe access to gas from the Caspian region. In order to put pressure on Europe, Vladimir Putin traveled to China in 2006 and announced that Moscow and Beijing would form an energy alliance. Gazprom and CNPC signed MoUs that envisaged building two gas pipelines from Siberia to China, with a total capacity of 68 bcm annually. While the eastern pipeline would pump gas from Eastern Siberia, the Western route going through Altai into China's Xinjiang province would pump gas from Western Siberia, the resource source for most of Gazprom's European customers. EU companies quickly got the message, and soon signed new long-term contracts with Gazprom. After this goal was achieved, Moscow again reduced its energy engagement with China, to Beijing's frustration. This Russian behavior actually prompted Chinese SOEs to look for alternative sources in Central Asia. Russia would later come to regret this type of 'bargaining chip' policy. If Russia had been strategic in its approach to the Chinese gas market already in 2006, it would probably have enabled Gazprom to decrease its dependency on European market while at the same time capitalizing on rising gas prices in Asia. But few people in Moscow were able to make sound judgments on China policy, and the Kremlin was at the time quite pleased with the way it was able to use the Chinese card to pressure the West.

Russia's View of China After 2009: Increasingly Important

Over the decade from 1997 to 2007, Russia's trade with China increased eightfold, from $6.1 billion to $48.2 billion.[7] However, as a share of Russia's total trade, China's position improved only marginally, from 4% of Russia's total trade in 1997 to 8.7% in 2007. Furthermore, Chinese FDI into Russia was still dwarfed by the EU's. Although Moscow and Beijing were partners in the Shanghai Cooperation Organization (SCO) and shared deep concerns about the U.S. presence in Central Asia, military and diplomatic cooperation was still rather hollow. For example, even though Russia used the platform of the SCO to issue joint warnings with China to the United States, and build a mechanism of joint military drills with the PLA, Russia still viewed its relationship with Beijing in Central Asia as competitive. As late as 2008, the economic and diplomatic relationship with China continued to be of a secondary priority to Moscow. Moreover, negative undercurrents still influenced the relationship, as Moscow became increasingly worried by the rise of Chinese power, including its military dimension. Around 2007, Russia stopped selling its most advanced weapons to China. This decision was partly a result of a revival of the Russian military as the largest customer of its national defense industry. However, it was also influenced by growing concerns that arms sales to China could boost a dangerous competitor, both in terms of international arms trade as well as a strategic rival.[8]

A change in attitude towards China started to happen in 2009, as Russia plunged into economic recession following the global credit crunch. Russia's GDP fell by 9.2%, the most drastic drop in GDP of all the G-20 nations. International demand for Russian commodities decelerated rapidly, and commodity prices were almost in freefall. Russian companies were unable to attract fresh money in Europe and the United States through IPOs or new loans, and refinancing previous credit lines became increasingly problematic. At the same time, China was demonstrating extraordinary success in combating the crisis, not least through a colossal Keynesian-like fiscal stimulus package totaling $585 billion. China managed to keep its GDP in 2009 growing by an impressive 9.2%, an achievement that greatly impressed President Medvedev.

In the summer and fall of 2009, the Russian elite started to seriously rethink its attitude to China. For the first time it became evident that China's market presented vast opportunities for Russian companies, and in particular commodity exporters. It was now also evident to the Russian elite that China, not Russia, would have the upper hand if the commercial ties with China were to be expanded. As a result of Moscow's hard nose "bargaining chip" energy policy, Beijing had already sent its national oil companies elsewhere. By 2009 China already had an operational pipeline pumping Central Asian oil from Atasu in Kazakhstan to Alashankou, and was finishing construction of a gas pipeline linking China to Turkmenistan. China's energy diplomacy engagement with Central Asia had happened on Moscow's watch, and the Kremlin was even quite happy about this development, because as Central Asian producers were finding new markets in China, they were less tempted to develop connections to energy markets in Europe and position themselves as competitors to Russia. But now, in 2009, Moscow suddenly discovered that Central Asian states were competitors after all, in an already very crowded Chinese energy market. As a consequence, Russia now had to go an extra mile to carve out its own place in the Chinese market.

In October 2009, Russia's two oil giants Rosneft, the largest state-controlled oil company, and the oil pipeline monopoly Transneft signed a contract with CNPC. Russia committed to build a direct pipeline to China. However, the 2009 credit crunch put this project at risk, as cash-strapped Rosneft and Transneft were struggling with the soaring construction costs of the East Siberia Pacific Ocean (ESPO) pipeline. Moscow and Beijing had been discussing such a branch pipeline going directly to China for several years, but to no avail. Moscow had not wanted to increase its vulnerability by building a pipeline leading to a single monopsonistic customer. But in 2009 Russia was out of options, because the Chinese were the only willing creditors. Russian companies took a $25 billion loan from the China Development Bank, backed by a contract to pump 15 million tonnes annually over the 2011–2030 period. The exact terms of the loan agreement and the oil contract have never been disclosed, but it is generally believed that the Russian side had to sell at a discount. Beijing squeezed additional concessions from Moscow in 2011, when the pipeline was completed. The Chinese side has used its position as Rosneft's and Transneft's creditor and the sole destination for oil going through the Skovorodino-Mohe pipeline to bargain an additional $1.5 per barrel discount by renegotiating the contract and threatening to abandon it altogether. The 2009 oil contract and bargaining process has come to symbolize Russia's growing asymmetric dependence on China.

Despite China's upper hand, other Russian SOEs soon followed Rosneft's and Transneft's example and flocked to Beijing in order to find long-term financing. Private Russian companies now looked to Hong Kong and even Shanghai as potential platforms for their IPOs. However, it was only UC Rusal, a company with its core business in Russia, but incorporated in Jersey, that actually made it to the Hong Kong Stock Exchange. This highly political deal made the company and its main stakeholder Oleg Deripaska quite happy, but upset investors. In fact, aluminum prices collapsed soon after the IPO, and so did Rusal's share price. Nevertheless, even this single deal had a huge demonstration effect on the Russian market, as it proved that capital platforms existed for Russian companies outside the EU and the U.S. These and other deals also had a transformative effect on Russia's trade with China. In 2009 China surpassed Germany to become Russia's largest country trade partner, a position it has occupied ever since. Russia was now certainly looking at China as a new engine of growth for its economy, but still saw it primarily as a market for Russian commodities and as a source of loans, and not as a source of high-end technologies for economic modernization—a view reflected in President Medvedev's Khabarovsk document. New heights of economic cooperation were reached in 2013 when Rosneft used Chinese loans again, this time in order to finance its domestic expansion in purchasing TNK-BP and Itera. And the same year Novatek, Russia's second-largest gas producer, sold 20% of its flagship project Yamal LNG in the Arctic to CNPC.

The increased awareness in Moscow about China's importance was mainly driven by economic realities, but also on the international stage Russia's cooperation with China deepened and broadened in scope. In 2009, Moscow hosted the first ever BRIC summit. BRIC as a concept of the four largest emerging economies—Brazil, Russia, India, China that was invented by Goldman Sachs' economist Jim O'Neill. It now came to life as a loose grouping of economic powerhouses demanding reforms of the Bretton-Woods institutions. The grouping expanded further into the BRICS in 2010 with the addition of South Africa. BRICS was not able to turn itself into a meaningful alternative to U.S.-led institutions, but it highlighted the fact that not all emerging powers were happy with the U.S.-led order and the role America played in world politics. Moscow and Beijing locked arms on a number of other international issues, including North Korea, global Internet governance, and opposition to Western meddling in the wake of the Arab Spring. However, elements of competition and mistrust were still present in the relationship, particularly with regard to Central Asia. Competing with growing Chinese influence in the region, Moscow prevented the creation of a free trade zone in the name of the SCO and blocked Beijing's efforts to establish the SCO Development Bank, while Russia pushed its own first Customs Union in the region, the Eurasian Economic Union (EEU). The global financial crisis had forced Russia to abandon decades of arrogance and neglect of its giant neighbor and view China more seriously as a market and partner. However, it was not prepared for how profoundly the year 2014 would transform its relationship with China.

Russia's View of China Post-2014: A Strategic Partner

When the crisis in Ukraine erupted in late 2013, no one in the Kremlin was expecting a prolonged confrontation with the West. But soon the political crisis caused by the fall of the Victor Yanukovich regime in Kiev led to the worst rift in Russia's relations with the West since the end of the Cold War. Responding to what it saw as a rude intrusion into its sphere of influence, Moscow moved to annex Crimea, and then initiated and supported a separatist movement in eastern Ukraine. By the fall of 2014, Russia was engaged in a full-scale regional war against Ukraine, though it was never officially announced. The West's initial reaction was a set of sanctions directed at people directly involved in the annexation of Crimea as well as some close friends and associates of Vladimir Putin. The Western sanctions toolkit, however, soon expanded to target key sectors of the Russian economy, including banking and energy, as well as arms sales. In the spring of 2014, following the initial round of Crimea-related sanctions, the Russian government organized a series of brainstorming sessions to analyze how different scenarios might hurt the economy. The conclusion was that Russia's near-total dependence on Western markets for its hydrocarbon exports, capital, and technology made the country extremely vulnerable, and that in order to withstand Western pressure the country needed a strong external partner. The only obvious candidate that fit the bill was China. China was the largest economy outside the Western coalition imposing sanctions on Russia, and it was also strong enough to resist U.S. attempts to include it into that coalition.

This was the context in which the Russian leadership in May 2014 embarked on a new and more ambitious pivot to China than ever before. The strategic goal was to deepen the political relationship, as well to gradually reorient the Russian economy towards the East. It was hoped that China would become a major buyer of Siberian hydrocarbons and other commodities; that Chinese financial hubs could replace the earlier role of London, Frankfurt, and New York for Russian companies; that Chinese investors would flock to buy Russian assets, provide cash, help to build and upgrade Russia's infrastructure; and that China would be willing to share critical technologies.

However, before rushing into Beijing's arms, Moscow wanted to make sure that this new pivot to China would not expose the country to even greater risks. Hence, throughout 2014 the Russian government conducted a confidential interagency process reviewing various challenges posed to Russia by a deeper engagement with China. This process, involving various government agencies, the business community and experts, was the first serious attempt on the Russian side to undertake a comprehensive review of its China policy. As a result, the Russian leadership came out of this exercise with a more clear-eyed view of its giant neighbor than ever before.

The most important conclusion reached in the Kremlin was that, although China would ultimately be more powerful than Russia, its rise does not pose an immediate challenge to Russian interests. Unlike the United States, China did not seek institutional or ideological hegemony, and would therefore not impose any political models or conditions on Russia in the way that the West had tried to promote democracy and undermine authoritarianism. The Kremlin acknowledged that China sought great power status in classical realpolitik terms, and that as its power grew so would the temptation to impose its will on others, including Russia. However, the thinking in Moscow was that Beijing would not be able to achieve hegemonic unipolarity, because its geopolitical ambitions would be checked by the United States and other great powers. This meant that China's rise would in the end lead to the construction of a non-ideological multipolar world order, an order in which Russia would play an important role as one of the great powers, second to the United States and China only, but powerful enough to maintain its sphere of influence and act independently when core national interests were at stake. Equally important was the conclusion reached in the Kremlin that many of the risks Moscow had previously associated with China had by now receded. These included in particular the perceived Chinese "demographic threat" to the Russian Far East, China's military modernization and copying of Russian military technology, and China's jostling for power and influence in Central Asia. Moscow's revised assessment was that none of these scenarios presented a great risk to Russia.

Increased Cooperation in the Russian Far East

Providing a fresh analysis of China's actual demographic and economic footprint in Siberia and the Far East was one of the key questions, since it had been the major source of Sinophobia in the Russian leadership. Looking into official figures and independent studies, Moscow concluded that Chinese migration into this region was marginal.[9] At any given moment, there were no more than 300,000 Chinese in Siberia and the Russian Far East, including tourists, exchange students, and temporary workers with legal work permits. Illegal migration had been curtailed towards the middle of the 2000s. Even more important were the structural trends on the Chinese side. With rising wages at home, Chinese in the border provinces preferred to migrate to the rich coastal regions of their Chinese motherland rather that to Russia's Far East. This trend has further accelerated since early 2015, as remittances sent back home by Chinese were halved by the sharp depreciation of the ruble. The Russian study noted that many Chinese were leaving Russia and returning to China. Moscow further concluded that it was possible to invite Chinese workers to Russia on short-term contracts working on large-scale infrastructure projects, like construction work during the Vladivostok APEC summit in 2012, and that most of the workers would return to China in orderly fashion. The overall assessment was that the "Chinese demographic threat" in the Russian Far East was just a myth, and that Russia should not let this be a stumbling block for bilateral cooperation.

Arms Exports Revitalized

The second important area under review in the 2014 study was Russia's informal ban on selling its most advanced military technology to China, originally introduced in the middle of the 2000s. Moscow's concerns at the time were both strategic and commercial. Russia feared that its own weapons sold to China might one day be used against it. Furthermore, the Chinese had a reputation within the Russian military-industrial complex for copying Russian equipment, and then positioning itself in the international arms sales market as a new competitor of Russian arms manufacturers in countries like Myanmar and Egypt.[10] Following the Ukrainian crisis, the Kremlin reconsidered its stance.

The 2014 review indicated that China's military industry sector was far more advanced than previously believed, and that the Chinese arms market offered only a brief window of opportunity for Russian producers. Within a decade or even less this window could close due to China's growing ability to develop the same weapons systems that Russia would like to sell. In addition, Moscow learned that many of the systems that the Chinese had allegedly stolen were actually developed by Russian engineers in the 1990s through contracts with Chinese military SOEs. Military technology transfer had been poorly regulated and lacked proper supervision at the time, and China, like many other countries, had simply taken advantage of the chaotic environment. Although this might not have been a very friendly act, it was definitely not illegal. In fact, these contracts had helped many Russian military enterprises and engineering teams to survive the severe disruptions of the 1990s.

On the military-strategic side, the Russian leadership now came to the conclusion that the 'China threat' had been exaggerated. First of all, since China didn't have a sizeable diaspora in Russia, any "hybrid operation" like the one that Russia itself undertook in Crimea capitalizing on pro-Russian sentiments of the majority of the peninsula's inhabitants and the presence of a Russian military base, was impossible in the Far East. Second, it became evident to Russian military planners that Moscow could in any case deter potential Chinese aggression through a combination of nuclear and conventional forces. Third, it was obvious that the PLA's priorities lay elsewhere, in the maritime domains of the East and South China Seas. The outcome of this revised thinking was that the Kremlin consented to the resumption of sales of high-end military technologies to China. Although new arms sales agreements with China didn't have major significance for Russia's national budget, they became a symbol of the restoration of political trust between the two countries.[11]

'Division of Labor' in Central Asia

Last but not least Moscow changed its view of China's growing influence in Central Asia. Since the collapse of the Soviet Union, Russia had regarded this region as its exclusive sphere of influence. It was happy to join hands with China in order to chase out America's military presence in Kyrgyzstan, and it wasn't opposed to Beijing's efforts to buy more oil and gas from Central Asian nations, since those deals were reducing incentives for local producers to seek routes to European market bypassing Russia. However, China's growing trade and investment flows with the region had caused a lot of concern in Moscow, particularly after Xi Jinping's maiden trip to Central Asia in September 2013 during which he announced China's Silk Road Economic Belt, which later became part of the Belt and Road Initiative.

A new debate about the Chinese presence in Central Asia started towards the end of 2014, and was chaired by First Deputy Prime Minister Igor Shuvalov, Putin's favorite economic troubleshooter. The conclusion of internal deliberations within the government was that China's economic dominance in Central Asia was inevitable due to structural reasons, as it was the only large potential buyer of and investor into the vast endowments of natural resources in the region. Other potential players were too far away, or their access to the region was blocked by conflicts like the war in Afghanistan or the geographic delimitation of the Caspian Sea. Furthermore, Russia and other players like Iran were in fact direct competitors of the Central Asian states in global energy markets. Finally, Russia's ability to buy commodities in the region and resell them to Europe was gradually diminishing due to Europe's efforts at diversification and the growth of renewables in the European energy mix. Against this backdrop, it was concluded that it would only be a matter of time before China became the dominant trade partner, investor and loan provider to the region, and that any economic competition with China for supremacy in Central Asia would be lost even before it started. Hence, Russia should seek a different approach by establishing a Sino-Russian condominium and division of labor in Central Asia, in which Moscow would play the role of security provider, while Beijing would be the economic engine for growth. As long as China formally respected the Russian-led EEU and did not seek bilateral free trade arrangements with Central Asian states that hurt Russia's interests, Russia would not object to Chinese economic activities in Central Asia.

Russia's Deeper Economic Engagement with China Post-Ukraine

The bar of expectation on the Russian side for cooperation with China was set very high in May 2014, as Vladimir Putin visited Shanghai. Putin and Xi Jinping presided over signing ceremonies for more than 30 bilateral agreements. These included the $400 billion gas deal between Gazprom and CNPC on the "Power of Siberia" pipeline that would pump up to 38 bcm annually to China starting in 2019, with full operational capacity to be reached in the second half of the 2020s. Half of Russia's ministers and many of its wealthiest men came home from the trip with MoUs, if not actual agreements or contracts. In September 2014, Gazprom CEO Alexey Miller told the Sochi investment forum that one couldn't apply European standards to doing business in the Asian gas market and stated that "in just one day, our esteemed Chinese partners did business amounting to the same level as Germany, our major gas consumer."[12] Many Russians were confident that China would take advantage of Russia's rift with the West by buying assets, issuing loans, and sharing technology.

The years 2015 and 2016 were to temper such expectations. It soon became evident that translating political messages into real contracts would be much more difficult than the Russian elite had hoped. In 2015, following a drop in the oil price and purchasing power of Russian companies and consumers after a devaluation of the Russian ruble, trade with China dropped by 28.6%. While this was understandable, what irritated Russian business people was the ultra-caution of Chinese financial players towards new opportunities in Russia. Russian bankers openly complained that their Chinese counterparts were de facto supporting Western sanctions through their very conservative loan policies towards Moscow, and careful monitoring of all transactions.

To be fair, this cool reaction from the Chinese side to the Russian offer of deepening economic ties should have come as no surprise. Russia had been neglecting the Chinese market for far too long, and most Chinese business players thus didn't consider Russia to be a safe place for investment. Besides, many Chinese companies were too globalized and too exposed to markets in the EU and the United States to ignore the tough stance of Western regulators on Russia, and this was particularly true for Chinese commercial banks. In addition, a number of factors in China led to reduced economic engagement with Russia in 2015–2017, such as the slowdown of the Chinese economy, and the massive anti-graft campaign announced by Xi Jinping. Beijing's efforts to stem capital outflow in 2017 had an effect on Russo-Chinese business ties too. The general mood of Russian oligarchs was captured by Victor Vekselberg, one of Russia's richest and most powerful men, talking in March 2016 at a high-level business conference attended by Vladimir Putin. "There was a certain level of optimism regarding Chinese companies. It was thought they were coming to the Russian market to spend big money. But the Chinese turned out to be very rational and very good businesspeople, so they wouldn't give money away for nothing."[13]

It is, however, important not to be misled by the complaints of Russian oligarchs and officials about Moscow's failed pivot to China. Replacing Russia's dependency on the West, which was built over centuries, with deepening ties to China will be a long process, and will require much more time than the short-term thinking of the Russian elite would allow. Nonetheless, if one zooms out and takes a larger view, it is quite clear that China's role in the Russian economy has increased significantly since 2014. First, China has decided to provide some critical technologies that are banned under Western sanctions. Although these deals are small in monetary terms, they carry large symbolic value. One such project is the Jiangsu Hengtong Power Cable Company Limited's agreement to supply high-voltage cable for the energy bridge that is intended to supply electricity to Crimea. Another example is Chinese engines for Russia's new Project 21631 Buyan-M corvettes that Russia originally planned to import from Germany. Russian government bodies and SOEs have also turned to Chinese producers like Huawei, ZTE and Inspur to purchase hardware for their IT systems, thus reducing dependency on Western suppliers. Since the disclosures of Edward Snowden in 2013, many Russians have come to believe that American and European IT equipment has backdoors that can be used by Western intelligence services.

Second, in 2016, according to data from the Russian Central Bank, China for the first time became the major loan issuer for the Russian economy, after Cyprus (and Cyprus shouldn't be seen as foreign money, since it's mostly Russian money parked in an offshore jurisdiction).[14] The amount of Chinese FDI into Russia remains highly contested. According to the Russian Central Bank, in 2015 and 2016 FDI from China amounted to only $645 million and $350 million, respectively.[15] However, figures provided by the Chinese Ministry of Commerce show a different picture, $3 billion in 2015, and $8 billion in 2016. The reason for this wide discrepancy is that the Chinese count deals known to Chinese regulators, but which go via tax havens. By the beginning of 2018, China's net accumulated FDI in Russia may exceed $50 billion, with nearly half of this entering Russia since the annexation of Crimea.[16] These figures may seem small in comparison to Western investments in Russia before the war in Ukraine. According to European Commission data, even in 2015 total EU FDI stock in Russia stood at 162 billion Euros.[17] But in the new reality of international affairs post-Ukraine, these Chinese investments represent a huge injection of money for a cash-strapped Russian economy, particularly since European FDI flows fell to 1.6 billion Euro in 2015 and 2.1 billion Euro in 2015.[18]

Third, the Chinese leadership has wisely decided to concentrate its limited resources on deals that involve members of Putin's entourage in order to win his trust. These deals included the Silk Road Fund (SRF) buying a 9.9% stake in Yamal LNG. Yamal LNG is co-owned by Gennady Timchenko, a long-time friend of Vladimir Putin, who was appointed by the President to chair the Russo-Chinese Business Council in April 2014. China Development Bank and Exim Bank also provided a $13 billion long-term loan to Yamal LNG. Another deal is the Sinopec and SRF purchase of two stakes in Sibur, Russia's largest petrochemical company. Again, Gennady Timchenko is one of the shareholders, together with Kirill Shamalov who is widely believed to be Putin's son-in-law.[19]

Beijing's focus on cementing bonds with the most powerful members of Putin's inner circle is paying off. Russian regulators have started to be more relaxed when it comes to Chinese bidding for sensitive projects in Russia, like the high-speed Moscow-Kazan train, a tender won by a Chinese company in 2016. Bilateral trade is now also bouncing back to pre-Crimea levels. In 2017, it increased by 20.8%. Russian imports of Chinese goods grew by 14.8% to $42.88 billion, while Russian exports to China increased by 27.7% to $41.2 billion. This also meant that the Russian trade deficit with China came down to just $1.5 billion. Bilateral trade is likely to increase in the coming years, primarily driven by growth in sales of Russian hydrocarbons to China. In January 2018, Russia announced the opening a second direct oil pipeline to China, which will double the capacity from 15 to 30 million tonnes a year. And towards the end of 2019 the Power of Siberia line will start pumping gas to China, entering full operational capacity by 2028. It is unlikely that Moscow and Beijing will be able to achieve the $200 billion trade benchmark by 2020, but without major drops in the oil price, this figure looks achievable by 2030.

Russia's Deeper Geopolitical Engagement with China Post-Ukraine

Before 2014, many Russians used to quote a Chinese saying that relations between Beijing and Moscow were "hot in politics but cold in the economy." And indeed before 2014 the number of bilateral summits and joint political statements far exceeded the number of business contracts.

Sino-Russian relations are no longer cold in the economy, but the aftermath of the war in Ukraine and Western sanctions has also witnessed tectonic shifts in Russian policy towards China. These events have closed a chapter in Russia's history, that of its attempts to become part of the Euro-Atlantic community. After several rounds of NATO expansion and the war in Georgia in 2008, this ambition already seemed unrealistic to many, but the developments of 2014 have set Russia on a path of confrontation with the West.

Moscow believes that Russia is defending the status quo, and that a hostile West seeks to impose its will on others. Undermining the political foundations of the U.S.-led international order is therefore seen as a good defense strategy, easing the pressure on Russia and its neighborhood. In order to achieve this new ambition Russia needs to boost the efforts of other great powers challenging American hegemony, and China is now seen as the main partner in this important undertaking. Consistent with this thinking, Russia cooperates with China in gradually revising some aspects of global governance. While the U.S.-led order was based on an idea of globalization and universal principles, including human rights and a level-playing field for businesses, Russia and China have a common narrative centered around sovereignty.

Russia's sale of its most advanced surface-to-air missile, the S-400, and its most advanced combat jet, the Su-35, to Beijing in 2015, should be seen as part of cementing mutual trust and closer political ties with China. These two weapons platforms directly influence the balance of military power in critical areas for the PLA in theaters like the East China Sea, the Taiwan Strait, and the South China Sea. The deepening of military ties is also reflected in the number of joint naval drills that Russia and China have held in recent years, in the Mediterranean Sea in 2015, in the South China Sea in 2016, and in the East China Sea and the Baltic Sea in 2017. Another area of military cooperation is missile defense. Russia and China held joint tabletop exercises on missile defense in 2016 and 2017, and in 2018 these may be expanded to include live-firing components. Such drills are clearly intended to counter expansion of American missile-defense installations in Europe and Asia, including deployments of THAAD in South Korea and Aegis Ashore in Japan.

Increased military cooperation does not mean that China and Russia are trying to build a formal military alliance. The cost of a military alliance still by far outweighs the benefits for both sides. Moscow does not want to be dragged into China's territorial conflicts in Asia, which involves important Russian partners like India and Vietnam. However, according to senior Russian military officials, the option of an alliance should not be excluded, and the practical foundation for an alliance thus needs to be established. The growing number of joint military drills will teach Russian and Chinese militaries to fight together and increase their interoperability. If the moment comes when political leaders in Russia and China decide that the simultaneous U.S. pressure on both is too hard, they need only sign a piece of paper to join forces, as the military foundation for an alliance will already be in place.

The deeper engagement post-Ukraine also stretches into the domestic politics of both countries. For example, while China has copied Russia's draconian NGO law in order to exert more control over its civil society, Russia is actively studying advanced Chinese practices of Internet governance. The Kremlin and Zhongnanhai have formed a joint mechanism for policy coordination[20] chaired by the respective leaders' chiefs of staff—a bureaucratic format China doesn't have with any other country. The mechanism chaired by the Head of the Presidential administration in Russia and the Director of the General Affairs Department of CPC has many subgroups, including regulation of the Internet, the fight against corruption, cadre development, etc. In these working groups, Russian and Chinese officials study the best practices of each other in various realms of state governance. As the Russian system becomes more authoritarian, Chinese bureaucratic authoritarianism increasingly appeals to the Kremlin as the way forward.

Conclusion: Towards Asymmetric Interdependence

For nearly two decades, Russia's policy towards China was mostly a function of Moscow's relations with its primary partners in the West. China was looked at with a mix of arrogance, fear and neglect. The crisis over Ukraine has brought Russia much closer to China, and the most important legacy of this shift in Russian foreign policy is the more nuanced approach that the Kremlin now takes towards Beijing, and not least the conclusion that China does not present an existential threat to Russia.

Russia never wanted a comprehensive pivot to China. After the global financial crisis, the Russian elite viewed China as a growing economic powerhouse that it needed to cooperate with in order to boost its own economy. However, the schism with the West over Crimea and Ukraine made Russia gravitate much closer to China than originally intended. One driver of deeper engagement with China is the transformation of Russian politics following the war in Ukraine. The country has become more authoritarian, with military and law enforcement agencies now playing an outsized role in every aspect of Russian politics, and security concerns trumping economic development. A second driver of closer engagement is the reaffirmed and increasingly widespread belief that the West is an adversary, and that Russia's mission is to push back against American hegemony. Before 2014, a "multipolar world order" was largely a slogan for Moscow, but it has now turned into a guiding principle of Russian foreign policy. This transformation of Russian thinking and policies has made it easier for Moscow to cooperate with Beijing.

Ironically, the policies of the new U.S. administration led by President Donald J. Trump have only moved Moscow closer to Beijing. On his campaign trail, Trump on numerous occasions stated that he wanted to improve ties with Russia and Putin, and that China was America's primary security concern. However, a year into his administration, U.S.-Russia ties have hit new lows. After new sanctions against Russia were codified in August 2017, it became clear to the Russian elite that the animosity between the two states was the new reality, one which could shape Russian foreign policy for years to come. A benchmark for the Russian side is the Jackson-Vanik amendment introduced in 1974 to punish USSR for preventing Jewish emigration. It was only in 2013 that this amendment was abolished by the U.S. Congress and replaced by the toxic, from the Kremlin's viewpoint, Magnitsky Act. As the sanctions are now set in stone, so is the conflict in U.S.-Russia relations. Given the role that American sanctions play for European companies, any hopes that the EU will revoke its sectorial sanctions against Russia, has also diminished.

The major strategic outcome of this fundamental shift in Russia's relations with the West is that Moscow has to redouble its efforts in partnering with China. This inevitably pushes Russia into a position of being China's junior partner. The ugly truth is that Moscow needs Beijing more than the other way around, and as the asymmetry between these two powers continues to increase, it will become cemented as the natural hierarchy in the relationship. However, Moscow is ready to live with that asymmetry as long as China at least pretends to respect Russia as a great power, and as long as the partnership with Beijing allows Moscow a certain degree of independence in its foreign policy.

Notes

1. Presidential Executive Office of Russia (2010).
2. This and many other parts of this chapter is based on a set of over 50 semi-structured interviews with Russian officials, business people and analysts conducted in 2014–2017, most of whom requested anonymity because they weren't authorized to discuss Sino-Russian relationship on the record. In order to save space and not overburden the reader with links to anonymous interviews with encrypted sources, we won't be referencing these interviews with footnotes unless needed.
3. Although, to be fair, historically by standards of unified Russian state dating to Ivan III after pushing back against Tatars in 1480, the border with China used to be one of the most peaceful. By comparison, Russia has been subjected to several military invasions from Europe, leading to the capture of its capital (in 1605 by Polish army and in 1812 by Napoleon), and nearly ending Russia as an independent state.
4. See Yeltsin's statement in *Kommersant Daily*, December 10, 1999, https://www.kommersant.ru/doc/232501.
5. Kashin (2012).
6. Gabuev (2014).
7. International Trade Centre (2018).
8. Kashin (2017).
9. See, for example, Balzer and Repnikova (2010).
10. Azar (2010).
11. Gabuev, Kashin (2017), Ibid.
12. Miller (2014).
13. Viktor Vekselberg's statement is quoted in RNS report: Vekselberg zayavil ob izmenenii trenda vzaimodejstvija s kitajskimi kompaniyami (Vekselberg has declared that the trend in cooperation with Chinese companies has changed). RNS, March 23, 2016. https://rns.online/economy/Vekselberg-zayavil-ob-izmenenii-trenda-vzaimodeistviya-s-kitaiskimi-kompaniyami---2016-03-23/.
14. Bank of Russia's data on Chinese loans in 2015 can be found at: https://www.cbr.ru/statistics/?PrtId=svs.
15. Ibid.
16. Author's interviews with Chinese officials conducted in October 2017 and March 2018 in Beijing.
17. Data accessed on European Commission's official website: http://trade.ec.europa.eu/doclib/docs/2006/september/tradoc_111720.pdf (last retrieved on January 31, 2018).
18. Ibidem.
19. Gabuev (2016).

20. This mechanism was formalized on March 24, 2016, by Director of the General Office of CPC Li Zhanshu and Kremlin Chief of Staff Sergey Ivanov. See the Kremlin's webpage report about signing a Memoranda of Cooperation between the two bodies: http://en.kremlin.ru/events/administration/51558.

Literature

Azar, Ilya. 2010. Nagleet Vostok: Rossija uvidela v Kitaje konkurenta na rinke vooruzheniy [The East is Getting Brazen: Russia Sees China as a Competitor in Arms Market]. Gazeta.ru, July 8. https://www.gazeta.ru/politics/2010/07/08_a_3396043.shtml.

Balzer, Harley, and Maria Repnikova. 2010. Migration Between China and Russia. *Post-Soviet Affairs* 26 (1): 1–37.

Gabuev, Alexander. 2014. Gosudarstvo ushlo iz kitaistiki [The State Has Abandoned Sinology]. *Kommersant-Vlast* (41), October 20. https://www.kommersant.ru/doc/2593673.

Gabuev, Alexander. 2016. China's Pivot to Putin's Friends. *Foreign Policy*, June 25. http://foreignpolicy.com/2016/06/25/chinas-pivot-to-putin-friends-xi-russia-gazprom-timchenko-sinopec/.

International Trade Centre. 2018. Bilateral Trade Between Russian Federation and China. TradeMap. https://www.trademap.org/Bilateral_TS.aspx?nvpm=1|643||156||TOTAL|||2|1|1|2|2|1|1|1|1. Accessed 31 Jan 2018.

Kashin, Vasily. 2012. Rossiya v poiskah ravnovesiya [Russia in Search of Balance]. *Vedomosti*, May 11, 2012. https://www.vedomosti.ru/opinion/articles/2012/05/11/rossiya_v_poiskah_ravnovesiya.

Kashin, Vasily. 2017. Vooruzhennaya druzhba: kak Rossija I Kitaj torgujut oruzhiem [Armed Friendship: How Russia and China Trade in Weaponry]. Carnegie Moscow Center, November 2. https://carnegie.ru/2017/11/02/ru-pub-74601.

Miller, Alexey. 2014. Miller's Report at "Sochi-2014" International Forum. Gazprom. http://www.gazprom.ru/press/news/miller-journal/2014/201583/. Accessed 31 Jan 2018.

Presidential Executive Office of Russia. 2010. Excerpts from Transcript of Meeting on the Far East's Socioeconomic Development and Cooperation with Asia-Pacific Region Countries, July 2. http://en.kremlin.ru/events/president/transcripts/8234.

PART II

Bilateral and Regional Developments

CHAPTER 4

Explaining the Emerging Sino-Russian Energy Partnership

Morena Skalamera

In terms of forging an energy partnership, China and Russia appear to be a perfect match. As China's economy boomed, its demand for natural resources became a major factor in the global economy, while Moscow has for some years stressed the "turn to the East" as it adjusts its strategic posture. But it was only in 2013–2014, when the two countries signed megadeals in oil and gas, that the China–Russia energy relationship reached the level of development their geographical proximity and economic complementariness had long implied.

In this chapter, I seek to explain the circumstances and timing of these key deals. I will also assess whether the emerging Sino-Russian energy partnership really transcends simple commercial interests, as some scholars have argued,[1] and to what extent energy cooperation points to a larger strategic convergence between Moscow and Beijing.

I argue that we need to look beyond geopolitics and economic complementariness to understand the true nature of Sino-Russian energy cooperation. While geopolitics has certainly played an influential role,

M. Skalamera (✉)
Belfer Center for Science and International Affairs, Harvard Kennedy School, Columbia, IL, USA
e-mail: Morena_Skalamera@hks.harvard.edu

J. I. Bekkevold and B. Lo (eds.), *Sino-Russian Relations in the 21st Century*, https://doi.org/10.1007/978-3-319-92516-5_4

other drivers have been no less important. Russia's energy turn to China occurred *before* the Ukraine crisis and had more to do with Moscow's assessment that Asia, and China in particular, would be the primary source of Russia's future growth.[2] Similarly, China's diversification oil and gas imports have been driven by both security concerns and profit interests.[3]

We also need to look at the nexus between domestic political conditions and foreign policy. The behavior of energy firms, like that of individuals and governments, reflects all kinds of baggage—preconceptions, biases, instincts and, in the case of National Oil and Gas Companies (NOCs), their distinctive relationships with the state. These inner workings in combination with material interests help explain the ups and downs of Sino-Russian energy cooperation.

An important academic debate is taking place about the growing interdependencies and subsequent restriction of national policies in gas as well as oil.[4] The international political economy of energy consists of actors that operate at various levels: companies; nation-states; supranational institutions, such as the European Union (EU); and international financial institutions.

The domestic-foreign policy nexus is furthermore married to the personalities of leaders. Individuals are keys to decision-making in all regimes, authoritarian and democratic. The primacy of personal pragmatism in determining policy outcomes is one of the most striking features of present-day Russia and China.[5] The different paths of Sino-Russian oil and gas trade cannot be understood without taking into account the vested interests of Russian and Chinese leaders, and the way these are shaped in turn by political institutions and conceptions of national identity.

The commercial interests of energy firms are critical in deciding the success (or failure) of specific energy projects.[6] Yet this offers only a partial explanation of the breakthroughs in 2013–2014.[7] Corporate decisions rarely, if ever, reflect "objective" commercial interests, but are made by individuals conditioned and driven by particular cultural references, vested interests, biases, and the peculiarities of their businesses.[8]

The chapter is divided into four parts. In the first two parts, I examine the contrasting paths—and fortunes—of Sino-Russian cooperation in oil and gas, respectively. In the third section, I explore developments in the energy relationship in the period following Moscow's annexation of Crimea and military intervention in Ukraine. Finally, I consider the current state and future prospects of Sino-Russian energy cooperation, and what they tell us about converging and diverging trends in the broader strategic partnership.

Oil Cooperation—A Success Story

Chinese and Russian officials and companies had been discussing the construction of a cross-border oil pipeline since the mid-1990s. The dynamics of the Sino-Russian energy relationship have always been shaped by fluctuations in world oil prices. In the 1990s, when prices were low and the Russian oil industry was starved for capital, Moscow was more interested in selling oil to China than the latter was in buying. Beijing was in no hurry to finalize negotiations, especially in the late 1990s when oil prices fell below $11 per barrel.

However, China's growing demand for oil and desire to diversify its sources of imports made the Russian pipeline alternative more attractive. Over the course of the 2000s, Chinese strategists became increasingly concerned about the security of oil transports as they traveled across the Indian Ocean and through the Strait of Malacca. They were especially worried that the United States might impose a blockade in the event of a crisis, for example over Taiwan.[9] Obama's policy of "rebalancing" towards Asia, which Beijing perceived as a broad-based effort to contain China, only strengthened its concerns about relying on sea-lanes primarily controlled by the US Navy. Meanwhile, Russia was seeking out new market opportunities for its oil and gas exports, as part of a gradual plan to shift domestic production centers to its eastern regions.[10]

The initial plan was for a pipeline from Angarsk in Eastern Siberia to Daqing in China's Heilongjiang province. However, Moscow became concerned about building a pipeline to a single monopsonic customer, and what it regarded as the excessive influence of Yukos, Russia's leading private oil company, in a deal of such strategic significance.[11] Rosneft, Russia's national oil company, subsequently swallowed Yukos's assets, and became the chief interlocutor in the discussions with CNPC.[12]

Protracted negotiations over pricing and the route of the East Siberia-Pacific Ocean (ESPO) oil pipeline then followed. In the wake of the 2008 global financial crisis, Moscow became somewhat more accommodating—a function of its acute dependence on energy export revenue, the need to compensate for slumping Western demand, and a requirement for capital to develop new oil fields. In 2009, work finally began on a pipeline spur from Skovorodino to Daqing, in exchange for $25 billion in Chinese loans to Rosneft and Transneft. It was anticipated that the deal would yield China an annual 15 million tonnes of crude oil over a period of 30 years. It would also help realize one of Russia's most important geoeconomic goals: increasing the production of oil for sale in Asian markets. This became the centerpiece of the Kremlin's development strategy towards Siberia and the Far East, and key to maximizing its economic and political weight in Asia.[13]

The Russian oil industry has been transformed into one of the most competitive sectors of the economy, and the power of Rosneft and its Executive Chairman Igor Sechin has soared. Sechin, arguably Putin's closest confidant, has positioned himself as the point man with Chinese energy firms, and a prime mover behind a burgeoning oil partnership. Since the late 2000s, this has continued to grow in scale and profitability, driven by China's insatiable growth and Russia's interest in ensuring a reliable oil market. In early 2013, Rosneft acquired TNK-BP in a $55 billion deal, adding about 9 million tonnes of oil to its production output and making Sechin the CEO of the world's largest listed crude oil producer. In June 2013, Rosneft and CNPC concluded an oil supply deal worth $270 billion over 25 years. In January 2014 Transneft opened its second and final branch of the ESPO pipeline, nearly doubling its capacity from 30 million tonnes a year to 50 million tonnes.[14] In June 2015, Russia surpassed Saudi Arabia to become China's top crude supplier.[15] And in March 2016 China overtook Germany as Russia's top crude consumer.[16]

Gas Cooperation and the Uneasy Birth of the Power of Siberia

May 2014 marked a historic moment in gas cooperation between China and Russia. After more than a decade of discussions and haggling, Gazprom and CNPC finally concluded a $400 billion supply agreement. This provided for the delivery of an annual 38 billion cubic meters of natural gas to China over a period of 30 years (beginning in 2018), to be transported through a new gas pipeline, the Power of Siberia.

Before exploring the drivers that led to this landmark agreement, it is important to note how gas cooperation differs from cooperation in oil. Unlike oil, gas is comparatively easy to produce but difficult and expensive to transport. Given that the value of what is being transported is also much lower, the sunk costs of building gas pipelines are higher. Gas pipelines create rigid relationships between suppliers and customers, making buyers potentially vulnerable to the geopolitical calculations of producers at the other end of the pipeline. Gas is more difficult than oil to replenish in response to arbitrary interruptions of supply, such as occurred in January 2006 and January 2009 when Russia and Ukraine were in dispute. Given the history of distrust between Moscow and Beijing, there were many twists and turns before the Power of Siberia gas pipeline was negotiated. In contrast to the oil sector, natural gas export infrastructure in Russia's eastern regions is insufficient to make use of the hitherto largely underdeveloped gas resources.[17]

Due to these differences, development of the gas sector in Russia has had a completely different institutional trajectory to oil. The government maintains tight control, which leads to the acute politicization of the gas business and puts Gazprom at the center of a very particular kind of state-market interaction. Since the end of the Soviet Union, Russia's oil and gas sectors have reflected opposing dynamics. Whereas decentralization of the oil sector stimulated a competitive centralization of Rosneft, the over-centralization of Gazprom's business weakened the company. In gas, commercial interactions are rarely independent from government,[18] but reflect the state's geopolitical priorities. Political control of exports remains important despite the lower profitability of gas as compared to oil.[19] The importance placed on Gazprom as the guarantor of gas to Russia's domestic market at regulated below-market prices,[20] coupled with its dependence on exports to Europe, ensures the politicization of EU–Russia gas relations. This is unheard of in the EU–Russia oil trade. Russian oil companies are commercial entities first and foremost, and geopolitical considerations play only a secondary role.

Although the share of non-Gazprom gas production has been growing, and independent companies such as Novatek play an increasingly important role both at home and in the export market, Gazprom retains a near-monopoly control on gas exports. In this connection, it has been accused by Rosneft of blocking access to the pipeline network. Since 2013, there has been a partial liberalization of Gazprom's export monopoly on LNG, although this has been limited to two companies only—Novatek, for the Yamal LNG project, and Rosneft.

Moscow has been aware for some time that the center of gravity in the global energy market has shifted to Asia, and that China, in particular, represents an enormous and fast expanding gas market.[21] Nevertheless, cooperation was slow to develop. Pricing proved a particularly contentious issue. Historically, CNPC has insisted that Gazprom sell natural gas to China at a price competitive with China's domestic coal, while Gazprom wanted CNPC to pay gas prices indexed to the oil price, as its European customers do. This, the Chinese were not prepared to accept due to their highly regulated (and subsidized) domestic gas market.

Another major difference between the two sides was over the route for transporting the gas from Russia to China. Gazprom had long wanted to pipe the gas from existing fields in Western Siberia to the western Chinese province of Xinjiang. Beijing, on the other hand, needs the gas for its populous coastal provinces. Unsurprisingly, then, there was little progress in negotiations.

Moscow's apparent stubbornness was motivated primarily by anxieties about an excessive China-dependence; it did not want to put all its eggs in the Chinese basket, especially given its view of natural gas as a vital foreign policy tool. For many years, these considerations outweighed the compelling economic rationale of opening up the China market. Gazprom was more concerned to use the notional "threat" of expansion to the East to strengthen its negotiating position with existing customers in Europe. Although its longer-term prospects depended on a turn to the East, this was slow to materialize. Little was done to upgrade Gazprom's woefully inadequate gas infrastructure in the eastern regions, which meant that it had little capacity to increase exports even after incentives emerged at the domestic level.[22]

Gazprom's fixation with Europe has led some experts to argue that it has acted as a brake on Russia's gas pivot to China.[23] Its Eastern Strategy reflects an obsolete corporate culture and anachronistic focus on the European market. It is typical of a state company that is slow to adapt to rapidly globalizing gas markets and technological innovation, both of which are critical to operating effectively in Asia.

Game-Changers?

Recent circumstances, however, have intervened to improve the chances of gas cooperation. In 2013, Russia's long-standing business model in Europe started to crumble, while the Chinese leadership stepped up efforts to find a cleaner fossil fuel alternative to polluting coal, which had become a politically sensitive issue.

Well before events in Ukraine, Russia's gas position in Europe was under pressure as a result of several factors: a growing emphasis on renewables and energy efficiency in customer-countries; European efforts to reduce energy dependence on Russia through diversification; and a prolonged economic crisis across the continent that depressed demand for Russian gas. At the same time, the EU's antitrust cases against Gazprom provoked serious resentment in Moscow, and intensified the search for alternative markets. These trends were accentuated by the Ukrainian conflict and the imposition of Western sanctions against Russia. By 2014, Moscow effectively had no option but to go cap in hand to Beijing. Just as important, Beijing shifted toward a more proactive stance on gas cooperation with Russia due to its own domestic environmental concerns, and desire to position itself as a "responsible ecologic power".[24] China was overly dependent on dirty coal, and it needed to incorporate cleaner natural gas into its primary energy mix.

But despite growing Chinese interest in Russian gas, Gazprom's woes in Europe made it harder for Moscow to conclude new accords with Beijing on favorable terms. The Chinese knew they could drive hard bargains with a Russia desperate for cash, credit, and new markets. They had also taken care to invest in alternative options. Thus, during the long years of negotiations with Gazprom, CNPC also financed and built a 30 bcm pipeline from Central Asia to service China's western provinces[25]; constructed a number of LNG terminals; and undertook exploration activity to develop China's shale gas reserves. As a result, by 2014 it had contracted sufficient gas imports to satisfy its supply needs, and was in no particular hurry to purchase piped gas from Russia. It could afford to wait for a good deal.

It has been claimed that the Power of Siberia pipeline demonstrates Russia's ability to develop new export markets outside of Europe, and marks what is just the beginning of a strategic gas relationship between Russia and China.[26] The project has been personally blessed by Xi as well as Putin,[27] and although there are reports of construction delays and spending cuts,[28] Gazprom insists that everything is on schedule.[29]

That remains to be seen. It is clear, though, that the 2014 Gazprom-CNPC agreement was less the result of commercial logic than the fortuitous outcome of new alignments among domestic interest groups, as well as external shocks such as the Ukraine crisis. Weakening gas interdependence with Europe reshaped the Russian political landscape, and empowered those elements of the elite whose interests were served by a hawkish, anti-Western policy that "looked East".[30] This trend became more pronounced as relations between Russia and Europe deteriorated.

In sum, a number of external shocks and internal developments within Russia combined to give new momentum to Sino-Russian gas cooperation. First, the economic crisis in Europe and the EU's shift toward greater use of renewables meant that Gazprom's traditional and most lucrative market was slipping away. Second, the US shale gas revolution led to a glut in the international LNG market. Third, new natural gas infrastructure such as interconnectors, better storage facilities and new LNG import terminals made the global gas market more interconnected, and the Europeans potentially less dependent on Russian gas supplies. Taken together with the changed domestic narrative about civilizational Eurasianism, this represented a real window of opportunity for policy adaptation and a strategic opening to the East.[31]

Energy Cooperation Post-Ukraine

Some observers regard the new gas relationship post-Ukraine as a major success for Moscow. Although Gazprom had to settle for a lower price for its gas than it had hoped, it still managed to strike the deal before the collapse of global oil prices, to which gas prices are indexed.[32] Other commentators argue, however, that the deal is not commercially sustainable, and is a disastrous money-losing project for Russia.[33] Still others point out that Kremlin insiders have benefited from the deal,[34] so from their point of view it is a more than viable enterprise.

What is beyond dispute is that the May 2014 gas deal has cemented Russia's turn to the East, and signaled a willingness to accommodate Beijing's priorities along the way. The fall in world oil prices from June 2014 enhanced China's leverage in the energy relationship. Prices are not likely to rebound to previous levels in the foreseeable future, and energy transition and climate change policies worldwide may further strengthen China's position. Russia's heavy dependence on energy exports makes it highly vulnerable to strategic shocks, such as the unconventional revolution and large price fluctuations.[35] More generally, oil supply is likely to remain significantly greater than global demand due to rationalization in the use of hydrocarbons and the discovery of new sources of fossil fuels around the world.[36] All this is bad news for Russia.

China's leverage might be even more pronounced in future gas negotiations. Whereas Russia will be unable to sustain a gas export policy that does not include China as its biggest market in Asia, China will have no problem satisfying its growing gas demand without Russia, at least until around 2030.[37]

In the aftermath of its annexation of Crimea, Russia hoped to gain Chinese support in its confrontation with the West, and counted in particular on new credits and investments to reduce its exposure to Western financial markets. Moscow's hopes were disappointed. The fall in global oil prices and the severely restricted access of Russian enterprises to Western credit finance[38] meant there was no compelling reason for the Chinese to fill the gap unless Moscow offered them particularly favorable terms. Better to wait and pick off Russian assets when these became available at much cheaper prices.[39] Furthermore, in the post-Ukraine world of sanctions, Chinese companies were leery about investing in upstream energy (and other) ventures, since this might harm their vastly more important economic ties with the United States.[40]

Beijing's record in this new role as principal valued customer and source of financing to Russia has been mixed. On the plus side, since 2014 several Russian NOCs have secured financing deals from Chinese state-owned banks.[41] For example, in March 2016 Gazprom arranged to borrow €2bn from the Bank of China in its largest ever bilateral loan.[42] However, except for the Yamal LNG venture, there has been no breakthrough on major infrastructure projects, highlighting the limits of a relationship that Moscow has cast as a counterweight to the West. While several major energy projects are currently being discussed, a closer look reveals that they do not constitute real alternatives, but will be at best supplements to Russia's European energy market. If completed, the Power of Siberia gas pipeline would provide China with a maximum 38 billion cubic meters (bcm) of gas per year, while the Altai project—a distant prospect today—would deliver only 30 bcm. Such figures pale in comparison with the 178.3 bcm that Gazprom exported to Europe in 2016.[43]

Meanwhile, most of China's FDI is flowing into the EU, the United States, and Asia, as it benefits from a buyer's market. Abundant energy supplies are available from plenty of other sources, including LNG from Qatar and Australia, and pipeline gas from Central Asia. LNG receiving terminals have mushroomed in China's coastal areas in recent years, with the total capacity increasing to approximately 56 bcm by the end of 2015.[44] According to BP's Energy Outlook to 2035, the share of pipeline gas supplies to China, including from Russia, will remain largely unchanged over the ten years from 2025, with the share of LNG and China's own gas output rising significantly. A desire to balance pipeline and LNG imports, in order to avoid the so-called Malacca dilemma, may encourage further negotiations with Russian exporters for pipeline gas.[45] But it is unclear whether these will achieve much, given Beijing's range of import options and development of renewables.

Russia is poised to become an important player in Asian energy markets through Novatek's Yamal LNG project in the Russian Arctic. In September 2013, CNPC bought a 20% share in Yamal LNG, while in March 2016 Novatek sold a further 9.9% stake to China's Silk Road Fund in a deal worth $0.2bn.[46] Other LNG projects, however, have fared less well. The Vladivostok LNG project was canceled. The Exxon-Rosneft joint LNG project, aiming to export natural gas produced in the Sakhalin-1 project, has also been shelved as a result of Western economic sanctions. The Altai pipeline has either been shelved indefinitely, or will at best be downsized into something more modest: a much smaller pipeline from Sakhalin to China's northeast.

So far, China has not proven to be a real substitute for Western technology or financing in Russia's large-scale infrastructure projects. It is hardly surprising, then, that several planned projects are losing momentum. To address this problem, Russia is on the lookout for new commercial opportunities in the Asia-Pacific, including with some of China's regional rivals.

Russia's Energy Diversification Strategy in Asia

In the aftermath of events in Ukraine, managing an effective energy policy has become an even bigger challenge for Russia, and a test of the strength and resilience of the Sino-Russian relationship. Russia's desperate need for financing has prompted it to look beyond China, and to deepen energy ties with other Asian powers, such as Vietnam, Japan, South Korea, and India. All these states have territorial disputes with China and oppose its behavior in the South China Sea.[47] Much of the oil and gas exported by sea from the Russian Far East, meanwhile, must cross the East China Sea, and energy deals with Vietnam give Russia an interest in the South China Sea as well.

Notwithstanding Japan's adherence to Western sanctions post-Ukraine, its investment in the Russian energy sector represents a potential complication in Sino-Russian cooperation. Revealingly, Moscow supported Japan's candidacy to join the Arctic Council as an observer, while it rejected China's for a long time.[48] However, although there is scope for increased Russian oil and gas exports to Japan, the latter's impact on regional market dynamics is limited given that its oil demand has already peaked and its natural gas demand has almost peaked, in contrast to China's surging demand for both.[49]

Many scholars believe that Moscow's energy "pivot to Asia" has delivered less than promised and will take longer to bear fruit than originally anticipated. Russia hopes to export oil and gas to the wider Asia-Pacific region, including Japan and South Korea, but is increasingly beholden to the Chinese energy market. As the Gazprom deal shows, bilateral cooperation in the gas sector is just now slowly emerging, and Russia has had to downsize its plans from pivoting to Asia to merely pivoting to China.[50] That said, Rosneft has sought to demonstrate that it is not completely reliant on China. It is looking for alternative buyers for its assets and has found an eager customer in India.[51]

Here, too, personal agency plays a critical role. Igor Sechin's close relations with his Chinese counterparts have helped forge the Sino-Russian oil partnership, and enabled him to extract tens of billions of dollars from CNPC to pay off Rosneft's debts. And in 2016, he successfully used Indian partners as a counterbalance to CNPC. Rosneft sold a 15% stake to ONGC (Indian Oil and Natural Gas Corporation) in Vankorneft, the Rosneft subsidiary that operates the Vankor field.[52] The move appeared to enhance Russian leverage vis-à-vis China. Following the Indian sale, the Beijing Gas Group bought 20% of a Russian equity field run by Rosneft for $1.1bn, in a deal that also gives the Russian oil conglomerate access to the Chinese domestic gas market.[53] Yet the Rosneft deal seems unlikely to herald a rush of similar agreements. The lack of progress on other deals, such as the Vladivostok LNG and Rosneft-Exxon LNG projects that were designated to ship LNG to other East Asian consumers, is indicative of the outsized influence of China and the absence of a genuine energy pivot to Asia. Indeed, the balance of power is tilting inexorably toward China. The Putin regime's need for continued growth in order to maintain domestic political and social stability creates a powerful incentive to seek some sort of alliance with China, even if that means accepting a subordinate economic relationship. Ultimately, Russia's presence in Northeast Asian energy markets depends on how China, the sole growing energy consumer in the region, arranges its own supply system.[54]

Conclusion

This chapter argues that we need to move away from the tendency to frame the debate over the Sino-Russian energy partnership in purely security or economic terms. The reality is that this has been driven by a mix of profit-seeking and security considerations, and domestic as well as foreign policy factors.

Energy firms are the real drivers of Sino-Russian energy cooperation. Gazprom and Rosneft have had contrasting fortunes in their dealings with Chinese companies. This is partly due to the intrinsic differences between the oil and gas sectors, but it is mainly because of the two companies' particular domestic roles and their ties to the Russian state. These help explain why Sino-Russian oil cooperation has been such a success story while gas cooperation has faltered. Personal agency, through strong individual personalities such as Sechin, has also been key.

The Russian energy shift towards China has been facilitated by the changing narrative in the Kremlin—the re-emergence of Eurasianism and the "turn to the East". For China, too, a growing emphasis on identity-based politics, for example cultivating an image as an "environmentally responsible power", and a heightened perception of the Malacca dilemma, have made it more disposed to reach deals with Russia.

Whether we characterize the Sino-Russian partnership as a soft alliance,[55] outright entente,[56] or conditional entente,[57] asymmetry defines the relationship. In the Sino-Russian energy trade, Beijing undoubtedly has the upper hand. Some Russians fret over their country's increased economic dependence on China, and such concerns may become more acute if Russia's political and economic circumstances deteriorate. Yet asymmetry does not in itself preclude constructive engagement.[58] Geopolitical and security concerns, market forces, and leaders' individual preferences may instead highlight converging interests and result in deep, sustainable cooperation. But there is a long way to go, and many hurdles to overcome, before such a vision can be realized.

Notes

1. Paik (2015), Røseth (2017).
2. Kokoshin (2011).
3. Bekkevold and Tunsjø (2018), Tunsjø (2013).
4. Belyi and Talus (2015), p. 3.

5. Lo (2015), p. 11, Easter (2008).
6. Abdelal (2015), Skalamera (2016a), See also the valuable contributions of Beth Simmons (2003), Patrick McDonald (2004), and Jonathan Kirshner (2007) within the literature on interdependence and conflict. These authors argue conflict ultimately depends on the domestic political balance between economic actors, such as bankers, who have a strong vested interest in pushing for peace versus those that do not. Energy companies, in the same vein, are a powerful domestic group that historically has been averse to conflict and to policies that limit cross-border energy trade.
7. Skalamera (2016b), Ziegler (2012).
8. Lo (2015), p. 5, Abdelal (2015).
9. Cohen and Kirshner (2012), p. 157. Some 80% of Chinese oil imports travel through the strait, a narrow 600-mile long waterway surrounded by Singapore, Malaysia, and Indonesia—all US allies—and plagued by piracy.
10. Shi Hongtao (2004), Liu Xiaoli (2009).
11. In 2002, Mikhail Khodorkovsky's Yukos held talks about engaging the Chinese in the development of Eastern Siberian upstream, and building an oil pipeline that would service the Chinese market from those fields. Such a proposition, however, ran against Putin's plans to build a pipeline all the way to the Pacific port of Nakhodka, thereby adding an extra 3000 km to the original Khodorkovsky plan. In 2004, Khodorkovsky was arrested and accused by the Russian government of, among other things, large tax evasion. The Yukos Affair marked the beginning of a large renationalization of Russia's oil and gas industry. For a detailed discussion see Skalamera (2016b).
12. Poussenkova (2013).
13. The Russian Far East is a huge, resource-rich region, but also very sparsely populated and remote from Russia's centers of power. It has lost a quarter of its population since the collapse of the Soviet Union and is now home to a little over six million people.
14. This was in exchange for an additional prepayment of $30 billion to Rosneft.
15. Bloomberg (2015).
16. RT (2016).
17. Itoh (2017).
18. Belyi and Talus (2015).
19. Belyi and Locatelli (2015).
20. As observed by a Russian energy analyst, Gazprom has always branded itself as a "socially responsible organization" accountable for Russian gas supplies. However, as the analyst notes, it is questionable whether this extra 'responsibility' justifies state's subsidies in favor of Gazprom. Interview with the author, September 2015, Moscow.

21. The International Energy Agency estimates that Asia's natural gas use will increase by a factor of more than 2.6 by 2035 (and that China's will quadruple), while demand in Russia's traditional European markets will grow only slightly. The EU's natural gas demand is expected to peak in 2025–2030.
22. Itoh (2017).
23. Johnson (2015).
24. Skalamera (2016b).
25. The delays over the gas deal were instrumental in pushing Beijing to turn to Central Asia, where, in 2007 it quickly negotiated and implemented long-term agreements with Turkmenistan, Kazakhstan, and Uzbekistan. This, in turn, led to China becoming the principal economic player in Central Asia and an emerging strategic actor there. The 4000 km pipeline became operational in 2009 and is to western China and transporting 30bcm a year over 30 years.
26. Trenin (2015).
27. Ibid.
28. Astakhova and Kobzeva (2017).
29. Elena Burmistrova, Head of Gazprom export, in conversation with the author, June 2016, Moscow.
30. Rozman (2014).
31. Calder and Ye (2004).
32. Trenin (2015), p. 7, Gabuev (2016).
33. Krutikhin (2014), Noel (2017).
34. Zaslavskiy (2014), Gabuev (2016).
35. In 2015, the oil and gas sectors accounted for 43% of the Russian federal budget and 53% of total exports—see Itoh (2017).
36. Maugeri (2017).
37. Itoh (2017).
38. Lo (2015), Abdelal et al. (2016).
39. That said, the leadership in Beijing told China's corporate players to avoid overtly exploiting Russia's difficult situation by seeking one-sided deals at knockdown prices. It worried that such behavior might cause unnecessary tensions and even encourage Russia to make another U-turn in order to mend relations with the West—see Gabuev (2016).
40. Khrennikova (2015).
41. Gabuev (2016).
42. Farchy (2016).
43. Gazprom.
44. Itoh (2017).
45. BP.
46. Buckley (2016).

47. Mankoff (2015).
48. Yahuda (2017).
49. Itoh (2017).
50. Skalamera and Goldthau (2016).
51. Henderson and Mitrova (2016).
52. Henderson and Mitrova (2016).
53. Foy (2017).
54. Itoh (2017).
55. Gabuev (2016).
56. Trenin (2015).
57. Lo (2017), p. 11.
58. Lo (2017), p. 26.

Literature

Abdelal, Rawi. 2015. The Multinational Firm and Geopolitics: Europe, Russian Energy, and Power. *Business and Politics* 17 (3): 553–576.

Abdelal, Rawi, Morena Skalamera, and M. Atnashev. 2016. Russia: Tribulations and *Toska. Harvard Business School Supplement*, March, 716–074.

Astakhova, Olesya, and Oksana Kobzeva. 2017. Russia–China Talks Over New Gas Routes Stalled: Sources. *Reuters*, June 7. https://www.reuters.com/article/us-russia-china-energy/russia-china-talks-over-new-gas-routes-stalled-sources-idUSKBN18Y1TX.

Belyi, Andrei V., and C. Locatelli. 2015. State and Markets in Russia's Hydrocarbon Sectors: Domestic Specificities and Interrelations with the West. In *States and Markets in Hydrocarbon Sectors*, ed. A. Belyi and K. Talus. London: Palgrave Macmillan.

Belyi, Andrei V., and Kim Talus (eds.). 2015. *States and Markets in Hydrocarbon Sectors*. London: Palgrave Macmillan.

Bekkevold, Jo Inge, and Øystein Tunsjø. 2018. Sustaining Growth: Energy and Natural Resources. In *Sage Handbook on Contemporary China*, ed. Mark Frazier and Wu Weiping. Sage, forthcoming.

Bloomberg. 2015. Russia Pips Saudi Arabia in Race to Grab China Oil Market Share, June 23. Available at https://www.bloomberg.com/news/articles/2015-06-23/russia-pips-saudi-arabia-in-race-to-grab-china-oil-market-share.

BP Energy Outlook to 2035.

Buckley, Neil. 2016. Sino-Russian Gas Deal: Smoke Without Fire. Inside Business. *Financial Times*, May 11. https://www.ft.com/content/eea4f2ec-16c0-11e6-b197-a4af20d5575e.

Calder, Kent, and Min Ye. 2004. Regionalism and Critical Junctures: Explaining the 'Organization Gap' in Northeast Asia. *Journal of East Asian Studies* 4 (2): 191–226.

Cohen, Danielle F.S., and Jonathan Kirshner. 2012. The Cult of Energy Insecurity and Great Power Rivalry Across the Pacific (Chapter 6). In *The Nexus of Economics, Security and International Relations in East Asia*, ed. Avery Goldstein and Edward D. Mansfield. Stanford, California: Stanford University Press.

Easter, Gerald M. 2008. The Russian State in the Time of Putin. *Post-Soviet Affairs* 24 (3): 199–230.

Farchy, J. 2016. Chinese Gas Company Buys 20% of Russian Field from Rosneft for $1.1bn. *Financial Times*, March 3.

Foy, Henry. 2017. Chinese Gas Company Buys 20% of Russian Field from Rosneft for $1.1bn. *Financial Times*, June 29. https://www.ft.com/content/b3fd1481-8f71-3326-9d92-9018fb6f4abc.

Gabuev, Alexander. 2016. Friends with Benefits? Russian–Chinese Relations After the Ukraine Crisis. *Carnegie Moscow Center*, June.

Gazprom Statistics. Accessed at http://www.gazpromexport.ru/en/statistics/.

Henderson, James, and Tatiana Mitrova. 2016. Energy Relations between Russia and China: Playing Chess with the Dragon. *OIES Paper*: WPM 67, August.

Itoh, Shoichi. 2017. Sino-Russian Energy Relations in Northeast Asia and Beyond: Oil, Natural Gas, and Nuclear Power. In *Japan and the Sino-Russian Entente: The Future of Major-Power Relations in Northeast Asia*, ed. Shoichi Itoh, Ken Jimbo, Michito Tsuruoka, and Michael Yahuda. NBR Special Report No. 64, April, National Bureau of Asian Research, Washington, DC.

Johnson, Keith. 2015. Russia's Stumbling Pivot to Asia. *Foreign Policy*, May 8. http://foreignpolicy.com/2015/05/08/russias-stumbling-pivot-to-asia-putin-xi-natural-gas-gazprom-altai/.

Khrennikova, Dina. 2015. China Wary of Closer Russia Energy Ties, Ex-CNOOC Economist Says. *Bloomberg Business*, July 2. https://www.bloomberg.com/news/articles/2015-07-02/china-wary-of-closer-russia-energy-ties-ex-cnooc-economist-says.

Kirshner, Jonathan. 2007. *Appeasing Bankers: Financial Caution on the Road to War*. Princeton, NJ: Princeton University Press.

Kokoshin, A. 2011. Сценарии развития Восточной Сибири и российского Дальнего Востока [Scenarios for the Development of East Siberia and the Russian Far East]. URSS.

Krutikhin, Mikhail. 2014. It's all about Russia's Incompetence. *Natural Gas Europe*, December 4. Available at https://naftogaz-europe.com/article/en/mikhailkrutikhin.

Liu, Xiaoli. (ed.). 2009. *Jundui yingfu zhongda tufa shijian he weiji feizhang-zheng junshi xingdong yanjiu* [A Study of Nonwar Military Operations by the Armed Forcees to Deal with Major Sudden Incidents or Crises]. Beijing: Guofang daxue chubanshe.

Lo, Bobo. 2015. *Russia and the New World Disorder*. Washington, DC: Brookings Institution Press.

Lo, Bobo. 2017. New Order for Old Triangles? The Russia–China–India Matrix. IFRI, Russia/NIS Center, April.

Mankoff, Jeffrey. 2015. Russia's Asia Pivot: Confrontation or Cooperation? *Asia Policy* 19: 65–87.

Maugeri, L. 2017. *OPEC's Misleading Narrative About World Oil Supply*, Harvard Kennedy School, Belfer Center for Science and International Affairs, Policy Brief, March.

McDonald, Patrick J. 2004. Peace Through Trade or Free Trade? *Journal of Conflict Resolution* 48 (4): 547–572.

Noel, Pierre. 2017. The Power of Siberia Natural-Gas Project: Commercial or Political? The Survival Editor's Blog, *IISS Comment*, January. Available at https://www.iiss.org/en/politics%20and%20strategy/blogsections/2017-6dda/january-7f20/power-of-siberia-2a1d.

Paik, K. 2015. Sino-Russian Gas and Oil Cooperation: Entering into a New Era of Strategic Partnership? *OIES Paper*: WPM 59, April.

Poussenkova, Nina. 2013. Russia's Eastern Energy Policy: A Chinese Puzzle for Rosneft. IFRI Russia/NIS Center, Paris, April. Available at https://www.ifri.org/sites/default/files/atoms/files/ifrirnv70poussenkovarosneftengapril2013.pdf.

Rozman, Gilbert. 2014. The Russian Pivot to Asia. *The Asan Forum*, December 1. http://www.theasanforum.org/the-russian-pivot-to-asia/.

Røseth, Tom. 2017. Russia's Energy Relations with China: Passing the Strategic Threshold? *Eurasian Geography and Economics* 58 (1): 23–55.

RT. 2016. China overtakes Germany as Russia's Top Crude Consumer, March 14. https://www.rt.com/business/335498-china-germany-oil-consumer/.

Shi, Hongtao. 2004. Zhongguo nengyuan anquan zaoyu 'Maliujia kunju' [China's Energy Security Encounters the "Malacca Predicament"]. *Zhongguo qingnian bao*, June 15.

Simmons, Beth. 2003. Pax Mercatoria and the Theory of the State. In *Economic Interdependence and International Conflict*, ed. Edward D. Mansfield and Brian M. Pollins. Ann Arbor: University of Michigan Press.

Skalamera, Morena. 2016a. Invisible but Not Indivisible: Russia, the European Union, and the Importance of "Hidden Governance". *Energy Research & Social Science* 12: 27–49.

Skalamera, Morena. 2016b. Sino-Russian Energy Relations Reversed: A New Little Brother. *Energy Strategy Reviews* 13–14: 97–108.

Skalamera, M., and A. Goldthau. 2016. Russia: Playing Hardball or Bidding Farewell to Europe? Discussion Paper, Belfer Center for Science and International Affairs, June.

Trenin, Dmitri. 2015. From Greater Europe to Greater Asia? The Sino-Russian Entente. *Carnegie Moscow Center*, April 9. Available at http://carnegie.ru/2015/04/09/from-greater-europe-to-greater-asia-sino-russian-entente-pub-59728.

Tunsjø, Øystein. 2013. *Security and Profit in China's Energy Policy: Hedging Against Risk.* New York: Columbia University Press.

Yahuda, Michael. 2017. Japan and the Sino-Russian Strategic Partnership. In *Japan and the Sino-Russian Entente: The Future of Major-Power Relations in Northeast Asia*, ed. Shoichi Itoh, Ken Jimbo, Michito Tsuruoka, and Michael Yahuda, NBR Special Report No. 64, April, National Bureau of Asian Research, Washington, DC.

Zaslavskiy, Ilya. 2014. Insiders Benefit from Gazprom-CNPC Gas Deal, But Russia's Budget Loses. *Chatham House*, London, June 2. https://www.chathamhouse.org/expert/comment/14633.

Ziegler, Charles E. 2012. Energy Pipeline Networks and Trust: The European Union and Russia. *International Relations* 27 (1): 3–29.

CHAPTER 5

The Military Dimension in Sino-Russian Relations

Paul N. Schwartz

Introduction

Russia's intervention in Ukraine in 2014 led to a fundamental shift in the post-Cold War international order. The effects of Ukraine were felt most immediately in Europe, where it led to a major deterioration in Russia's relations with the West. Over time, however, Ukraine brought about a significant shift in Russia's relations with China as well, as Moscow sought to upgrade relations with Beijing to obtain economic and diplomatic support needed to offset Western sanctions and avoid isolation.

The results of these efforts have been mixed. In areas such as trade and financing, Chinese support has consistently failed to live up to the Kremlin's expectations. In areas such as energy, Beijing has been notably more cooperative, although it has driven hard bargains with Russia to secure favorable terms. By contrast, military relations have been a distinct area of success.

P. N. Schwartz (✉)
Center for Strategic and International Studies (CSIS),
Washington, DC, USA
e-mail: PSchwartz@csis.org; pnschwartz@verizon.net

J. I. Bekkevold and B. Lo (eds.), *Sino-Russian Relations in the 21st Century*, https://doi.org/10.1007/978-3-319-92516-5_5

Arms trade has risen sharply since Ukraine, highlighted by two major arms agreements in 2015 for the sale of Russia's S-400 air defense system and Su-35 combat aircraft.[1] Joint military exercises have expanded as well, as the two have held some of their largest joint exercises to date. Increasingly, they have been holding such exercises in more provocative locations as well, such as the Baltics and the South China Sea. Finally, despite, the growing military imbalance between Russia and China, the two continue to maintain a relatively demilitarized border, allowing them to concentrate most of their forces elsewhere.

Still, this is not the first time that Russia and China have upgraded their military relationship. From 1991–2005, Moscow and Beijing were engaged in a comparably high level of defense cooperation, highlighted by large-scale arms transfers and military-to-military engagement. Over time, however, this enhanced level of cooperation proved to be unsustainable due to growing divergence between Russia and China over a range of issues. As a result, starting around 2006, military relations entered into a relative down period, where they remained for several years.[2]

Given this recent history, is it realistic to expect things to turn out any differently this time around? Take arms sales, for example. For the moment at least, they have returned to their previous high levels. But how sustainable is this likely to be? The answer will depend on several factors. Will Russia now be more willing to sell advanced military technology to China? Or were these sales simply one-time events driven by Russia's momentary desperation? And what about the problems that have hindered arms sales in the past, such as China's reverse engineering practices? Have the two finally overcome these problems or have they simply been suppressed for the moment?

By the same token, Russian–Chinese joint military exercises also appear to be reaching new heights post-Ukraine. But again, how sustainable will this prove to be? Much will depend on the perceived value of these exercises for both countries. Do they see them as a useful mechanism for boosting their respective military capabilities? Or are they viewed primarily as a political tool for sending signals to others about the strength of their strategic partnership? And what have the two gained by holding joint naval exercises in places such as the Baltics and the South China Sea?

The two countries' defense postures continue to be directed primarily toward other countries, especially the United States. If anything, Ukraine seems to have reinforced this policy. Yet questions remain about the long-term durability of this policy in light of China's growing military power. Until recently, Russia had been holding large-scale military exercises in the Russian Far East as a means of hedging against China. Given Russia's increased dependence on China, will Moscow now abandon this policy? And, over the long run, will the growing military imbalance between the two countries eventually force Russia to adjust its defense posture?

The recent upgrade in military relations between Russia and China has also raised questions of a more fundamental nature, questions about the character of their relationship and the degree to which the two are becoming more aligned. Until recently, most analysts tended to discount the military significance of the Russia–China strategic partnership due to conflicting interests and persistent mistrust.[3] For the same reasons, the likelihood that the two might become true allies has tended to be discounted as well.[4]

Since Ukraine, however, there have been growing signs of convergence between the two countries, and this has sparked much debate about the extent to which the two are now aligning. For the first time since the Cold War, there is serious debate about the potential for the two to form a de facto security alliance if not an outright military alliance.[5] Most observers still tend to discount this possibility, seeing the recent increase in defense cooperation as noteworthy, but still falling within well-circumscribed limits.[6] Others are less confident, however, viewing this increase as a powerful indicator of a deepening security relationship between Russia and China.[7]

This chapter will attempt to shed light on the foregoing questions by examining the development of Russian–Chinese military relations over the past decade. It will conclude by evaluating the extent to which this reflects a fundamental shift in the overall relationship toward closer alignment.

Military-Technical Cooperation

Arms sales continue to occupy a central place in the military relationship. Since 1992, Russian arms sales to China have exceeded $33 billion. Russia is by far China's largest arms supplier, accounting for nearly 80% of its total imports since 1991. Over the same period, Beijing has been one of Russia's leading arms clients, accounting for nearly a quarter of its total arms sales (Fig. 5.1).[8]

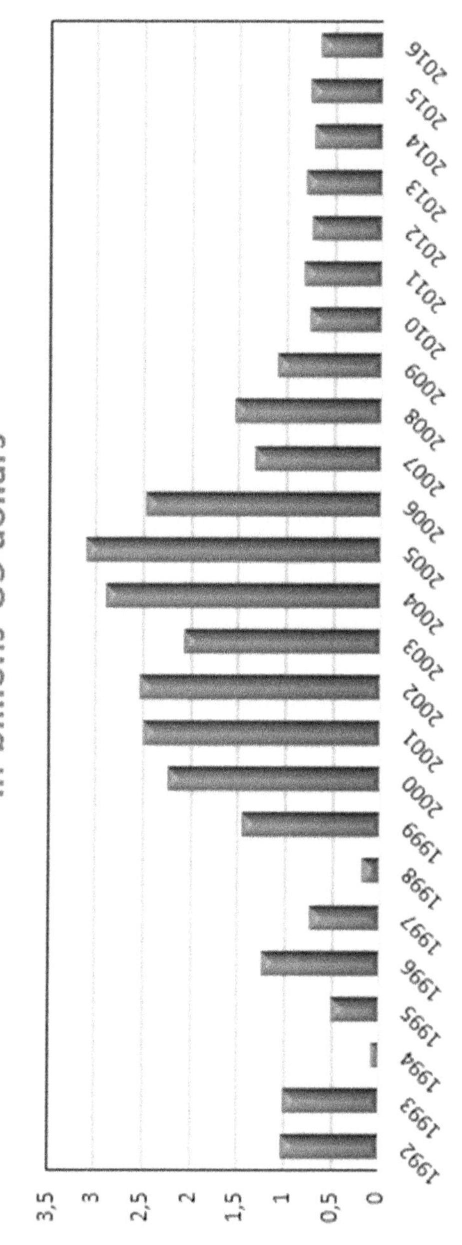

Fig. 5.1 Russian Arms Sales to China 1992–2016

The Unexpected Decline of Russian Arms Sales

Between 1991 and 2006, Russia arms sales to China were conducted on a massive scale, as the PLA sought to rapidly boost its military capabilities. Over this period, Beijing purchased Kilo submarines, Sovremenny destroyers, Su-27/Su-30 combat aircraft, and several other Russian systems. Russia transferred substantial amounts of military technology as well.[9] As a result, arms sales to China averaged over $1 billion dollars per year during the mid-1990s, and over $2 billion per year during the early-2000s.[10]

Starting in 2006, however, Russian arms sales to China declined abruptly. From 2006–2010, the two failed to enter into a single new arms sale agreement of any substance, although sales of aircraft engines and components continued. This led some observers to predict the beginning of the end for Russian platform sales to China.[11]

There were several reasons for this sharp decline. China was unhappy with Russian pricing policies as well as the poor maintenance record of Russian equipment. It was also unhappy about Russia's failure to deliver on a contract to sell Il-76 transport aircraft to China due to supply problems.[12]

Moreover, though China was still subject to a Western arms embargo, by 2006 its defense industry was increasingly able to satisfy the military's basic requirements.[13] China now wanted to buy more advanced Russian systems, and it wanted more of the underlying technologies as well.[14]

However, by 2006 Russia was increasingly reluctant to transfer additional weapons to China. Having diversified its customer base, Russia's defense industry was now less dependent on Chinese arms sales. China's reverse engineering practices were another major factor, especially after China introduced the J-11B fighter, an obvious clone of Russia's Su-27 Flanker.

Moscow was also increasingly concerned about China's emerging arms export activities. Some feared that Beijing would use previously transferred Su-27 technology to compete with Russia for exports of advanced combat aircraft.[15] Moreover, although Chinese arms sales were still relatively modest, Russian defense firms were already facing increased competition from China in traditional Russian markets such as Egypt and Myanmar.[16]

Concerns over China's rising military power contributed to the decline as well. Such concerns had always been present to some extent. Moscow had long maintained a ban on sales of strategic bombers to

China, and had been reluctant to transfer its most advanced conventional weapons as well, although they had often been freely sold to India, much to Beijing's chagrin.[17] Since the early-2000s, however, concerns over the security risks of selling weapons to China had been growing among some Russian observers.[18]

Nevertheless, such worries probably contributed less to the slowdown than the other concerns mentioned above. Much of the Russian elite still believed that selling weapons to China actually enhanced Russia's security, at least in the short run, by helping to maintain Beijing's goodwill.[19] They were also inclined to discount the near-term risks, since arms sales were limited primarily to defensive weapons, and since Beijing was still focused too heavily on Taiwan to worry about Russia.[20]

Thus, Moscow tended to see China as more of a long-term security challenge. In 1998, for example, General Baluevsky, the head of the General Staff Main Directorate, predicted that it would take until 2050 for China to become a serious military power.[21] Over the short term, however, arms sales still yielded substantial benefits for Russia. Ultimately then, Russia's fear of arming a potential future adversary was at most a secondary factor in the decline in bilateral arms trade.

The Revival of Arms Sales

After a prolonged period of decline, arms sales between Russia and China finally began to improve from 2011.[22] They received a further boost after Xi came to power a year later, as both sides sought to upgrade relations in the face of increasing competition with the West.[23] For the Kremlin, concerns over NATO's intervention in Libya and perceived U.S. support for the anti-Putin demonstrations in 2011–2012 were just the latest in a long list of grievances. For China, the recently announced U.S. pivot to Asia led to a sharp increase in tensions between Washington and Beijing in the Western Pacific.

Despite the improved political climate, arms sales increased only gradually at first, highlighted by two sizable agreements for the sale of Al-31 aircraft engines in 2011 for USD $500 million, and Mi-17 combat helicopters in 2012 for USD $660 million.[24] Signs of real progress emerged in April 2013, however, when Chinese media reports indicated that Beijing had agreed in principle to purchase Su-35 combat aircraft, Lada-class submarines, and possibly S-400 air defense systems from Moscow.[25]

Over the next two years, however, these transactions became stuck in protracted negotiations. Russia wanted Beijing to commit to buy minimum numbers of each system as assurances against reverse engineering. For their part, the Chinese sought additional price concessions and probably technology transfers as well.[26] As talks dragged on, many observers doubted whether these sales would ever take place.

Finally, in 2015 Moscow and Beijing announced two major new arms agreements, one for the sale of the S-400 for a total of $3 billion, and another for the sale of the Su-35 Flankers for a total of $2 billion.[27] Not only were these the largest transactions between the two since the early 2000s, they also ended Russia's informal ban on sales of advanced weapon systems to China. Russia's intervention in Ukraine had much to do with breaking the logjam. Moscow now urgently needed Beijing's support to help counter Western sanctions and diplomatic pressure, and it was willing to make concessions on arms sales to obtain this. The desire for revenue was also an important factor, especially since Russia's defense industry was facing sustained budget cuts due to the country's ongoing economic problems.[28]

A growing need for Chinese defense technologies likely played a role as well. Due to Western sanctions over Ukraine, Russia had been forced to turn to China for certain dual-use items it could no longer obtain from the West, including electronic components for Russia's aerospace programs, and marine diesel engines for the Russian Navy.

Anger at the United States was yet another factor. In the past, Moscow had often pressed for greater military cooperation with China during times of increased tensions with Washington, as this was seen as a way of imposing additional costs on the West for its policies toward Russia.[29]

In the face of such exigencies, long-standing concerns over intellectual property and security simply appear to have been overridden. According to Alexander Gabuev, the Kremlin conducted a policy review prior to approving the Su-35 sale and determined that the associated intellectual property risks were minimal because China had virtually closed the technology gap with Russia anyway.[30]

However, the Kremlin's logic seems strained at best. If the PRC was truly so technologically advanced, then why would it want to buy these systems in the first place, especially given its long-standing desire for self-sufficiency? More telling is the fact that Russia required China to sign yet another intellectual property agreement prior to the sale.[31]

Concerns over rising competition from Chinese arms exports were also discounted, since Moscow still views this as more of a long-term problem, given that the two countries occupy different segments of the global arms trade.[32]

Nor was Moscow particularly swayed by the dangers of selling such advanced weapons to a rising regional superpower either. The fact that Russia offered these systems in the first place says a lot about the Kremlin's priorities. According to Gabuev, the Kremlin was no longer worried about a Chinese incursion in the Russian Far East because Chinese immigration had declined significantly and was no longer seen as a major problem.[33] But this sounds more like a Kremlin rationalization than a sound assessment, given the enduring realities of China's rising military power. Instead, the Kremlin seems once again to have emphasized short-term gains over long-term security implications.

Thus, despite the considerable risks involved for Russia, arms sales to China were restarted. By all indications, they are likely to continue as well, as all of the conditions driving such sales are still in place. According to reports, Russia and China have already entered into several new arms sales agreements. In 2017, new contracts were reportedly signed for the sale of additional D-30 aircraft engines for $658 million and for the transfer of AL-31 aircraft engines for a comparable amount.[34] Technology transfers are also on the rise, as indicated by a recent Russian announcement that several joint projects are currently proceeding.[35]

Yet it is likely that arms transfers will continue to be limited by various factors. For one, it is unclear as yet whether Russia will supply more of its most advanced weapons systems to China, as subsequent sales have focused primarily on the transfer of components. Even if it did, due to China's increased self-sufficiency, it is highly unlikely that arms sales will ever reach the high sustained levels achieved in the early 2000s. Most importantly, it is not at all clear how long this renewed arms trading relationship will last, as all of the problems that led to the original slowdown in 2006 are still present. They have simply been pushed into the background for now.

Joint Military Exercises

Military exercises constitute the second major area of Russia–China military relations. Moscow and Beijing currently maintain two principal joint exercise programs, the Peace Mission counter-terrorism exercises in

Central Asia, which have been held since 2005, and the Joint Sea naval exercises, which were added in 2012. Recently, Moscow and Beijing have been conducting other joint exercises as well. As a result, the scale and pace of their joint exercise activity have been increasing rapidly.

The Peace Mission Program

Since 2005, Russia and China have been holding Peace Mission exercises under the auspices of the Shanghai Cooperation Organization (SCO). The founding of Peace Mission was an important milestone for the two countries as it constituted a significant expansion of their military relationship beyond arms sales. That the Peace Mission program has been sustained for more than a decade is testament to their commitment to it.

The program commenced in 2005, partly in response to U.S. policies. By then, Moscow and Beijing were increasingly dissatisfied with Washington over issues such as Western support for the "Color" revolutions, arms sales to Taiwan and the establishment of U.S. military bases in Central Asia.[36] The launch of Peace Mission coincided with other joint actions aimed at the United States, including the release of a Russian–Chinese declaration repudiating the U.S.-led international order and an SCO declaration calling for the United States to close its military bases in Central Asia.[37] Thus, from its very inception, Peace Mission has had a certain anti-U.S. character.

Peace Mission was also intended to provide a venue for the Russian and Chinese militaries to gain greater operational experience. To this end, the two have held nine separate exercises to date. While ostensibly focusing on counter-terrorism, these exercises have encompassed a wide range of military activities.

Up to a point, Peace Mission exercises have been useful in allowing the two militaries to gain operational experience, especially as their level of complexity and joint activity has increased. During Peace Mission 2014, for example, participants conducted a range of joint air-ground exercises involving a wide array of advanced weapons.[38]

Overall, however, the operational benefits of the Peace Mission exercises have been limited, largely due to shortcomings in their design, which has often led to them being overly scripted and poorly coordinated. Though recent exercises have been better designed, such problems continue to surface. During Peace Mission 2014, for example, the level of interoperability, though improved, still remained relatively limited, especially in comparison with comparable exercises held within Western alliances.[39]

Peace Mission's value has also been undermined by persistent mistrust and geopolitical rivalry. Prior to Peace Mission 2005, Moscow and Beijing spent months wrangling over the location of the exercise. Beijing wanted to hold it in Zhejiang province near the Taiwan Straits, but this was deemed too provocative for Moscow, which did not want to become entrapped in China's Taiwan dispute.[40] Ultimately, Moscow insisted that it be held further north.

A similar incident occurred prior to Peace Mission 2007 when Russia pushed for the exercise to be held within a joint SCO-CSTO framework. By so doing, Moscow hoped to use the exercise as a means of strengthening the CSTO, a rival security organization controlled by Russia. However, Beijing rejected the idea because it wanted to enhance the security role of the SCO, in which it maintained a leading role.[41]

Ongoing rivalry between Russia and China over the CSTO and SCO continues to undermine the Peace Mission program. Russia remains deeply ambivalent about the SCO. On the one hand, it would like the SCO to take on a more anti-American character by emphasizing its potential as a military alliance. On the other, Moscow's preference for the CSTO has left it with little interest in actually improving the SCO's military capacity.[42]

By contrast, China has shown little interest in using the SCO as a vehicle for overtly challenging the West. Instead, Beijing has preferred to use it as an instrument for making further economic inroads into Central Asia, to Russia's detriment. At the same time, Beijing has been pushing for the SCO to take on a greater security role in Central Asia, as that would further boost China's influence in the region.

Such rivalry helps to explain why the SCO still lacks a unified command structure, and why the operational benefits of Peace Mission have been so limited as well. Moscow's reluctance to support the SCO has led it to underinvest in the Peace Mission program.[43] Thus, Peace Mission has been undermined by internal divisions, lack of sophistication, poor planning, and lack of a joint command structure.[44]

Since Ukraine, however, Russia has chosen to downplay its differences with China over Central Asia while recommitting to the Peace Mission program, at least rhetorically. The Russian media cited Peace Mission 2014 as evidence that Moscow still has important allies.[45] Consequently, so long as Russia's relations with the West remain strained, its interest in the Peace Mission program will likely remain strong as well.

Joint Sea Naval Exercises

In 2012, Russia and China added the Joint Sea naval exercise series to their growing defense portfolio. Joint Sea provides a forum for the Russian and Chinese navies to engage in a wide range of joint activities. Thus far, the two navies have conducted seven such exercises in total.

In comparison with Peace Mission, Joint Sea has been a greater success. Right from the start, these exercises have been relatively sizable affairs. Joint Sea 2013 involved a total of 12 Russian and 6 PLA warships, and this has been fairly typical.[46] Moreover, each country has been willing to contribute sizable forces to these exercises, especially when it is hosting the exercise.[47]

The exercises have also been better designed than the Peace Mission exercises. Recently, they have increased in complexity as well, as demonstrated by the combined air-sea amphibious exercise held during Joint Sea 2016. They have also been exhibiting greater realism, as shown by use of so-called "back to back" exercises held during Joint Sea 2016, in which participants conducted maneuvers with minimal pre-planning.[48]

In short, Joint Sea has been an effective vehicle for each side to gain operational experience. Thus far it has also been relatively unaffected by geopolitical rivalry of the kind that has hindered Peace Mission. Moreover, the need for the program is greater, since both countries face similar naval challenges from the United States. Both lack meaningful alternatives in any event, since most Western countries refuse to engage in comparable naval exercises with either Russia or China, out of reluctance to help them build up their combat capabilities.[49]

Nevertheless, there have been clear limits to the Joint Sea program. Due to the limited emphasis on interoperability, the program has done little to prepare the two navies to conduct joint naval operations against a real-world adversary.[50] Since the two are not currently allies, however, this has not been a priority. Instead, both navies have been content to use these exercises as a means to gain operational experience and exchange technical know-how.

Joint Sea's operational benefits have also been constrained by the limited scope and duration of these exercises. On average, a Joint Sea exercise lasts around seven days, which is significantly shorter than the typical U.S./allied naval exercise.[51] Joint Sea exercises also tend to be smaller than their U.S./allied counterparts.[52] Given these limitations, the operational benefits from Joint Sea have failed to match those provided by comparable exercises held in the West.

So far, fear of China's rising military power has not been a significant limiting factor, even though Joint Sea has the potential to create security problems for Russia. As Russian analyst Alexander Khramchikhin recently warned, by exercising with China in the South China Sea, Russia risked becoming entrapped in China's territorial disputes in the region. He also warned that Joint Sea would enhance China's naval capabilities in ways detrimental to Russia's security interests.[53]

Instead of heeding such warnings, the Kremlin has chosen to double down on Joint Sea post-Ukraine. Surprisingly, so has China, as the two countries have increasingly been holding these exercises in controversial locations, such as the Baltic and the South China Sea. In essence, they have been using these exercises quite provocatively to signal their growing power, their expanding security ties, and their mutual displeasure with the United States. Given the high geopolitical value obtained from these exercises, and the limited blowback they have provoked until now, it seems likely that such exercises will not only continue, but may soon be held in even more controversial locations such as the Indian Ocean and perhaps even the Western hemisphere.

Recent Developments

Since Ukraine, Russia and China have begun to hold additional joint military exercises as well. By far the most important of these has been the joint missile defense exercise held in May 2016 in response to the U.S. decision to deploy THAAD in South Korea. The Chinese were especially rattled by this decision, out of fear that THAAD would undermine China's ability to deter Taiwan from declaring independence.

Designated "Aerospace Security-2016," this six-day tabletop exercise was designed for the use of "rapid reaction anti-aircraft and anti-missile defense units of Russia and China in a bid to defend the territory from occasional and provocative strikes by ballistic and cruise missiles."[54] The two later announced that they would hold a second missile defense exercise sometime in 2017, although this has yet to take place. The decision to launch this new exercise program reflects a growing level of convergence between the two on countering U.S. missile defense.

In addition to this exercise, Russia and Moscow have recently been holding other kinds of joint exercises, such as the counter-terrorism exercise held near Moscow in 2016 involving members of their respective internal security forces, and the joint border defense exercise held in 2014.[55] It is highly likely that joint military exercises will continue at their current high levels, as they are providing substantial military and political benefits for both countries. In fact, they are likely to expand even further. In July 2017, the Russian and Chinese defense ministers signed a new "Road Map for Military Cooperation" scheduled to run through 2020. While details were not disclosed, Chinese defense minister Chang Wangqan announced that Russia and China "are planning to carry out very large and important events this year."[56]

Defense Posture

The extent to which Russian and Chinese leaders have adapted their respective defense postures to take account of each other's evolving military capabilities and strategic intentions represents the third major dimension of Russia–China military relations. Over the last decade, both countries have experienced major increases in military power, though China's gains have been more impressive. Thus far, however, the orientation of their respective defense postures has been only marginally affected by these developments.

The Enduring Impact of Normalization

During the Cold War, the Soviets maintained 56 divisions and thousands of tanks and warplanes stationed along their shared border, while the Chinese fielded an even larger force.[57] Following normalization in 1989, Russia and China began to gradually draw down their forces. By 2000, Russia's forces had been reduced by as much as 85%; PLA forces in the region were also significantly reduced, though less dramatically.[58] The reduction in forces coupled with various confidence-building measures adopted since the Cold War drastically reduced the sense of mutual threat.[59] The net effect was to convert their respective border regions into relatively quiet strategic rear areas, which they have remained ever since.

Maintaining a quiet border has enabled both Russia and China to achieve substantial cost savings. More importantly, it has allowed Russia to concentrate its forces in the West where it has faced numerous challenges in Chechnya, Georgia, Ukraine, and from NATO. Likewise, China has been able to concentrate its forces to the East and the South, where it has faced various maritime challenges with respect to Taiwan, the United States and the South China Sea. At times, Russian arms sales to China have encouraged the latter process by bolstering the PLA's maritime forces, thus helping to fuel ongoing competition between China and the United States.[60]

The Shifting Military Balance

Up until the late 2000s, the general orientation of the two countries' defense postures remained relatively unchanged, despite the fact that the military balance between Russia and China had shifted dramatically.[61] Fed by double-digit increases in defense spending, the PLA, already the largest military in the world, was rapidly transforming itself into a modern, sophisticated force with increasingly advanced military capabilities.[62] By contrast, over the same period, the once mighty Soviet military had nearly collapsed due to severe and sustained budget cuts and as of the mid-2000s had barely begun to turn things around.[63] As a result, by 2008 the PLA had made enormous progress in narrowing the gap with the Russian military.

More critically still, by the late 1990s the military balance in the Russian Far East had also shifted decisively in favor of China, as Russian forces in the region were no longer sufficient to defend against a large-scale Chinese incursion absent reinforcement from the West.[64] This shift had major repercussions for both sides. For China, it fundamentally altered its perspective in the region, as it no longer considered Russia to be a serious threat.[65] Consequently, while Beijing continued to maintain large forces within striking distance of Russia, most were relocated well outside the border regions where they focused primarily on other challenges, such as North Korea.[66]

For Moscow, however, the change in the military balance created a serious security dilemma. To remedy the problem, as early as 2001, some Russian military experts began advocating for "the creation in the Far Eastern region of a powerful general-purpose force."[67] At the time, however, this option was simply unaffordable for Moscow, so it chose instead to rely on a strategy of rapid reinforcement from the West in the event of a crisis.[68]

Soon, however, doubts arose about the viability of this strategy as well, since Russia's airlift capacity was insufficient to transport large military units, while its railway systems to the east were all highly vulnerable to interdiction.[69] Lacking a viable conventional option, the Kremlin soon realized that it would have to rely on nuclear weapons to deter a potential Chinese attack.[70]

Given its limited military options, Moscow chose instead to rely primarily on maintaining good relations with China as its principal means for heading off potential security challenges from Beijing. Ultimately, this proved to be a sound policy, as neither side had any interest in renewed confrontation. Moreover, both were still benefiting too much from arms sales and other forms of cooperation to risk undermining the relationship. Both also still had more pressing security challenges to deal with, especially from the United States. Thus, despite the growing military imbalance between Russia and China, neither country felt compelled to make any fundamental changes in its defense posture until the late-2000s.

The Impact of Military Reforms

Starting in 2008, Russia's military footprint in the RFE finally began to change, though this had less to do with China and more with major military reforms that were introduced after the 2008 Georgia War. These reforms were intended to transform the old Soviet-era mass mobilization military into a leaner, more agile force better suited to meeting Russia's current security challenges. As part of reforms, Russia's forces, including those in the RFE, were thoroughly reorganized, as old military districts were merged, new army headquarters were established, and divisions were converted into brigades.

These changes did not significantly alter the military balance in the east. Although Russian forces were finally undergoing modernization, the number of units assigned to the region did not really change all that much. If anything, the overall reduction in troop size as a result of reforms, and the shift from divisions to lighter brigades less suited to defending the vast reaches of the RFE, likely reduced Russia's defense capabilities in the east, at least initially.[71]

While this was taking place, the PLA Army (PLAA) was shifting to a "transregional" defense strategy, to increase its ability to rapidly move forces from one military region to another as needed to meet contingencies. To achieve this objective, the PLAA focused on improving mobility through increased emphasis on "air-ground integrated operations, long-distance maneuvers, rapid assaults, and special operations."[72] This new emphasis on mobility was on full display during the Stride

2009 military exercises, when four Chinese divisions were rapidly shifted to different locations across the country.

To Russian observers, however, Stride 2009 looked very much like a rehearsal for a potential Chinese intervention in Russia.[73] This was especially alarming to those already concerned about the PLAA's large footprint in northern China and its rapid advances in network-centric capabilities.[74] Fueled by concerns such as these, the Kremlin finally began to revise its strategy toward China. While continuing to engage fully with Beijing, it started to hedge militarily as well. In 2009, for example, the Russian army redeployed two newly formed brigades closer to the Russian–Chinese border.[75] In 2010, an additional combined arms army was established near Chita to handle reinforcements from the West in a future crisis.[76]

Russia also began holding large-scale military exercises in the RFE, including most notably Vostok 2010, which to that point was the largest exercise held by Russia since Soviet times. Although pegged as a counter-terrorism exercise, Vostok 2010 was clearly aimed at China. In fact, prior to the exercise, a Russian military commander stated that "despite friendly relations with China, our army command understands that [it is sometimes necessary to] quiet a friend down with a conventional or nuclear club."[77] This message was further reinforced by Vostok 2014, an even larger exercise with up to 100,000 troops.

Still, it would be easy to overstate the implications of these new military measures. For one, they had little real effect on the underlying military balance. Since 2009 in fact there have been virtually no additions to Russian ground forces stationed in the RFE, although they have been substantially modernized. Moreover, while exercises such as Vostok have demonstrated Russia's ability to rapidly reinforce the RFE during peacetime, it is doubtful whether such moves could be replicated in wartime.

Even if they could, the amount of forces that Russia could shift to the east would hardly be sufficient to materially affect the outcome. The PLAA still maintains four entire group armies in its Northern Military Region alone, far outnumbering the opposing Russian ground forces located in the Eastern Military District.[78] Still, the demonstrated ability to rapidly shift forces to the RFE coupled with Russia's growing long-range conventional strike capabilities have likely strengthened its ability to deter China to some degree. Moreover, in a future crisis, they might also buy Russia additional time to defuse the crisis. Nevertheless, for the time being, Russia will still have to rely primarily on its non-strategic nuclear weapons to deter Chinese aggression.[79]

The Effects of Ukraine

Given their limited military options, Russia's leaders have continued to place higher priority on engaging with Beijing as the primary means of addressing potential security challenges from China. This has been even more the case since the Ukraine crisis, as Moscow has prioritized expanding cooperation over military hedging.[80]

To improve relations with China, Moscow has repeatedly compromised on long-held positions since Ukraine (e.g., natural gas prices; sales of advanced weapon systems), thereby further reducing the grounds for potential conflict. Thus far, this strategy has proven effective, as both sides have reinforced their strategic partnership in order to increase their leverage in dealings with the United States. Moscow has also continued to benefit from the fact that China's military build-up is still focused primarily on the Western Pacific.

Given current geopolitical conditions, therefore, it seems unlikely that Russia or China will alter their respective defense postures any time soon. Both countries continue to focus on countering Western military power in areas of greater importance to each of them. Moreover, given the collapse of President Trump's efforts to improve relations with Moscow, there seems little likelihood that a change in U.S. policy will alter the strategic calculus of either Moscow or Beijing in the near term. Yet as China's military power continues to increase, at some point the Kremlin is likely to reconsider its overall defense posture toward China.

Conclusion

Having now surveyed the three principal areas of Sino-Russian military relations, this chapter will conclude by evaluating the extent to which recent developments in defense cooperation reflect a growing strategic alignment between Russia and China. As we have seen, military relations between the two countries have increased dramatically since the Ukraine crisis. Collectively, these developments reflect a substantial upgrade in the overall military relationship. Moreover, although clear limits remain, recent developments strongly indicate a growing strategic alignment between the two countries as well.

The resumption of arms sales is especially notable in this regard, as it reflects a decision by both countries to restore arms trade as a central pillar of their relationship. Moreover, the sheer volume of the increase is another strong indicator of the degree to which the two have recommitted to this aspect of the relationship. It shows that both countries are willing to make compromises to move beyond the problems that have plagued arms sales in the past.

The expansion of joint military exercise programs is yet another clear indicator of growing alignment between Russia and China. Recent decisions to expand the size and complexity of existing joint exercise programs, and to add new programs represent a substantial commitment by both sides to increased cooperation in this area. Likewise, efforts to breathe new life into the Peace Mission exercises demonstrate an increased willingness by both sides (especially Moscow) to move beyond the geopolitical rivalry that has hindered security cooperation in Central Asia. Collectively, these developments have further reinforced military relations, while confirming that Russia and China will continue to act as each other's primary exercise partners.

A further indication of their growing military alignment is the increased propensity by Russia and China to hold joint naval exercises in highly sensitive locations, such as the Baltics and the South China Sea. By doing so, they demonstrate an increased willingness to tacitly support one another in their respective disputes with the West (and others), something they had previously been unwilling to do.

Growing alignment is also evident in their respective defense postures. As each country has found itself locked into increasingly competitive strategic relationships with the West, they have found it expedient to maintain a quiet strategic rear area on their shared border in order to concentrate their forces in more pressing locations. That neither country has seen fit to materially alter its defense posture despite recent increases in military power by both countries demonstrates a relatively high degree of trust.

Nevertheless, clear limits remain regarding the degree to which the two sides are willing to pursue military alignment. Notably, much of the recent increase in defense cooperation has taken place as a result of the Ukraine crisis, under conditions in which Moscow has had to compromise on long-held positions to obtain crucial support from Beijing. Absent Ukraine, it is not at all clear that the Kremlin would have agreed to sell two of its most advanced military systems to Beijing.

The fact that Moscow only agreed to do so after Ukraine indicates that the recent increase in defense cooperation still masks a degree of underlying discomfort on Moscow's part, something which calls into question how durable the upgrade in military relations will be. For its part, China continues to harbor its own set of concerns over enhanced military relations with Russia, concerns over Russia's pricing practices, its willingness to transfer more of its advanced military technology to Beijing, and the potential for further rivalry in Central Asia.

Such problems were on full display during the Su-35 sale, which took nearly two years to complete. This sale was nearly derailed due to Moscow's persistent concerns over China's reverse engineering practices, and Beijing's concerns over pricing.[81] The limits of cooperation have also been evident in their joint military exercises. The low priority placed on achieving greater interoperability during joint military exercises is a prime example, as it reflects an enduring lack of interest by both sides in developing the kind of integrated military capability needed to conduct effective joint military operations, something which would be necessary if the two ever decided to form a true military alliance.

Yet neither country has demonstrated any real interest in forming a true military alliance, despite the recent upgrade in military relations. This can be explained by several factors. First, neither wants to become entrapped in a dispute involving a third party, especially the United States, over issues that do not affect their vital interests. Second, both countries are capable of defending themselves against external attack and thus view a purely defensive alliance as unnecessary. Finally, neither country wants to foreclose its opportunities to engage with third countries, including the United States, which would be put off by an outright military alliance between Russia and China.[82]

Despite these limitations, the recent upswing in military relations is a clear indicator of growing alignment between Russia and China, and this trend is likely to continue, at least over the near term, as the conditions driving the two toward closer defense cooperation still remain in place. The possibility that the United States might pursue rapprochement with Russia, a policy strongly advocated by President Trump, might have changed the current dynamics to some degree by reducing Moscow's dependence on Beijing. However, with the collapse of that policy due to widespread opposition in the U.S. Congress, it is hard to foresee any other short-term development that has the potential to alter the conditions currently driving the two toward closer alignment.

Notes

1. SIPRI (2018).
2. Schwartz (2014).
3. Kaczmarski (2015), pp. 25–27.

4. Kuhrt (2014), p. 100.
5. Lukin (2014), p. 31.
6. See for example Hiroshi (2015).
7. See for example Sutter (2017), p. v.
8. SIPRI (2018).
9. Rangsimaporn (2006), p. 481.
10. SIPRI (2018).
11. Jakobsen, et al. (2011), p. 14.
12. Kuhrt (2014), p. 99.
13. Yuan (2010), p. 216.
14. Lague (2008).
15. Rangsimaporn (2006), p. 484.
16. Weitz (2008), p. 31.
17. Weitz (2017), p. 30, Blank and Levitsky (2015), p. 67.
18. Rangsimaporn (2006), pp. 480, 485.
19. Ibid., pp. 482, 485.
20. Ibid., pp. 480, 481.
21. Ibid., p. 488.
22. Yu (2013).
23. Lukin (2014), p. 12.
24. SIPRI (2018).
25. Choi (2013).
26. "Russia–China's Su35 Complex and International Relations in Next Five Years," *Kanwa Asian Defence Review*, no. 137 (March 1, 2016), 13–14.
27. Meick (2017), pp. 14–15.
28. Zamakhina (2016).
29. Rangsimaporn (2006), p. 482.
30. Gabuev (2016), p. 23.
31. Yu (2013).
32. Bitzinger (2016).
33. Gabuev (2016), p. 23.
34. Nikolsky (2016).
35. Ibid.
36. Yu (2005), p. 3.
37. Ibid., p. 1.
38. Weitz (2015), pp. 28–32.
39. Urchek (2016).
40. Engelbrekt and Watts (2015), p. 6.
41. Haas (2013), p. 22.
42. Hartnett (2012), p. 242–433.
43. Ibid.

44. U.S.–China Economic and Security Review Commission (2015), p. 407, Weitz (2015), pp. 54–55, Allen, Saunders, and Chen (2017), p. 28.
45. Weitz (2014).
46. Meick (2017), p. 26.
47. Ibid., p. 26.
48. Ibid., p. 9.
49. Allen, et al. (2017), pp. 3, 26.
50. Yu (2015).
51. The average Joint Sea exercise lasted seven days. By contrast RIMPAC 2016 lasted 35 days. See "Rim of the Pacific," National Defence and the Canadian Armed Forces, http://www.forces.gc.ca/en/operations-exercises/rimpac.page.
52. There were a total of 45 ships in RIMPAC 2016. Ibid.
53. Cited in Kozyrev (2017), p. 22.
54. TASS (2016).
55. See Meick (2017), pp. 24–27.
56. Sputnik (2017). As things turned out, the only notable additional exercise held by the two following this announcement was a joint missile defense exercise conducted in December 2017. For more on this exercise, see Gady (2017).
57. Mahnken (1987), pp. 96, 99.
58. Wilson (2004), p. 50.
59. Rangsimaporn (2006), p. 480.
60. Schwartz (2014).
61. Lo (2008), pp. 75–76.
62. Anderson and Engstrom (2009), pp. 1–2.
63. Felgenhauer (2007).
64. Chang (1999), p. 267.
65. Donaldson and Donaldson (2003), p. 720.
66. See Wood (2017).
67. Rangsimaporn (2006), p. 487.
68. Chang (1999), p. 267.
69. Karnaukov and Tseluiko (2011), p. 105, Khramchikhin (2010).
70. Saradzhyan (2010).
71. Thornton (2011), pp. 28–29.
72. Blasko (2007), p. 282.
73. Khramchikhin (2010).
74. Kipp (2013), p. 51.
75. Ibid.
76. Sakaguchi (2012), p. 50.
77. Kipp (2013), p. 51.
78. Wood (2017).

79. Gabuev (2015), p. 7.
80. Klein and Westphal (2016), p. 2.
81. Schwartz (2017).
82. Goldstein (2017).

Literature

Allen, Kenneth, Phillip C. Saunders, and John Chen. 2017. Chinese Military Diplomacy, 2003–2016: Trends and Implications. *INSS: China Strategic Perspectives* 11. http://ndupress.ndu.edu/Media/News/Article/1249864/chinese-military-diplomacy-20032016-trends-and-implications/.

Anderson, Eric C., and Jeffrey G. Engstrom. 2009. Capabilities of the Chinese People's Liberation Army to Carry Out Military Action in the Event of Regional Conflict. *SAIC*, March.

Bitzinger, Richard A. 2016. China's Military Is Getting Strong (So Why Aren't Chinese Weapons Selling?). *The National Interest*, September 17. http://nationalinterest.org/blog/the-buzz/chinas-military-getting-strong-so-why-arent-chinese-weapons-17746.

Blank, Stephen, and Edward Levitsky. 2015. Geostrategic Aims of the Russian Arms Trade in East Asia and the Middle East. *Defence Studies* 15 (1): 63–80.

Blasko, Dennis. 2007. PLA Ground Force Modernization and Mission Diversification. In *Right Sizing the People's Liberation Army*, ed. Roy Kamphausen and Andrew Scobell. Carlisle Barracks, PA: Army War College Strategic Studies Institute.

Chang, Felix K. 1999. The Unraveling of Russia's Far Eastern Power. *Orbis* 43 (2): 257–284.

Chi-Yuk, Choi. 2013. China to Buy Lada-Class Subs, Su-35 Fighters from Russia. *South China Morning Post*, March 27. http://www.scmp.com/news/china/article/1199448/china-buy-russian-fighters-submarines.

Donaldson, Robert H., and John A. Donaldson. 2003. The Arms Trade in Russian–Chinese Relations: Identity, Domestic Politics, and Geopolitical Positioning. *International Studies Quarterly* 47 (4): 709–732.

Engelbrekt, Kjell, and John Watts. 2015. Sino-Russian Strategic Collaboration: Still an "Axis of Convenience"? *Swedish Defence University*, February 12.

Felgenhauer, Pavel. 2007. Russian Military: After Ivanov. *Perspective* 17 (3). https://open.bu.edu/handle/2144/3641.

Gabuev, Alexander. 2015. A Soft Alliance? Russia–China Relations After the Ukraine Crisis. *European Council on Foreign Relations*, February.

Gabuev, Alexander. 2016. Friends with Benefits? Russian–Chinese Relations After the Ukraine Crisis. *Carnegie Moscow Center*, June. http://carnegie.ru/2016/06/29/friends-with-benefits-russian-chinese-relations-after-ukraine-crisis-pub-63953 http://carnegieendowment.org/files/CEIP_CP278_Gabuev_revised_FINAL.pdf.

Gady, Franz-Stefan. 2017. China, Russia Kick Off Anti-Ballistic Missile Defense Exercise. *The Diplomat*, December 12. https://thediplomat.com/2017/12/china-russia-kick-off-anti-ballistic-missile-defense-exercise/.

Goldstein, Lyle. 2017. A China–Russia Alliance? *The National Interest*, April 25. http://nationalinterest.org/feature/china-russia-alliance-20333.

Haas, Marcel de. 2013. Russian–Chinese Security Relations. *Netherlands Institute of International Relations*, March 27.

Hartnett, Daniel M. 2012. Looking Good on Paper: PLA Participation in the Peace Mission 2010 Multilateral Military Exercise. In *Learning by Doing: The PLA Trains at Home and Abroad*. Carlisle, PA: Strategic Studies Institute.

Hiroshi Yamazoe. 2015. The Prospects and Limits of the Russia–China Partnership. *RUFS Briefing*, No. 32, December.

Jakobsen, Linda, Paul Holtom, Dean Knox, and Jingchao Peng. 2011. China's Energy and Security Relations: Hopes, Frustrations and Uncertainties. SIPRI Policy Paper 29, October.

Kaczmarski, Marcin. 2015. *Russia–China Relations in the Post-crisis International Order*. London and New York: Routledge.

Karnaukov, Anton, and Vyacheslav Tseluiko. 2011. Russian Military Doctrine and the State of its Armed Forces. In *Russia's New Army*, ed. Mikhail Barabanov. Moscow: Center for Analysis of Strategies and Technology.

Khramchikhin, Alexander. 2010. Neadekvatnyi vostok [The Inadequate East]. *Nezavisimaya Gazeta*, July 23. http://nvo.ng.ru/eventsnvo/2010-07-23/1_vostok.html.

Kipp, Jacob. 2013. Russia as a Nuclear Power in the Eurasian Context. In *Strategic Asia 2013–2014: Asia in the Second Nuclear Age*. Seattle, WA and Washington, DC: The National Bureau of Asian Research.

Klein, Margarete, and Kirsten Westphal. 2016. Russia: Turn to China? *SWP Comments* 7: 1–8. https://www.swp-berlin.org/fileadmin/contents/products/comments/2016C07_kle_wep.pdf.

Kozyrev, Vitaly. 2017. Whose Pacific Century? *2017 ISA Conference*, Panel 'China and Its Neighbors'.

Kuhrt, Natasha. 2014. Russia and China: Strategic Partnership or Asymmetrical Dependence. In *Russia and East Asia: Informal and Gradual Integration*, ed. Tsuneo Akaha and Anna Vassilieva. New York: Routledge.

Lague, David. 2008. Russia and China Rethink Arms Deals. *New York Times*, March 2. http://www.nytimes.com/2008/03/02/world/asia/02iht-arms.1.10614237.html?mcubz=3.

Lo, Bobo. 2008. *Axis of Convenience: Moscow, Beijing, and the New Geopolitics*. London: Chatham House.

Lukin, Artyom. 2014. The Emerging Anti-American Axis of Russia and China: Implications for Asia. *American Studies Institute* 37 (2): 5–43.

Mahnken, Thomas. 1987. Current Sino-Soviet Military Relations. *Asian Affairs* 14 (2): 91–105.

Meick, Ethan. 2017. China–Russia Military-to-Military Relations: Moving Toward a Higher Level of Cooperation. *Staff Research Report of the U.S.–China Economic and Security Review Commission*, March 20.

Nikolsky, Alexander. 2016. Kitay vernulsya v pyaterku krupneyshikh importerov rossiyskogo oruzhiya [China Returns to Five Largest Importers of Russian Weapons]. *Vedomosti*, November 2. http://www.vedomosti.ru/politics/articles/2016/11/02/663309-kitai-krupneishih-importerov.

Rangsimaporn, Paradorn. 2006. Russia's Debate on Military-Technological Cooperation with China: From Yeltsin to Putin. *Asian Survey* 46 (3): 477–495.

Sakaguchi, Yoshiaki. 2012. Russia's Military Reform and Changes in the Russian Military in the Russian Far East. In *Neighbourhood Watch: Japanese and Swedish Perspectives on Russian Security*, ed. Shinji Hyodo and Carolina Vendil Pallin. Stockholm Sweden: Swedish Defence Research Agency.

Saradzhyan, Simon. 2010. The Role of China in Russia's Military Thinking. *Belfer Center*, May 4. https://www.belfercenter.org/publication/role-china-russias-military-thinking.

Schwartz, Paul. 2014. Evolution of Sino-Russian Defense Cooperation Since the Cold War. *ASAN Forum*, June 13. http://www.theasanforum.org/evolution-of-sino-russian-defense-cooperation-since-the-cold-war/.

Schwartz, Paul. 2017. Russia–China Defense Cooperation: New Developments. *The ASAN Forum*, February 9. http://www.theasanforum.org/russia-china-defense-cooperation-new-developments/.

SIPRI. 2018. *Arms Transfer Database*. Stockholm International Peace Research Institute. Available at https://www.sipri.org/databases/armstransfers.

Sputnik. 2017. Russian, China Deepen Military Cooperation with Mutually Beneficial Road Map, July 6. https://sputniknews.com/world/201706071054403535-china-russia-military-road-map/.

Sutter, Robert. 2017. Forward. *In Russia–China Relations: Assessing Common Ground and Strategic Fault Lines*. Washington, DC: National Bureau of Asian Research.

TASS. 2016. Russia, China Launch First Computer-Enabled Anti-Missile Exercises, May 26. http://tass.com/defense/878407.

Thornton, Robert. 2011. *Military Modernization and the Russian Ground Forces*. Carlisle Barracks, PA: Army War College Strategic Studies Institute.

Urchek, Daniel. 2016. Looking Towards The SCO Peace Mission 2016. *Real Clear Defense*, July 25. https://www.realcleardefense.com/articles/2016/07/26/looking_towards_the_sco_peace_mission_2016_109623.html.

U.S.–China Economic and Security Review Commission. 2015. *2015 Report to Congress*, November. Available at https://www.uscc.gov/sites/default/files/annual_reports/2015%20Annual%20Report%20to%20Congress.PDF.

Weitz, Richard. 2008. *Sino-Russian Security Relations*. Carlisle, PA: Strategic Studies Institute.

Weitz, Richard. 2014. SCO Security Cooperation Has Multiple Motives. *Hudson Institute*, September 25. https://www.hudson.org/research/10667-sco-security-cooperation-has-multiple-motives.

Weitz, Richard. 2015. *Parsing Chinese–Russian Military Exercises*. Carlisle, PA: U.S. Army War College, Strategic Studies Institute.

Weitz, Richard. 2017. Sino-Russian Security Ties. In *Russia–China Relations: Assessing Common Ground and Strategic Fault Lines*, NBR Special Report #66, July.

Wilson, Jeanne L. 2004. *Strategic Partners: Russian–Chinese Relations in the Post-Soviet Era*. Armonk, New York, and London, England: M. E. Sharpe.

Wood, Peter. 2017. Strategic Assessment: China's Northern Theater Command. *Jamestown Foundation*, May 15. https://jamestown.org/program/strategic-assessment-chinas-northern-theater-command/.

Yu, Bin. 2005. The New World Order According to Moscow and Beijing. *Comparative Connections* 7 (3). http://cc.csis.org/2005/10/new-world-order-according-moscow-beijing/.

Yu, Bin. 2013. Tale of Different Pivots. *Comparative Connections* 14 (3). January. https://www.csis.org/programs/pacific-forum-csis/publications/comparative-connections/volume-14-2012/vol-14-no-3-january.

Yu, Bin. 2015. Tale of Two Parades, Two Drills, and Two Summits. *Comparative Connections* 17 (2), September. http://cc.csis.org/2015/09/tales-two-parades-two-drills-two-summits/.

Yuan, Jing Dong. 2010. Sino-Russian Defense Ties. In *The Future of China–Russia Relations*, ed. James Bellacqua. Kentucky: University Press of Kentucky.

Zamakhina, T. 2016. Masshtab imeyet znacheniye [Scale Matters]. *Rossiyskaya Gazeta*, 27 November. https://rg.ru/2016/11/27/putin-prizval-obespechit-shirokij-vyhod-predpriiatij-rf-na-vneshnie-rynki.html.

CHAPTER 6

Tending the Eurasian Garden: Russia, China and the Dynamics of Regional Integration and Order

Alexander Cooley

[W]e understand [that Central Asia is your backyard].
But you [Russia] are supposed after all to look after your own yard,
water the flowers. Please excuse my frankness.
—Chinese official responsible for Eurasian policy[1]

Central Asia remains a critically important region to both Moscow and Beijing. Publicly, Moscow and Beijing project an aura of friendly cooperation and a rather neat division of labor: Russia is Central Asia's privileged caretaker, responsible for maintaining order and guaranteeing security, while China focuses on economic investment and upgrading regional infrastructure, with regional development the perceived key to stabilizing its restive western province of Xinjiang that borders the region. But as the opening quote suggests, even within these

A. Cooley (✉)
Political Science Department at Barnard College,
Columbia University's Harriman Institute, New York, NY, USA
e-mail: ac210@columbia.edu; acooley@barnard.edu

J. I. Bekkevold and B. Lo (eds.), *Sino-Russian Relations in the 21st Century*, https://doi.org/10.1007/978-3-319-92516-5_6

publicly acknowledged parameters, mutual frustrations and strategic concerns percolate. The Russia–China relationship in Eurasia is more akin to "public cooperation and private rivalry" (Cooley 2012a), with growing divergences in regional priorities and goals unlikely to be publicly voiced or acknowledged.[2]

This chapter interrogates the unspoken politics, rivalries and strategic interaction of Russia and China in Central Asia. There is some important and substantive regional cooperation, much of it initiated by mutual concerns about the influence and long-term intentions of the United States in the region as part of its campaign in Afghanistan. However, a close study of their respective approaches to Eurasian regional integration, and the organizations they each champion, reveals important caveats and an underlying divergence of preferred integration modes.

More broadly, Moscow and Beijing's Eurasian interactions reveal much about their respective broader international priorities and foreign policy orientations. Russia sees itself as a great power in an increasingly multipolar world of declining Western power and moral authority, with the right to set its own rules and reject, by any means necessary, the encroachment of Western institutions, actors and norms into the post-Soviet space. Its agenda is classically revisionist or "counterhegemonic" in international relations jargon, challenging both the efficacy and legitimacy of the existing Western-led order and its institutional architecture.[3] In this respect, Russia approaches regional integration projects—including its participation in the Shanghai Cooperation Organization (SCO) and leadership of the Collective Security Treaty Organization (CSTO) and Eurasian Economic Union (EEU)—as instruments to institutionalize its privileged status in Eurasia and underscore its great power status outside it.

China, as others have pointed out, does not share Russia's fundamental counterhegemonic disposition towards the West, having developed within the economic opportunities afforded by the liberal international order.[4] But Beijing does prioritize cooperative overseas ties, developing new regional vehicles for its development initiatives—the SCO or the Asian Infrastructure Development Bank (AIIB)—not only to increase connectivity between regions, but also to develop a political community of surrounding states that will remain sensitive to Beijing's interests and priorities.

Post-2014, the crisis in Ukraine and the US drawdown from Afghanistan have accelerated both Russian and Chinese regional engagement initiatives. But as Moscow has pushed to increase its cooperation with Beijing, in part to signal it can withstand Western economic sanctions and has credible alternative geopolitical partners, the asymmetry of capabilities and influence across the region is also becoming more noticeable. China's counter-order institutions[5] have infringed on Russia's perceptions of the region as its own sphere of influence, but instead of confronting Beijing in the wake of US disengagement, Moscow appears to have pragmatically accommodated itself to China's new ambitions like the Belt and Road Initiative (BRI). In short, the Sino-Russian "strategic partnership" in Central Asia takes place increasingly on Beijing's terms.

I begin this essay by outlining the particular national interests, goals and frames of reference that Moscow and Beijing respectively place on Eurasian integration, and briefly identify their preferred institutional vehicles. The next section explores the development of Eurasia's regional architectures in the 2000s, noting how the Central Asian republics mostly welcomed them as extensions of their multivector foreign policies, and traces how their institutional development interacted with the security and political engagement of the United States following the events of 9/11. The following section focuses on Russian and Chinese attitudes towards the SCO's development during the decade, demonstrating how this grouping embodied some common aspirations but also reflected divergences rooted in Moscow and Beijing's respective counterhegemonic and counter-order goals. I conclude by examining Eurasian regional relations in the wake of the 2014 Ukraine crisis and US disengagement from the region. These developments have accelerated Russian and Chinese engagement with the region through new regional initiatives, but also underscored China's growing regional power and influence.

Russia and China's Regional Goals and Preferred Vehicles for Eurasian Integration

The Russian Approach: Primacy Through New Regional Organizations

It is important to note how Moscow and Beijing view their respective goals of Eurasian integration. For Moscow, in both the economic and security spheres, deepening Eurasian integration has emerged as a central foreign policy goal. Defending its "sphere of privileged interests," as President Dmitry Medvedev proclaimed in the aftermath of the 2008 Georgia War, and the countering of Western influence and encroachment are key objectives. In turn, retaining Eurasian primacy justifies Russia's status and self-identification as a great power and indispensable player in the international order.[6]

Moscow's chosen vehicles for pursuing this primacy have been the CSTO in the security sphere, and the Eurasian Union (EEU) in the economic and legal spheres. CSTO membership comprises Russia, Armenia, Belarus, Kazakhstan, Kyrgyzstan, and Tajikistan. Uzbekistan, which had joined in 2006 when it tacked away from security cooperation with the United States, exited the group in 2012. At its 2002 founding, President Putin introduced the CSTO's mission as combating terrorism and new transnational threats.[7] But as relations with the United States deteriorated from 2003, the CSTO came to position itself as a counter to NATO. In terms of its institutional design and functions, the security group boasts a unified command and a rotating chairmanship. Moscow operates its foreign military bases in Armenia and Kyrgyzstan under CSTO auspices and oversees a common air defense system, while member states are afforded the benefit of purchasing military hardware at the same prices as the Russian military. Moscow also led the creation of the group's integrated Collective Rapid Reaction Forces, a clear attempt to emulate NATO's rapid reaction force.[8] In response to the Arab Spring and concerns about street-led uprisings, the group also enhanced its counterintelligence and cybersecurity activities, particularly its targeting of social media.[9]

The foundational agreement of the EEU was signed in May 2014, and the organization is the successor to the Eurasian Customs Union (founded in 2010) and the Eurasian Economic Community (EurAsEC).[10] Like the CSTO, the EEU is modeled on a Western counterpart—the European Union. It has introduced an integrated internal market and common tariff area, overseen by a set of supranational institutions such as a tariff-sharing formula and the Eurasian Economic Commission headquartered in Moscow. The three founding members of the Eurasian Union—Russia, Belarus, and Kazakhstan (later joined by Armenia and Kyrgyzstan)—do not have classically complementing economies, but membership of the organization affords access to subsidized Russian energy imports, provided by Russia's side-payments in negotiations.[11] Preliminary studies indicate that the EEU has increased economic integration among its core states, reversing the post-Soviet trend of de-coupling. But the regional project has also initiated more of a domestic backlash, especially in Kazakhstan, and debates about whether its regional architecture serves all members' national interests.[12]

Two points are especially relevant about these Russian-led regional organizations. First, contra current Western commentary that these organizations seek to re-establish the Soviet Union, they are actually modeled on contemporary Western counterparts, mimicking, respectively, the organizational forms of NATO and the European Union.[13] Indeed, both the CSTO and the EEU can be contrasted to the initial attempts to promote post-Soviet cooperation via the Commonwealth of Independent States (CIS). In retrospect, the CIS did not successfully create new institutional forms to manage relations among Russia and the newly independent states, but rather was an attempt to preserve as many of the previous cooperative practices, interdependencies and ties as possible.[14] But the CIS's practical irrelevance during the 1990s also conditioned many scholars and commentators to skeptically view all subsequent Russian-led integration efforts. Second, the intensification of rivalry between Russia and the West as a result of the 2014 Ukraine crisis has more clearly designated these organizations as geopolitical groupings designed to project Moscow's influence across the region.

The Chinese Approach: A Multilateral Front for Regional Engagement

For China, engagement with Eurasia, especially Central Asia, and the promotion of regional integration are not just matters of foreign policy, but also an extension of its domestic policy towards its restive western province of Xinjiang. The collapse of the Soviet Union generated new independent countries that suddenly shared an unresolved Soviet-era border with China and heightened concerns that regional Uighur groups might mobilize externally to destabilize the political situation in China.[15]

Beijing's preferred vehicle for fostering this regional security and economic cooperation has been the SCO, headquartered in Beijing.[16] Comprising China, Russia, Kazakhstan, Kyrgyzstan, Tajikistan, and Uzbekistan (with India and Pakistan joining in 2017), the SCO was formed in June 2001 as the successor to the Shanghai Five forum, a group charged with concluding the lingering Soviet-era boundary dispute. The official narrative is that the Shanghai Five was such a success, that its members resolved to create a permanent organizational structure and add Uzbekistan in order to tackle broader issues of regional security and stability.[17] The organization claims to embrace the civilizational diversity of its members of the "Shanghai Spirit," implicitly contrasting its doctrine of sovereign non-interference in the internal affairs of its members with the economic and political conditions imposed by Western international groups working in the region.[18]

On the security side, the SCO has some notable achievements, creating a distinct normative framework for addressing transnational security threats and institutionalizing novel forms of internal security cooperation within a new regional legal framework.[19] From the outset, the SCO adopted as its institutional mission, seemingly straight from the Chinese MFA, the mandate to cooperatively combat the "three evils" of "terrorism, separatism and extremism."[20] In 2004, the member states' Ministries of Interior established the Regional Anti-Terrorist Structure (RATS) based in Tashkent, whose purpose was to facilitate cooperation and information-sharing about regional transnational threats. Since its founding, the organization has maintained a comprehensive regional blacklist of banned individuals and groups, engaging in a type of authoritarian reciprocity and logrolling, where each country places its own pet transnational threat on the list in exchange for recognizing everyone else's. Not surprisingly, even after major combat operations had subsided in Afghanistan, the blacklist grew.[21] The 2009 SCO Counterterrorism Treaty goes several steps further, allowing for a number of extra-territorial measures, enshrined at the treaty level, such as mandating that member states hand over suspects to another member state within 30 days and allowing security services to carry out operations on each other's territory.[22] SCO member states also hold regular military exercises, usually dominated by Russian and Chinese forces, known as SCO Peace Mission, which usually focus on an "antiterrorism" scenario in the region.

Beyond its security cooperation, Beijing has tried to push the organization to play a leading role in fostering regional economic integration, proposing a series of "public goods" type roles. Beijing considers the economic development of the Central Asian region critical in promoting regional stability.[23] At different times, Chinese policymakers have pushed for the organization to create the legal framework for a free trade zone, a business council, a regional development bank and even, during the economic downturn, an anticrisis fund. But Beijing's economic initiatives have been met with opposition and foot-dragging by Moscow and the Central Asian states themselves. Central Asian governments not only fear formalizing China's growing regional economic power, but Moscow is loath to establish any SCO forum that would signal formal acquiescence to Beijing's regional economic hegemony. As a result, Beijing has adopted the curious position of funding a range of bilateral economic initiatives, but referring to them post hoc as SCO projects, a practice that causes considerable confusion among the international media and even scholars familiar with the region.

China's attempt to use the SCO as a development projects vehicle has been paralleled by a flurry of activity to establish new regional development mechanisms. In 2013, Beijing established the New Silk Route Fund, under the management of the people's Bank, dedicated to funding projects in Central Asia. In 2014, it announced the establishment of the New Development Bank, under the BRICS, and the Asian Infrastructure Investment Bank (AIIB), which Kazakhstan, Tajikistan, and Uzbekistan joined. SCO initiatives in the area of official youth groups, election observation missions, cultural exhibitions and educational/university exchanges round out what is the organization's rather eclectic portfolio.

Regional Integration in Practice: Multiple Initiatives and the Multivector 2000s

Throughout the 2000s, these Russian and Chinese-led Eurasian integration projects evolved and co-existed. Their mutual accommodation was in part driven by some functional differentiation—for example, the SCO appeared to focus on cooperation among internal security services while the CSTO focused on military planning and integration. In turn, these reflected the different security priorities of Beijing and Moscow and their mutual accommodation. However, accommodation was also a function of the Eurasian states themselves wanting to maintain engagement with multiple external patrons. Two important factors created the conditions for these multivector foreign policy orientations: the entrance of the United States as a major security player in Central Asia after 9/11 and China's meteoric economic rise.

The Eagle Has Landed: 9/11 and the Impact of the US Regional Entry

The US entry into Central Asia following the attacks of 9/11 gave Moscow and Beijing renewed impetus to pursue these regional projects. For Moscow, 9/11 and Operation Enduring Freedom was initially perceived as a political opportunity to partner with the West. President Putin was the first world leader to have talked with President George W. Bush after the 9/11 attacks when he offered his support to defeat a common "civilizational enemy." Moscow consented to the stationing of US forces in Uzbekistan and Kyrgyzstan in the fall of 2001 and officially accepted the United States sending Special Forces and trainers to Georgia in 2002 to clear the Pankisi Gorge of militants that had been spilling over from the North Caucasus.

This brief period of active Russian support of the US military presence in Eurasia lasted about 18 months. By summer of 2003, the Kremlin had grown increasingly frustrated with US unilateralism and what it perceived as Washington's dismissal of Russian interests and concerns. Far from offering partnership on equal footing, the Bush Administration had withdrawn from the ABM treaty, pushed for yet another expansion of NATO to include the Baltic States, and intervened in Iraq without United Nations authorization.[24] In Central Asia itself, the US military had simply bypassed Russia and was not only using the Central Asian states as logistical hubs, but also providing bilateral military assistance and training.[25] As Jason Lyall has shown, public talk of a common civilizational struggle quickly gave way to a new enduring narrative that the United States was intent on using its new bases to project its influence within Central Asia itself and pry these states away from Moscow.[26]

Lesser known, but equally important, is how the sudden US military presence propelled the SCO to deepen its institutional structures. The organization had only been in existence for three months prior to 9/11 and Beijing feared that the US military presence would become permanent, thereby almost completing the encirclement of China from the West and providing a platform for surveillance and even destabilizing operations in Xinjiang. Fearing their potential exclusion from a new Russian–US partnership in Central Asia, Chinese officials feverishly held a number of SCO meetings the following spring on security-related topics such as Afghanistan, border issues, and counterterrorism.[27] By the June 2002 summit in Saint Petersburg, Beijing had lined up support among member states to establish the SCO's regional antiterrorism structure and adopt a number of organizational initiatives and working committees.

But perhaps the most significant series of events in terms of their impact on Russian and Chinese integration efforts were the so-called Color Revolutions of 2003–2005 that swept out of power entrenched post-Communist rulers in Georgia (2003), Ukraine (2004), and

Kyrgyzstan (2005), and replaced them with more Western-oriented figures.[28] Moscow's alarm at the Orange Revolution is well-documented, but Beijing's response to the Kyrgyz Tulip revolution (a state that shares a border with Xinjiang) showed an almost similar level of alarm. Both countries denounced these uprisings and condemned these regime changes as the outcomes of unwarranted foreign interference. Within the CSTO and the SCO, planners supported a number of countermeasures to confront such outside influences, while throughout Eurasia worried governments placed new restrictions on the media and the operations of foreign-backed NGOs.[29]

Then in May 2005, forces from Uzbekistan's Interior Ministry brutally cracked down on hundreds of protestors in the eastern city of Andijon. While the Uzbek government was severely criticized by the West, which called for an international investigation into the repression and sanctioned leading Uzbek officials, Moscow and Beijing strongly supported Uzbek President Islam Karimov. Two months later, Uzbekistan evicted US forces from their base at Karshi-Khanabad (K2) and announced that it would rejoin the Russian-led CSTO (Fumagalli 2007). From that point, both the SCO and CSTO would invoke the threat of further Color Revolutions to justify their security activities.

Beyond fears of Western interference, some of the West's own regional integration plans caused concern in Moscow and Beijing. Chief among these was the US decision to encourage links, especially in infrastructural development, between Central Asia and Afghanistan. In 2006, the State Department formally moved the administration of the Central Asian states from the Eurasian Bureau to a newly constituted Bureau for South and Central Asian Affairs. Both Moscow and Beijing viewed the move with suspicion, as signaling a geopolitical intent to re-orient the region. In fact, the United States made very little progress towards this goal, even as leading policymakers such as Secretary of State Hillary Clinton publicly proclaimed that Washington would back efforts to establish a "New Silk Route."

China's Economic Rise in Central Asia: Enter the Public Goods Provider

As the US presence in Central Asia gave impetus to many CSTO and SCO initiatives in the security sphere, China's dramatic economic rise in the 2000s made it Central Asia's dominant external economic player.

The financial crisis thrust China into the role of the region's "public goods provider," offering emergency loans, development financing, and building new regional infrastructure projects. At the same time, though, China has struggled to gain formal Russian acceptance for the institutionalization of this role within regional organizations.

First, the stark "facts." As Fig. 6.1 points out, the level of trade according to IMF data between the Central Asian states and China/Russia simply exploded in the 2000s, but China's rise increased at a greater rate. In the year 2000 (note: not 1990), China's official trade volume with the region was around $1bn, while by the end of the decade this had increased at least 30 times over, probably much more if we consider the statistical anomalies in trade data that tend to be underreported by Central Asian customs authorities. Russia's trade with the region also increased significantly to about $22bn by 2010, from a baseline of about $4bn in 2000. The key inflection point was the great financial crisis of 2008, when China's regional trade volumes surpassed Russia's. Notably, the peak volume of trade with both external powers was reached in 2013, after which volumes diminished, in large part due to the regional economic crisis unleashed by the Ukraine conflict and the resulting sanctions and countersanctions.

The financial crisis also spurred major investments by China. Chief among them were the three major loans for energy deals around 2009

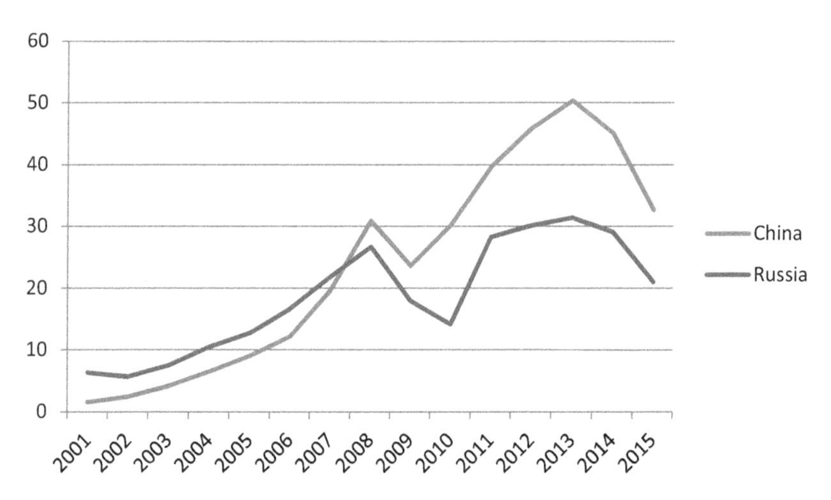

Fig. 6.1 Central Asian trade with Russia and China, annual, 2001–2015 (*Source* International Monetary Fund 2017)

that Beijing concluded with Russia ($25bn), Kazakhstan ($10bn), and Turkmenistan, in each case providing financing in exchange for long-term energy supply.[30] China also completed the construction of two important new pipelines: one oil pipeline, originating in the Caspian, and traversing Kazakhstan, and the landmark Central Asia–China gas pipeline (CAGP). The latter was the region's first high volume gas pipeline built in the post-Soviet era, originating in Turkmenistan, and traversing Uzbekistan and Kazakhstan before going on to China.

Beyond the sheer volume of China's economic engagement has also come a qualitative shift in its role. By the late 2000s, China was not only a large investor and trading partner, but had become the region's creditor. Much like the hegemons in the international political economy literature, China was offering a market for Central Asian "distress goods" through its burgeoning trading hubs of Kashgar and Urumqi. It assumed the classic roles of providing credit for infrastructure and development projects in Kyrgyzstan and Tajikistan, and acting as a lender of last resort by extending credits through loans-for shares agreements with energy producing countries. For example, by the end of 2013, one report estimated that China's Ex-Im Bank would own 70% of Tajikistan's external debt.[31] Similarly, the $8bn extended to Turkmenistan during the financial crisis, secured by supplies of Turkmen gas via the newly constructed CAGP, provided a financial lifeline to Ashgabat.

On the energy front, the legal structure of the CAGP, an agreement comprising three separate joint ventures (China–Turkmenistan, China–Uzbekistan, China–Kazakhstan) with China a 50% partner in each, has ensured that China acts as the project's chief mediator should disputes arise over price, volume, environmental issues or repairs. In Kazakhstan, the construction of an additional spur by CNPC from Beineu-Borzoi-Shymkent is actually gasifying Kazakh cities, while line D of the international pipeline has been planned to pass through Tajikistan and Kyrgyzstan, giving China a gas pipeline network for export and distribution throughout the region. Although construction on the line was halted in 2017, by January 2018 work on the Tajik section had restarted.[32]

Despite Multiple Regional Integration Initiatives, Central Asian Economic Integration Remains Low

One final point bears emphasis: the actual impact of all these different regional integration projects on economic cooperation in Central

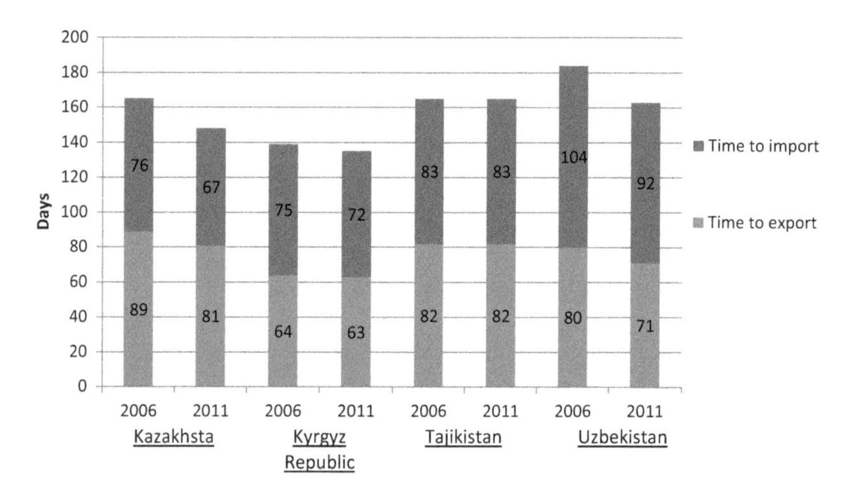

Fig. 6.2 Time required for import/export in Central Asia, 2006 and 2011 (*Source* World Bank doing business data. Modified from Cooley 2012)

Asia itself has been minimal. Despite the intensification of Chinese and Russian economic activity in Central Asia, overall trade barriers within the Central Asian region remain prohibitively high. As Fig. 6.2 highlights, despite the rise of the SCO, the EurAsEC/Customs Union and even Western-backed initiatives meant to spur regional economic integration throughout the 2000s, the informal barriers to trade remain substantial, with none of the Central Asian countries demonstrating improvements.

As Fig. 6.3 further shows, Central Asia is not only a poor imitation of Silk Routes of the past, it is the most trade unfriendly region in the world. Between 2006 and 2011, according to the World Bank's data on trading across borders, average import/export times in Central Asia were 85/79 and 79/74 respectively, more than triple the comparable times in the Middle East and North Africa or Latin America and the Caribbean. In fact, times in all these other regions showed more relative improvement than in Central Asia. The establishment of the Eurasian Customs Union in 2010 actually placed a trade barrier on the Kazakh–Kyrgyz border that until then was relatively open and had been the key to Kyrgyzstan's emerging role as a re-exporter of Chinese goods to the rest of the CIS states.[33]

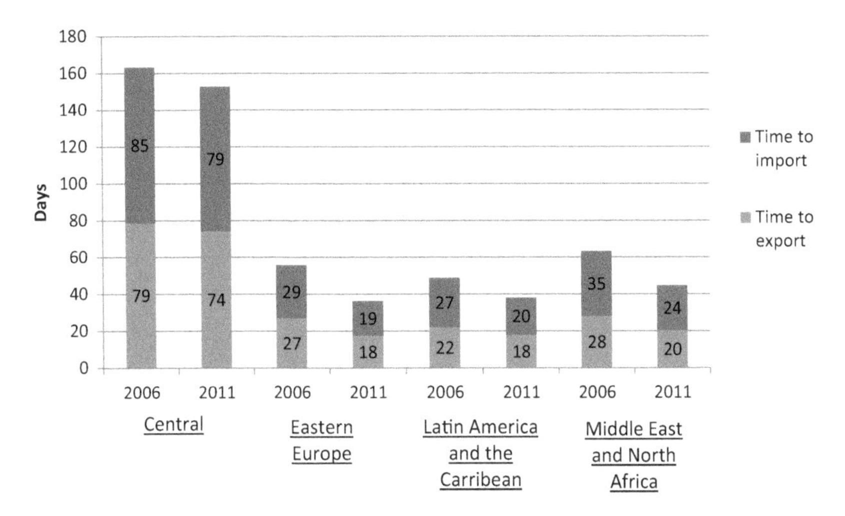

Fig. 6.3 Comparative regional times required for import/export, 2006 and 2011 (*Source* World Bank doing business data. Modified from Cooley 2012)

The 2000s that saw the evolution and consolidation of Russian and Chinese regional integration projects also marked the seeming peak of the "multivector" foreign policy era in the region, during which multiple external powers each promoted their own regional integration schemes. With the United States and NATO engaged in the region because of Afghanistan, Russia still developing its instruments of influence, and China rapidly increasing its economic footprint, the Central Asian states felt empowered to pursue cooperative ties with multiple partners.

Case Study: Cooperation and Hidden Tensions in the SCO

The trials and tribulations of the SCO during the 2000s highlight how the contrasting regional integration agendas and world views of Russia and China have played out in practice. Along with Moscow and Beijing's differing security agendas, member states' concerns about China's growing economic power have hindered the organization's economic agenda. As a result, for all the public talk about the SCO being a new-style organization, embodying different norms and practices, the main factor inhibiting its development is well known to scholars if regional integration: concerns about the potential relative gains from cooperation,[34] specifically Russian fears of institutionalizing Chinese economic dominance.

Whose Security, Whose Principles? The Georgia War and Splits Over Splittism

The SCO's "three evils" mantra was initially a convenient way for Moscow to attract Beijing's support for its campaign in Chechnya and operations in the North Caucasus. The previous section has noted how the Color Revolutions galvanized the two sides to oppose Western influence in Eurasia, especially the West's "values" agenda of promoting human rights and democracy.

But beyond these common concerns, intra-SCO politics exposed many of the schisms between Moscow and Beijing regarding the group's purpose and role. Its anti-Western tone was accommodated somewhat by Beijing, notably in the now infamous 2005 Astana Declaration against US military bases that was interpreted by many in the West as evidence of their growing counterhegemonic cooperation.[35] However, since that declaration, or perhaps because of it, Chinese officials have taken great care to emphasize that, as a security organization, the SCO neither seeks to counterbalance NATO nor is intended as a counterhegemonic platform against the West.

Consider the SCO's very mixed response to Russia's military campaigns in Georgia 2008 and Ukraine 2014, compared with China's crackdown in Xinjiang following the Urumqi incidents of 2009.[36] In both 2008 and 2014, Russian officials tried to use the organization as a platform to issue a strong statement affirming the Russian position and recognizing these sovereign boundary changes—independence for Abkhazia and South Ossetia in 2008 and the annexation of Crimea into the Russian Federation in 2014. It received no such support in 2008 at the SCO summit in Dushanbe, when China rebuffed requests by then Russian president Dmitry Medvedev to recognize the independence of the Georgian breakaway territories. President Hu Jintao stated instead that "China has noticed the latest developments in the region, expecting all sides concerned to properly settle the issue through dialogue and coordination."[37] According to the newspaper *Kommersant*, Medvedev had travelled to the Dushanbe summit confident of securing the backing normally reliable Kazakhstan and Kyrgyzstan, but the Central Asian states were united in their opposition to extending legal recognition to Abkhazia and South Ossetia, even as they expressed understanding for the Russian position on the war.[38] Similarly, in 2014, despite deep concern about the potential for other Western-supported Maidan-type movements to topple other regional governments, the organization has not legitimized Russia's actions. And just like 2008, Beijing released statements of understanding of the Russian position, but chose to abstain in the March 2014 UN vote on the Crimean annexation—while Kyrgyzstan and Tajikistan failed to vote altogether.

In contrast, following the 2009 violence in Urumqi that led to over a 100 deaths as Chinese security services cracked down on Uighur protestors, the Chinese MFA almost immediately crafted a strong statement in support of Beijing's right to deal with this "internal matter". Within 24 hours, all the other SCO members had agreed to it and the statement was issued by the SCO Secretariat a couple of days later.[39] Tellingly, after the 2008 rebuff Russian officials publicly backed the position that the CSTO, rather than the SCO, should be the primary security partner for Western engagement on regional security issues such as Afghanistan, even though its members, most notably Belarus, refused to recognize the independence of the Georgian breakaway territories.

True, the SCO has regularly accommodated Moscow's emerging counterhegemonic worldview, by issuing statements against intervention in Syria, deployment of the US missile defense system, and the Arab Spring. But in terms of substance it has been unable to develop any major new initiatives beyond internal security cooperation.

For a while, Beijing also pushed the possibility that the SCO could become more actively involved in Afghanistan following NATO's 2014 withdrawal, mostly by offering platforms for internal political dialogues, providing technical assistance and providing training to Afghan police forces. But despite President Hamid Karzai's enthusiastic embrace of the organization and acceptance of observer status, the Central Asian states' deep ambivalence about actively involvement in Afghanistan coupled with Moscow's preference for the CSTO ensured that the organization has played only a limited role in post-2014 Afghanistan. In fact, China's position itself appears to have shifted somewhat, going from advocating a role for the SCO to now focusing on the need to ensure P5 agreement about Afghanistan's future regional partnerships.[40]

Not Acknowledging China's de Facto *Economic Hegemon's Role*

Fundamental disagreements over the SCO's economic role have also continued to hamper the organization's development. When the group first formed, various initiatives such as an Interbank Association, business council and free trade project were mooted, but none of these have materialized. At core, and as admitted by Russian SCO officials, Moscow opposes such ideas, which would in practice establish a set of governance institutions, or counter-order bodies, that would lock in Chinese economic power and governance across the region.

This divergence between Beijing and Moscow was magnified by the global financial crisis. After the extent of the crisis became clear, Beijing approached Moscow and other SCO members with a proposal to create an emergency "crisis fund." This would have been similar to its own project-based domestic stimulus package, offering countercyclical lending for regional infrastructure projects. Moscow rejected these calls in the fall of 2008 and winter of 2009.[41] When in June 2009, Beijing once again broached the topic, it offered a 50–50 split, proposing that each of the regional powers provide $5bn in financing and that the two jointly select all regional projects.[42] Moscow refused again, this time citing an obscure Russian legal restriction on contributing to multilateral lending institutions without Duma consent. Frustrated, the Chinese shelved the proposal for two years, after which they unilaterally proceeded to allocate funds, but labeled these loans as "SCO projects."

Then again in the lead-up to the high-profile 2012 SCO Summit in Beijing, the organization had been on track to finally announce the establishment of an SCO Regional Development Bank, a vehicle for regional project finance proposed by China and supported by the Central Asian members. But the announcement and plan was halted, and then tabled, after the Russian delegation announced that it needed more time to consider the initiative. As with the other disagreements over China's "public goods" role, these tensions were buried under the official pomp and ceremony of the Beijing meeting. A similar thing happened in the lead-up to the 2014 Dushanbe Summit. The Russian delegation proposed that the existing Eurasian Development Bank (a Russian–Kazakh project) sponsor regional development projects, instead of a new SCO financing vehicle which China has continued to push.[43]

In sum, while Beijing has been reluctant to present the SCO security mission as a counterhegemonic agenda, Moscow has refused to allow Beijing a formal platform to become the region's economic public goods provider. Such disagreements and internal political tensions within the organization do not necessarily reduce the SCO to a "paper tiger." The organization has been successful in pushing itself as a non-Western regional organization that promotes regime stability and norms of sovereignty, and its expansion to include India and Pakistan makes the group symbolically important. The SCO has also enabled individual states to push back against Western criticisms and normative agendas, encouraging the Central Asian governments to deflect external criticisms and to demand the paring down of political and human rights conditions in organizations like the OSCE. In this respect, the SCO's presence as a non-Western "alternative" for its members to leverage is more significant than its actual organizational coherence or policy accomplishments. But the fundamental tensions at the core of the institution have endured.

Pivotal 2014: Intensifying Russian and Chinese Engagement Within Continued Asymmetry

The year 2014 marked a watershed in the international relations of Eurasia. The start of the formal US withdrawal from Afghanistan, accompanied by perceptions of its disengagement from the region, had already prompted both Moscow and Beijing to deepen their regional engagement. But the Ukraine conflict unleashed a wave of regional political and economic uncertainty, as Central Asian states feared both Russia's new interventionism and the regime threats posed by Maidan-like street protests. The net result has been that the "multivector equilibrium" that characterized the region's external relations in the 2000s—balancing relations among Russia, China, and the West—appears to be giving way to greater regional Russian and Chinese dominance, but with Russia increasingly having to accept a growing asymmetry in its relations with Beijing.

China's March Westward and the Belt and Road

In September 2013, at a speech at Nazarbayev University in Astana, Chinese President Xi Jinping announced plans to promote a "Silk Road Economic Belt" across neighboring Eurasian states. Over the next few months, Chinese policymakers and analysts further outlined ambitious plans to promote regional cooperation, economic integration, and connectivity by funding large-scale infrastructure and development projects throughout the region. These include a series of land routes and high-speed rail links intended to connect East Asia with Europe (via Eurasia), South Asia and the Middle East, as well as an accompanying maritime belt, supported by upgrades to ports and logistical hubs. Collectively these two belts have been described as the One Belt One Road (OBOR) or BRI and, according to the *South China Morning Post*, the initiative represents the, "most significant and far-reaching project the nation has ever put forward."[44]

The BRI is consistent with the idea, first articulated by Chinese IR scholar Wang Jisi, about the need for China to "march west" and increase its engagement with Central Asia and the Middle East, in order to fill the vacuum left by a vacating United States (he curiously makes no reference to Russia) and escape the competitive box of a military build-up in East Asia.[45] According to Wang, increased involvement in Central Asia would also offer Beijing the opportunity to partner with the United States on regional issues and could even become a bargaining chip in the event that US–Chinese relations deteriorated.

The drivers of the BRI also include perennial Chinese imperatives like stabilizing Xinjiang and placing it at the core of new inter-regional links; creating a new political community among China's neighbors sensitive to Beijing's concerns; and offering new external market opportunities for Chinese economic actors that are struggling with a slowing domestic economy already at investment overcapacity.[46] Beyond the proposed land bridge rail network through Kazakhstan, most of the large BRI projects in Central Asia appear to be continuations of previous Chinese initiatives—including expanding the CAGP and building a high-speed rail network. But the BRI offers an important hook to various Chinese companies and local governments to promote their regional initiatives as nationally important.

Despite the upbeat tone to coverage of the BRI, China's experiences in Central Asia point to a number of potential challenges confronting Beijing.[47] These include dealing with a graft-prone region in which elites use foreign-sponsored infrastructure to generate private revenue streams, and border and customs officials collect large informal payments. Meanwhile, growing Sinophobia, especially in Kazakhstan, Kyrgyzstan, and Tajikistan is being fueled by Russian-language media, coverage of Chinese corruptions scandals, and resurgent domestic illiberal and nationalist movements.

The recent establishment of new regional organizations and funding vehicles for these initiatives, including the Silk Road Fund and the AIIB, suggest that Beijing is also broadening its institutional engagement for the region beyond just relying on the SCO. Indeed, China's agreement to expand the SCO's membership to include Pakistan and India in 2017 appears to have been an acknowledgement that the SCO will remain largely a ceremonial and symbolic grouping and that Beijing's economic agenda in Central Asia will be best pursued via the BRI even as the organization remains officially committed to fostering regional integration and cooperation. Practically speaking, the SCO's consensus norm means that the organization is even less likely to develop into a problem-solving body, while some of its more successful security agenda might be compromised by the inclusion of the South Asian nuclear rivals.

The Ukraine Crisis and Moscow's Renewed Regional Engagement

The Ukraine crisis of 2014 also sent shockwaves throughout Eurasia. Russia's willingness to use force to annex Crimea and destabilize Ukraine alarmed all the Central Asian states, many which host Russian military facilities. Moscow's effective media and information campaign was almost as concerning to states like Kazakhstan and Kyrgyzstan that are consumers of Russian satellite television and local broadcasting. At the same time, authoritarian fears of a Maidan-style uprising, backed by the West, has also alarmed regional governments, leading to a new wave of regime insecurity.

Already, beginning in about 2012, Moscow had begun to engage more robustly with selected Central Asian states, treating them as clients. Perceptions of a looming US withdrawal prompted Russia to renew its long-term overseas basing agreements with Kyrgyzstan, Tajikistan, and Armenia, and these states also received promises of significant military assistance and investments in strategic sectors. With Uzbekistan's exit from the CSTO, that organization appears more coherent. The publicly-feared threat of "spillover" from Afghanistan plays a useful political role by giving Russian military facilities an actual strategic purpose (as opposed to just operating as a marker of prestige and influence), while some instability on the Afghanistan–Central Asian border justifies growing Russian security cooperation with the Central Asian republics, both within the CSTO and bilaterally with Turkmenistan and Uzbekistan.

The meme of Afghan spillover also allows Russian officials to highlight the regional costs and destabilizing effects of American global military interventions.

On the economic front, the crisis in Moscow's relations with the West has accelerated Russian efforts to advance the EEU as the preferred regional economic architecture, and deepen relations with China. However, both of these have come at a price. On the EEU front, Russian negotiators appear to have granted Belarus, Kazakhstan, Armenia, and Kyrgyzstan a host of concessions in their desire to maintain the political momentum of formalizing the EEU in May 2014. For example, Belarus was allowed to maintain its energy re-export trade, Armenia allowed hundreds of exemptions from the regional tariff for politically and socially sensitive consumer goods, while Kazakhstan effectively blocked any forms of political cooperation from moving forward such as the EEU parliament. At the same time, the fallout from Western sanctions and Russian countersanctions generated new concerns over re-export within EEU borders, and the repositioning of customs officials on the Russian border with Belarus and Kazakhstan, leading to a certain amount of de-integration in 2014 compared to 2013.[48]

Reconciling the BRI and EEU: Can There be a Coherent Greater Eurasia?

On the China front, Russian officials appear increasingly willing to deepen cooperation, although this is happening more and more on Beijing's terms. Morena Skalamera's chapter has detailed important concessions made by Moscow on price and side payments to secure the Power of Siberia gas deal in 2014. But China is being granted access to Russian strategic sectors, most notably new Chinese investments in Russian energy production (including Rosneft and Novatek projects), while Russian advanced weapons systems sales have resumed. Tellingly, Russia signed onto the AIIB in 2015 only after President Putin overrode an initial rejection of the organization by the Russian Ministry of Finance bureaucracy.[49]

Discussions over cooperative mechanisms between the EEU and China (including BRI) continue, though the exact forms and terms of these institutional interactions remain uncertain. Philosophically, the major aspects of these two integration projects seem to be in tension: while the BRI views Central Asia mostly as a transit corridor to strengthen China's connectivity with Europe, the Middle East and South Asia,

Russia's EEU views Central Asia as a space to be protected from competing external influences by a common tariff and regulatory framework. Simply put, China seeks to facilitate *moving through* Central Asia, just as Russia wishes to lock it into its regional economic orbit.

Tellingly, neither side publicly acknowledges any frictions or contradictions in their respective visions for Eurasian integration. Despite early concerns, Moscow now accepts public declarations of cooperation between the EEU and the BRI as a substitute for any actual joint planning. It also appears to grasp that the BRI will have many non-Russian routes and projects. Viewed from this perspective, Russia's adoption of a "Greater Eurasia" initiative in 2016 that seeks to promote greater integration and connectivity throughout the Eurasian landmass implicitly concedes that the BRI represents the core of future integration efforts. Though Russian analysts talk up the potential of North–South forms of integration, the renewed opportunities for cooperation with Iran, and the ever closer relationship with Turkey, Greater Eurasia appears to bury, as opposed to confront, the dilemmas posed by China's growing continental dominance and construction of new regional counter-order institutions within Russia's sphere of influence.

Given the geopolitical shift to the east that Russian policymakers are so keen to signal in the wake of the Ukraine crisis, Moscow finds itself "rhetorically entrapped," unable to publicly voice any misgivings about Chinese plans. Instead, it embraces an axiomatic faith that these regional frameworks will eventually converge in a manner that promotes Russian interests.[50]

Conclusions

The 2000s in Central Asia were characterized by a broad regional multipolarity and a type of multivectorism practiced by all the Central Asian states that wanted to maintain ties with Russia, China and the West. Within this political environment, the Central Asian states were happy to join regional organizations such as the SCO, as long as doing so did not undermine sovereign choice or otherwise constrain governmental action. As a result, the decade was characterized by what one scholar has aptly referred to as "virtual regionalism" (Allison 2008), with the Central Asian states joining a host of regional forums and integration initiatives with few tangible results. Throughout this time, China's role in the region grew, even as Beijing and Moscow were publicly careful to present a neat division of labor in the region.

Events of 2014 have upset what seemed like a relatively stable set of affairs. Perceptions of US withdrawal and even US geopolitical disengagement have removed a critical vector for the Central Asian governments. Given the difficulties of maintaining basing access and managing relations with these authoritarian regimes, Washington policymakers had already developed an acute sense of "Central Asia fatigue" even prior to the Trump administration. But Trump's self-declared isolationism seems readier still to concede Central Asia as a zone of Russian and Chinese influence. And although the Pentagon in the summer 2017 announced that it would increase the US troop presence in Afghanistan by 4000 to roughly 14,000 without a timetable for their removal, such a footprint is still comparatively light and unlikely to result in Central Asia once again becoming a US security or logistical partner.

Ultimately, Russia's current acute need for non-Western geostrategic partnership means that it is likely to accept partnership with China increasingly on Beijing's terms. This may well extend to granting Beijing a larger role in security affairs. The September 2016 suicide bombing of the Chinese Embassy in Bishkek and Beijing's intensifying border cooperation with Tajikistan suggest that if Russian-led high-profile security efforts cannot address sources of instability within the region, China will take its own measures to ensure the stability of its borders. Judging by recent trends, Moscow is more likely to adapt its own view of Beijing's acceptable field of action and redefine its own perceptions of national interests, than to confront or challenge China's growing regional influence.

Notes

1. Quoted from "Россииско-китаиские-семинар 'Россия и Китаи в новои между народнои среде'" ["Russian–Chinese seminar: 'Russia and China in the new international environment'"], Council for Foreign and Defence Policy, Moscow, Chinese Institute of International Strategic Studies, RIA Novosti, March 20–22, 2009, www.svop.ru/meeting/meeting117.htm. As published in Crisis Group (2013), 9.
2. Cooley (2012b).
3. Lukin (2014).
4. Kotkin (2009), Lo (2008). On China and liberal order, see Ikenberry (2011).
5. By counter-order, I refer to the newly created non-Western international institutions, organizations, and rule-sets established for the exercise of global governance.

6. Tsygankov (2012), Larson and Shevchenko (2010).
7. Allison (2004).
8. Flikke (2009), pp. 30–33.
9. Kucera (2011).
10. On competing logics of post-Soviet economic integration, see Darden (2009).
11. Dragneva and Wolczuk (2013).
12. For integration data, see Vinokurov (2012). A critical Kazakhstani perspective is provided in Kassenova (2012).
13. See Nikitina (2009).
14. For a critical assessment, see Olcott et al. (1999).
15. See especially Clarke (2011).
16. Coverage of the SCO is a growth industry. Important works include Aris (2011) and Bailes (2007).
17. For a critical rejoinder, see Gavrilis (2008).
18. Ambrosio (2008).
19. On the development of SCO norms, see Ambrosio (2008) and Lewis (2012).
20. See Aris (2011).
21. See data reported in Human Rights in China (2011).
22. In response, prominent international human rights organizations have argued that these practices violate central international human rights treaty commitments and norms, such as political asylum norms or the convention against torture, going so far as to claim that the treaty is a vehicle for human rights violations. See Cooley (2013), and FIDH (2012).
23. Zhao (2006).
24. For an overview, see Mankoff (2009).
25. For details, see Cooley (2012).
26. See Lyall (2004) for a fascinating content analysis of how Russian officials changed their framing of the US presence in Central Asia.
27. See Nadine's (2007) cataloguing of these efforts.
28. Beissinger (2007), Mitchell (2012).
29. Cooley (2012), Appendix 1.
30. Downs (2011).
31. Crisis Group (2011).
32. Eurasianet (2018).
33. On Kyrgyzstan's re-export trade, see Kaminski and Raballand (2009).
34. Grieco (1988).
35. Walt and Pape (2005) both cite the episode, and subsequent eviction from K2, as evidence of "soft-balancing" against the US. In fact, according to inside accounts, the statement was initially placed on the agenda by

Uzbek President Karimov who, in turn, was supported by Putin. Beijing was nervous about the declaration, but went along with it in the interest of preserving unity, but allegedly removed reference to "US bases" in favor of the language "foreign military bases" so as to not single out the United States. See Cooley (2012).
36. This section draws on Cooley (2009).
37. Weitz (2008).
38. Author's communication with *Kommersant* correspondent Alexander Gabuev. Moscow, June 2009.
39. Author's interviews with SCO Secretariat. Beijing, October 2009.
40. Author's interviews with Chinese MFA advisors and CASS officials, August 6–10, 2014 Beijing.
41. Author's observations and interviews at Annual SCO Academic conference, Shanghai Academy of Social Sciences, July 2009.
42. Cooley (2009).
43. Gabuev (2015).
44. South China Morning Post (2015).
45. Wang (2012).
46. For an overview of Chinese perspectives, see Swaine (2015).
47. On the challenges facing the BRI in Central Asia, see Clarke (2016) and Cooley (2016).
48. Schenkkan (2014).
49. The Finance Ministry had apparently viewed the outlay for AIIB membership as excessive given overall budgetary pressures, Gabuev (2015).
50. On Russia's changing view of the BRI, see Peyrouse (2017).

Literature

Allison, Roy. 2004. Regionalism, Regional Structures and Security Management in Central Asia. *International Affairs* 80: 463–483.

Allison, Roy. 2008. Virtual Regionalism, Regional Structures and Regime Security in Central Asia. *Central Asian Survey* 27 (2): 185–202.

Ambrosio, Thomas. 2008. Catching the 'Shanghai Sprit': How the Shanghai Cooperation Organization Promotes Authoritarian Norms in Central Asia. *Europe–Asia Studies* 60: 1321–1344.

Aris, Stephen. 2011. *Eurasian Regionalism: The Shanghai Cooperation Organization*. London: Palgrave Macmillan.

Bailes, Alyson J.K., et al. 2007. *The Shanghai Cooperation Organization*. Stockholm: Stockholm International Peace Research Institute.

Beissinger, Mark R. 2007. Structure and Example in Modular Political Phenomena: The Diffusion of Bulldozer/Rose/Orange/Tulip Revolutions. *Perspectives on Politics* 5: 259.

Clarke, Michael E. 2011. *Xinjiang and China's Rise in Central Asia—A History.* New York and London: Routledge.
Clarke, Michael. 2016. Beijing's March West: Opportunities and Challenges for China's Eurasian Pivot. *Orbis* 60 (2): 296–313.
Cooley, Alexander. 2009. Cooperation Gets Shanghaied: China, Russia and the SCO. *Foreign Affairs* [Online], December 14. https://www.foreignaffairs.com/articles/china/2009-12-14/cooperation-gets-shanghaied.
Cooley, Alexander. 2012a. *Great Games, Local Rules: The New Great Power Contest in Central Asia.* New York: Oxford University Press.
Cooley, Alexander. 2012b. In Central Asia, Public Cooperation and Private Rivalry. *New York Times,* June 8. Available at https://www.nytimes.com/2012/06/09/opinion/in-central-asia-public-cooperation-and-private-rivalry.html.
Cooley, Alexander. 2013. The League of Authoritarian Gentleman. *Foreign Policy* [Online], January 31. http://foreignpolicy.com/2013/01/30/the-league-of-authoritarian-gentlemen/.
Cooley, Alexander. 2016. *The Emerging Political Economy of OBOR: The Challenges of Promoting Connectivity in Central Asia and Beyond.* Washington, DC: CSIS, October, at https://csis-prod.s3.amazonaws.com/s3fs-public/publication/161021_Cooley_OBOR_Web.pdf.
Crisis Group. 2011. *Central Asia: Decay and Decline.* Asia Report No. 201. Brussels: ICG.
Crisis Group. 2013. *China's Central Asia Problem.* Asia Report No. 244. Brussels: ICG.
Darden, Keith A. 2009. *Economic Liberalism and Its Rivals: The Formation of International Institutions Among the Post-Soviet States.* New York: Cambridge University Press.
Downs, Erica. 2011. *Inside China Inc: China's Development Bank's Cross-Border Energy Deals.* Washington, DC: Brookings.
Dragneva, Rilka, and Kataryna Wolczuk (eds.). 2013. *Eurasian Economic Integration: Law, Policy and Politics.* Cheltenham: Edward Elgar.
Eurasianet. 2018. Tajikistan Resumes Building Turkmenistan–China Pipeline. January 31. Available at https://eurasianet.org/s/tajikistan-resumes-building-turkmenistan-china-pipeline.
FIDH. 2012. *The Shanghai Cooperation Organization: A Vehicle for Human Rights Violations.* Paris: FIDH.
Flikke, Geir. 2009. *Balancing Acts: Russian–Chinese Relations and Developments in the SCO and CSTO.* Oslo NUPI Report.
Fumagalli, Matteo. 2007. Alignments and Realignments in Central Asia: The Rationale and Implications of Uzbekistan's Rapprochement with Russia. *International Political Science Review* 28: 253–271.

Gabuev, Alexander. 2015. Why Did It Take Russia So Long to Join the Asian Infrastructure Investment Bank? *Carnegie Moscow*, March 30. https://carnegie.ru/commentary/59554.

Gavrilis, George. 2008. *The Dynamics of Interstate Boundaries*. New York: Cambridge University Press.

Grieco, Joseph. 1988. Anarchy and the Limits of Cooperation: A Realist Critique of the Newest Liberal Institutionalism. *International Organization* 42: 485–507.

Human Rights in China. 2011. *Counterterrorism and Human Rights: The Impact of the Shanghai Cooperation Organization*. New York: HRC.

Ikenberry, G. John. 2011. Future of the Liberal World Order: Internationalism After America. *Foreign Affairs* 90: 56–68.

International Monetary Fund. 2017. Direction of Trade Statistics. Available at http://www.imf.org/en/Data.

Kaminski, Bartłomiej, and Gaël Raballand. 2009. Entrepot for Chinese Consumer Goods in Central Asia: The Puzzle of Re-exports Through Kyrgyz Bazaars. *Eurasian Geography and Economics* 50: 581–590.

Kassenova, Nargis. 2012. Kazakhstan and Eurasian Economic Integration: Quick Start, Mixed Results and Uncertain Future. *Russie.NEI. Visions* 14.

Kotkin, Stephen. 2009. The Unbalanced Triangle: What Chinese–Russian Relations Mean for the United States. *Foreign Affairs* 88 (5): 130–138.

Kucera, Joshua. 2011. With Eye to Arab Spring, CSTO Strengthens Cyber, Military Powers. *Eurasianet*, August 15. Available at https://eurasianet.org/s/with-eye-to-arab-spring-csto-strengthens-cyber-military-powers.

Larson, Deborah Welch, and Alexei Shevchenko. 2010. Status Seekers: Chinese and Russian Responses to US Primacy. *International Security* 34 (4): 63–95.

Lewis, David. 2012. Who's Socialising Whom? Regional Organisations and Contested Norms in Central Asia. *Europe–Asia Studies* 64: 1219–1237.

Lo, Bobo. 2008. *Axis of Convenience: Moscow, Beijing, and the New Geopolitics*. Washington, DC: Brookings Institution Press.

Lukin, Alexander. 2014. What the Kremlin is Thinking: Putin's Vision for Eurasia. *Foreign Affairs* 93: 85–93.

Lyall, Jason. 2004. Great Games: Russia and the Merging Security Dilemma in Central Asia. Paper Delivered to the Annual meeting of the American Political Science Association, Washington, DC.

Mankoff, Jeffrey. 2009. *Russian Foreign Policy: The Return of Great Power Politics*. Lanham, MD: Rowman & Littlefield.

Mitchell, Lincoln A. 2012. *The Color Revolutions*. Philadelphia: University of Pennsylvania Press.

Nadine, Rebecca Louise. 2007. China and the Shanghai Cooperation Organisation: 1996–2006. PhD dissertation, University of Sheffield.

Nikitina, Yuliya. 2009. Никитина Ю.А. ОДКБ и ШОС: модели регионализма в сфере безопасности [CSTO and SCO: Models of Regionalism in the Security Sphere]. Moscow: MGIMO and Navona.

Olcott, Martha Brill, Anders Åslund, and Sherman W. Garnett. 1999. *Getting It Wrong: Regional Cooperation and the Commonwealth of Independent States.* Washington, DC: Carnegie Endowment for International Peace.

Pape, Robert A. 2005. Soft Balancing Against the United States. *International Security* 30: 7–45.

Peyrouse, Sebastien. 2017. The Evolution of Russia's Views on the Belt and Road Initiative. *Asia Policy* 24 (1): 96–102.

Schenkkan, Nate. 2014. Band of Outsiders: How Sanctions Will Strengthen Russia's Economic Clout. *Foreign Affairs*, August 27.

South China Morning Post. 2015. "One Belt, One Road" Will Define China's Role as World Leader. SCMP Leader, April 2. Available at http://www.scmp.com/comment/insight-opinion/article/1753773/one-belt-one-road-initiative-will-define-chinas-role-world.

Swaine, Michael D. 2015. Chinese Views and Commentary on the 'One Belt, One Road Initiative.' *China Leadership Monitor* 47: 2.

Tsygankov, Andrei P. 2012. *Russia and the West from Alexander to Putin: Honor in International Relations.* New York: Cambridge University Press.

Vinokurov, Evgeny. 2012. The Customs Union and the Single Economic Space: Towards the Eurasian Economic Union. In *EDB Eurasian Integration Yearbook*, ed. Evgeny Vinokurov. Almaty: Eurasian Development Bank.

Wang, Jisi. 2012. *'Marching Westward': The Rebalancing of China's Geostrategy.* International and Strategic Studies Report No. 73, Peking University.

Weitz, Richard. 2008. Beijing–Moscow Rift Over Georgia War Deepens. *World Politics Review*, September 19.

Zhao, Huasheng. 2006. The Shanghai Cooperation Organization at 5: Achievements and Challenges Ahead. *China and Eurasia Forum Quarterly* 4: 3.

CHAPTER 7

China, Russia and the Great Power Contest in the Middle East

Jo Inge Bekkevold

Great powers have shaped events in the Middle East ever since the decline of Ottoman power in the eighteenth century.[1] During the Cold War, the United States and the Soviet Union contended for influence in the region through their respective client states. Following the Soviet collapse and the end of the Cold War, the influence of the United States became paramount and many Middle Eastern countries bandwagoned with the hegemon.[2] Today we see the contours of a new great power contest in the Middle East,[3] with the United States being challenged by Russia and China.

The balance of power in the Middle East depends on the polarity—the number of great powers—and nature of engagement, whether it is competitive, cooperative or hegemonic. If one of the great powers attempts to dominate the region, the others tend to increase their support for local allies to prevent these from bandwagoning with the would-be hegemon.[4] Since the 1990–1991 Gulf War, the United States has dominated the Middle East. However, the durability of the post-Cold War unipolar US-led international system is increasingly in question.[5]

J. I. Bekkevold (✉)
Norwegian Institute for Defence Studies, Oslo, Norway
e-mail: jib@ifs.mil.no

J. I. Bekkevold and B. Lo (eds.), *Sino-Russian Relations in the 21st Century*, https://doi.org/10.1007/978-3-319-92516-5_7

We are now returning to a new bipolar system, with China emerging as a peer of the United States.[6]

If we are on the verge of a new bipolarity, revolving around the United States and China, it seems likely that Russia will have to play second fiddle. However, the regional picture can diverge from the global pattern, with other powers enjoying considerable influence in a particular theater of international relations. For instance, East Asia was characterized by the U.S.–China–Soviet great power triangle during the second half of the Cold War, and has been characterized by U.S.–China bipolarity since the end of the Cold War.[7] In this chapter, I argue that we are witnessing just such a case in the emerging U.S.–Russia–China great power triangle in the Middle East.

U.S. hegemony in the Middle East has stemmed from its unipolar position in the international system, and its willingness to play the role of regional leader.[8] However, the Middle East is now losing some of its earlier importance for American interests, as reflected in the decline of U.S. crude oil imports from the region. In 2012, Zbigniew Brzezinski observed that whereas in the mid-1970s the United States had strong relationships with the four most important countries in the Middle East–Iran, Saudi Arabia, Egypt, and Turkey–U.S. influence in all four countries has since fallen substantially.[9] And as the United States began to lose ground, China and Russia stepped up their engagement in the region.[10]

Russia is the weakest component of the global triangle, but the Middle East's relative geographic proximity to it makes it important to Moscow. Russia's willingness to use traditional balancing tools such as arms sales, and its military intervention in Syria, signal that it is keen to be seen as a great power in the Middle East. It is setting the policy agenda in Syria, and has reinforced its military presence there, establishing an airbase outside Latakia and upgrading its naval base in Tartus. At the same time, it has developed a close working relationship with Tehran, and is using an Iranian airbase for bombing raids against the Syrian opposition.

China is also increasing its footprint in the region. In January 2016, as Xi Jinping paid a landmark visit to Iran, Saudi Arabia, and Egypt, it launched its first ever White Paper on the region—the Arab Policy Paper. China is the only great power with equal access to Saudi Arabia and Iran, two of its most important sources of crude oil, and through its Belt and Road Initiative (BRI) it is getting ready to invest huge sums in infrastructure in the Middle East. Although China engages the region mainly in geo-economic terms, it has for a number of years contributed naval vessels and crew to the multilateral anti-piracy effort in the Gulf of Aden. It is also building a naval repair facility in Djibouti, which will be its first ever overseas military base.

This chapter examines whether the United States, China and Russia have predominantly competitive or cooperative policies in the Middle East. Competitive intervention by several great powers in a region is likely to entrench balance of power politics.[11] I also consider to what extent Chinese and Russian interests converge in the Middle East. Beijing and Moscow have on a number of occasions since 2011 jointly vetoed US and Western-led UN Security Council resolutions on Syria, they both have a close relationship with Iran, and in 2015 Russia invited China to hold their first ever joint naval drills in the Mediterranean Sea, leaving the impression that these two countries have a coordinated approach in the Middle East, and that their policies in the Middle East are part of a larger objective limiting the influence of the United States. Even though it is assumed that regions where great powers are actively involved are not sufficiently autonomous to create their own balances of power,[12] it is important to take into account how local actors in the Middle East can influence the great power contest. The role of local countries in a region shaped by great power competition is also emphasized in Cooley's analysis of Sino-Russian relations in Central Asia in this volume.[13] Accordingly, the chapter begins with an outline of Beijing's and Moscow's respective approaches, ambitions, and recent initiatives towards the Middle East. It then explores their policies towards the war in Syria, and with key countries such as Iran, Turkey, Saudi Arabia, and Egypt. Finally, it assesses the great power contest between the United States, Russia and China, with a particular emphasis on the dynamics of the Sino-Russian relationship.

Russia in the Middle East

Tsarist imperialism made the Ottoman Empire and Persia (Iran) the principal focus of Russia's interests on its southern flank. Even in the early years of the Cold War, Moscow had few geopolitical interests in the Middle East beyond Turkey and Iran.[14] However, this changed with Nikita Khrushchev and Soviet support for Egyptian leader Nasser's pan-Arab nationalism from the mid-1950s.[15] And despite Egypt's decision in

1972 to expel Russian military advisors and later abandon their friendship treaty, the USSR continued to be a significant player in the Middle East as it became a major theater of Cold War rivalry with the United States.

Although Russia's influence in the Middle East collapsed following the end of the Cold War, in recent years it has acquired renewed strategic leverage as a result of its military campaign in Syria. U.S. and European reluctance to be drawn into yet another lengthy military operation has played a role in this reversal of fortunes. Yet Russia's recent gains in the Middle East are not simply opportunistic, but reflect a degree of strategic planning.[16] Moscow began to rebuild damaged relations in the Middle East in the early 2000s as a stepping stone to reasserting Russia's great power status and gaining international respect.[17] As Walter Russell Mead has noted, "[b]eating Barack Obama like a brass drum doesn't just help Putin at home. It helps him re-establish Russia's prestige in the Middle East. … It helps drive a wedge between the U.S. and our allies in Europe. It helps persuade rulers all over the world that the U.S. is a weak and ineffective power, encouraging them to look to rising powers like China, Iran and, of course, Russia as better partners for the future."[18] With U.S. leadership and engagement in the Middle East in decline, Russia is better able to shape policy in the Middle East, and do so "on the cheap."[19] In terms of financial costs, Russia's military operation in Syria is comparable to an ongoing military exercise and does not require a special budget.[20]

The geographical proximity of the Middle East to Russia's southern flank makes it important for Moscow to secure a sphere of influence in this region, in particular through a military presence.[21] With the annexation of Crimea, establishment of bases in Syria, and access to air bases in Iran, Russia has increased its power projection capability and diplomatic leverage in the Middle East.[22] Nikolai Kozhanov, a leading Russian expert on the Middle East, has rightly observed that "Moscow's appetite is growing according to [its] achievements on the ground. Syria is now considered as a kind of means to further regional influence rather than a goal itself".[23] In fact, Russia can arguably extend its military reach into the Gulf region, and pose an anti-access area denial (A2/AD) threat that the United States and its allies have not faced on NATO's southern flank for decades.[24]

Russia also seeks to exploit the Middle East as an expanding market for arms sales. Imports by Middle Eastern states are growing, and accounted for 29% of total global arms imports in the period

2012–2016. However, most of these states continue to rely primarily on the United States and Europe for the acquisition of advanced military capabilities. The ten largest arms importers in the Middle East during this time—Saudi Arabia, the United Arab Emirates, Egypt, Iraq, Turkey, Israel, Qatar, Oman, Kuwait, and Jordan—all had the United States and NATO allies as their main suppliers of weapons.[25] But this picture may change as Russia becomes a power broker in the region, and uses arms sales to this purpose.[26]

Another strategic interest of Russia in the Middle East is to contain Islamist extremism. With a sizeable Muslim population, and fighters from North Caucasus joining the ranks of Islamic State (IS) in Syria, Moscow is worried about the spread of Islamist terrorism to the Caucasus and wider Eurasia.[27] Finally, Russia's Middle East policy is driven by what Bobo Lo has called "the fear of democratic contagion".[28] With the color revolutions in several former Soviet states and Western interventionism in Iraq and Afghanistan still fresh in Putin's mind, Moscow's support to the Assad regime in Syria should also be seen as an effort to turn back the tide of grassroots democratization.[29] It is pertinent that the Syrian uprising gained momentum during the second half of 2011, around the same time as popular protests in Russia erupted against Putin's decision to stand for a third presidential term.[30]

Both Dmitri Trenin and Stephen Blank argue that Russia does not have any permanent allies in the Middle East, and that Moscow's policy is situational and conditional depending on its interests at any given time.[31] Talal Nizameddin, by contrast, argues that in recent years it has tried to pursue a more balanced approach to countries in the region.[32] Nevertheless, Putin's Russia continues to align itself with the Iran–Syria-Hezbollah axis—a response in part to the latter's desire for Moscow to counterbalance American influence in the Middle East.[33]

China in the Middle East

In 1955, China took part in the Bandung Conference in Indonesia, a gathering to which the Soviet Union was not invited. The Conference enabled China to achieve a diplomatic breakthrough with a number of Third World countries, and in 1956 Egypt established diplomatic relations with China, soon followed by Syria and Yemen.[34] Beijing saw the newly decolonized states as important supporters for the recently established People's Republic of China.

In January 2016, 60 years after China established diplomatic relations with Egypt, it launched its first White Paper on the region—the Arab Policy Paper.[35] China's interests in the Middle East have evolved greatly over these six decades. It has become the world's number one importer of crude oil, and the number one trader of manufactured goods. Much of China's seaborne trade passes through the Middle East region and the Suez Canal. China's Middle East policy is also increasingly linked to the BRI. These developments give it greater leverage in the region.

China's most influential foreign affairs official in the post-Mao era, Qian Qichen, wrote in his memoirs that "The Gulf is a place of strategic importance. Any crisis there affects the strategic balance of the whole world."[36] Qian argued that China as a large country and one of five permanent members of the UN Security Council should play an important role in safeguarding regional stability in the Middle East. That said, China's legacy in the Middle East is very different from that of Russia or the United States. It is no stranger to providing arms to regimes and opposition groups, but it has played only a minor role in the region's Cold War proxy wars, instead positioning itself as one of the leaders of the non-aligned movement in the 1950s and 1960s. Consequently, countries in the Middle East can identify with China's history of anti-imperialist struggle in a way they do not with Russia or the United States.[37] This, combined with a certain degree of anti-Americanism that China (and Russia) shares with many Middle East countries,[38] could give Beijing an advantage. As Xi Jinping put it in his speech at the Arab League headquarters in Cairo in January 2016: "Instead of looking for a proxy in the Middle East, we promote peace talks; instead of seeking any sphere of influence, we call on all parties to join the circle of friends for the BRI; instead of attempting to fill the "vacuum," we build a cooperative partnership network for win-win outcomes."[39] Nevertheless, behind the rhetoric great power rivalry has always played a role in Beijing's Middle East policies, best exemplified by its relationship with Iran where China has moved from countering Soviet expansionism to resisting U.S. unilateralism.

The Arab Policy Paper links Chinese interests in the Middle East with Xi's China Dream of national rejuvenation, which seeks to build a strong and prosperous country. The Paper puts energy cooperation at the core of cooperation with the region. Indeed, China's emphasis on energy bears some resemblance to how the United States used to look upon the Middle East as a strategic supplier of oil.[40] Although China has pursued a successful diversification strategy in its oil imports,[41] the Middle East will continue to be the main source of these for the foreseeable future.[42] China now imports more oil from the Middle East than does the United States, which has Canada as the most important source of crude oil imports. In 2016, the six Middle East OPEC countries (Kuwait, Iran, Iraq, Qatar, Saudi Arabia, and United Arab Emirates) exported an average 2.95 million barrels per day (b/d) of crude oil to China, more than to Europe (2.54 million b/d) and North American (1.85 million b/d).[43]

Since Xi launched the idea in 2013, the BRI has become China's most ambitious undertaking, and it is highlighted in the Arab Policy Paper. The seventh ministerial meeting of the China–Arab States Cooperation Forum in 2016 agreed to "advance the joint construction of the Belt and Road between China and Arab states."[44] Through its two legs the Silk Road Economic Belt and the twenty-first Century Maritime Silk Road, the BRI encapsulates the ongoing reconfiguration of China's geostrategy—balancing its traditional role as a land power with its new role as a sea power. In addition to finding new outlets for excess industrial capacity, the BRI is driven by a desire to stabilize China's western frontier, secure access to energy and mineral resources, establish land transit routes through Eurasia, and build facilities in the Indian Ocean that can assist China's trade interests. Finally, the BRI could help Beijing to manage great power relations in Central and South Asia, and even to carve out a potential sphere of influence.[45]

The strategic drivers behind the BRI now increasingly shape China's interests in the Middle East as well, especially as a gateway for trade. China has emerged as one of the largest trading partners in the region. As illustrated in Table 7.1, its trade in 2016 with Egypt, Iran, Israel, Saudi Arabia and Turkey was almost five times larger than Russia's trade with the same countries, and also considerably larger than that of the United States. Yet China's commercial interests extend well beyond its growing bilateral trade with the region. In 2015, trade with Europe and Africa accounted for 15.9 and 4.5%, respectively, of China's total foreign trade.[46] Increasing uncertainty over U.S. foreign policy has moved Europe up the strategy ladder in Beijing. The fact that Egypt, Saudi Arabia and Turkey are all represented in the 12-member strong Board of Directors of the China-initiated Asian Infrastructure Investment Bank (AIIB), whose main purpose is to finance infrastructure projects in BRI partner countries, shows the importance of the Middle East as a gateway.[47]

Table 7.1 Foreign trade of selected countries in the Middle East, 2016 (in million USD)

	China	*United States*	*Russia*
Egypt	8049	4109	2476
Iran	22,492	184	2771
Israel	9224	25,696	1560
Saudi Arabia	44,036	36,118	740
Turkey	27,771	17,538	16,896
Total 5 countries	*111,572*	*83,645*	*24,443*

Source International Monetary Fund (2017). Direction of Trade Statistics, accessed 9 July 2017 at http://www.imf.org/en/Data

Some of China's trade with Europe and Africa will transit over land through Iran and Turkey, but much of the trade in goods and oil is seaborne. China also imports a large amount of oil from African countries in addition to the Middle East. Hence it has a direct interest in the stability of the world's most important strategic chokepoint by volume of oil transit, the Strait of Hormuz, as well as in the Arabian Sea, the Gulf of Aden, and the Suez Canal. This interest is reflected in China's engagement in the multilateral Gulf of Aden anti-piracy operation, its decision to build a naval facility in Djibouti, and its increased naval presence in the Indian Ocean Region, which includes submarine patrols.[48] According to the Defense Ministry in Beijing, the Djibouti support facility will mainly provide rest and recreation for Chinese troops taking part in U.N. peacekeeping and Humanitarian Assistance and Disaster Relief (HADR) missions in the region.[49] However, China's expanding international economic interests are also increasing demands for its armed forces to protect Chinese citizens, investments, and critical sea lines of communication (SLOC), a priority identified in its 2015 Defense White Paper.[50]

Finally, China's interest in the Middle East also stems from fears about the spread of Jihadist ideology among its Muslim population, and for the stability of its Muslim borderlands in the face of Turkestan separatism. China has in recent years seen large-scale unrest in Xinjiang and several violent incidents in other provinces, and some Chinese Uighurs and Muslim Huis have reportedly joined IS.[51] This explains Beijing's emphasis combating the so-called "three evils"—religious extremism, ethnic separatism and international terrorism—in the Central Asian region through cooperation between Shanghai Co-operation Organization

(SCO) member-states.[52] The Middle East in this context is an extension of China's periphery, with the Arab Policy Paper emphasizing anti-terrorism and police cooperation.

Syria

On 4 October 2011, China and Russia vetoed a UN Security Council resolution that would have condemned human rights violations in Syria and foreshadowed potential action against the government of President Bashar al-Assad. The European-drafted resolution had been watered down to try to avoid the vetoes, for example dropping a direct reference to sanctions against Damascus, but Moscow and Beijing argued that the draft contained no provision against outside military intervention in Syria. The U.S. envoy to the UN at the time, Susan Rice, stated that opposition to the resolution was a "cheap ruse by those who would rather sell arms to the Syrian regime than stand with the Syrian people."[53] However, Beijing and Moscow were motivated by much more than just commercial gain. In justifying their veto, they stressed the importance of defending the principles of non-intervention in domestic affairs, and respect for the sovereignty and territorial integrity of Syria.[54]

Since that time, Russia has vetoed seven more draft resolutions on Syria, with China joining it on five occasions.[55] Moscow backs Damascus both in order to promote Russia's influence in the region, and to prevent Western-backed regime change. By engaging militarily in Syria, it has effectively strong-armed itself back onto center stage after its ostracization by the West post-Crimea. From co-chairing the Geneva peace talks on Syria with the U.S., Russia in late 2016 took the lead with the Astana peace process, facilitating negotiations between the Assad government and Syrian opposition groups. In the Astana talks, Russia is the pivotal player, while the United States, the EU, Saudi Arabia, and the UN are largely marginalized.[56]

Moscow is conscious, too, that the fall of the Assad regime would significantly weaken Iran's regional position.[57] Indeed, Tehran encouraged Russia to enter the Syrian theatre to shore up Assad's position, as illustrated by the Iranian decision to allow Russian troops to use the air base in Hamedan.[58] However, as we shall see, Russia's alignment with the Iran–Syrian axis creates problems in Russia's relationship with Turkey and in particular Saudi Arabia.

Beijing shares many, but not all, of Moscow's motives for supporting the Assad regime. Syria has less geopolitical value for China than for Russia; it is scarcely relevant to China's self-perception as a great power. Despite appointing a special envoy on Syria, and consulting with both the Syrian government and opposition, China has kept a low profile lest its support for the Iran–Syrian axis jeopardize its relations with Saudi Arabia. Beijing's decision to join Moscow in vetoing the draft UN Security Council resolution on Syria in October 2011 may have been motivated by considerations of Sino-Russian solidarity, and by the potential prospect of future quid pro quo.[59] But more likely is that China shared Russia's view that it was vital to maintain the balance of power in the Middle East. A Western-backed regime in Syria would not only seriously weaken Iran's position, but also grant the United States excessive leverage. Beijing and Moscow also accuse NATO of misusing the March 2011 UN Security Council resolution on a Libyan no-fly zone in order to overthrow the Gaddafi regime.[60] At the time, they abstained rather than used their veto, due largely to the influence of the Arab League.[61] China's abstention raised speculation about whether it was abandoning its long-held stance on non-interference.[62] In reality, it has a flexible approach to non-intervention.[63] But within the framework of the United Nations Beijing and Moscow uphold traditional principles of state sovereignty, non-intervention, and non-interference in other countries' domestic affairs. They viewed the October 2011 veto on Syria as critical in preventing the legitimization of military intervention to remove a sovereign government in conflict with Western values.[64]

Iran

Iran was aligned with the West during the Cold War, and following the 1979 revolution Ayatollah Khomeini crushed the communist movement in the country. This appeared to kill off any possibility of cooperation between the Soviet Union and Iran. But with the United States supporting Saddam Hussein during the 1980–1988 Iran–Iraq War, Khomeini decided to approach Moscow. The two sides signed a military cooperation agreement, and the Kremlin supported Tehran's nuclear project.[65] Russia–Iran relations were further boosted after the U.S. invasion of Iraq in 2003,[66] and, more recently, the war in Syria and the gathering crisis between Moscow and the West.

Russia sees Iran as an important partner in achieving its goals in Eurasia and the Middle East. It finds Iran's anti-Americanism useful to balance U.S. influence in the region, and to promote its own vision of a multipolar world order. For Russia, "its policy towards Iran is not an end in itself, but rather one piece of a larger puzzle involving multiple actors."[67] Moscow has used Iran's nuclear program as a bargaining chip with Washington, but within limits. In 2006, Russia joined UN Security Council resolutions imposing economic sanctions against Iran, and it later played an important role in the P5+1 nuclear deal negotiations.[68]

For China, cooperation with Iran ticks many boxes—access to crude oil, a gateway for the BRI, a partner in managing great power relations. Sino-Iranian relations have boomed over the past decade, and in January 2016 Xi Jinping became the first foreign leader to visit Tehran after confirmation of the Joint Comprehensive Plan of Action (JCPOA) on Iran's nuclear program. Xi signed a strategic partnership with Iran that stated China's support for its application for full membership of the SCO, and a Memorandum of Understanding (MoU) on jointly pursuing the BRI. Iran was initially hesitant to embrace the Chinese Belt and Road Initiative out of fears that this should cause problems in Western powers' policy on lifting economic sanctions on Iran.[69] China has emerged as Iran's biggest trading partner, aided by Western sanctions. Further Chinese investments into railways, highways, and container ports, and access to Iranian ports for the servicing of PLA Navy (PLAN) warships, could turn Iran into an important logistical hub within the BRI. Beijing and Tehran have also expanded into previously taboo areas, such as military cooperation. Two PLAN destroyers visited the Iranian port of Bandar Abbas in 2014, the first-ever visit by Chinese warships to an Iranian port.[70]

Like Moscow, Beijing views Iran as a useful partner in challenging the dominant power of the United States, and has used arms sales and nuclear assistance to boost ties, and even as bargaining chip. China was instrumental in developing Iran's nuclear program, although it ended its support in 1997 in order to improve relations with the United States, a vastly more important economic partner. Over time, Beijing has become adept at complying with U.S. demands, while figuring out ways to help Tehran (and itself).[71] Scobell and Nader argued in a recent Rand report that Chinese policies toward Iran continues to be a cautious balance between supporting Iran without damaging its relationship with the United States.[72] However, with its growing economic and military muscle, it is more willing to pursue its own foreign policy interests regardless of U.S. sensitivities. It is aware of Saudi concerns about Sino-Iranian relations, but for the time being has been able to manage this tension.

Iran hoped that the JCFOA would open the way to greater European and even American investment, and enable it to achieve a more balanced foreign policy. However, if President Trump follows through on his threats to withdraw from the agreement, it will have no choice but to lean towards Russia and China. In the long term, China is better positioned to develop a strong relationship with Iran. Tehran values Moscow's security assistance, but Beijing has much more to offer in terms of economic cooperation. Furthermore, Iran has a legacy of historical mistrust towards Russia that does not exist in Sino-Iranian relations.

Turkey

Russia and Turkey have been traditional rivals since the eighteenth century.[73] Lenin supported the Ataturk revolution, but relations between the Soviet Union and Turkey grew more distant during the Cold War as Turkey joined NATO and became the alliance's southern bulwark against communist expansion.[74] After the end of the Cold War, Ankara's pan-Turkish policies in the post-Soviet space led to further tensions in the relationship, with significant policy disagreements over the "frozen conflict" between Armenia and Azerbaijan, the Chechen wars, and Georgia.

Today, Moscow and Ankara view the conflict in Syria very differently, with Turkey seeking the removal of the Assad regime, and opposing Russian support to the Syrian Kurdish Democratic Union Party (PYD). Moscow, like Washington, sees the PYD as key to fighting IS. Yet despite these disagreements, the historical baggage between them, and Turkey's membership of NATO, Russia and Turkey have moved closer to each other since the early 2000s, as disappointment in their respective relations with the United States and the EU has paved the way for practical cooperation.[75] Lack of U.S. and European support during the coup in July 2016 and continued U.S. military support for the Kurds in Syria and Iraq, have encouraged Ankara to gravitate towards Moscow in an "Axis of the Excluded."[76] Even the 2015 Turkish downing of a Russian jet on the Syrian–Turkish border, and the assassination of Russia's ambassador to Turkey in Ankara in December 2016, did not stop Putin from inviting

Turkey to be a core member of the Moscow-led Astana peace process on Syria. By engaging Ankara, Moscow hopes to strengthen Russia's position not just in Syria but also the "Greater Middle East," including the Caucasus and Eurasia. And with good cause. At the first Astana meeting in January 2017, Turkey replaced its earlier demand for Assad to stand down with a more pragmatic policy.[77]

The announcement in September 2017 that Turkey is purchasing a Russian surface-to-air missile system is a clear sign that Erdogan is losing faith in the United States and NATO.[78] Acquisition of a Russian missile system undermines NATO interoperability—the very reason why Washington had previously stopped Ankara from buying missiles from China.[79] Nevertheless, although Turkey wishes to stay on good terms with its largest neighbor, it would be surprising if it decides to leave NATO and bandwagon with Russia.

China initially shared Russian concerns about Ankara's pan-Turkish policies in Central Asia. Turkish criticism of Beijing's treatment of its Uyghur minority peaked during the 2009 riots in Xinjiang province when Erdogan likened the Chinese government's actions to "genocide."[80] In 2015, anti-Chinese sentiment in Turkey was once again in evidence following reports that Uighurs in China had been banned from fasting during Ramadan.[81] However, Beijing (like Moscow) finds it more useful to influence Turkish policy through bilateral cooperation. A strategic partnership agreement was concluded in 2010, and during the 2016 G20 Summit in China, Beijing and Ankara signed an MOU on bilateral cooperation under the BRI.[82] In 2012, Turkey became a "dialogue partner" of the SCO, and has since expressed interest in full membership. At the opening ceremony of the Belt and Road Forum in May 2017, Putin and Erdogan sat on either side of Xi Jinping, highlighting the importance China attaches to Turkey's contribution to the BRI as a gateway linking China and Europe. The idea of Turkey as a gateway, however, is contingent on cordial relations between Ankara and Europe, a goal which is essentially incompatible with Russia's desire to undermine Turkey's relationship with NATO.

Saudi Arabia

Russia and China both established diplomatic relations with Saudi Arabia in 1990. During the Soviet occupation of Afghanistan, Saudi Arabia was along with the United States the largest supporter of the Afghan mujahideen.

The end of the Cold War and Saddam Hussein's invasion of Kuwait convinced Riyadh to engage with Moscow. But despite the normalization of relations, Russian policy in Chechnya, and the revival of the Russian Orthodox Church and Russian nationalism, have led the Saudis to view Russia as an anti-Muslim country.[83] Moscow, for its part, has regarded Saudi support for the re-Islamization of Central Asia with considerable suspicion.[84] The U.S. invasion of Iraq in 2003 opened the way for closer collaboration between the two countries, and Putin took the opportunity to pursue a more balanced policy towards Saudi Arabia.[85] However, with Russia backing Iran and the Assad regime in Syria, the outlook for relations remains uncertain. Although Riyadh is increasingly concerned about the future of American engagement in the region, with U.S. crude oil imports shrinking and Washington's global leadership in decline, it is more likely to see China rather than Russia as an alternative partner to the United States.

Since the end of the Cold War, Beijing has managed to build a close relationship with Riyadh. Although the Chinese cannot provide security in the form of boots on the ground, it was actually Beijing's willingness to provide Saudi Arabia with intermediate range ballistic missiles (IRBMs) in the 1980s, when the U.S. refused to do so because of Israeli opposition that opened the door for Chinese–Saudi diplomatic relations in 1990.[86] Today, China continues to supply Saudi Arabia with weapons it cannot buy from the United States, including drones that can carry cameras and missiles. The two sides have agreed to manufacture Chinese drones in Saudi Arabia,[87] and there are reports of China providing Saudi Arabia with missile systems.[88] Meanwhile, crude oil and related products remain the cornerstone of the economic relationship. Saudi Arabia was China's top source of imported crude oil from 2002 until Russia overtook it for the first time in 2016, and their bilateral energy cooperation also includes refineries, petrochemicals, and natural gas. China is expected to be one of the principal investors in the planned initial public offering (IPO) of Saudi Arabia's state-owned oil company Saudi Aramco.[89]

Egypt

With more than 90 million inhabitants, Egypt is the most populous country in the Middle East, but its role and influence in the region has been declining as it slides into stagnation and faces the threat of domestic implosion.[90] Although Donald Trump received Egyptian President

Sisi in Washington in April 2017, some American commentators view the once close relationship as "a relic of a bygone era,"[91] and even argue that "there are no longer any compelling reasons for Washington to sustain especially close ties with Cairo"[92] Post-Mubarak, Egypt has tried to balance its great power relationships, and both Sisi and his predecessor Mohamed Morsi visited Moscow and Beijing early in their presidencies. Russia and China are eager to deepen their relations with Egypt. Putin has from the outset supported Sisi's presidency, and looked for opportunities to expand economic and military ties. Russian arms sales to Egypt are growing, and in 2015 the two countries conducted their first joint naval exercise in the Mediterranean. Moscow seeks Cairo's support for its Libya policy and the Astana peace process, and Egypt has reportedly allowed Russia to use its military bases to deploy forces into Libya.[93] In May 2017, Russian Defense Minister Sergei Shoigu and Foreign Minister Sergey Lavrov travelled to Cairo for a 2+2 meeting with their Egyptian counterparts.

Unlike Russia who "lost" Egypt to the United States during the Cold War, Egypt has always been a pillar of Chinese engagement in the Middle East. Egypt was the only Middle Eastern country visited by Jiang Zemin, Hu Jintao and Xi Jinping on each leader's first trip to the region. Thanks to the strategic importance of the Suez Canal, Egypt, like Turkey and Iran, is seen as a gateway to Europe.[94] It also plays an important role in China's Africa policy, and is involved in the Forum on China–Africa Cooperation. During Sisi's visit to China in December 2014 the two sides agreed to establish a "comprehensive strategic partnership." Although Russia is also increasing its economic cooperation with Egypt, and has invested in the Suez Canal Economic Zone, its investments are dwarfed by Chinese aid programs, grants, and loans. As early as 2012, China surpassed the United States as Egypt's largest trading partner.[95] And while it is still a small player in the Egyptian arms market, there is movement also in this area.[96]

Assessing Great Power Contest

The geopolitical configuration of the Middle East is changing. As during the Cold War, it is once again shaped by great power rivalry, with China and Russia becoming more prominent and U.S. influence declining.

Washington continues to support Israel, and combating terrorism and Islamist extremism has moved up the policy agenda. Despite reduced oil imports from the region, the United States still identifies a vested interest in safeguarding international sea-lanes. It retains a strong military presence, and it is still the major arms provider to most countries in the Middle East. Nevertheless, there is a growing sense that Washington is less committed to the region. As a result, a number of Middle Eastern countries are seeking to develop closer relations with China and Russia in order to reduce their dependence on the United States. This is true even of long-standing U.S. allies such as Egypt, Saudi Arabia, and Turkey. Meanwhile, a U.S. pull-out from the JCFOA would push Tehran further towards Beijing and Moscow.

Moscow and Beijing share many views on the Middle East. They have coordinated their policies on Syria, and believe that a diminished U.S. influence in the region is to their advantage. The Kremlin is especially keen to exercise leverage against Washington, and assert Russia's great power credentials.

Moscow and Beijing both seek to contain Islamist extremism, and the SCO is pivotal in this connection. With India and Pakistan joining the organization in 2017, and with Iranian membership gaining momentum and Turkey's a real possibility, China and Russia have an instrument with which to coordinate anti-terrorism efforts in Central Asia, and possibly even in parts of the Middle East.

At the same time, some fundamental strategic interests in the region divide China and Russia. Although Russia coordinates oil output with Saudi Arabia and other OPEC members to prop up international oil prices, Beijing has been better able than Moscow to balance relations with Tehran and Riyadh. China's ability to maintain close links with both is unique and could position it as a possible power broker in the future. The Middle East supplies half of China's crude oil imports, and is a gateway for its economic interests, notably through the BRI. China's increasing dependence on stability in the Middle East versus Russia's tactical maneuvering is pushing the policies of Beijing and Moscow in different directions.

Moscow and Beijing adhere to traditional interpretations of state sovereignty and non-interference, not least in relation to the Middle East. But as China expands its economic and military engagement in the region, it will find it difficult to maintain this stance. Through its good relations with Israeli and Palestinian leaders, as well as with Iran and Saudi Arabia, it may be tempted to "venture into the maelstrom."[97] China portrays itself as a different great power in the Middle East from the United States, Russia and the leading Europeans. That said, Xi has abandoned "keeping a low profile" as the guiding principle of Chinese foreign policy, and foreshadowed a much more ambitious and assertive approach to international relations.

Indeed, China's current attitude towards the Middle East bears some resemblance to the earlier position of the United States. After WWII, when it replaced Great Britain as the dominant power in the region, the United States was looked upon as a neutral contributor to development—or at least until its involvement in the overthrow of Mossadegh in Iran.[98] Revealingly, before 1980 almost no American soldiers were killed in action while serving in the Greater Middle East.[99] But since 1990, almost no American soldiers have been killed in action anywhere else. With the end of the Cold War, the role and position of the United States in the Middle East changed, and the same thing could happen with China. True, it has no experience or tradition of military intervention, and for now does not have the power projection capability to deploy large forces the Middle East. However, recent Defense White Papers and China's 2015 counter-terrorism law leave open the possibility that the PLA could undertake overseas operations. The pressure for China to play a more active role would increase if the United States or Russia were not able or willing to be a security provider in the region.

Conclusion

The hegemonic position of the United States in the Middle East is giving way to a new great power triangle consisting of the United States, Russia, and China. The relationship between these three great powers will be characterized more by competition than cooperation. Russia and China have more in common with each other than with the United States, but Beijing is more concerned with stability and economic cooperation in the region than is Moscow. Russia's relations with countries in the Middle East are mostly one-dimensional, revolving around security and arms trade. China's relationships are more multi-dimensional, encompassing major investments, infrastructural development, crude oil imports, a steadily expanding arms trade, and growing security footprint. With the American commitment to the region in doubt, Middle Eastern states are likely to increase their cooperation with China (and Europe) to balance Russia. And this, along with China's growing influence across Eurasia, could lead to tensions in the Sino-Russian partnership as Beijing finds it increasingly difficult to assuage Moscow's strategic concerns.

Notes

1. Salem (2008), p. 3.
2. Miller (2004), p. 260.
3. The Middle East is here defined as including the following countries and areas; Jordan, Syria, Lebanon, Israel, Iraq, Iran, Turkey, Egypt and the Arabian Peninsula.
4. Miller (2004), pp. 240–241.
5. See for instance Zakaria (2017), Rachman (2011), and Layne (2009a, b).
6. Tunsjø (2018).
7. Ross (2004).
8. Miller (2004), p. 248.
9. Brzezinski (2012), p. 100.
10. Russell Mead (2016).
11. Miller (2004), p. 239.
12. Paul (2004), p. 21.
13. See also Cooley (2012).
14. LeDonne (1997).
15. Mansfield (2013), pp. 283–286.
16. Blank (2014), p. 9.
17. Nizameddin (2013), Trenin (2016).
18. Russell Mead (2016).
19. Baev (2015), p. 9.
20. Trenin (2016).
21. Trenin (2016).
22. Blank (2014).
23. Hille et al. (2017).
24. Hannah (2016).
25. Fleurant et al. (2017).
26. Blank (2014), Russel Mead (2016).
27. Nizameddin (2013), p. 292, Trenin (2016), Flanagan (2013), p. 166.
28. Lo (2015), p. 37.
29. Baev (2015), p. 11, Stepanova (2016).
30. Nizameddin (2013), pp. 297–299.
31. Trenin (2016), Blank (2015).
32. Nizameddin (2013), p. 5.
33. Nizameddin (2013), p. 158.
34. Garver (2016a), pp. 106, 122–124.
35. China State Council (2016).
36. Qian (2005), p. 57.
37. Garver (2016a).
38. Alterman and Garver (2008), pp. 2–3, 10.

39. Xi (2016).
40. Bacevich (2017), p. 3.
41. Tunsjø (2013), pp. 85–86.
42. US Energy Information Administration (2017).
43. OPEC (2017), pp. 56–57, 62.
44. China Ministry of Foreign Affairs (2016).
45. Bekkevold and Engh (2017).
46. China National Bureau of Statistics (2017).
47. AIIB (2017).
48. Department of Defence (2016), pp. 21–22.
49. Jacobs and Perlez (2017).
50. China State Council Information Office (2015).
51. Scobell and Nader (2016), pp. 13–14.
52. Bekkevold and Engh (2017).
53. Trevelyan (2011).
54. United Nations (2011).
55. Besides the joint vetoes on, China and Russia have aligned on two additional UN Security Council vetoes, in 2007 on a proposal that called for a democratic transition amid the Myanmar military junta, and a 2008 proposal that threatened sanctions against the government of Zimbabwe (United Nations 2017).
56. Wintour (2017), Al Jazeera (2017).
57. Geranmayeh and Liik (2016), p. 3.
58. Geranmayeh and Liik (2016), p. 4.
59. Yun (2012).
60. Trevelyan (2011), Yun (2012). The strong Chinese reaction to the NATO bombing in Libya was confirmed to the author in interviews in Beijing in June 2011.
61. Borger (2011).
62. Yun (2012).
63. Ren (2014).
64. Yun (2012).
65. Legvold (2007), p. 5.
66. Nizameddin (2013), p. 259, Legvold (2007), p. 9.
67. Geranmayeh and Liik (2016), p. 6.
68. Geranmayeh and Liik (2016), p. 2, Nizameddin (2013), p. 265, Flanagan (2013), p 172.
69. Iran was initially hesitant to embrace the BRI for fear this could inhibit the lifting of Western economic sanctions against Iran. See Garver (2016b).
70. Scobell and Nader (2016), Garver (2016b).
71. Scobell and Nader (2016), p. 56, Garver (2006, 2016b), Hiim (2015).

72. Scobell and Nader (2016).
73. Legvold (2007), LeDonne (1997).
74. Flanagan (2013), p. 164.
75. Flanagan (2013), p. 164.
76. Hill and Taspinar (2006).
77. Wintour (2017).
78. Gall and Higgins (2017).
79. Ibid.
80. Hindy (2017).
81. Girit (2015).
82. Zhou Rong (2017).
83. Nizameddin (2013), p. 238.
84. Trenin (2016).
85. Nizameddin (2013), pp. 240–241.
86. Crucially, too, Riyadh severed diplomatic ties with Taiwan. Scobell and Nader (2016), p. 25.
87. Hindy (2017).
88. Scobell and Nader (2016), p. 44.
89. "Aramco" is derived from the original "Arabian-American Oil Company" founded in 1933 as a joint venture with American interests. Saudi Arabia took full control of the company in 1980. U.S. interests in Saudi Arabia goes beyond oil, but if China becomes the principal investor in the planned IPO of Aramco it will still be seen as an indicator of shifting interests in the region.
90. Benaim et al. (2017), p. 3.
91. Tamkin (2017).
92. Hanna (2015).
93. Luhn (2017).
94. Tiezzi (2016).
95. Chaziza (2016).
96. Nader (2015), Theohary (2016).
97. Dorsey (2016).
98. The Central Intelligence Agency played a central role in the 1953 coup that brought down Iranian Prime Minister Muhammad Mossadegh, fueling a surge of nationalism which culminated in the 1979 Iranian Revolution and shaping U.S.–Iran relations for decades. See Allen-Ebrahimian (2017) and Kinzer (2003).
99. Bacevich (2017).

Literature

AIIB. 2017. Asian Infrastructure Investment Bank Homepage. https://www.aiib.org/en/about-aiib/governance/board-directors//. Accessed 9 July 2017.

Al Jazeera. 2017. Astana Hosts Eighth Round of Talks on Syria's War. *Al Jazeera News*, December 20. https://www.aljazeera.com/news/2017/12/astana-hosts-eighth-talks-syria-war-171220093245167.html. Accessed 27 Feb 2018.

Allen-Ebrahimian, Bethany. 2017. 64 Years Later, CIA Finally Releases Details of Iranian Coup. *Foreign Policy*, June 20. http://foreignpolicy.com/2017/06/20/64-years-later-cia-finally-releases-details-of-iranian-coup-iran-tehran-oil/. Accessed 27 Feb 2018.

Alterman, Jon B., and John W. Garver. 2008. *The Vital Triangle: China, the United States, and the Middle East*. Washington, DC: CSIS Paperback, Center for Strategic & International Studies.

Bacevich, Andrew J. 2017. *America's War for the Greater Middle East: A Military History*. New York: Random House.

Baev, Pavel K. 2015. Russia as Opportunist or Spoiler in the Middle East? *The International Spectator* 50 (2): 8–21.

Bekkevold, Jo Inge, and Sunniva Engh. 2017. Silk Road Diplomacy: China's Strategic Interests in South Asia. In *South Asia and the Great Powers: International Relations and Regional Security*, ed. Sten Rynning. London: I.B. Tauris.

Benaim, Daniel, Mokhtar Awad, and Brian Katulis. 2017. Setting the Terms for U.S.–Egypt Relations. Center for American Progress, February 21. https://www.americanprogress.org/issues/security/reports/2017/02/21/426654/setting-the-terms-for-u-s-egypt-relations/. Accessed 19 Aug 2017.

Blank, Stephen J. 2014. Russian Strategy and Policy in the Middle East. *Israel Journal of Foreign Affairs* VIII (2): 9–23.

Blank, Stephen J. 2015. Russia's New Presence in the Middle East. *American Foreign Policy Interests* 37: 69–79.

Borger, Julian. 2011. Libya No-Fly Resolution Reveals Global Split in UN. *The Guardian*, March 18. https://www.theguardian.com/world/2011/mar/18/libya-no-fly-resolution-split. Accessed 1 May 2017.

Brzezinski, Zbigniew. 2012. *Strategic Vision: America and the Crisis of Global Power*. New York: Basic Books.

Chaziza, Mordechai. 2016. Comprehensive Strategic Partnership: A New Stage in China–Egypt Relations. *Middle East Review of International Affairs* 20 (3): 41–50.

China Ministry of Foreign Affairs. 2016. The 7th Ministerial Meeting of the China–Arab States Cooperation Forum Concludes in Doha, May 12. http://www.fmprc.gov.cn/mfa_eng/zxxx_662805/t1363599.shtml. Accessed 5 July 2017.

China National Bureau of Statistics. 2017. *China Statistical Yearbook 2016*, Beijing. http://www.stats.gov.cn/tjsj/ndsj/2016/indexeh.htm. Accessed 9 July 2017.

China State Council. 2016. China's Arab Policy Paper. Xinhua, January 13. http://news.xinhuanet.com/english/china/2016-01/13/c_135006619.htm. Accessed 18 Apr 2017.

China State Council Information Office. 2015. China's Military Strategy. Xinhua, May 26. http://www.chinadaily.com.cn/china/2015-05/26/content_20820628.htm. Accessed 08 July 2017.

Cooley, Alexander. 2012. *Great Games, Local Rules: The New Great Power Contest in Central Asia*. New York: Oxford University Press.

Department of Defence. 2016. *Military and Security Developments Involving the People's Republic of China 2016*. Annual Report to Congress, Office of the Secretary of Defense, April 26.

Dorsey, James M. 2016. China and the Middle East: Venturing into the Maelstrom. RSIS Working Paper, No. 296, March, S. Rajaratnam School of International Studies, Singapore.

Flanagan, Stephen J. 2013. The Turkey–Russia–Iran Nexus: Eurasian Power Dynamics. *The Washington Quarterly* 36 (Winter): 163–178.

Fleurant, Aude, et.al. 2017. Trends in International Arms Transfers, 2016. *SIPRI Fact Sheet*, February.

Gall, Carlotta, and Andrew Higgins. 2017. Turkey Signs Russian Missile Deal, Pivoting from NATO. *New York Times*, September 12. https://www.nytimes.com/2017/09/12/world/europe/turkey-russia-missile-deal.html. Accessed 5 Oct 2017.

Garver, John W. 2006. *China and Iran: Ancient Partners in a Post-imperial World*. Seattle: University of Washington Press.

Garver, John W. 2016a. *China's Quest: The History of the Foreign Relations of the People's Republic of China*. New York: Oxford University Press.

Garver, John W. 2016b. India and the Emerging Sino-Iranian Partnership. Paper presented at the conference 'India and the Great Powers: Continuity and Change', Institute for Defence Studies and Analyses, New Delhi, 21 November.

Geranmayeh, Ellie, and Kadri Liik. 2016. The New Power Couple: Russia and Iran in the Middle East. *European Council on Foreign Relations Policy Brief*, September.

Girit, Selin. 2015. China–Turkey Relationship Strained Over Uighurs. *BBC News*, Istanbul, July 9, 2015. http://www.bbc.com/news/world-asia-china-33440998. Accessed 25 June 2017.

Hanna, Michael Wahid. 2015. Getting Over Egypt: Time to Rethink Relations. *Foreign Affairs*, November/December. https://www.foreignaffairs.com/articles/egypt/getting-over-egypt. Accessed 18 Aug 2017.

Hannah, John. 2016. Russia's Middle East Offensive. *Foreign Policy*, September 13. http://foreignpolicy.com/2016/09/13/russias-middle-east-offensive/. Accessed 20 June 2017.

Hiim, Henrik S. 2015. *Selective Assistance: China and Nuclear Weapons Proliferation*. Unpublished PhD thesis submitted to the Faculty of Social Sciences, University of Oslo, October.

Hill, Fiona, and Omer Taspinar. 2006. Turkey and Russia: Axis of the Excluded? *Survival* 48 (1): 81–92.

Hille, Kathrin, Erika Solomon, Heba Saleh, and John Reed. 2017. Russia's Middle East Ambitions Grow with Syria Battlefield Success. *Financial Times*, January 19. https://www.ft.com/content/c131d7c2-dda7-11e6-9d7c-be108f1c1dce. Accessed 20 June 2017.

Hindy, Lily. 2017. A Rising China Eyes the Middle East. *The Century Foundation*, April 6. https://tcf.org/content/report/rising-china-eyes-middle-east/. Accessed 27 June 2017.

International Monetary Fund. 2017. Direction of Trade Statistics. http://www.imf.org/en/Data. Accessed 9 July 2017.

Jacobs, Andrew, and Jane Perlez. 2017. U.S. Wary of Its New Neighbor in Djibouti: A Chinese Naval Base. *New York Times*, February 25. https://www.nytimes.com/2017/02/25/world/africa/us-djibouti-chinese-naval-base.html. Accessed 5 July 2017.

Kinzer, Stephen. 2003. *All the Shah's Men: An American Coup and the Roots of Middle East Terror*. Hoboken, NJ: Wiley.

Layne, Christopher. 2009a. The Waning of U.S. Hegemony—Myth or Reality? A Review Essay. *International Security* 34 (1): 147–172.

Layne, Christopher. 2009b. America's Middle East Grand Strategy After Iraq: The Moment for Offshore Balancing Has Arrived. *Review of International Studies* 35: 5–25.

LeDonne, John P. 1997. *The Russian Empire and the World, 1700–1917: The Geopolitics of Expansion and Containment*. New York and Oxford: Oxford University Press.

Legvold, Robert (ed.). 2007. *Russian Foreign Policy in the 21st Century and the Shadow of the Past*. New York: Columbia University Press.

Lo, Bobo. 2015. *Russia and the New World Disorder*. London: Chatham House; Washington, DC: Brookings Institution Press.

Luhn, Alec. 2017. Russian Special Forces Sent to Back Renegade Libyan General—Reports. *The Guardian*, March 14. https://www.theguardian.com/world/2017/mar/14/russian-special-forces-deployed-in-egypt-near-libyan-border-report. Accessed 19 Aug 2017.

Mansfield, Peter. 2013. *A History of the Middle East*, 4th ed., revised and updated by Nicolas Pelham. New York: Penguin Books.

Miller, Benjamin. 2004. The International System and Regional Balance in the Middle East. In *Balance of Power: Theory and Practice in the 21st Century*, ed. T.V. Paul, James J. Wirtz, and Michel Fortmann. Stanford, CA: Stanford University Press.

Nader, Aya. 2015. Egypt, China Sign New Weapons Deal. *Daily News Egypt*, May 2. https://dailynewsegypt.com/2015/05/02/egypt-china-sign-new-weapons-deal/. Accessed 22 Aug 2017.

Nizameddin, Talal. 2013. *Putin's New Order in the Middle East*. London: Hurst & Company.

OPEC. 2017. *OPEC Annual Statistical Bulletin 2017*, 52nd ed. Vienna: Organization of the Petroleum Exporting Countries.

Paul, T.V. 2004. Introduction: The Enduring Axioms of Balance of Power Theory and Their Contemporary Relevance. In *Balance of Power. Theory and Practice in the 21st Century*, ed. T.V. Paul, James J. Wirtz, and Michel Fortmann. Stanford, CA: Stanford University Press.

Qian, Qichen. 2005. *Ten Episodes in China's Diplomacy*. New York: HarperCollins.

Rachman, Gideon. 2011. American Decline: This Time It's for Real. *Foreign Policy* 184 (January/February): 59–65.

Ren, Mu. 2014. China's Non-intervention Policy in UNSC Sanctions in the 21st Century: The Cases of Libya, North Korea, and Zimbabwe. *Ritsumeikan International Affairs* 12: 101–134.

Ross, Robert S. 2004. Bipolarity and Balancing in East Asia. In *Balance of Power: Theory and Practice in the 21st Century*, ed. T.V. Paul, James J. Wirtz, and Michel Fortmann. Stanford, CA: Stanford University Press.

Russell Mead, Walter. 2016. Russia Re-emerges as a Great Power in the Middle East. *The American Interest*. https://www.the-american-interest.com/2016/09/12/russia-re-emerges-as-a-great-power-in-the-middle-east/. Accessed 20 June 2017.

Salem, Paul. 2008. The Middle East: Evolution of a Broken Regional Order. Carnegie Papers, Carnegie Middle East Center, Number 9, June, Carnegie Endowment for International Peace, Washington, DC.

Scobell, Andrew, and Alireza Nader. 2016. *China in the Middle East: The Wary Dragon*. Santa Monica, CA: RAND Corporation.

Stepanova, Ekaterina. 2016. Russia in the Middle East: Back to a "Grand Strategy"—Or Enforcing Multilateralism. *politique étrangerè* 2: 1–14.

Tamkin, Emily. 2017. Time to Rethink the U.S.–Egypt Relationship, Experts Tell Senate. *Foreign Policy*, April 25. http://foreignpolicy.com/2017/04/25/time-to-rethink-the-u-s-egypt-relationship-experts-tell-senate/. Accessed 19 Aug 2017.

Theohary, Catherine A. 2016. *Conventional Arms Transfers to Developing Nations, 2008–2015*. Washington, DC: Congressional Research Service (December 19).

Tiezzi, Shannon. 2016. The Belt and Road and Suez Canal: China–Egypt Relations Under Xi Jinping. *China Policy Institute: Analysis*, February 16. https://cpianalysis.org/2016/02/16/87681/. Accessed 25 June 2017.

Trenin, Dmitri. 2016. Russia in the Middle East: Moscow's Objectives, Priorities, and Policy Drivers. Carnegie Task Force White Paper. Carnegie Endowment for International Peace, April 5. http://carnegieendowment.org/files/03-25-16_Trenin_Middle_East_Moscow_clean.pdf. Accessed 20 June 2017.

Trevelyan, Laura. 2011. China and Russia Have Vetoed a UN Security Council Resolution Condemning Syria Over Its Crackdown on Anti-government Protesters. *BBC News*, New York, October 5. http://www.bbc.com/news/world-middle-east-15177114. Accessed 1 May 2017.

Tunsjø, Øystein. 2013. *Security and Profit in China's Energy Security Policy: Hedging Against Risk*. New York: Columbia University Press.

Tunsjø, Øystein. 2018. *The Return of Bipolarity in World Politics: China, the United States and Geostructural Realism*. New York: Columbia University Press.

United Nations. 2011. Security Council Fails to Adopt Draft Resolution Condemning Syria's Crackdown on Anti-government Protestors, Owing to Veto by Russian Federation, China. SC/10403, October 4. https://www.un.org/press/en/2011/sc10403.doc.htm. Accessed 12 July 2017.

United Nations. 2017. *Security Council—Veto List*. Dag Hammarskjold Library. http://research.un.org/en/docs/sc/quick. Accessed 7 Aug 2017.

US Energy Information Administration. 2017. More Chinese Crude Oil Imports Coming from Non-OPEC Countries. *Today in Energy*, April 14. https://www.eia.gov/todayinenergy/detail.php?id=30792. Accessed 7 July 2017.

Wintour, Patrick. 2017. Russia in Power-Broking Role as Syria Peace Talks Begin in Astana. *The Guardian*, January 23. https://www.theguardian.com/world/2017/jan/22/russia-syria-talks-astana-kazakhstan-. Accessed 15 Aug 2017.

Xi, Jinping. 2016. Work Together for a Bright Future of China–Arab Relations. Speech at the Arab League Headquarters, Cairo, January 21. http://www.chinadaily.com.cn/world/2016xivisitmiddleeast/2016-01/22/content_23191229.htm. Accessed 5 July 2017.

Yun, Sun. 2012. Syria: What China Has Learned from Its Libya Experience. *Asia-Pacific Bulletin*, Number 152, East–West Centre, February 27.

Zakaria, Fareed. 2017. "Say Hello to a Post-America World. *Washington Post*, July 27. https://www.washingtonpost.com/opinions/say-hello-to-a-post-america-world/2017/07/27/aad19d68-7308-11e7-8f39-eeb7d3a2d304_story.html?utm_term=.33426f643548. Accessed 3 Oct 2017.

Zhou, Rong. 2017. B&R Can Help Strengthen China–Turkey Ties. *Global Times*, May 24. http://www.globaltimes.cn/content/1048523.shtml. Accessed 25 June 2017.

CHAPTER 8

The Arctic Dimension in Sino-Russian Relations

Christopher Weidacher Hsiung and Tom Røseth

Sino-Russian interaction in the Arctic region[1] constitutes a new dimension in their relationship. Russia possesses the largest Arctic territory and has significant civilian and military assets in the region. For Moscow, the Arctic has great strategic value and is increasingly important for Russia's economic development. Although Beijing does not place the Arctic at the top of its agenda, in recent years it has become much more engaged in the region. Not being an Arctic littoral state, China has defined itself as a "near-Arctic state" and is keen to consolidate its position as an Arctic stakeholder. Russian natural resources and Chinese capital to develop those resources would seem a perfect match, but Moscow was initially reluctant to accommodate and accept an expanded Chinese Arctic presence and influence. Russian foot-dragging was most clearly expressed in its late acceptance of China as a permanent observer state to the Arctic Council. Some parts of the Russian military and political

C. W. Hsiung (✉)
Norwegian Institute for Defence Studies, Oslo, Norway
e-mail: ChristopherDaniel.WeidacherHsiung@ifs.mil.no

T. Røseth
Norwegian Defence University College, Oslo, Norway
e-mail: troseth@fhs.mil.no

J. I. Bekkevold and B. Lo (eds.), *Sino-Russian Relations in the 21st Century*, https://doi.org/10.1007/978-3-319-92516-5_8

establishment even saw China's involvement in developing Arctic resources as a potential threat.[2] But in 2013 China, together with India, Japan, Singapore, and South Korea, was finally admitted into the Arctic Council as a permanent observer.

In this chapter we explore the challenges and opportunities for Sino-Russian cooperation in the Arctic. Our main argument is that, despite initial reluctance, Moscow has come to accept China as an Arctic player. It recognizes that Russia needs foreign assistance to realize its Arctic potential, be it from Western countries or Asian states such as China. We identify Russia and China's Arctic interests, and investigate four crucial issue areas of Sino-Russian dynamics in the region: Russia's acceptance of China into the Arctic Council; the potential for cooperation over the Northern Sea Route (NSR); energy cooperation; and security relations.

Russian and Chinese Interests in the Arctic

Russia is one of five Arctic littoral states, together with Canada, Denmark, Norway, and the United States. These five littoral states (aka the 'Arctic Five') and the three Nordic countries, Finland, Iceland and Sweden, are regarded as the traditional Arctic players. They also constitute the members of the Arctic Council. The melting of the massive ice cap covering the Arctic Ocean enhances opportunities for commercial activities, allowing easier access to energy, minerals and migrating fishing stocks, as well as the development of a possible new shipping route between the Pacific and the Atlantic Oceans, most notably the NSR. Another important project is the Northeast Passage fiber-optic cable route under the Arctic Sea, intended to link Japan to the United Kingdom via China, Russia, Finland and Norway. These new opportunities have renewed international interest in the region among both traditional Arctic players and non-Arctic countries in Europe and Asia.

Nevertheless, increased activity also brings challenges in terms of environmental concerns, search and rescue, as well as more traditional security issues. One vital question is how such activity and the entry of new actors will shape cooperation and conflict. The Arctic has mainly been characterized by cooperation, where shared interests and a number of institutions and international regimes like the UN Convention on the Law of the Sea (UNCLOS) tie the actors together and facilitate collaboration.[3] In Greenland in May 2008 the five Arctic littoral states, including Russia, adopted the "Ilulissat Declaration" committing themselves to peaceful cooperation.[4] Much attention is focused on the potential for extracting petroleum; a much cited 2008 study conducted by the United States Geological Survey (USGS) found that the Arctic contains up to 30% of the world's undiscovered gas and 13% of its undiscovered oil.[5] However, most Arctic oil reserves are to be found within the territorial waters of the Arctic littoral states, and as much as 80% is thought to be located within Russian territory. At the same time, the Arctic cannot be viewed in isolation, and conflicts in other parts of the world could have repercussions in the region.[6] The Ukraine crisis and the ensuing confrontation between Russia and the West have already had a negative impact on Arctic cooperation and business opportunities, and, conversely, increased collaboration between Moscow and Beijing.

Russian Interests

Russia stated in its Arctic strategy of 2008 that developing the Arctic is a national priority, focusing on resource development, ensuring security and stability, developing the NSR, and achieving sustainable development. The strategy was updated in 2013.[7] The 2009 Russian energy strategy identified the Arctic as a future resource base.[8] And Russia's maritime doctrines of 2001 and 2015 task the Navy to protect and promote its interests in the Arctic.[9]

Increased usage of the NSR is expected to boost the Arctic's strategic importance. The ice-free harbours of the Kola peninsula provide access to the Atlantic Ocean and are the base of the Northern Fleet, a vital component of Russia's nuclear deterrence strategy. In April 2015, Russia reorganized its coast guard under a new Coast Guard Command for the Western Arctic in Murmansk and another in Petropavlovsk-Kamchatsky for the Eastern Arctic.[10] Central in the strategy is to ensure territorial claims according to its right as a coastal state. In August 2015, Russia submitted to the UN Commission on the Limits of the Continental Shelf a claim of 1.2 million square kilometres on the continental shelf beyond 200 nautical miles in the Arctic Ocean. The submission and approval process will be concluded by 2019 at the earliest.[11] Russia's revised claim was far better scientifically documented than its earlier and rejected submission in 2001. With the new documentation, it is likely that Russia's claim will be accepted.

Russian President Vladimir Putin has on several occasions called for a stronger military presence in the Arctic.[12] In September 2013, the

Northern Fleet patrolled along the NSR with its flagship, the cruiser *Petr Veliky*. Later, as part of a larger Arctic military exercise in August 2015, a navy vessel group sailed the same route with personnel from the Arctic Brigade based in Alakurtti.[13] The Russian Navy has reopened seven former Soviet military bases, among them a base in the New Siberian Islands, an archipelago crucial for monitoring the NSR.[14] The Northern Fleet is in the process of preparing for more commercial activity along the NSR and to protect Russian strategic interests in the Arctic. Russia has also deployed new long-range surface-to-air missile systems to the Kola Peninsula and Novaya Zemlya.[15] Although military deterrence through new deployments, capabilities and exercises is directed mainly towards the US and its NATO allies, it also conveys to other states such as China that Russia is securing its national interests and sovereignty in the Arctic.

Chinese Interests

China's interest and engagement in the Arctic region has increased substantially in the last few years. In January 2018, China released its first white paper on the Arctic, titled "China's Arctic Policy" where China defined itself as a "near-Arctic state". The document represents the most authoritative statement of China's Arctic policy and is much a response to growing concerns in the international community over China's intentions in the Arctic. Broadly speaking, the document spelled out four main focus areas for China's Artic interest and engagement. The first is scientific research as part of efforts to understand the impact of climate change on China, That said, research on the Arctic constitutes just one leg of its wider polar research program, and its Antarctic research program is more comprehensive and better funded.[16] Second, China has an interest in the Arctic shipping routes. Particular emphasis is put on utilizing the NSR which China wishes to develop into a "Polar Silk Road" as part of its "Belt and Road Initiative" (BRI) between China and Europe. China's third focus area is access to Arctic natural resources, principally oil, natural gas, minerals and fisheries but also developing tourism. And, finally, China wishes to consolidate its position as a constructive Arctic stakeholder through participation in relevant global and regional institutions and regimes and through bilateral engagement with Arctic states.[17]

As China's interest in the Arctic has increased, so have concerns among the Arctic states, including Russia, over its intentions. It has been suggested that, in time, Beijing will pursue a more assertive approach to promoting its interests, especially in relation to energy and maritime rights.[18] Security concerns have also been raised. For instance, China's Defence White Paper for 2010 identified outer space, cyber space and the polar regions as new domains of intensified international military competition.[19] But this referred primarily to US activities, such as the development of new military capabilities and operational concepts, missile defense systems, global battlefield reconnaissance and surveillance, and the establishment of the United States Cyber Command.[20] Crucially, there is no indication an assertive approach by China in the Arctic. China has mainly been engaged in scientific activities in the Arctic and commercial interests have been conducted in cooperation with littoral states. Moreover, Beijing has at numerous occasion, often through statements by government officials confirmed that it respects the sovereignty of the Arctic states and their legal rights based on UNCLOS.[21] Further, the 2018 white paper confirms China's commitment to the legal and institutional framework governing the Arctic and the rights of the littoral Arctic states.[22]

Russian Acceptance of China's Observer Status in the Arctic Council

The Arctic Council, founded in 1996, is the main international forum for coordinating Arctic policies, in particular with regard to environmental protection and sustainability (It does not deal with military security issues.). The Arctic Council is not a decision-making body, although the possibility of it evolving in this direction is being discussed.[23] Anton Vasiliev, Russia's Ambassador to the Arctic Council, stated in 2014 that Russia seeks to enhance the Council's role through cooperation with other Arctic states and legally binding agreements.[24] At the Arctic Council Ministerial Meeting in Kiruna in May 2013, the eight member-states voted in favour of accepting China, India, Italy, Japan, Republic of Korea, and Singapore as new observer states while deferring a final decision on the European Union (EU). Russia's position had previously been to oppose China and the EU becoming members, a position it shared with Canada. Moscow was sceptical about bringing in large powers that could then complicate the work of the Council. By contrast, the Nordic countries together with the United States had a more positive view towards accepting new observers, including China's application.[25]

Russia did not want to undermine the position of the "Arctic Five", and also argued that the three other Nordic member countries, Finland, Sweden and Iceland, should play a lesser role in the Council. The Russian position changed, however, and at the Kiruna meeting Foreign Minister Lavrov stated that Russia welcomed observers who accepted the criteria for entry approved at the Arctic Council meeting in Nuuk in 2011.[26] These criteria bind observer states to respect the sovereign rights of the Arctic states and abide by UNCLOS. When Canada indicated that it was open to admitting new observers to the Council, Russia did not want to be left isolated. Furthermore, the overall positive trend in Sino-Russian relations made it difficult for Moscow to refuse China observer status. A few days before the Kiruna meeting, Russian and Chinese energy companies had agreed significant oil deals, and a gas pipeline agreement was under negotiation, finalized a year later in May 2014.[27]

The level of Sino-Russian co-operation in the Arctic Council has to be evaluated on the basis of their different status within it. So far, however, Russia and the other permanent members are satisfied with Chinese participation in the Council.[28] China weighs its actions carefully, tries to work constructively in the different working groups, and has kept a comparatively low profile.[29]

The Northern Sea Route (NSR)

The European Union is China's biggest trading partner.[30] Utilizing the NSR will shorten the sailing distance between Europe and the three Northeast Asian economies of China, Japan, and South Korea. For instance, the route from Shanghai to Hamburg will be 6400 kilometres shorter, or around 15 sailing days, than the route via the Suez Canal.[31] From a strategic point of view, the NSR offers China an alternative sea line of communication to the traditional route through the Indian Ocean and the Suez Canal, where China is concerned about instability in the Middle East, piracy in East Africa, the so-called "Malacca dilemma",[32] and US command of sea-lanes. Moscow sees the development of the NSR as a potentially profitable new global trade route, under conditions defined by Russian national legislation. Moscow recognizes, however, the need for foreign involvement in developing the NSR and has at different occasions invited outside parties, including China.[33] Several countries are interested in a commercially sustainable NSR, but as the world's number one trading nation, and largest ship-owning country in terms of vessel numbers and third largest in terms of tonnage, China would play a pivotal role.

China and Russia have already begun to cooperate on the NSR. A first trial transit by sea of liquefied natural gas (LNG) from Murmansk in Russia to Ningbo in China was conducted in August 2010.[34] It was followed by a commercial agreement between Russia's largest shipping company Sovcomflot Group and the China National Petroleum Corporation (CNPC) in 2010, establishing a long-term framework for oil transport along the NSR that included the training of Chinese personnel on Arctic navigation.[35] Since 2011, several bulk ships have sailed from Murmansk along the NSR to Chinese ports carrying iron ore. In addition, several oil tankers and LNG carriers travelled between the Russian port of Vitino in the White Sea and China in 2012 and 2013.[36] The Chinese company SVA Mining Ltd concluded an agreement in 2012 with the Yakutia authorities for coal shipments and investments in infrastructure at the port of Verkhoyansk.[37] The following year, the China Ocean Shipping Company (COSCO) vessel *Yong Sheng* became the first foreign container ship to complete the NSR.[38] The purpose of the trip was to explore the benefits and challenges of using the NSR as a commercial route. COCSO followed up with another transit in 2014, increasing to around five vessels for 2016 and 2017. At the Arctic Circle Meeting in Reykjavik in October 2016, Ding Nong, Executive Vice President of COSCO, expressed optimism regarding the future of NSR shipping.[39] Relatedly, in 2014 China issued its first Arctic navigation guidelines for the NSR,[40] and in December 2015 the Ministry for Development of the Russian Far East and the Chinese National Development and Reform Commission (NDRC) signed a Memorandum of Understanding on the NSR, and agreed to establish a joint working group to study feasibility models.[41] Moreover, in July 2017 China and Russia agreed to carry out cooperation on the NRS and jointly build an "Polar Silk Road" as part of China's BRI.[42] Finally, China's Poly Technologies has been involved in Arctic infrastructure construction, notably the Belkomur railway and the Arkhangelsk deep-water harbour.[43]

Three elements are critical in assessing Sino-Russian interaction in Arctic shipping: the commercial feasibility of the NSR; China and Russia's respective positions on freedom of navigation in Arctic waters; and Russia's tariff regime. Despite Russia's ambitions to develop the NSR, the number of transits is still very low, with 41 in 2011, 46 in 2012, 46 in 2013, 31 in 2014, and less than 20 in 2015, 2016, and 2017.[44]

In addition to depressed commodity prices, Russian authorities point to difficult ice conditions and the cancellation or rerouting of mineral and gas shipments as the main explanations for the drop in the number of transits.[45] Notwithstanding the trial transits, most Chinese shipping companies remain reluctant to incorporate the Arctic in their global shipping network.[46] The Chinese Ministry of Commerce (MOFCOM) has identified unpredictable ice conditions, environmental concerns, lack of basic infrastructure, and difficulties in predicting delivery times as factors that might influence the decisions of Chinese commercial operators.[47]

It is also questionable how much China would actually benefit from using the NSR instead of sailing though the Suez Canal. Ships sailing from ports in southern and central China to destinations in Europe would save much less time and fuel through the NSR than those sailing from the northern Chinese provinces, or from Japan or South Korea.[48] Four of China's five busiest ports, Shanghai, Shenzhen, Ningbo-Zhoushan, and Guangzhou, are located in its southern or central coastal provinces.[49] This suggests there is less potential for China to utilize the route than for South Korea and Japan. That said, its northern regions could benefit if it is able to develop ports in North Korea (Rajin) and Russia (Zarubino), opening up landlocked areas and saving shipping time instead of sailing around the Korean Peninsula.[50] China's BRI could also potentially develop an Arctic route. According to the government document, "Vision for Maritime Cooperation under the BRI", published by the NDRC and the State Oceanic Administration in June 2017, the Arctic was officially incorporated into the BRI.[51] It remains unclear, however, what that incorporation would entail in practice.

Second, China and Russia have different positions interpreting freedom of navigation in Arctic waters.[52] A potentially more serious issue concerns different interpretations of certain provisions under UNCLOS. Russian legislation treats the archipelagos along the NSR as internal waters and claims sovereignty over them.[53] Moscow cites special conditions and national legislation with reference to UNCLOS' so-called "ice article" 234, under which coastal states are given the right to enforce non-discriminatory laws within their Exclusive Economic Zones (EEZ) in ice-covered areas where environmental and navigation concerns are vital.[54]

China interprets UNCLOS differently. It upholds that Chinese vessels should enjoy freedom of navigation through the EEZ of littoral states and international straits. Nevertheless, it is unlikely that these divergent interpretations will become a major point of friction. When China was admitted to the Arctic Council in 2013, it accepted UNCLOS as the legal framework for the Arctic and agreed to respect the sovereign rights of Arctic states. Beijing also assured Moscow that it had no intention of challenging Russian positions in this area.

Third, China questions the tariff regime for shipping in Russia's territorial waters and EEZ, although Chinese analysts claim this matter can be resolved through bilateral consultations.[55] Moscow is aware that unreasonable conditions would push freighters to use other sea routes. Another potential issue is that as China increases its own ice-breaker fleet, it may start to challenge Russia's nationalization of marine traffic with monopoly on ice-breaker support and obligatory use of Russian ships for oil products in its Arctic.[56]

Energy Cooperation

Russia has traditionally been reluctant to invite Chinese companies into Arctic energy projects, especially on the production side. But given China's thirst for oil and natural gas, and its financial muscle, voices in Beijing argue that China could provide Russia the necessary capital to develop the region.[57] Russia has long worked with Western companies in the Arctic, especially on offshore projects that require foreign competence, technology and investments.[58] But following Western sanctions in the aftermath of the Ukraine crisis, it has become much more open to Chinese energy engagement in the region.

China's Arctic oil and gas interests are more limited than is commonly supposed, but cooperation with Russia stands out as the most significant development.[59] As part of a larger deal in May 2013,[60] Rosneft invited CNPC to explore three offshore fields in the Barents and Pechora Seas as well as an onshore field in Nenetsk. Igor Sechin, head of Rosneft, confirmed in 2014 that the company was committed to working with China on Arctic offshore projects.[61] Besides geological explorations, though, there has been little concrete progress. In September 2016, Gazprom Neft offered China National Offshore Oil Corporation (CNOOC) and CNPC ownership of two Arctic shelf license blocks in the Barents and Chukchi seas.[62] However, Chinese companies remain reluctant to become too involved in Arctic offshore investments. The technology and know-how of Western companies are still needed for these types of projects. Factor in low (or non-existent) profit margins in these high-cost ventures, and it becomes hard for Russia to attract Chinese partners.[63] That said, in the summer of 2017 Russian energy companies contracted China Oilfield Services Ltd (COSL) to perform seismic surveys and exploration drilling in the Barents and Kara seas—the first time a Chinese company had been chosen for such a purpose.[64]

A far more successful Sino-Russian energy project in the Arctic is the LNG terminal on the Yamal peninsula in Northwest Siberia. The LNG-project ended Gazprom's monopoly on Russian gas exports, at least on shipping, and is politically important for Russia as it seeks a role in the global LNG market. With its opening in December 2017, the terminal provides summer season shipments of LNG to Asia and a year-round route westwards. The first load of LNG was sold to Vitol in January 2018.[65] The project is run by Yamal LNG, a joint-venture company with Russia's Novatek owning 50.1%, France's Total 20%, CNPC 20%, and the China Silk Road Fund 9.9%.[66] The Silk Road Fund investment indicates that China is incorporating the Arctic within the BRI. In April 2016, Yamal LNG signed credit line facilities with the China Exim Bank and the China Development Bank for a total of 19.1 billion euros.[67] China has now provided about 60% of the capital to implement the Yamal LNG project. To expand LNG-cooperation CNPC also in November 2017 agreed to initiate cooperation with Novatek on the development of Arctic LNG 2 project. The China Development Bank will provide for up to 3 billion USD in financing.[68]

Security Relations

The Ukrainian crisis has led other Arctic states to freeze most of their military ties with Moscow. The souring relationship between Russia and the West started well before Ukraine; in particular, the 2008 war in Georgia dealt a severe blow to Russia–NATO cooperation. That war also revealed significant flaws in the Russian military's performance, which led to a major modernization program.[69] Today, Russia's military posture represents a real challenge to NATO in the Arctic.[70] The alliance has responded, mainly by bolstering air and land defense capabilities in the Baltic States and Poland, but it is also looking to counter Russia's improved anti-access area-denial (A2/AD) capabilities in the North Atlantic and the Arctic Ocean.[71] NATO officials still meet with their Russian counterparts within the framework of the Arctic Council, and regional coast guard cooperation is continuing.[72] But the deteriorating relationship between Russia and the West is clearly limiting security and economic cooperation.

Against this background, and expanding Sino-Russian military ties, it is possible that Moscow may accept some form of security activities with China in the Arctic. In September 2015, PLA Navy ships passed through the Bering Sea in the North Pacific for the first time,[73] and in July 2017 the two sides conducted a joint naval exercise in the Baltic Sea.[74] Given these developments, the previously unthinkable idea of Sino-Russian naval exercises in the Arctic has become a possibility, for example in the Barents Sea or Chukchi Sea.

On the other hand, the Chinese are well aware of Russian sensitivities about the presence of other powers in the Arctic, particularly when this has a military dimension. They understand the key role the Arctic plays in Russian national security thinking, and in Putin's promotion of Russia as a great power.[75] They also know that historically Russia has been suspicious of Chinese interest in the region.[76] Nevertheless, some Chinese analysts have called on Beijing to monitor Russian military developments and their impact on Chinese interests.[77]

If Russia-West relations continue to deteriorate, Sino-Russian security cooperation in the Arctic could increase. However, it is also possible that Russia will strengthen its military presence in the region, and become even more defensive on sovereignty and security issues. Increased militarization of the area would inhibit commercial interests, including those of China, and the future of the NSR would become highly problematic.

Conclusion

Russian suspicion toward Chinese engagement in the Arctic has started to give way to substantive cooperation, with Moscow seeking Chinese investment in Arctic infrastructure and energy. It recognizes that in order to develop the Arctic, Russia needs foreign capital, technology and assistance from Arctic and non-Arctic states. Moreover, its ongoing crisis with the West has given momentum to interaction with China in the Arctic (as elsewhere), a trend that could be reinforced and even accelerated over time.

However, it is premature to conclude that Chinese and Russian interests are convergent given several ongoing challenges. First, with the exception of the Yamal LNG project, most of the Sino-Russian projects in the region are progressing very slowly. Second, China still lacks the necessary technology and know-how to replace Western energy companies in offshore and high-tech onshore projects, and the low oil price has reduced profit margins. Third, many Chinese shipping companies have adopted a wait-and-see attitude with regard to the NSR. Fourth, the Arctic is far less important for China than it is for Russia. And, finally, the strategic significance of the Arctic for Russia suggests that Moscow will retain strong reservations about a significant Chinese presence in the region, however good their relationship may be in other respects.

Notes

1. The Arctic is here defined as all areas (oceans and territories) north of the Arctic Circle.
2. Tulupov (2013).
3. Stokke and Hønneland (2006).
4. The Ilulissat Declaration (2008).
5. USGS (2008).
6. Tamnes and Offerdal (2014).
7. Russian Government (2008, 2013).
8. Russian Institute for Energy Strategy (2009).
9. Russian MFA (2001), Kremlin (2015).
10. Murmanskiy Vestnik (2015).
11. RIA Novosti (2016), Chekalin (2017).
12. Sputnik International (2013).
13. Pettersen (2015).
14. Staalesen (2013a).
15. Staalesen (2015).
16. Up to the end of 2017 China had undertaken eight research expeditions to the Arctic and 33 to the Antarctic.
17. China State Council (2018).
18. Blank (2013), Rainwater (2013).
19. China State Council (2011).
20. Chase (2011), Anthony H. Cordesman and Nicholas S. Yarosh (2012).
21. China MFA (2013).
22. China State Council (2018).
23. Graczyk and Koivurova (2013).
24. Røseth (2014).
25. Lunde (2014).
26. Lavrov (2013).
27. Paik (2015).
28. Statement by senior Norwegian Foreign Ministry official, Oslo, April 2015.

29. Interview with U.S. Diplomat, Beijing, June 2015.
30. European Commission (2017).
31. *The Economist* (2012).
32. Most of China's sea transport moves through the narrow Malacca Straight and represent a potential vulnerability. Seen from Beijing, in the event of a confrontation with the U.S., Washington could severely disrupt China's trade.
33. Rosbalt (2017).
34. Huang et al. (2014).
35. Sovcomflot (2010).
36. Alexei Bambulyak et al. (2015).
37. Neftegaz (2012).
38. Staalesen (2013b).
39. Staalesen (2016a).
40. China State Council (2014).
41. Centre for High North Logistics (2015).
42. Xinhua (2017).
43. Staalesen (2016b).
44. Transits as defined by Russian NSR Administration, between the Kara gate and Cape Dezhnev. Centre for High North Logistics (CHNL) (2017), Northern Sea Route Administration (2018).
45. Pettersen (2014).
46. Huang et al. (2014).
47. China Ministry of Commerce (2013).
48. Lee and Song (2014).
49. World Shipping Council (2016).
50. Jakobson and Lee (2013), p. 10, Chen (2012).
51. Xinhua (2017).
52. Blunden (2012), Wright (2011).
53. Internal waters include the sea lanes going through to the archipelagos of Novaya Zemlya, Severnaya Zemlya and the East Siberian Islands and their connection to the mainland. The area between Wrangel Island and the mainland is not defines as internal waters, See Østreng et al. (2013).
54. UNCLOS PART XII.
55. This was also alluded to in private conversations during the "Asian Countries and the Arctic Future" conference in Shanghai organized by Shanghai Institutes for International Studies and Fridtjof Nansen Institute, 23–26 April, Shanghai, 2014.
56. Staalesen (2018).
57. Li (2014), pp. 133–135.
58. Øverland (2014).
59. Hsiung (2016).

60. The 2013 Rosneft-CNPC deal set the stage for a doubling of Russian oil exports to China by 2018 through the expansion of East Siberian and Pacific Ocean (ESPO) pipeline, with an estimated value of $270 billion, See Røseth (2017), pp. 38–39.
61. Klimenko (2014), p. 20.
62. Kozlov (2017).
63. Yakovlev (2015).
64. Filimonova (2017), Staalesen (2017).
65. Neftegaz (2018).
66. CNPC got involved in 2013 buying a 20% stake from Novatek, and the China Silk Road Fund followed in CNPC's footsteps, obtaining its stake in the project in September 2015 through a 15-year loan of around 730 million euros. See Xinhua (2015).
67. LNG World News (2016).
68. Humpert (2017).
69. Zysk (2015).
70. Efjestad (2017).
71. Tamnes (2017).
72. Skram and Gade (2016).
73. Cooper (2015).
74. Majumdar (2017).
75. Lu (2010), Qian (2014).
76. Zuo (2012), p. 139, Xu (2014).
77. Li and Zhan (2013).

Literature

Bambulyak, Alexei, Are Kristoffer Sydnes, Aleksandar Saša-Milakovic, Bjørn Frantzen. 2015. Shipping Oil from the Russian Arctic: Past Experiences and Future Prospects. In *Proceedings of the 23rd International Conference on Port and Ocean Engineering Under Arctic Condition*, June 14–18, Trondheim, Norway.

Blank, Stephen. 2013. China's Arctic Strategy. *The Diplomat*, June 20. http://thediplomat.com/2013/06/chinas-arctic-strategy/. Accessed 1 June 2014.

Blunden, Margaret. 2012. Geopolitics and the Northern Sea Route. *International Affairs* 88 (1): 115–129.

Centre for High North Logistics (CHNL). 2015. Ministry for Development of Russian Far East Prepares the NSR Development Model Up to July 2016, December 31. http://www.arctic-lio.com/node/232.

Centre for High North Logistics (CHNL). 2017. Transit Statistics. http://www.arctic-lio.com/nsr_transits. Accessed 5 Sept 2017.

Chase, Michael S. 2011. China's 2010 National Defense White Paper: An Assessment. *China Brief* 11 (7). Jamestown Foundation.

Chekalin, Dennis. 2017. РФ представит ООН заявку на расширение границы шельфа в Арктике [The Russian Federation Introduce to the UN Its Application to the Inquires of the Continental Borders in the Arctic]. *Rossiskaya Gazeta*, August 17. https://rg.ru/2017/08/17/rf-predstavit-oon-zaiavku-na-rasshirenie-granicy-shelfa-v-arktike.html. Accessed 17 Sept 2017.

Chen, Gang. 2012. China's Emerging Arctic Strategy. *The Polar Journal* 2 (2): 358–371.

China Ministry of Foreign Affairs. 2013. Foreign Ministry Spokesperson Hong Lei's Remarks on China Being Accepted as Observer in the Arctic Council, May 15. http://www.fmprc.gov.cn/mfa_eng/xwfw_665399/s2510_665401/2535_665405/t1040943.shtml. Accessed 2 July 2014.

China Ministry of Commerce. 2013. 北极航道商业化运营的前景 [The Commercial Prospects of the Arctic Northern Sea Route], September 11. http://www.mofcom.gov.cn/article/i/dxfw/jlyd/201309/20130900299022.shtml.

China State Council. 2011. *China's National Defense in 2010*, State Council Information Office, March 31. http://www.china.org.cn/government/whitepaper/node_7114675.htm. Accessed 30 Aug 2017.

China State Council. 2014. 北极航行指南（东北航道）》出版发行 [Arctic Navigation Guidelines on the Northern Sea Route Published], September 18. http://www.gov.cn/xinwen/2014-09/18/content_2752215.htm. Accessed 30 June 2017.

China State Council. 2018. *China's Arctic Policy*. State Council Information Office, January 26. http://english.gov.cn/archive/white_paper/2018/01/26/content_281476026660336.htm. Accessed 15 Feb 2018.

Cordesman, H. Anthony, and Nicholas S. Yarosh. 2012. *Chinese Military Modernization and Force Development. A Western Perspective*, Center for Strategic & International Studies. https://www.csis.org/analysis/chinese-military-modernization-and-force-development-0.

Cooper, Helene. 2015. In a First, Chinese Navy Sails Off Alaska. *The New York Times*, September 2. https://www.nytimes.com/2015/09/03/world/asia/in-a-first-chinese-navy-sails-off-alaska.html?mcubz=1.

European Commission. 2017. Countries and Regions: China. http://ec.europa.eu/trade/policy/countries-and-regions/countries/china/. Accessed 4 Sept 2017.

Efjestad, Svein. 2017. Norway and the North Atlantic: Defence of the Northern Flank. In *NATO and North Atlantic. Revitalising Collective Defence*, ed. John Andreas Olsen, RUSI Whitehall Paper, No. 87.

Filimonova, Nadezda. 2017. Gazprom and China's 'Breakthrough' in the Russian Arctic. *The Diplomat*, August 8. http://thediplomat.com/2017/08/gazprom-and-chinas-breakthrough-in-the-russian-arctic/. Accessed 8 Aug 2017.

Graczyk, Piotr, and Timo Koivurova. 2013. A New Era in the Arctic Council's External Relations? Broader Consequences of the Nuuk Observer Rules for Arctic Governance. *Polar Record* 50: 1–12.

Hsiung, Weidacher Christopher. 2016. China and Arctic Energy: Drivers and Limitations. *The Polar Journal* 6 (2): 243–258.

Huang, Linyan, Frederic Lasserre, and Olga Alexeeva. 2014. Is China's Arctic Interest Driven by Arctic Shipping Potential. *Asia Geographer* 32 (1): 59–71.

Humpert, Malte. 2017. China to Expand Role in Novatek's Arctic Gas Development. *High North News*, November 3. http://www.highnorthnews.com/china-to-expand-role-in-novateks-arctic-gas-development/. Accessed 16 Feb 2018.

Jakobson, Linda, and Seong-Hyon Lee. 2013. The North East Asian States' Interests in the Arctic and Possible Cooperation with the Kingdom of Denmark. *SIPRI Report*, April.

Klimenko, Ekaterina. 2014. Russia's Evolving Arctic Strategy: Drivers, Challenges and New Opportunities. *SIPRI Policy Paper*, No. 42, September 1–25.

Kremlin. 2015. Морская доктрина Российской Федерации [The Marine Doctrine of the Russian Federation], See (in Russian). http://static.kremlin.ru/media/events/files/ru/uAFi5nvux2twaqjftS5yrIZUVTJan77L.pdf. Accessed 5 Sept 2017.

Kozlov, Dmitry. 2017. Aziatam kholodno v Arktike [Asians Are Cold in the Arctic]. *Kommersant Newspaper*, September 7, 2016. http://politarktika.ru/news/aziatam_kholodno_v_arktike/2016-09-07-751. Accessed 6 Sept 2017.

Lavrov, Sergey. 2013. Speech of Russian Foreign Minister Sergey Lavrov at the Eighth Ministerial Session of the Arctic Council, Kiruna, May 15. http://www.mid.ru/en/press_service/minister_speeches/-/asset_publisher/7OvQR5KJWVmR/content/id/110214. Accessed 6 Sept 2017.

Lee, Sung-Woo, and Ju-Mi Song. 2014. Economic Possibilities of Shipping Through Northern Sea Route. *The Asian Journal of Shipping and Logistics* 30 (3): 415–430.

Li, Jiangmin. 2014. 俄罗斯北极开发战略与中俄合作 《俄罗斯黄皮书, 俄罗斯发展报告, 2014/李永全主编》 [Russia's Strategy for Developing the Arctic and Sino-Russian Cooperation]. In *Yellow Book of Russia. Annual Report on Development of Russia*, ed. Li Yongquan, 124–135. Beijing: Shehui kexue wensan chubanshe.

Li, Jingyu, and Longlong Zhan. 2013. 我国开拓北极东北航道的战略思考《中共中央党校学报》 [Considerations for China's Strategy in Developing Its Northeast Arctic Shipping Lane]. *Journal of the Party School of the Central Committee of the C.P.C.* 17 (6): 108–112.

LNG World News. 2016. Yamal LNG Secures $12 Bln from Chinese Banks. *LNG World News*, April 29. http://www.lngworldnews.com/yamal-lng-secures-12-bln-from-chinese-banks/.

Lu, Junyuan. 2010. 北极地缘政治与中国应对 [Geopolitics in the Arctic and China's Response]. Beijing: Shishi chubanshe.

Lunde, Leiv. 2014. The Nordic Embrace: Why the Nordic Countries Welcome Asia to the Arctic Table, Roundtable: Polar Pursuits: Asia Engages the Arctic. *Asia Policy* 18 (July): 39–45.

Majumdar, Dave. 2017. Russia and China Are Sending Their Navies to the Baltic Sea: Is a Formal Alliance Next? *The National Interest*. http://nationalinterest.org/blog/the-buzz/russia-china-are-sending-their-navies-the-baltic-sea-formal-21669. Accessed 30 July 2017.

Murmanskiy, Vestnik. 2015. 1 апреля 2015 года был образован новый орган безопасности [On April 1st 2015 a New Organ for Security Was Estabslihed]. *Murmanskiy Vestnik*, April 1. http://www.mvestnik.ru/shwpgn.asp?pid=2015041554. Accessed 5 Sept 2017.

Neftegaz. 2012. Якутия, уголь и Северный морской путь [Yakutia, Coal and the NSR]. *Neftegaz.ru*. http://neftegaz.ru/news/view/102170. Accessed 5 Sept 2017.

Neftegaz. 2018. Ямал СПГ осуществил 1-ю поставку газового конденсата [Yamal LNG Carried Out Its First Supply of Gas Condensate]. *Neftegaz.ru*. https://neftegaz.ru/news/view/168719-Teper-i-zhidkie-uglevodorody.-Yamal-SPG-osuschestvil-1-yu-postavku-gazovogo-kondensata. Accessed 16 Feb 2018.

Northern Sea Route Administration of the Russian Federation. 2018. Summing Up Activity of Administration NSR for 2017, January 12. http://www.nsra.ru/en/glavnaya/novosti/n19.html. Accessed 16 Feb 2018.

Østreng, Willy, et al. 2013. *Shipping in Arctic Waters: A Comparison of the Northeast, Northwest and Trans Polar Passages*. Heidelberg: Springer.

Øverland, Indra. 2014. Russia's Energy Arctic Policy. *International Journal* 65: 865–878.

Pettersen, Trude. 2014. Northern Sea Route Traffic Plummeted. *Barents Observer*, December 16. http://barentsobserver.com/en/arctic/2014/12/northern-sea-route-traffic-plummeted-16-12. Accessed 7 May 2015.

Pettersen, Trude. 2015. Arctic Brigade Joins Northern Fleet Exercise Along Northern Sea Route. *Barents Observer*, August 17. http://barentsobserver.com/

en/security/2015/08/arctic-brigade-joins-northern-fleet-exercise-along-northern-sea-route-17-08. Accessed 25 Jan 2016.

Paik, Kuen-Wook. 2015. *Sino-Russian Gas and Oil Cooperation: Entering into a New Era of Strategic Partnership?* OIES PAPER: WPM 59. Oxford: The Oxford Institute for Energy Studies.

Qian, Zongqi. 2014. 俄罗斯: 加快维护北极新利益步伐 《中国海洋报》 [Russia: Accelerating the Pace of Protecting Arctic Interests]. *China Ocean News*, May 27. http://www.chinaislands.gov.cn/contents/20243/15425.html. Accessed 29 Apr 2015.

Rainwater, Shiloh. 2013. Race to the North: China's Arctic Strategy and Its Implications. *Naval War College Review* 66 (2): 62–82. Naval War College Press.

RIA Novosti. 2016. РФ 9 февраля презентует в ООН заявку на расширение шельфа в Арктике [Russian Federation on the 9th February Presents in UN Its Application on the of Inquries on the Contintenal Shelf in the Arctic]. *RIA Novosti*, Janurary 22, See (in Russian) RIA Novosti. http://ria.ru/arctic/20160122/1363388896.html. Accessed 5 Sept 2017.

Rosbalt. 2017. Президента Путина встретили и выслушали в Китае [They Met and Listened to President Putin in China]. *Rosbalt*, May 17, See (in Russian). http://www.rosbalt.ru/world/2017/05/14/1614826.html. Accessed 5 Sept 2017.

Russian Government. (2008, 2013). *The 2008 Strategy*: Основы государственной политики Российской Федерации в Арктике на период до 2020 года и дальнейшую перспективу [The Principals of the Russian Federation State Policies' in the Arctic for the Period Until 2020 and Beyond], September 18. http://government.ru/info/18359/. Accessed 5, 20 Sept 2017. The Updated 2013 Version: Стратегия развития Арктической зоны Российской Федерации и обеспечения национальной безопасности на период до 2020 года [Strategy for the Development of the Arctic Zone of the Russian Federation and National Security for the Period up to 2020]. http://government.ru/info/18360/. Accessed 5, 20 Sept 2017.

Russian Institute for Energy Strategy. 2009. The Russian State Energy Strategy for the Period Up 2030. http://www.energystrategy.ru/projects/es-2030.htm. Accessed 5 Sept 2017.

Russian MFA. 2001. For the 2001 Doctrine, See the *Security Council of the Russian Federation*: Морская доктрина Российской Федерации на период до 2020 года [The Marine Doctrine of the Russian Federation for the Period Up to 2020]. http://www.mid.ru/foreign_policy/official_documents/-/asset_publisher/CptICkB6BZ29/content/id/462098. Accessed 5 Sept 2017.

Røseth, Tom. 2014. Russia's China Policy in the Arctic. *Strategic Analysis* 38 (6): 841–859.

Røseth, Tom. 2017. Russia's Energy Relations with China: Passing the Strategic Threshold? *Eurasian Geography and Economics* 58 (1): 23–55.

Skram, Arild-Inge, and Jo G. Gade. 2016. The Role of Coast Guards in Conflict Management: The Norwegian Experience. In *International Order at Sea: How It Is Challenged. How It Is Maintained*, ed. Jo Inge Bekkevold and Geoffrey Till. London: Palgrave Macmillan.

Sovcomflot. 2010. руппа компаний Совкомфлот и Китайская национальная нефтегазовая корпорация договорились о стратегическом партнерстве [Sovcomflot Group and China National Petroleum Corporation Become Strategic Partners]. *Press-Centre Sovcomflot.* http://www.sovcomflot.ru/about/scf_group/novoship/official_information/item478.html. Accessed 5 Sept 2017.

Sputnik International. 2013. Putin Orders Strong Military Presence in Arctic. *Sputnik International*, December 10. https://sputniknews.com/russia/20131210185429796-Putin-Orders-Strong-Military-Presence-in-Arctic/.

Staalessen, Atle. 2013a. In Remotest Russian Arctic, a New Navy Base. *Barents Observer*, September 17. http://barentsobserver.com/en/security/2013/09/remotest-russian-arctic-new-navy-base-17-09. Accessed 15 Feb 2014.

Staalesen, Atle. 2013b. First Container Ship on Northern Sea Route. *Barents Observer*, August 21. http://barentsobserver.com/en/arctic/2013/08/first-container-ship-northern-sea-route-21-08. Accessed 8 Aug 2014.

Staaleen, Atle. 2015. Russia Deploys S-300 in Novaya Zemlya. *The Barents Observer*, December 9. https://thebarentsobserver.com/en/security/2015/12/russia-deploys-s-300-novaya-zemlya. Accessed 6 Sept 2017.

Staalesen, Atle. 2016a. COSCO Sends Five Vessels Through Northern Sea Route. *Barents Observer*, October 10. https://thebarentsobserver.com/en/arctic-industry-and-energy/2016/10/cosco-sends-five-vessels-through-northern-sea-route.

Staalesen, Atle. 2016b. Russian, Chinese Officials Hold Talks on Arctic Railway Project. *Radio Canada International, Eye on the Arctic*, May 24. http://www.rcinet.ca/eye-on-the-arctic/2016/05/24/railway-russian-chinese-arctic-railway-project-beijing-belkomur/. Accessed 6 Sept 2017.

Staalesen, Atle. 2017. Russians Choose Chinese Explorers for Arctic Oil. *Barents Observer*, April 27. https://thebarentsobserver.com/en/industry/2016/04/russians-choose-chinese-explorers-arctic-oil. Accessed 9 Aug 2017.

Staalesen, Atle. 2018. These Are China's Top 10 Keywords for the Arctic. *Barents Observer*, January 30. https://thebarentsobserver.com/en/arctic/2018/01/these-are-chinas-top-keywords-arctic. Accessed 16 Feb 2018.

Stokke, Olav Schram, and Geir Hønneland (eds.). 2006. *International Cooperation and Arctic Governance: Regime Effectiveness and Northern Region Building*. New York: Routledge.

Tamnes, Rolf. 2017. The Significance of the North Atlantic and the Norwegian Contribution. In *NATO and North Atlantic. Revitalising Collective Defence*, ed. John Andreas Olsen, RUSI Whitehall Paper.

Tamnes, Rolf, and Kristine Offerdal (eds.). 2014. *Geopolitics in the Arctic: Regional Dynamics in a Global World*. New York: Routledge.

The Economist. 2012. Snow Dragons. *The Economist*, September 1. http://www.economist.com/node/21561891.

The Ilulissat Declaration. 2008. Original Document. http://www.oceanlaw.org/downloads/arctic/Ilulissat_Declaration.pdf.

Tulupov, Dmitry. 2013. Time for Russia and China to Chill Out Over the Arctic. *Russia Direct*, December 5. http://www.russia-direct.org/content/time-russia-and-china-chill-out-over-arctic. Accessed 10 Sept 2014.

UNCLOS PART XII: Protection and Preservation of the Marine Environment. http://www.un.org/depts/los/convention_agreements/texts/unclos/part12.htm. Accessed 26 Feb 2014.

USGS—United States Geological Survey. 2008. Fact Sheet 2008-3049: Circum-Arctic Resource Appraisal: Estimates of Undiscovered Oil and Gas North of the Arctic Circle. http://pubs.usgs.gov/fs/2008/3049/fs2008-3049.pdf.

World Shipping Council. 2016. Top 50 World Container Ports. http://www.worldshipping.org/about-the-industry/global-trade/top-50-world-container-ports. Accessed 26 Jan 2016.

Wright, David Curtis. 2011. *The Panda Bear Readies to Meet the Polar Bear: China and Canada's Arctic Sovereignty Challenge*, 1–10. Calgary: Canadian Defense and Foreign Affairs Institute.

Xinhua. 2015. China's Silk Road Fund to Buy into Russian LNG Project. *Xinhua*, December 19. http://europe.chinadaily.com.cn/business/2015-12/19/content_22750174.htm. Accessed 20 Jan 2016.

Xinhua. 2017. China, Russia Agree to Jointly Build "Ice Silk Road". *Xinhuanet*, July 4. http://www.xinhuanet.com/english/2017-07/04/c_136417241.htm. Accessed 16 Feb 2018.

Xu, Bo. 2014. 中俄北极合作的基础与路径思考,《东北亚论坛》 [Reflections on the Foundations and Paths of Sino-Russian Cooperation in the Arctic]. *Northeast Asia Forum* (3): 61–63.

Yakovlev, Vadim. 2015. According to Deputy Director Vadim Yakovlev in Gazprom Neft. http://www.gazprom-neft.ru/press-center/lib/1108572/. Accessed 6 Sept 2017.

Zuo, Fengrong. 2012. 俄罗斯海洋战略初探《外交评论》 [Primarily Study on Russia's Maritime Strategy]. *Foreign Affairs Review* (5): 125–139.

Zysk, Katarzyna. 2015. Managing Military Change in Russia. In *Security, Strategy and Military Change in the 21st Century: Cross-Regional Perspectives*, ed. Jo Inge Bekkevold, Ian Bowers, and Michael Raska. London: Routledge.

PART III

China, Russia and the World

CHAPTER 9

From Global Governance to Global Disorder? Implications for Russia and China

Bin Yu

A quarter of a century after the end of the bipolar system, the global liberal order, which has been sustained by American primacy, is said to be "weakened and fractured at its core."[1] The "end" of the post-WWII liberal international order[2] may well be an intellectual over-spin in the aftermath of Brexit and the rise of Trumpism in 2016. But regardless of the validity of this new "endist" discourse,[3] Russia and China are singled out as the causes, directly or indirectly, for the alleged "ending" of the liberal order.[4]

Why has there been such a steep descent to pessimism across the West from the jubilant triumphalism of just a few years ago? What is the relationship between the notion of global governance—which is directed at the vast non-West including the post-Soviet space—and the current sense of disorder[5] and malaise of the West? What does global governance mean for Russia and China? What are the sources and incentives for Moscow and Beijing to work with, or depart from and even undermine, these global mechanisms? How do they view and engage global governance

B. Yu (✉)
Department of Political Science, Wittenberg University,
Springfield, OH, USA
e-mail: byu@wittenberg.edu

J. I. Bekkevold and B. Lo (eds.), *Sino-Russian Relations in the 21st Century*, https://doi.org/10.1007/978-3-319-92516-5_9

institutions? What are the similarities and differences between Russia and China in their respective dealings with the global liberal order and its governance, and how and why do they differ? What does the future hold for their policies on the global liberal order and on specific global governance issues such as the "governing deficit"?[6]

This chapter begins with an overview of the unanticipated arrival of the "global governance" age in a paradoxical world of unipolarity and fragmentation, particularly on the vast Eurasian landmass where the forces of change have gathered momentum. The format, direction, and degree of Russian and Chinese engagement with existing global governing mechanisms, however, were largely driven by their historical departure from their respective communist legacies. The chapter will examine the socio-political dynamics inside both countries that have shaped their different approaches to global governance. The gradualist reform and rebuilding process in China helped it join the capitalist world trading system, albeit in its own way. Rapid change in the former Soviet Union left considerable contradictions in Russia and its "near-abroad," orienting the post-Soviet space more toward geopolitical frictions than economic interdependence. Next, the chapter will compare and analyze similarities and differences in Russian and Chinese approaches to global governance: Russia's emphasis on global security governance and China's interest in economic governance. Although both countries face an increasingly unfriendly West, they have so far resisted the temptation to form a formal alliance—largely as a result of the historical learning experience from their volatile interactions during the Cold War, and of their extensive ties with the Western liberal international order thereafter.

Between a "New World Order" and the Age of Great Mess

"The world is a mess. I inherited a mess," complained President Donald Trump just a few months into the White House.[7] One wonders what has led to the current "mess" from the "New World Order" (NWO) declared by US President George H.W. Bush on September 11, 1990.[8] A pivotal point for this NWO was US–Soviet partnership, a sharp contrast to the widespread hostility toward Moscow in the West today. In a strikingly similar way to Woodrow Wilson's 1919 rhetoric on the principle of collective security through the League of Nations, Bush's NWO speech stressed the role of the United Nations (UN), whose goals were now within reach for the first time since its inception at the end of World War II, thanks to Soviet cooperation. No one, including Bush himself, anticipated the sudden Soviet implosion a year later. For most Western political and intellectual elites,[9] the NWO was already in place and there was, therefore, no need for any governance.

The NWO, however, ushered in a string of US-led wars, most of which were initiated without UN authorization: the Bosnian war in 1992–1995, the Kosovo war in 1998–1999, and the Afghan, Iraqi, and Libyan wars in the twenty-first century. The last three, plus the ongoing civil wars in Syria and Yemen, have laid waste to much of the Middle East and North Africa. The dismantling of ruling regimes without replacing them with effective government essentially paved the way for extremist groups such as Islamic State (IS).

The combination of Western triumphalism (endism), globalized capitalism, and unrelenting interventionism led to general instability in many parts of the world, and underlined the need for effective global governance in the aftermath of the Cold War.[10] The ending of bipolarity also made it possible for more collective management of the world's problems. There was a surge of ideas and policies on global governance to the point that a prominent scholar claimed that it had become, "in an extraordinarily short time ... the dominant motif of contemporary social sciences."[11] In the new millennium, the international community seemed to have reached a consensus regarding the definition of global governance: "the collective management of common problems at the international level...includes all the institutions, regimes, processes, partnerships and networks that contribute to collective action and problem solving at an international level."[12]

Tales of Two Communist Reforms: Building Up vs. Breaking Down

Years prior to the end of the Cold War, Russia and China started to reach out to the outside world because of their own internal dynamics and reforms. The origin, format, process, and outcomes of their outreach were, however, very different, leading to different approaches toward global governance.

China's Slow Rebuild

In retrospect, China's outreach had more to do with global engagement than with the notion of "governance." The process started long before the end of the Cold War for several reasons. One was China's departure from the Soviet camp—and the ensuing Sino-Soviet-US strategic triangle—leading to the first significant breakdown of the highly rigid, ideologized, and militarized Cold War order between two rival alliances. Second, China's domestic economic system remained largely outside the two existing camps for much of the Cold War. Separation from the then Soviet-led economic bloc gave China both the flexibility and opportunity to adapt itself to the West-dominated international trading system at a much earlier stage (1978) than other Soviet bloc members. Third, the existence of overseas Chinese communities in Hong Kong, Taiwan, and Southeast Asia contributed significantly to China's opening to the outside world. Finally, Deng's reforms from 1978 onward saw a gradual building-up out of the ashes of Mao's anti-bureaucratic and populist campaigns. As a result, there was relatively little bureaucratic resistance to reforms compared to the strong, all-encompassing, and rigid bureaucracy facing Gorbachev. For the same reason, China was able to seek, as well as experiment, with different types of economic models including those practiced in the West. In Deng's words, China should "wade across the stream by feeling the way" (摸着石头过河). If there is anything that constitutes a so-called China model, it is this open-ended, experimental, and pragmatic approach that has shaped China's perceptions of, and relations with, the outside world.

None of these ideational changes and policy outcomes by China were anticipated or explained by the leading IR theories prior to the end of the Cold War. Indeed, these West-centric theories were designed for and by the West. There is, perhaps, nothing right or wrong about this. The point, however, is that to understand China's approach to global governance, China's own discourse is at least as important as those of Western theorizing.

Chinese efforts at reaching out did not guarantee a smooth transition to global standards or expectations. The process of China's economic reform was full of twists and turns, and its political elite had no ready blueprint for reforms to such a large economy and society. Until the late 1970s, the economy was centrally managed and largely closed to outsiders. US–China rapprochement did open a window to the West, and this remained open largely for geostrategic purposes. The Chinese economic system and its operating principles had to undergo painful adjustments. Despite some early success in rural reforms, urban reforms quickly led to higher inflation, job insecurity, corruption, and social instability.[13] It took almost 15 years for China to join the World Trade Organization (WTO) in December 2001, mainly because the United States, Europe, and Japan insisted on changes to the Chinese economy before accepting China as a WTO member. Among these preconditions were tariff reductions, open market imperatives, and industrial policies. Lower tariffs, however, meant China would have to trim or reform government-run enterprises, with unknown social and political consequences. Following protracted internal deliberation and preparation, China took the plunge. This essentially meant that China applied external standards, practice, and incentives to shape the domestic landscape, favoring efficiency over equality.

The world that China has tried to enter and engage, however, is far from ideal. The notion of global governance is riddled with contradictions, if not traps, in the eyes and minds of the Chinese. The issues of who should govern whom and what, as well as how to govern, remain elusive. Furthermore, the ultimate goal of the West appears to be the conversion of the non-West to a one-size-fits-all model of Western democracy and the free market. The concepts of governance, leadership, and dominance, therefore, are West-centric with many blind spots regarding the non-West, including China.

Despite the challenges of joining the international system, China has gradually integrated itself into the world's governing bodies, including the UN and many other forums. Within these institutions, China has transformed itself from a passive participant in the early years to a more active player. The so-called rise of China means, to a large degree, a gradual process of learning about and integrating itself into international governing institutions. In the new millennium, the concept, scope, and methods of global governance have been extensively discussed by the policy and academic community in China. In the ten years between 2004 and 2013, Chinese scholars published more than 200 articles on global governance. Various think-tanks have invested huge resources into the subject. The Chinese Academy of Social Sciences (CASS), for example, started a multi-year project, "The Strategic Environment and Choices for China's Participation in Global Governance [中国参与全球治理的战略环境与战略选择]." Following the 2008 financial crisis, the People's University in Beijing launched a forum for think-tanks for G-20 countries.[14] The Translation Bureau of the Chinese Communist Party [中共中央编译局] also set up a Center for Global Governance and Developmental Strategy [全球治理与发展战略研究中心].[15] Similar think-tanks have been created around China by both government agencies and institutions of higher learning to the point that the official *People's Daily* declared in late July 2014 that China is now entering a period of "think-tank spring." Most of these research centers and institutions focus on global governance issues such as economic development, the environment, sustainable development, renewable energy, finance, trade, etc.[16]

By late 2015, the Chinese political elite had embraced global governance,[17] only to be surprised by the West's regression to populism, nativism, protectionism, and anti-foreigner/immigrant sentiments (Brexit, Trumpism, etc.). Beijing nonetheless strengthened its commitment to globalization and global governance. President Xi Jinping highlighted these themes during his speech at the Davos Economic Forum in January 2017,[18] in sharp contrast to the America-first motif of President Trump's inauguration speech a month later.[19]

Russia's Exit to Where?

170 years before the 74-year-old Soviet Union broke apart, US President James Madison prophesied:

> I cannot but think…that the future growth of Russia…[is] not a little overrated. Without a civiliz[ing] of the hordes nominally extending the Russian dominion over so many latitudes and longitudes, they will add little to her real force, if they do not detract from it; and in the event of their civiliz[ing], and consequent increase, the overgrown empire, as in so many preceding instances, must fall into separate and independent states.[20]

Madison's prophecy, however, never factored in the unprecedented scale and style of the Soviet implosion, particularly in three areas. One was that it happened not because of its systemic exhaustion through over-expansion but mainly as a result of the decisions, and indecision, of its political elite. It was also the first time in history that an empire had collapsed while in possession of tens of thousands of nuclear weapons. Lastly, what collapsed was a separate trading system outside the West. Once Vladimir Lenin took Russia out of World War I, the country never really attempted to rejoin international society until 74 years later in the wake of its implosion. In between, it created and managed its own trading system with other Warsaw Pact members.

Despite the many deficiencies of this centralized and bureaucratic system, the Soviet Union became a superpower rivaling the US, particularly in the area of strategic weapons. This was at a time when Mao's China was either bypassing (in 1958) or later dismantling (in 1966–1976) central bureaucracies. The trajectory of Soviet development was linear in comparison with China's roller-coaster development under Mao. Indeed, many Chinese analysts who emerged out of the Cultural Revolution (1966–1976) found that the Soviet Union was faring much better than China both politically and economically, and thought that China should, therefore, revert to the "good old days" of the 1950s when it briefly adopted many features of the Soviet administrative-command system.

The exit from the Soviet system turned out to be painful and costly for Russia. The Western-style political experiment (Gorbachev's *glasnost* and *perestroika*) and economic transition (Yeltsin's "shock therapy") proved to be at once "romantic" and tragic as the Soviet empire disintegrated. The rise of Vladimir Putin as a strong leader 17 years ago proved the maxim that social chaos produces strong leaders [乱世出英雄]. In between, the Russians fought hyperinflation,[21] two bloody wars in Chechnya,[22] recurring terrorism, the loss of identity,[23] and finally reemerged as a reasonably strong major power at the 2014 Sochi Olympics, only to be frustrated by the Ukraine crisis with its Western "partners."[24]

Russia's internal transition from a centralized, stable, and static mode of governance to its sudden death followed a totally different trajectory from China' rebuilding process. Russia has had to devote considerable attention and resources to addressing the problems of political transition, and therefore, has prioritized "high politics" in its engagement with the outside world. In turn, NATO expansion,[25] and to a lesser extent EU enlargement, have compelled Moscow to maintain a geostrategic outlook, often at the expense of an economically oriented developmental strategy.

Global Governance and Two Newcomers

Regardless of the different processes, postures, and priorities in China and Russia's integration with the existing international system, the two large Eurasian powers have significantly adapted themselves to its institutions and various regional multilateral forums. These include the IMF,

World Bank, APEC, WTO, G-20, nuclear security summits,[26] and the two "six party talks" on the nuclearization of the DPRK (from 2003) and Iran (since 2006). Without China and Russia's adaptation to and participation in global institutions, however uncomfortable, the world would be a very different place. But engagement has yielded mixed results for their respective interests.

Russia's Unrequited Love?

As a security-oriented country, Russia seems more interested in, and perhaps capable of, interacting with multilateral forums for global security governance. This is no surprise because Russia is one of the world's two nuclear superpowers. Aside from participating in the two six-party talks, Moscow has also been more proactive than Beijing on broader issues of military and civilian nuclear security. In 2006, Putin and Bush initiated the Global Initiative to Combat Nuclear Terrorism (GICNT), which now includes 82 member-states. The mission of the GICNT is to strengthen global capacity to prevent, detect, and respond to nuclear terrorism by conducting multilateral activities that strengthen the plans, policies, procedures, and interoperability of partner nations.[27]

Russia's more proactive posture on nuclear security governance is not just a matter of expertise developed through its Cold War arms control negotiations with the West. More importantly, it perceives such governance as imperative at a time when Russia is much weaker in terms of both comprehensive national power and military capabilities than in Soviet times. Rules-based international security mechanisms, therefore, would alleviate its security concerns. For the same reasons, Moscow has also gone beyond Beijing in committing itself to several global security mechanisms such as the Proliferation Security Initiative, a US-led group that attempts to prevent the trade of weapons of mass destruction[28]; the Missile Technology Control Regime (MTCR)[29]; and the Treaty on Open Skies, which allows NATO countries and former Soviet states to carry out aerial reconnaissance over each other's territory. Russia has also ratified the Comprehensive Nuclear Test Ban Treaty (CTBT), which China has yet to do.

Beyond engaging these security mechanisms, Russia's post-Cold War cooperation with NATO had been quite fruitful as the two sides explored more meaningful ties. In 1994, Russia joined NATO's Partnership for Peace program. And in May 2002, the NATO-Russia Council was created during the NATO summit in Rome. It envisaged cooperation in many areas of common interest, ranging from fighting terrorism to joint military exercises, personnel training, and Afghanistan.

Occasionally, Moscow's efforts to integrate Russia into global and regional institutions exceeded the expectations of the West. In 2000, the newly elected Russian president Vladimir Putin went so far as to seek Russian membership of NATO, but was "rebuffed" by Madeleine Albright, then US Secretary of State. Western officials and media tended to dismiss Putin's "suggestions" as "mischievous,"[30] particularly against the backdrop of the second round of NATO enlargement in May 2000. But Putin's interest in NATO membership may have been more serious than is often credited. In 2001, he revealed a declassified Soviet document indicating that Soviet leaders had asked to join NATO in 1954, a year after Stalin's death and a year before the Warsaw Pact was established.[31] Putin also offered to jointly develop a missile defense system with NATO and the United States. His bold statement shocked Beijing because just a few days before, the Russian Security Council Secretary, Sergey Ivanov, assured the press that a compromise with the U.S. regarding missile defense was "unlikely."[32]

Much has happened since those "good old," and perhaps more "innocent," days when the Russian political elite was still toying with the idea of joining the West. Then, US President George W. Bush was perhaps not too far from the truth when he claimed to see into Putin's soul at their June 2001 summit in Slovenia.[33] Putin was ready to cooperate and reciprocate, perhaps more than the West expected. Three months later, he was the first foreign head of state to call the US president after the 9/11 terrorist attacks, and this was followed by Russia's active intelligence-sharing and logistical support for NATO forces in Afghanistan. To the Kremlin's dismay, Bush's response to Putin's overtures was to withdraw three months later from the ABM Treaty, a cornerstone of strategic stability between the United States and Russia.

At a more fundamental level, it is in Russia's interests to maintain a working relationship with the West, particularly the United States. This is why Putin chose not to immediately retaliate against the sanctions imposed by the Obama administration at the end of 2016, although he eventually did following US Congress approval of additional sanctions in July 2017.[34] The Kremlin's unprecedented restraint was further highlighted by its continuing cooperation with Washington on Syria, Iran, North Korea, and counter-terrorism, all areas which have direct implications for global governance with the West.[35]

Non-proliferation and Arms Control: Beijing Style

Compared to Moscow's active participation in global security institutions, China's involvement has been more selective. It has been active in the two six-party talks. It also joined the Nuclear Suppliers Group (NSG) in 2004, and signed the Biological Weapons Convention and Chemical Weapons Convention. Together with Russia, it participated in the removal and elimination of chemical weapons in Syria. Perhaps the biggest difference between China and Russia is that Beijing has not engaged with Washington in arms control negotiations—for several reasons. One is China's unique nuclear posture. China has never provided details about its nuclear arsenal. Various Western estimates indicate a range of 80–300 warheads ready for deployment and in storage. The 2008 Chinese Defense White Paper uses "lean and effective" to describe China's small strategic force.[36] It should be noted that the decision to maintain a small nuclear force was made in the late 1950s and early 1960s when China was plagued by economic constraints. In the twenty-first century when China's economy is much larger and more robust, the size of its strategic forces remains limited (Fig. 9.1).[37]

China's low inventory of nuclear weapons has been accompanied by its declared No First Use (NFU) strategy. It maintains that all nuclear-weapon states should adopt NFU, as China has done, in order to lower their nuclear thresholds, leading eventually to an international legal accord on NFU. In this context, China considers its NFU policy as its closest connection with nuclear arms control.

China's low-inventory, high-threshold nuclear posture has, however, come under question domestically following the 2016 US presidential

Country	**Active**	**Total**
United States	1650	6600
Russia	1710	6800
UK	120	215
France	280	300
China	270	270

Fig. 9.1 Nuclear Warheads—the five nuclear-weapon states under the NPT (2017) (*Source* Kristensen and Norris 2017)

election. A heated debate erupted in reaction to Trump's "strategic arrogance" towards China and his Russia-warm, China-cold rhetoric on trade, Taiwan, and nuclear armaments. Some commentators have called for a Russian-style nuclear deterrence—high-inventory and low-threshold—so that China is both respected and feared.[38] In this context, China's mobile DF-31AG ICBM, which made its debut in the PLA's ninetieth anniversary military parade on 30 July 2017, has been described as a much needed remedy to narrow the "missile gap" between China's minimalist nuclear inventory and the huge US and Russian stockpiles.[39]

But even with a much larger nuclear inventory, it is unlikely Beijing will reverse its current NFU nuclear strategy. In this regard, China's long-term security can, and perhaps should, be enhanced at the global level through a nuclear arms control regime comprising three major components: multilateralism, differentiated responsibility and reduction, and maintenance of strategic stability. For Beijing, the UN's role in this area should be maximized, and the legitimate and reasonable security concerns of all countries should be respected and accommodated. Accordingly, China remains active in the review process for the Treaty on the Non-proliferation of Nuclear Weapons (NPT), particularly the 8th NPT Review Conference in 2010. It advocates the early entry into force of the CTBT, and early negotiations on the Fissile Material Cut-off Treaty at the Conference on Disarmament in Geneva. Regionally, China supports establishing nuclear weapon-free zones in the ASEAN area and Central Asia, as well as efforts to create a nuclear weapon-free zone in the Middle East. As part of the requirements of the Preparatory Commission of the CTBT, it has set up 12 international monitoring stations and laboratories including six primary seismological monitoring stations, three radionuclide stations, the Beijing Radionuclide Laboratory, the China National Data Center, and one infrasound station.

More generally, China insists that the countries possessing the largest nuclear arsenals should bear primary responsibility for nuclear disarmament. This should be done in a verifiable, irreversible, and legally-binding manner. When conditions are "appropriate," other nuclear-weapon states including China may join in multilateral negotiations on nuclear disarmament.

Finally, Beijing, together with Moscow, maintains that the US global missile defense (MD) program is detrimental to international strategic stability, in particular China's minimalist deployment policy. It fears that other nuclear powers may be inclined to strike first at China if they believe their MD can neutralize its retaliatory capabilities.

In an asymmetrical world of nuclear overkill capacity, preemption, and nuclear first use, China's nuclear goals are not altruistic. Nevertheless, its NFU policy offers the least provocative and most direct path to nuclear disarmament.[40]

China's WTO Wonder vs. US' TPP Exit

In contrast to Russia's predominantly security-based engagement with the world, Beijing's global outreach has been largely economic. Since its WTO membership in 2001, it has become the world's largest trading nation with a total volume of $4.28 trillion in 2017 (exports totaling US$2.36 trillion and imports amounting to US$1.92 trillion).[41]

In 2013, Beijing launched its ambitious Belt and Road Initiative (BRI) for trade, connectivity, and infrastructure development across the Eurasian continent and beyond. This was followed immediately by the creation of the Asian Infrastructure Investment Bank (AIIB). By early 2017, Chinese companies had made over $50 billion of investment under the BRI, and are expected to invest $750 billion around the world in the next five years (2017–2021).[42]

Fifteen years after it entered the WTO, a more involved China in global trade is alarming both liberal-internationalists (Ferguson), who claim that China is the only winner in the West's liberal world order,[43] and Trump, the populist-nativist who prescribes "America first" policies instead of US global leadership.

Washington's earlier response to the phenomenal growth of Chinese economic activity around the world was to create a separate and exclusive trading system (Trans-Pacific Partnership—TPP) outside the WTO without China. In May 2013 when China finally expressed interest in joining the TPP talks, some "insiders" reacted with skepticism and raised concerns about its "ill-intentions" to "spoil" the TPP. As James Parker observed in *The Diplomat*, "one of the most important aspects of the TPP may well be its role as a divider, with who may be excluded perhaps as important as who may end up on the inside."[44]

America's efforts to exclude China from the TPP seemed to go hand in hand with its heavy lobbying to prevent allies from joining the AIIB. For Washington, the AIIB threatened to displace the US-created and US-dominated global financial institutions (WB, IMF and the

Asian Development Bank, or ADB). However, the US blocking effort crumbled on 12 March 2015 when the United Kingdom broke ranks by announcing its decision to join the AIIB. It was followed by Italy, Germany, and France.[45]

The real purpose of the TPP was less economic and more political or geopolitical. In contrast to Washington's us vs. them approach to multilateral trade regimes, Beijing's AIIB and BRI are inclusive—conceptually, structurally, and operationally—and open to anyone including the United States and its allies. Xi Jinping declared as early as 2014 that "[a]ll countries are welcome to board the train of China's development ... [e]ither for a fast ride or for a free ride."[46] China's overarching goal has been to sustain, and even broaden and deepen, the existing liberal mechanism of reciprocity and connectivity, albeit with some reforms. In this regard, TPP's demise on the first day of Trump's presidency may have unwittingly saved the global trading system from further fragmentation and politicization.

Russia and China's Road to the World: An Assessment

Washington's unsuccessful opposition to the AIIB won't be the last obstacle to "outsiders" in the current global governing system. There are also broader and long-term trends outside the West. Decades after their respective reforms led them away from orthodox communism, Russia and China have taken different paths toward the West-centered global system and its governance. The degree and direction of their participation in existing institutions, however, have been largely determined by their unique national characteristics. This is despite the many similarities between them and their expanding strategic partnership.

A recent *Global Times* commentary argues that, for Russia, there is no "life-or-death" [生死攸关的] need to open itself to the outside world, given its huge territory (more than two times larger than China's), abundant natural resources, its early industrialization, and a population one tenth that of China's. In other words, Russia can always retreat into itself if necessary. China's reforms, however, dictate that it must open itself to the outside world for technology, modern concepts, and, increasingly, natural resources. Otherwise, it cannot even feed itself. As a result, China's modernization means a "one-way" ticket to global engagement, no matter how difficult the process is.

The *Global Times* piece argues, further, that Putin's recent assertiveness, although frustrating to Washington, has yet to yield any strategic payoff. By contrast, China's cooperative efforts, huge trade volume, and emphasis on a "new type of major power relationship" have considerably diluted elements of contradiction with Washington, and enabled Beijing to avoid the "historical traps" of confrontation between rising and declining powers. That said, the rise of China has been a gradual process, and its approach not always perfect. Foreign engagement has forced domestic changes to the point that the phrase "reform and opening up to the outside world" [改革开放] should be reversed as "foreign engagement and reform" [开放改革].[47]

The *Global Times* assessment may be overly generalized, though it is far from the deterministic structural Marxism of the 1970s[48] and the more recent geopolitical "code" discourse of the twenty-first century[49] with its ideational/civilizational fatalism. But it does encapsulate the divergent regional economic strategies of Russia and China, specifically the former's Eurasian Economic Union (EEU) and the latter's BRI. Russia's reaction to the BRI has been a complex learning and adapting process shaped by both internal and external stimuli. Moscow's reaction to Xi Jinping's September 2013 launch of the BRI in Kazakhstan was cautious at best,[50] despite Xi's promised "three Nos": no interference in the internal affairs of Central Asian countries; no attempt to seek a dominant role in regional affairs; and no desire to carve out a sphere of influence.[51] Despite agreement in May 2015 to develop a partnership between the EEU and the Silk Road Economic Belt (SREB)—part of the BRI—Putin seems set to retain Russia's bottom line. "We agree only to those proposals that benefit us," he told journalists at the Beijing BRI Forum in May 2017. He stated further that "… all … existing integration structures in Eurasia and any new initiatives [should] be based on universal and generally recognized foundations. They must also take into account the specifics of the member states' national development models and be developed openly and transparently."[52] At the same time, "[i]t would be a shame not to make use of the opportunities this cooperation creates. Russia is open for cooperation with all countries, and today China is demonstrating its openness to the entire world."[53]

It remains to be seen how the EEU and BRI interact over the next few years. Judging by the current trajectory, the BRI is set to expand, regardless of what Russia does. Chinese decision-makers have been careful to manage Moscow's sensitivities over the BRI, in sharp contrast to Washington's cruder and often hostile approach toward Russia.[54] Putin remains popular in the Chinese public space, being seen as a strong and capable head of state as well as a symbol of masculinity. For Moscow, there is perhaps no alternative but to embrace the BRI given an unfriendly West and recent US sanctions imposed by the Trump administration. Between China's open-ended and promising BRI and the West's theoretically open but actually closed "liberal" international order, Moscow's choice of the BRI is both rational and practical. For the West, the question is to what extent this economic partnership will lead to further geopolitical and even military alignment between the two large Eurasian powers.

Beijing and Moscow: Reluctant "Allies"?

2016 may well prove a turning point for the liberal international order and its governance, or ungovernability. This is not necessarily because of the West's retreat from its long-held leadership (Brexit and Trumpism), but also its growing concern over an emergent Sino-Russian "alliance." There are plenty of signs of just such a partnership: the "best ever" relationship repeatedly asserted by both sides; their "comprehensive partnership of strategic cooperation" (CPSP, 全面战略协作伙伴关系)[55]; frequent summits; and the growing institutionalization of inter-governmental exchanges. Military-military ties, too, are progressing toward closer interoperability. Aside from regular exercises at the bilateral and multilateral (Shanghai Cooperation Organization—SCO) level, the two militaries held their first ever joint command/headquarters missile defense exercise on May 26–28, 2016, in response to the accelerated deployment of the US missile defense systems in Europe and Asia. Code-named "Aerospace Security 2016," the drill was held in Moscow at the Aerospace Defense Forces Central Scientific Research Institute, with the second one was conducted on December 11–15, 2017 in the PLA Air Command Institute in Beijing.[56] Almost every year since 2012, the two navies have conducted their "Joint-Sea" exercises, with recent drills taking place in sensitive areas such as the South China Sea (September 2016) and the Baltic Sea (July and September 2017). Russian arms transfers to China have also turned the corner with the sale of high-end items such as the Su-35 multi-role fighter/bomber and S400 SAM batteries.

There is no question that the perceived challenges to their respective national interests and strategic space by Western alliances seem to have led to more proactive and coordinated actions between Beijing and Moscow. Both sides, however, continue to resist a formal alliance, which could impose binding obligations vis-à-vis a third party. This restraint was evident during the Ukraine crisis when there was much talk in Russia and China about elevating the strategic partnership into an alliance. Putin, however, reiterated many times during 2014 that Russia sought no such thing, while other senior Russian figures were similarly wary about incurring the obligations of a formal alliance. In his July 2014 visit to China, Presidential Administration Head Sergei Ivanov stated that Russia and China had no intention of building a military alliance, and that Sino-Russian mutual trust had no connection with Ukraine.

The scholarly community in China has been debating the pros and cons of an alliance. While some argue that Beijing should not get too close to Moscow lest this alarm the West, the consensus seems to be that the current strategic partnership—short of a formal alliance—is just right.

At a more historical and philosophical level, China and Russia remain reluctant to move toward a formal alliance. During the Cold War, bilateral ties between Moscow and Beijing had swung from heart-melting "honeymoon" (1949–1959) to heart-breaking "divorce"/confrontation (1960–1989). The Sino-Soviet alliance was saturated with ideological components that first exaggerated the commonalities between the two communist giants in the 1950s and then the differences in the 1960s and 1970s. Neither was normal. Both positions were highly emotional and even irrational, preventing pragmatic compromise and conflict management. It is not surprising that the process of normalizing Sino-Russian relations began with minimizing and eventually neutralizing the ideological factor. Without a binding alliance and the highly intrusive influence of ideology, China and Russia were able to develop and manage their relations with greater pragmatism and flexibility.

Such a healthy "distance" between Beijing and Moscow and mutual tolerance of each other's differences constitute the basis for the "new major power relationship" [新型大国关系] between them. Its strategic, historical, and ideational foundation is, therefore, not easily influenced either by Trump's Russia-friendly rhetoric[57] or by any US attempt to exploit differences between Moscow and Beijing.[58] The perceived loss of the US pivotal position in the current "not-so-strategic" triangle[59] may be rectified only if Washington reins back its interventionist impulse, which has cost it so much and for so long.

In the final analysis, a genuine alliance between Moscow and Beijing, similar to NATO and other US-led groupings, is neither likely nor necessary in the short to medium term. That is, unless the core interests of both are seen to be jeopardized at the same time by the same third party. The Obama administration fell into this trap. By punishing Russia and hedging China with a largely militarized Asia pivot, it drove them into each other's arms. Six months into office, Trump was boxed in by the beltway establishment with a new sanctions bill to punish Russia. His attempts at a rapprochement with Moscow were (and continue to be) undermined by growing anti-Kremlin sentiment in Washington. The new sanctions bill against Moscow, which Trump reluctantly signed, has only driven Russia further toward China.

A century after the outbreak of World War I, a hypothetical question remains: what if China and Russia do form a tighter and interlocking alliance, similar to those of the pre-World War I European blocs that directly led to war in the fateful summer of 1914? Moscow and Beijing seem more keenly aware of the likely consequences of such a move than their Western partners. By not allying with each other, they are actually slowing the march down that fateful path to hell in the era of weapons of mass destruction.

In this connection, what James Madison prophesied almost two hundred years ago about the constantly expanding Russian empire is perhaps more applicable to today's NATO and EU, at least from the Russian and Chinese perspectives. The West's tireless expansion to the east—aggravated by Obama's militarized "rebalancing" to the Asia-Pacific, Trump's idiosyncratic impulses, the enhanced freedom of action of the US military—has resulted in new space to conquer and defend. Few, if any, in the West seemed to be bothered by the instability, chaos, failed states, terrorism, and refugee flows in much of the non-West. But excessive Western interventionism, resisted by Russia and China in the post-Cold War decades, has generated the ultimate blowback.[60] During 2016–2017, populism, nativism, hardcore nationalism, xenophobia, anti-globalization, and anti-establishment forces have engulfed the West itself. The alleged "loss" of the liberal international order to China and Russia[61] is perhaps the latest addition to those mythical historical "losses": China (and McCarthy's witch-hunt), Vietnam,[62] Russia,[63] Iraq,[64] Libya,[65] Syria, the US-always-won-the-war-but-lost-the-peace,[66] and the "loss" of the 2016 US presidential election to Russia. Welcome to a brave new world of ungovernability and irresponsibility.

Notes

1. Kagan (2017).
2. Ferguson and Zakaria (2017). For a more thorough discussion of the "lost" liberal order, see Foreign Affairs Special Issue "What Was the Liberal Order? The World We May Be Losing", March 2017, https://www.foreignaffairs.com/system/files/pdf/anthologies/2017/b0033_0.pdf.
3. The first, and optimistic, "endism" discourse was articulated by Francis Fukuyama in his, "The End of History?" from 1989.
4. Ferguson insisted that China is the winner of the global liberal order, which is being lost. See Ferguson and Zakaria debate, Lo (2015), and Kagan (2017).
5. Isaac (2016).
6. The notion of "governing deficit" [全球治理赤字] was first used by scholar Jin Canrong in 2017, see Jin (2017).
7. Schwartz (2017).
8. Bush (1990).
9. A notable exception was Z, "To the Stalin Mausoleum", published in Daedalus in 1990. Mr. Z's real name was Martin Malia, a University of California Berkeley historian. See Z (1990).
10. Blin and Marin (2007).
11. James and Soguk (2014).
12. EUISS and US NIC (2010), p. 17.
13. See also Barry Naughton, Growing Out of the Plan: Chinese Economic Reform, 1978–1993 (1996).
14. "People's University established think tank for G20 summit [人民大学发起建立 G20 智库年会机制] September 3, China News Net [中国新闻网], http://www.chinanews.com/gn/2014/09-03/6559886.shtml.
15. www.cctb.net/zzjg/yjzx/qqzl/.
16. "People's University's think tank: a brave new world" [人民大学智库建设令人耳目一新], *People's Daily*, July 24, 2014, http://news.ruc.edu.cn/archives/85956.
17. "Focusing on Global Governance: Politburo's Study Sessions" [中共中央政治局集体学习两次聚焦"全球治理"], Strategy and Policy Forum, 8 October 2016, https://freewechat.com/a/MzAxMDQ5ODMxOQ==/2654743486/1; Jin (2017), op. cit.
18. Xi Jinping (2017).
19. Trump (2017).
20. Madison to Richard Rush, November 20, 1821, in David Mattern et al. (2013), pp. 420–422.
21. More than 2000% in 1992. See Remington (2010), p. 388.
22. 1994–1996 and 1999–2009.

23. Billington (2004).
24. Russian Foreign Minister Lavrov's habitual reference to Western Europeans and Americans.
25. Soviet leaders were promised that NATO would not expand to the East, according to Joshua Shifrinson. See Shifrinson (2016).
26. Russia and China participated the three nuclear summits in 2010 (Washington), 2012 (Seoul) and 2014 (Hague). In November 2014, however, Russia informed the US that it won't attend the 2016 summit in Chicago, See *Reuters* (2014).
27. US Department of State.
28. US Department of State (2014).
29. See Missile Technology Control Regime website http://mtcr.info/.
30. Traynor (2001).
31. Traynor (2001), op. cit.
32. Yu (2000).
33. Kempe (2007).
34. Moscow expelled 755 American diplomats, reducing US diplomatic staff in Russia to 455 people, the number of Russian diplomats left in the US after Washington expelled 35 staff in December 2016. See Mohammed (2017).
35. Pitalev (2017).
36. State Council (2009).
37. Various Western sources attribute China's small number of China's nuclear warheads to China's limited stocks of military plutonium, which is estimated to be adequate for a few to several hundred new warheads, see Kulacki (2011).
38. *Global Times* (2017). For details, see Bin Yu (2017).
39. Xi Yazhou (2017).
40. State Council (2011).
41. Liu (2018).
42. Xi Jinping (2017).
43. Ferguson and Zakaria (2017), op. cit.
44. Parker (2013).
45. Mahbubani (2015), Higgins and Sanger (2015), p. A4.
46. Xi Jinping (2014).
47. *Global Times* (2015).
48. Wallerstein (1974).
49. Katzenstein and Weygandt (2017).
50. Bin Yu (2014).
51. Xi Jinping (2013), *Global Times* (2013).
52. Putin (2017a).

53. Putin (2017b).
54. In his last press conference as US president, Obama said that Russia "doesn't produce anything that anybody wants to buy, except oil, gas and arms." See Vielma (2016).
55. For an analytical comparison of various kinds of China's strategic partnership relationships and evolution of the Sino-Russian partnership relations, see Zhang and Ma (2014).
56. *People's Net* (2017).
57. *The Economist* (2017).
58. See a recent research project by NBR, Chase et al. (2017).
59. The Nixon-Kissinger type of strategic triangular politics seems to have been replaced by a "not-so-strategic" triangle, in which games played by the three parties are non-zero-sum. Part of the reason is that Russia and China have developed extensive ties with the international order, no matter how complicated these can sometimes be. Decades after their initial departure from communist orthodoxy, both Beijing and Moscow have enormous stakes in the existing world order, though in different areas and to different degrees. For the concept of the "not-so-strategic" triangle, see Bin Yu (2004), p. 5.
60. Johnson (2000).
61. Ferguson and Zakaria (2017), op. cit.
62. Galloway (1998).
63. "The 'Who Lost Russia' Debate", see *Newsweek* (1992).
64. Sky (2014).
65. Chollet and Fishman (2015).
66. LaFeber (2008), p. 1.

Literature

Billington, James. 2004. *Russia in Search of Itself.* Washington, D.C.: Woodrow Wilson Center Press.

Blin, Arnaud, and Gustavo Marin. 2007. *Rethinking Global Governance.* Paris: Forum for a New World Governance.

Bush, George H.W. 1990. Address Before a Joint Session of the Congress on the Persian Gulf Crisis and the Federal Budget Deficit, Bush Presidential Library and Museum, September 11. http://bushlibrary.tamu.edu/research/public_papers.php?id=2217&year=1990&month=9.

Chase, Michael S., Evan S. Medeiros, J. Stapleton Roy, Eugene B. Rumer, Robert Sutter, and Richard Weitz. 2017. *Russia–China Relations: Assessing Common Ground and Strategic Fault lines*, NBR Special Report #66, July, National Bureau of Asian Research, Washington, D.C.

Chollet, Derek H., and Ben Fishman. 2015. Who Lost Libya? Obama's Intervention in Retrospect. *Foreign Affairs*, May/June. https://www.foreignaffairs.com/articles/libya/2015-04-20/who-lost-libya.

EUISS, and US NIC. 2010. *Global Governance 2025: At a Critical Juncture*, The EU Institute for Security Studies and US National Intelligence Council, Paris, December. Available at http://www.iss.europa.eu/uploads/media/Global__Governance_2025.pdf.

Ferguson, Niall, and Fareed Zakaria. 2017. The Future of Geopolitics: Be It Resolved, the Liberal International Order Is Over…, The Munk Debates, April 28. http://munkdebates.com/.

Fukuyama, Francis. 1989. The End of History? *The National Interest* 16 (Summer): 3–18.

Galloway, Joseph L. 1998. Who Lost Vietnam? *The New York Times*, September 20. http://www.nytimes.com/books/98/09/20/reviews/980920.20gallowt.html.

Global Times. 2013. 社评:在中亚"三不", 中国拒绝帝国思维 [China's Three Nos for Central Asia: China Rejects Imperialist Mindset]. *Global Times*, Editorial, September 10. http://opinion.huanqiu.com/editorial/2013-09/4339509.html.

Global Times. 2015. 中俄不同开放度对应各自国情 [Degree of China and Russia's Opening to the Outside World Determined by Their Respective Domestic Situation], March 20. http://opinion.huanqiu.com/editorial/2015-03/5959919.html.

Global Times. 2017. 中国的军费和战略核力量都还不够 [Deficit: China's Military Spending and Nuclear Forces]. 环球时报 [*Global Times*], January 24. http://opinion.huanqiu.com/editorial/2017-01/10010425.html.

Higgins, Andrew, and David Sanger. 2015. 3 European Powers Say They Will Join China-Led Bank. *New York Times*, March 18.

Isaac, Jeffrey C. 2016. The Politics of Global Disorder. *Perspectives on Politics* 14 (1): 1–4.

James, Paul, and Nevzat Soguk (eds.). 2014. *Globalization and Politics, Volume I, Global Political and Legal Governance*. Thousand Oaks, CA: SAGE Publications.

Jin, Canrong. 2017. 金灿荣: 未来10年的世界大变局 [Mega Changes in the World for the Next Decade]. 观察者网 [*The Observer*], August 1. http://www.guancha.cn/JinCanRong/2017_08_01_420867_s.shtml.

Johnson, Chalmers. 2000. *Blowback: The Costs and Consequences of American Empire*. New York: Metropolitan Books.

Kagan, Robert. 2017. Backing into World War III. *Foreign Policy*, February 6. http://foreignpolicy.com/2017/02/06/backing-into-world-war-iii-russia-china-trump-obama/?utm_content=bufferd07ea&utm_medium=social&utm_source=facebook.com&utm_campaign=buffer.

Katzenstein, Peter J., and Nicole Weygandt. 2017. Mapping Eurasia in an Open World: How the Insularity of Russia's Geopolitical and Civilizational Approaches Limits Its Foreign Policies. *Perspectives on Politics* 15 (2): 428–442.

Kempe, Frederick. 2007. Bush Can Take Another Look Into Putin's 'Soul'. *Bloomberg*, June 6. http://www.bloomberg.com/apps/news?pid=newsarchive&sid=aWrjoiCIMmL8.

Kristensen, Hans M., and Robert S. Norris. 2017. Status of World Nuclear Forces, Federation of American Scientists, December. https://fas.org/issues/nuclear-weapons/status-world-nuclear-forces/.

Kulacki, Gregory. 2011. *China's Nuclear Arsenal: Status and Evolution*. Cambridge, MA: Union of Concerned Scientists, October.

LaFeber, Walter. 2008. *America, Russia, and the Cold War, 1945–2006*, 10th ed. New York: McGraw-Hill.

Liu. (ed.). 2018. China's Foreign Trade up 14.2 Pct in 2017. *Xinhua*, January 12. http://www.xinhuanet.com/english/2018-01/12/c_136890444.htm.

Lo, Bobo. 2015. *Russia and the New World Disorder*. London, UK: Chatham House.

Mahbubani, Kishore. 2015. Why Britain Joining China-Led Bank Is a Sign of American Decline. *Huffington Post*, March 16. www.huffingtonpost.com/kishore-mahbubani/britain-china-bank-america-decline_b_6877942.html.

Mattern, David, et al. (eds.). 2013. *The Papers of James Madison*, Vol. 2. Charlottesville, VA: The University of Virginia Press.

Mohammed, Arshad. 2017. US Senate Looks to Have Ended Trump's Honeymoon with Russia. *Reuters*, July 29. http://www.atimes.com/article/us-senate-looks-ended-trumps-honeymoon-russia/.

Naughton, Barry. 1996. Growing Out of the Plan: Chinese Economic Reform, 1978–1993. Cambridge, UK: Cambridge University Press.

Newsweek. 1992. The 'Who Lost Russia' Debate. *Newsweek*, Staff, March 22. http://www.newsweek.com/who-lost-russia-debate-196204.

Parker, James. 2013. China and the TPP: The Trojan Horse Option. *The Diplomat*, September 24. http://thediplomat.com/2013/09/china-and-the-tpp-the-trojan-horse-option/.

People's Net. 2017. 中俄 '空天安全-2017'联合反导演习今日开启 [Sino-Russian 'Aerospace Security 2017' Joint Anti-Missile Drill Starts Today]. 人民网 [*People's Net*], December 11. http://military.people.com.cn/n1/2017/1211/c1011-29698446.html.

Pitalev, Iliya. 2017. Russia 'Sends Very Careful Message' to Trump by Targeting Obama-Era Sanctions. *Sputnik*, July 29. https://sputniknews.com/russia/201707291055987722-russia-us-sanctions-obama-trump/.

Putin, Vladimir. 2017a. Roundtable Meeting of Leaders at Belt and Road International Forum, Executive Office of the President of Russia, May 15. http://en.kremlin.ru/events/president/news/54496.

Putin, Vladimir. 2017b. Vladimir Putin Answered Media Questions Following a Working Visit to China, Executive Office of the President of Russia, May 15. http://en.kremlin.ru/events/president/news/54499.

Remington, Thomas. 2010. Politics in Russia. In *Comparative Politics Today: A World View*, Updated 9th ed., ed. Gabriel Almond. Boston: Pearson Education, Inc.

Reuters. 2014. Russia Told U.S. It Will Not Attend 2016 Nuclear Security Summit. *Reuters*, Staff, November 5. www.reuters.com/article/2014/11/05/us-nuclear-security-usa-russia-idUSKBN0IP24K20141105.

Schwartz, Ian. 2017. Trump: The World Is a Mess, I Inherited It, and I Will Fix It, Blog Posted from Joint News Conference with King Abdullah II of Jordan. *Real Clear Politics*, April 5. Available at www.realclearpolitics.com/video/2017/04/05/trump_the_world_is_a_mess_i_inherited_it_and_i_will_fix_it.html.

Shifrinson, Joshua. 2016. Deal or No Deal? The End of the Cold War and the U.S. Offer to Limit NATO Expansion. *International Security* 40 (Spring): 7–44.

Sky, Emma. 2014. Who Lost Iraq? And How to Get It Back. *Foreign Affairs*, June 24. https://www.foreignaffairs.com/articles/iraq/2014-06-24/who-lost-iraq.

State Council. 2009. *China's National Defense in 2008*. Beijing: State Council Information Office of the People's Republic of China, January 20. http://www.china.org.cn/government/whitepaper/node_7060059.htm.

State Council. 2011. *China's National Defense in 2010*. Beijing: State Council Information Office of the People's Republic of China, March 31. http://www.china.org.cn/government/whitepaper/node_7114675.htm.

The Economist. 2017. Donald Trump Seeks a Grand Bargain with Vladimir Putin. *The Economist*, Leader, February 11. www.economist.com/news/leaders/21716609-it-terrible-idea-donald-trump-seeks-grand-bargain-vladimir-putin.

Traynor, Ian. 2001. Soviets Tried to Join Nato in 1954. *The Guardian*, June 16. http://www.theguardian.com/world/2001/jun/17/russia.iantraynor.

Trump, Donald. 2017. Inaugural Address, January 20. https://www.whitehouse.gov/inaugural-address.

US Department of State. Global Initiative to Combat Nuclear Terrorism. https://www.state.gov/t/isn/c18406.htm.

US Department of State. 2014. Proliferation Security Initiative Participants, June 4. www.state.gov/t/isn/c27732.htm.

Vielma, Antonio José. 2016. Obama Says Russia Is a Smaller, Weaker Country than the US. *CNBC*, December 16. https://www.cnbc.com/2016/12/16/obama-says-russians-cant-change-us-or-weaken-us.html.

Wallerstein, Immanuel. 1974. The Rise and Future Demise of the World Capitalist System: Concepts for Comparative Analysis. *Comparative Studies in Society and History* 14 (4): 387–415.

Xi, Jinping. 2013. 习近平发表重要演讲 吁共建"丝绸之路经济带 [Xi Jinping's Speech Calling for Joint Construction of a 'Silk Road Economic Belt']. 中国新闻网 [*China News Net*], September 7. http://www.chinanews.com/gn/2013/09-07/5257748.shtml.

Xi, Jinping. 2014. Speech at the State Great Hural of Mongolia, August 22, Available at Chinese Ministry of Foreign Affairs Webpage. www.fmprc.gov.cn/mfa_eng/wjdt_665385/zyjh_665391/t1185662.shtml.

Xi, Jinping. 2017. Keynote at the World Economic Forum, Davos, Switzerland, January 17. https://www.weforum.org/agenda/2017/01/full-text-of-xi-jinping-keynote-at-the-world-economic-forum.

Xi, Yazhou. 2017. 八一 "实战化" 大阅兵中 "低调炫耀" 的部分 [The Less Visible Hardware in the August 1 Anniversary Parade]. 观察者网 [*The Observer*], July 31. http://www.guancha.cn/XiYaZhou/2017_07_31_420634_s.shtml.

Yu, Bin. 2000. China–Russian Relations: Strategic Distancing…or Else? *Comparative Connections* 2 (2). http://csis.org/files/media/csis/pubs/0002qchina_russia.pdf.

Yu, Bin. 2004. The Three Players: Moscow, Beijing, and Washington in the Era of Preemption. *Harvard International Review* 26 (2): 5.

Yu, Bin. 2014. Putin's Glory and Xi's Dream. *Comparative Connections* 15 (3). http://cc.csis.org/2014/01/putins-glory-xis-dream/.

Yu, Bin. 2017. Trilateral Politics: Trump Style. *Comparative Connections* 19 (1): 113–122. http://cc.csis.org/2017/05/trilateral-politics-trump-style/.

Z. 1990. To the Stalin Mausoleum. *Daedalus* 119 (1): 295–344.

Zhang, Lei, and Ma Jun [张雷、马骏]. 2014. 中俄关系为什么叫 "全面战略协作伙伴关系" [Why is Sino-Russian Relationship Called 'Comprehensive Partnership and Strategic Collaboration'], February 7. http://opinion.cntv.cn/2014/02/07/ARTI1391781363647600.shtml.

CHAPTER 10

Triangularism Old and New: China, Russia, and the United States

Stephen Blank

The concept of the strategic triangle comprising China, USSR or Russia, and the US originated in the 1970s. It stipulates that each party tries to manipulate the triangle in its favour, that is, to be closer to the other two sides than they are to each other.[1] However, this only works if the two closest players can pursue mutually reinforcing or at least congruent policies at the bilateral, regional, and global levels. If they are unable to achieve this, then they cannot maximize the benefits of the evolving triangular dynamic. Therefore, in order to grasp the triangular dynamic, this paper first analyses U.S. policy and then focuses on Sino-Russian relations regarding regional Asian security issues.

Triangular relationships are dynamic and unpredictable, and depend greatly on individual leaders. In 2012, Putin had already heralded pro-Chinese policies as Russia sought to "catch the wind of China's growth in its sails."[2] In 2016 Putin stated that,

This work was supported by the National Research Foundation of Korea Grant funded by the Korean Government [grant number NRF-2015S1A3A2046684].

S. Blank (✉)
American Foreign Policy Council, Silver Spring, MD, USA
e-mail: traininblank@aol.com

J. I. Bekkevold and B. Lo (eds.), *Sino-Russian Relations in the 21st Century*, https://doi.org/10.1007/978-3-319-92516-5_10

> As we know the Sino-Russia relationship is now at its best. We often call it the strategic partnership which I think is not only at a political level but also at the economic one. China is Russia's largest trading partner, although bilateral trade volumes have dropped a little due to the sluggish oil prices. To my delight, our cooperation has continued to diversify. Recently, trade volumes in high-tech and manufacturing fields have grown significantly. The large cooperation projects in aviation, aerospace, energy and nuclear power look promising. — We share common views in a series of international issues. Undoubtedly, it's a key factor in maintaining stability. We cherish the relationship with China and hope to further push it forward.[3]

Russia's deepening structural economic-political crisis paralleled and intensified Putin's policy, leading to another decade of stagnation from 2008–2017 and further decline relative to China. Consequently, the most critical element in Sino-Russian relations is the growing asymmetry of power between China and Russia in China's favour.[4] Indeed, Russia has frequently solicited China for a formal alliance. And China's practical response conforms to alliance dynamics even if it formally eschews alliances.

The hallmarks of this alliance dynamic are reversals of Russian policies to China's benefit, support for China on Asian regional issues, and Russia's asymmetrical dependence upon Chinese economic, political, and military support. Despite difficulties in economic issues and particularly in Central Asia, the evidence for all three hallmarks even in these domains is quite strong. Thus, to use Bismarck's metaphor, China is the rider and Russia the horse in this alliance. Indeed, by 2009 economic weakness forced Moscow had to reverse past policy and admit China into its plans for developing Russia's Far East.[5] And by 2012, analysts noticed China's ability to impose its agenda on Russia and gain disproportionate benefits from Russia while avoiding any lasting commitment to Russia's calls for an alliance.[6] This is even truer today.[7]

Therefore, the triangular concept currently reflects not a predictable trilateral relationship but an immensely volatile relationship among three states and at least for some U.S. analysts may no longer apply.[8] Meanwhile, this de facto if not formal Sino-Russian alliance derives from geopolitically and ideologically congruent perspectives aiming squarely at America's values, interests, and the world order it largely created. Admittedly, these are contentious claims for many, possibly most, analysts deny that an alliance is occurring or is sustainable.[9] They invoke Putin and Xi Jinping's statements against alliances.[10] Many also flatly deny any ideological congruence between China and Russia despite the solid evidence of congruent modes of self-presentation and of portraying contemporary international relations.[11] Nevertheless, analysts like Artem Lukin, Rens Lee, Gilbert Rozman, and this author believe the evidence clearly shows an evolving alliance along with bilateral ideological and strategic congruence.[12] Moreover, the actual evidence shows all the signs of an alliance. Indeed, Trenin admits China gets most if not all that it wants from China without a formal alliance.[13]

Since 2012, Putin has accelerated the development of this informal Sino-Russian alliance. He denies the existence of a potential China threat. Moscow and Beijing constantly reiterate that relations have never been better,[14] and that they are "natural partners and natural allies".[15] In the wake of the war in Ukraine, the Kremlin conducted an inter-agency study of potential risks of partnership with Beijing. The overall conclusion was that Moscow had little to fear from China. We have seen important Russian concessions to Chinese policies and interests that Moscow had hitherto resisted. These are evident in many areas of the relationship: arms sales, China equity in Russian energy and Arctic infrastructure projects, Chinese investment in Russia, Central Asia, Moscow's backing for Beijing on East Asian security issues, and even in strategic arms control, where the Kremlin no longer insists on the multilateralization (i.e., involvement of China) in disarmament negotiations with the United States.[16] Military cooperation has expanded, with joint naval operations in the Mediterranean in 2015 and the Baltic in 2017, and Russian participation in exercises in the South China Sea in 2016.[17] Moscow's support for a Chinese role in Syrian reconstruction also highlights a need for Beijing's support for its Middle Eastern policies.[18] Russian concessions accentuate China's already superior bilateral position, and Russia's growing dependence on Chinese economic, political, and military support.[19]

U.S. Policy

The Obama administration ignored Russia in Asia.[20] Neither did it take the Sino-Russian partnership seriously. Indeed, it favored China over Russia in Central Asia, notably supporting Beijing's Silk Road Economic Belt (SREB).[21] Whatever Russian threats Washington perceived were in Europe or Eurasia, not East Asia. As *The Economist* reported, "Barack Obama has blithely regarded Russia as an awkward regional power, prone to post-imperial spasms but essentially declining."[22]

American officials professed disappointment and surprise that Russia rejected Washington's liberal integrationist view of world politics, thereby displaying their tone deafness towards Russia.[23] Obama neither addressed the question of Sino-Russian collaboration nor exploited Russian concerns about China's growing nuclear and military capabilities.[24] Washington preferred dealing separately with each state rather than reckoning with their strategic partnership, which was founded in a shared resentment of Washington.

Obama rejected the strategic logic of the triangle and zero-sum politics embraced by Russia and China.[25] While Washington and Beijing viewed each other as their principal interlocutor on Asian if not global issues, the Obama White House made it clear that it needed Moscow's help only with Afghanistan and Iran, and shunned cooperation with Russia against ISIS.[26] Secretary of Defense Chuck Hagel's outline of U.S. defense policy in Asia to the 2013 Shangri-La Dialogue omitted to mention Russia at all, as if it was absent from Asia's strategic equation. [27] Instead of seeing it as a potential challenger to Chinese power in Asia or as a consequential Asian actor, Hagel implied that Russia was merely an instrumental regional actor. In the process, he dismissed out of hand Moscow's fundamental foreign policy project of securing recognition of its global great power status and primacy in Eurasia.[28] Obama's neglect of the Sino-Russian relationship precluded both cooperation with Russia in Asia and Chinese cooperation on Ukraine.

Trump's ascension to power portended major changes in the triangle. As one Russian commentator noted, Moscow hoped for a new era in Russo-US relations, in which Washington would focus on national interests rather than seek to expand U.S. global hegemony.[29] Other reports claimed that Trump's team had discussed rapprochement with Moscow, including the rollback of sanctions, in order to undermine the Sino-Russian partnership.[30] However, the domestic furor in the U.S. over the Trump campaign's contacts with Russia and subsequent attempts at cover-up has so poisoned domestic politics that there is no support for improved relations with Russia.[31] Indeed, sanctions have been reinforced and expanded.[32]

Meanwhile, Sino-American relations are deteriorating. Beijing predictably played Washington on North Korea. The Chinese will not coerce Pyongyang to abandon nuclear weapons, and their limited gestures have not persuaded anyone that US–China partnership is viable.[33] That said Beijing could achieve a genuine rapprochement with Washington without consulting Moscow. A new U.S.–China trade deal may not alleviate bilateral economic tensions,[34] but it could stimulate a renewed dialogue and strike at Russia's economic ties to Beijing, for example through increased U.S. LNG exports to China.[35]

Unsurprisingly, Asian allies and publics regard Trump as a "sucker," and have lost confidence in him and in U.S. policy more generally.[36] Russia, too, has little faith in U.S. policy.[37] America acts not strategically but reactively, and its policies show no sign of any strategic vision or coherence. Trump can neither control himself nor his administration, and is being pulled in opposite directions by his desire for cooperation with Russia and China, and impulses to lash out at them.[38]

Towards an Alliance: The Regional Dimension Basis of Sino-Russian Relations

Although a close Sino-Russian partnership predated events in Ukraine, before 2014 Moscow pursued an independent position on key Asian security issues and sought a reliable partnership with Washington. Today, however, the picture has changed. Clear movement towards a Sino-Russian alliance is discernible, despite visible tensions in their relations.[39] Russian commentators and officials view China's rise calmly and see no particular threats. More than ever, they are unlikely to downgrade ties with China in order to pursue an inconstant and fragile rapprochement with Washington.[40]

As Vasily Kashin has noted, Moscow and Beijing avoid using the term alliance but the relationship already far exceeds "neighborliness" or even "strategic partnership."[41] In 2014, Foreign Minister Lavrov remarked on the emergence of a new type of alliance, "not in the sense of tough bloc discipline when NATO was against the Warsaw Pact ... but [of] flexible network alliances."[42] This alliance need not be formally codified, but can remain a flexible alignment with room for separate, parallel, or convergent initiatives and even occasional disagreements.[43]

Since 2014, Moscow has sought such an alliance. In October that year, Putin described Russia and China as natural allies.[44] A month later, Defense Minister Sergei Shoigu contended that both countries not only faced U.S. threats in the Asia-Pacific but also U.S.-orchestrated "color revolutions" and Islamic terrorism. He called for enhanced cooperation in response, both bilaterally and within the Shanghai Cooperation Organization.[45] Shoigu identified "good-neighborly relations" with

China as key "to ensuring peace throughout the Eurasian continent and beyond."[46] This marked a reversal of previous Russian policy, which had sought to exclude the PLA from Central Asia and claim sole rights of military intervention in the region. Neither was it the only example of solicitation of an alliance with China. Putin recently noted that:

> As we had never reached this level of relations before, our experts have had trouble defining today's general state of our common affairs. It turns out that to say we have strategic cooperation is not enough anymore. This is why we have started talking about a comprehensive partnership and strategic collaboration. "Comprehensive" means that we work virtually on all major avenues; "strategic" means that we attach enormous inter–governmental importance to this work.[47]

This is too close for advocacy of an alliance to be coincidental. But the alliance Moscow seeks need not be formally codified like NATO or pre-World War I alliances. Rather this alliance can remain a de facto flexible alignment with room for separate, parallel, or convergent, initiatives or even occasional disagreements in keeping with Russian views on the contemporary world order.[48] This conforms to Kashin, Putin, and Lavrov's observations on the bilateral relationship's tendencies.[49] Michael Yahuda also observes that Russian elites very much favor-enhanced collaboration.

> Moscow believes that bolstering China's military position in East Asia is very much in Russian interests. As the official in charge of Russian arms exports stated in April 2015, "if we work in China's interests, that means we also work in our interests." In other words, the U.S.-led economic sanctions on Russia have made Sino-Russian strategic interests more congruent.[50]

More recently Russian Defense Minister Shoigu remarked that,

> Russia's strategic partner is the People's Republic of China. Bilateral military cooperation is developing actively. Primarily it is focused on the fight against international terrorism. Joint actions are regularly practiced during the military exercises Naval interaction and Peaceful Mission. The Russian Federation continues to prepare specialists for the People's Liberation Army of China. In total more than 3,600 Chinese servicemen have been trained in the universities of the Ministry of Defense of the Russian Federation.[51]

This solution meets China's refusal to join formal alliances and Chinese leaders' repeated calls upon Moscow to forge ever closer ties and cooperation regarding Asian and international security, support China's vital national interests, and even build a new world order based on. "global strategic stability."[52] It also allows Putin (and Xi Jinping) to pretend that there is not an alliance and that Russia is expanding its ties in Asia. Yet "Russia and China stick to points of view which are very close to each other or are almost the same in the international arena," Putin said, in 2016.[53]

Moscow favors enhanced collaboration with China in East Asia, believing that U.S.-led economic sanctions against Russia have made Sino-Russian strategic interests more congruent, and that bolstering China's military position in the region is, therefore, very much in Russia's interests.[54] The trend towards alliance relations is reflected in the expansion of Sino-Russian military cooperation, involving joint exercises and the training of Chinese officers in Russian defense universities.[55] These developments reinforce closer security and strategic ties between Moscow and Beijing, and foreshadow the emergence of a new world order based on "global strategic stability"[56] by highlighting their convergent views on many international issues.

Although Russia and China sometimes find cooperation difficult, what counts more is their commitment to emphasizing the positives in the relationship, rather than labouring over any differences. This approach has been facilitated by the steady institutionalization of bilateral ties. This encompasses summits between heads of state; regular meetings of prime ministers and foreign ministers; and consultations on strategic stability (at the level of deputy foreign minister), military cooperation (at the level of defense ministers), and broader security issues (between national security advisors).[57] These institutional ties have grown significantly in recent years, especially at the highest level; since 2013 Putin and Xi Jinping have met 22 times.

The frequency (and closeness) of Sino-Russian contacts has translated into real policy coordination—whether it is on general questions of global order, or in more specific areas, such as the Middle East, North Africa, or the Korean peninsula.[58] In the process, Russia's Asia policy (the so-called "turn to the East") has retreated into mainly a pivot towards China, despite Putin's efforts to preserve an independent position by balancing the Sino-Russian partnership with ties with other Asian countries.[59]

Regional Trade Blocs

Deputy Prime Minister Igor Shuvalov's team fought hard to overcome resistance to Russian membership of China's Asian Investment and Infrastructure Bank (AIIB). Yet even though Russia decided to join the new organization it was slow to play an active role in it.[60] Likewise, notwithstanding grandiose plans for connecting with China's Belt and road Initiative (BRI), little concrete has been achieved.[61] Russia, China, and four Central Asian states discussed for years a possible free trade agreement, but this, too, went nowhere due to Russian anxieties about Chinese economic might.

Today, however, there has been a notable shift in Moscow's position, whereby it tacitly acknowledges Chinese dominance of Central Asian external trade and investment, and the need to accommodate itself to Beijing.[62] Some Russian commentators argue that the BRI is fundamentally different from Russia's integration efforts in the former Soviet Union, or that these projects are complementary.[63] But the evidence points to China's unrelenting subordination of Russian interests to its own goals. In 2014, Chinese investors announced their interest in investing in a high-speed Moscow-Kazan railway that would become the foundation of a rail line from Beijing to Europe. Yet while the original Memorandum of Understanding (MOU) envisaged that it would pass through Siberia, it was later revealed that the line would go instead through Xinjiang to Astana, bypassing Russia, and cutting the travel time by two-thirds.[64]

Southeast Asia

Until 2014–15 Russia pursued an independent policy in Southeast Asia, seeking naval bases in Cam Ranh Bay (Vietnam) and Singapore, as well as farther afield in the Seychelles, Latin America, and the Middle East.[65] In particular, it increased support for Vietnam in energy exploration in the South China Sea, arms sales, and defense cooperation.[66] In 2012, the two countries upgraded their relationship to a "comprehensive strategic partnership".[67] Vietnam's defense minister, General Phung Quang Thanh, called Russia "Vietnam's primary strategic military partner in the sphere of military and technical cooperation."[68] Moscow later helped Hanoi to build a submarine base and repair dockyard to provide maintenance support for other naval platforms. The submarine base will host the Kilo-class subs that Vietnam has bought from Russia to protect its interests in the South China Sea.[69] In 2015, both sides began discussing regular Russian port visits to Cam Ranh Bay for maintenance, rest, and relaxation.[70] They also announced a third tranche of the sale of 12 new SU-30MK2 fighter aircraft that can target ships, aerial, and ground targets. And Hanoi ordered six new Varshavyanka-class submarines that will improve on its existing Kilo-class submarines and conduct anti-submarine, anti-ship, general reconnaissance, and patrols missions in the relatively shallow waters of the South China Sea.[71] Most strikingly, Prime Minister Dmitry Medvedev approved a draft military cooperation pact in 2015. This envisaged various information confidence-building measures, and cooperation on counter-terrorism and arms control.[72] A Free Trade Agreement (FTA) was also concluded between the Moscow-led Eurasian Economic Union and Vietnam in 2016.[73]

Russia's activities clearly surprised and dismayed China. In 2012, the Chinese media called them "unrighteous" and criticized Moscow for preferring cooperation with "ill-doers" instead of China, with whom it professed an identity of interests. They noted that Russo-Vietnamese military and energy cooperation would allow Hanoi to extend energy exploration into disputed waters, and accused Russia of seeking a return to the former Soviet base at Cam Ranh Bay.[74] Russia's "chess moves" suggested that Sino-Russian amity, at least in regard to the Asian regional security agenda, was something of a sham.[75]

Yet, since 2015, Russian policy has undergone a transformation. Growing dependence on China has forced Moscow to curtail all criticism of Beijing's policies in Asia. Deputy Prime Minister Dmitry Rogozin observed that "Russia and China are now becoming *as we wanted, not only neighbors but deeply integrated countries*"[76] (author's italics). Andrei Denisov, Russia's ambassador to China, not only described their partnership as a model for great power relations, he also supported Beijing's demand that the U.S. refrain from involvement in the South China Sea.[77] At the 2015 Shangri-La Conference Moscow announced joint Sino-Russian naval exercises in the South China Sea in 2016.[78] Deputy Defense Minister Antonov criticized Washington's Asian missile defense deployments, and called U.S. policies a "systematic containment" of Russia and China. He attacked Washington for pressuring Hanoi to prevent Russia from basing long-range aircraft in Cam Ranh Bay, from where they flew missions against the United

States and Japan.[79] And when the U.S. military challenged Chinese claims of sovereignty over its artificial islands in the South China Sea, Antonov accused Washington of forming military blocs in Southeast Asia.[80] Tellingly, since 2015, Russia has agreed no new arms deals with Vietnam.

Moscow's unwillingness to recognize Chinese threats has only grown with its dependence on China. This makes it virtually impossible for Russia to develop an effective response to Chinese power.[81] By 2016, despite its efforts to expand economic ties with ASEAN members through economic integration plans, energy, and arms deals, it became apparent that Moscow was inclining increasingly to Beijing's views on the South China Sea. On April 14, 2016, Lavrov stated that,

> ... China and the respective ASEAN states are now developing a legally binding code of conduct in the South China Sea. We actively welcome this process. We won't interfere in it. We believe that other countries [i. e the U.S.] should also encourage these efforts and refrain from taking sides or using these ongoing disputes to get any geopolitical unilateral advantage in the region or to isolate one country or another.[82]

And in September 2016, Putin and Lavrov formally supported Beijing's defiance of the International Court of Justice ruling against its claims in the South China Sea.[83]

Japan

In 2010–11, Russia and China jointly proposed a multipolar Asian order, declaring that the world was steadily evolving towards multipolarity, and that their comprehensive partnership was a factor for peace in Asia. Both governments openly recognized their respective territorial claims vis-à-vis Japan on the South Kurile (Northern Territories) and Senkaku (Diaoyu) islands, and denounced efforts to "undo" the territorial status quo. They agreed to promote multilateral mechanisms throughout Asia, based on "mutual trust, mutual benefit, equality, and cooperation." All states would respect each other's sovereignty and territorial integrity, and adhere to non-bloc principles and the ideal of equal and indivisible security.[84] Russia sought India's assent to this formulation, and covertly solicited Japan's endorsement even while publicly humiliating it over the disputed islands and continuing regular overflights into Japanese air space. These telltale signs of its desire to play everyone against the middle[85] highlighted its unreliability as an ally to China.

Moscow found it hard to maintain this agreement when in 2012 Beijing called its sovereignty over the Senkakus a core interest. Nikolai Patrushev, head of Russia's Security Council, told Tokyo that Russia would not take sides in the dispute; Japan and China must solve this problem through mutual dialogue. Meanwhile, Moscow and Tokyo agreed to "strengthen the bilateral dialogue in a bid to expand cooperation in the fields of security and defense amid the rapidly changing security environment in the Asia-Pacific region."[86] Clearly, Russia did not subscribe to China's territorial claims.[87] And in 2013 as Chinese threats against Japan mounted, it conspicuously undertook to normalize relations with Japan and attract Japanese investment. Lavrov said Russia would not ally with any one party against another. In early 2014, Moscow rejected Chinese offers of support for its position on the South Kuriles in return for supporting China's position on the Senkakus. Putin told Prime Minister Abe that Russia and Japan were "natural partners" and that normalization and partnership had every reason to succeed. These remarks not only indicated Moscow's desire for normalization with Japan, but also represented a signal to Beijing.[88]

Moscow refrained from commenting on Japan's intention to revise its "pacifist" constituion even while Beijing denounced Tokyo.[89] Although the Russian Ministry of Foreign Affairs indicated its "wariness" about Japan's evolving defense policies, it reserved judgment while urging Tokyo not to join Western sanctions against Moscow.[90] And when Japan finally introduced sanctions, these were relatively mild and left room for a resumption of dialogue.[91]

Yet the Russo-Japanese rapprochement soon ran aground.[92] Moscow joined Beijing in opposing deployment of the US THAAD missile defense system that protects Japan and South Korea from North Korea. Tokyo disagreed strongly with Moscow's view that the Korean crisis originated in Washington's threat to unseat the regime in Pyongyang.[93] More generally, Russia has shown little understanding of Japan's security anxieties vis-à-vis North Korea and China, while the impasse on the disputed islands precludes any early territorial settlement (and peace treaty). In short, Moscow has stonewalled Tokyo, demanding unreciprocated unilateral concessions—another clear indication of the power of the China lobby in Moscow.[94]

North Korea

In 2010–11, Russia, alarmed at the deteriorating security situation on the Korean peninsula, launched its own initiative to repair ties with North Korea.[95] But despite some initial success, by 2016, this initiative had been stymied by North Korean obstruction and Russia's lack of influence. As a result, throughout this period Moscow continued to associate itself with Beijing's initiatives[96]—a position that dismayed some Russian experts who felt that it should assert its own position on Korean issues.[97]

Today, Moscow supports the latest Chinese "compromise" advocating a simultaneous freeze of North Korean nuclear testing and U.S.-ROK military exercises, a proposal that would leave Pyongyang's nuclear program intact while diminishing South Korean readiness.[98] Russia and China also reject THAAD and the presence of U.S. troops on the Korean peninsula.[99] Beijing long ago grasped the desirability of access to North Korean ports in order to exploit the Arctic commercially—a prospect that causes Moscow some concern, given its desire to maintain control over the developing Northern Sea Route. China's Arctic reach is growing, while Russia has cut its spending on Arctic transport infrastructure by 90%.[100] This suggests that beneath the surface of Sino-Russian amity, China is marching forward commercially while Russia is failing.

Arms Sales

Russia's arms transfers to China undoubtedly benefit the buyer more than the seller. Apart from money, gaining some insight into China's military, and proving Russia's bona fides to Beijing, it is hard to see how Moscow benefits from the ensuing destabilization of Asian security. Arms sales to China have clearly enhanced the PLAN's ability to threaten the U.S. and its allies in the Asia-Pacific region. China is moving from anti-access/sea denial (A2/AD) in the Yellow and East China seas to a much more ambitious "second island chain" strategy that aims to project power throughout the Western Pacific.[101]

Russian arms transfers have been critical in this connection. They have improved Chinese ship design, cruise, and ballistic anti-ship and anti-air missiles; sharpened the PLAN's ability to detect and track moving ships and airplanes at sea and strike them from distance; and expanded China's naval air defense umbrella, potentially threatening US, and Japanese fleet operations in the Western Pacific.[102] Russia is reportedly developing a naval version of the S-400 air defense system to sell to China, which would double the effective range of Chinese naval-based air defenses. The PLA has already started taking delivery of the land-based S-400.[103] Acquiring the S-400 is a major blow to Taipei, since it will allow China to strike anywhere on Taiwan, in addition to covering the Senkakus, and reaching targets as far as Kolkata, Hanoi, and Seoul.[104] When Chinese statements, exercises, and fleet deployments are taken into account, we can see that these improved capabilities significantly increase the threat posed by the PLAN and PLAAF to Japan and other Asian states.[105] Similarly, the YJ-12 and YJ-18 cruise missiles from Russia enable a qualitative leap forward in Chinese cruise missile projection capabilities.[106] Then there is the prospect of the sale of the Amur-class submarine to China, which would further enhance the PLAN's reach,[107] while delivery of the Sukhoi Su-35 multi-purpose fighter provides the Chinese with a major boost in air combat quality.[108]

The size and frequency of Sino-Russian naval exercises has increased substantially.Some observers estimate that the joint exercises of August 2015 were the largest ever between the two countries. They were significant not only for the size of the contingents involved, but also for the quality of interaction, which resembled the U.S. Navy's structured drills with its Asia-Pacific partners. The exercises provide a framework within which Russia and China can develop their individual and collective defensive capabilities, and challenge the U.S.-led maritime order in the Asia-Pacific.[109] Most recently, the Baltic Sea exercise in July 2017 points to a new-found strategic boldness in Beijing, as it seeks to alleviate U.S. pressure in the South China Sea by projecting (symbolic) power into the Baltic.[110]

Conclusion

Current trends in energy cooperation and arms sales, Chinese investment in Central Asia, and Asian regional security suggest that Beijing is increasingly able to exploit Russian policies to its advantage. While both sides offer each other substantial benefits, China, not Russia, retains the greatest freedom of maneuver in the triangle, and is able to maximize its gains while keeping Moscow on a short leash. China, not Russia, can make major deals with the U.S. against the backdrop of U.S. strategic incoherence and Putin's ongoing failure to modernize Russia, Sino-Russian strategic, and ideological convergence will continue as China's leverage over Russia grows, and Moscow becomes more estranged from the West.[111]

Sino-Russian ties may be transactional but they are also deeply ideological.[112] Neither are they static. Chinese power is rising while Russia stagnates and even declines. That dynamic, despite the congruence of Russo-Chinese views, will have serious consequences in coming years.

China may still be Russia's gateway to Asia.[113] But obtaining recognition as a bona fide Asian power is becoming harder for Russia as it slips into an ever greater dependence on China. Its previous hedging strategy has failed, and it is losing ground to China politically as well as economically. Putin has made restoring Russia as a great power his mission, yet his system and domestic policies preclude realization of that goal. Whereas Russia enjoys the status of a great power, China has become a great power both in name and substance—a transformation that has come at least partly at Russia's expense. This asymmetry, together with the failings of American foreign policy, should warn us not to be complacent about the future of the U.S.-China-Russia strategic triangle, or the prospects for international security.

Notes

1. According to Gilbert Rozman the continuation of the concept of the triangle underscored every Chinese calculation of great power relations since the 1970s (Rozman 2010), p. 53.
2. Putin (2012).
3. Putin (2016a).
4. Lo (2017).
5. Blank (2011).
6. Kaczmarski (2012), p. 5.
7. Trenin (2017).
8. Wishnick (2015), and author's conversations with Wishnick July 18–19, 2017 in Washington, DC.
9. Trenin (2017), Lo (2017), Bond (2016).
10. Putin (2014a). Lee (2015), pp. 132–133.
11. Leichtova (2014), p. 147.
12. Rozman (2014), Lee and Lukin (2015), Lukin (2017b), Blank (2016), Wimbush and Portale (2017).
13. Trenin.
14. An (2017).
15. Lukin (2017b), p. 202.
16. Tennis (2017), TASS (2017).
17. Weitz, forthcoming.

18. Blank (2015a), *Daily Sabah* (2017).
19. Blank (2011), Kaczmarski (2012).
20. Blank (2012a).
21. See statements from Deputy Secretary of State Blinken (2015) and Principal Deputy Assistant Secretary, Bureau of South and Central Asian Affairs, Hoagland (2015).
22. The View From the Kremlin: Putin's War on the West, www.theeconomist.com, http://www.economist.com/news/leaders/21643189-ukraine-suffers-it-time-recognise-gravity-russian-threatandcounter, February 14, 2015.
23. See interview with Celeste Wallander, senior director for Russia and Eurasia, National Security Council (2015).
24. Oswald (2013).
25. In 2009 Deputy Assistant Secretary of Defense Celeste Wallander stated: "We see [with Russia] lots of areas where our interests overlap and where it's possible to find cooperation and coordination. We don't accept a zero-sum frame, but this is a frame that everyone keeps trying to force on the United States ... the United States expects Russia to abide by the same rules of the game that Russia expects the rest of the international of the international community to approach Russia with" (Wallander 2009). See also Mitchell (2014), Keating (2013) and Rozman (2010), p. 53.
26. Testimony of Victoria Nuland, Assistant Secretary, Bureau of European and Eurasian Affairs Before the House Foreign Affairs Committee (2015), Wroughton and Spetalnik (2014).
27. Hagel (2013).
28. Zezima (2014).
29. Kireeva (2017).
30. McLaughlin and Tamkin.
31. Apuzzo et al. (2017).
32. Lamothe (2017), Fishman (2017).
33. Friedman (2017), Landler (2017).
34. Kawanami and Harada (2017).
35. Harder (2017), Sharma (2017).
36. Friedman (2017), Panda (2017).
37. Hudson (2017), Kilina (2017).
38. Murray and Bash; Landler (2017).
39. Lo (2017), Bond (2016).
40. Luzyanin and Zhao (2017), pp. 18–19, Radio Free Europe (2014), Trenin (2016).
41. Kashin (2016).
42. Interfax (2014a).

43. Silaev and Sushentsov (2017), Bordachev (2017).
44. Radio Free Europe (2014).
45. Interfax (2014b).
46. Ministry of Defense of the Russian Federation (2014b).
47. Putin (2016b).
48. Silaev and Sushentsov (2017), Bordachev (2017).
49. Kashin (2014).
50. Yahuda (2017), p. 6.
51. Shoigu (2017).
52. Putin (2015).
53. *The Straits Times* (2016).
54. Yahuda (2017), p. 6.
55. Shoigu (2017), Ministry of Defense of the Russian Federation (2014b).
56. Rinna (2016), Putin (2015).
57. Kaczmarski (2008).
58. Ministry of Foreign Affairs of the Russian Federation (2015).
59. Putin (2014b).
60. Gabuev (2016).
61. Ibid.
62. Einhorn (2016), Gabuev (2015a).
63. Bordachev et al. (2016), pp. 20–28, Makarov and Sokolova (2016), pp. 29–42.
64. Ibid., pp. 33–34.
65. RIA Novosti (2014), Blank (2012b).
66. Blank (2012b).
67. Thayer (2012).
68. Mukhin (2013).
69. Gravatt (2010).
70. Mukhin (2013).
71. Vietnam Net (2013).
72. Interfax (2013).
73. TASS (2016).
74. Radyuhin (2010).
75. Mankoff (2013).
76. Bodner (2017).
77. Ria Novosti (2015).
78. Gabuev (2015b), Panda (2015).
79. Mehta (2015), Nguyen (2015).
80. Antonov (2015).
81. Gabuev (2015b).
82. Lavrov (2016).
83. Tran (2016), Lukonin (2017), p. 5.

84. China Daily (2010), Ministry of Foreign Affairs of the People's Republic of China (2008).
85. Authors conversations with U.S. analysts, Washington, DC, March, 2011, Lavrov (2011).
86. Blank (2012c).
87. Ibid.
88. Blank (2014b).
89. Interfax (2014c).
90. Lukashevich (2014).
91. Fackler (2014), Blank (2014a).
92. Blank (2017b).
93. Blank (2015b), Rozman (2015), Putin (2017).
94. Brown (2017), Brown (2016).
95. Blank (2015b), Blank (2015c).
96. Vorontsov and Toloraya (2014), Zhebin (2015).
97. Ibid., Lukin (2017a), Toloraya and Gabetts (2017).
98. BBC Monitoring (2017).
99. Lukin (2017a), p. 9.
100. Blank (2017a).
101. For one recent example see Schwartz (2015).
102. Ibid., Barabanov (2009).
103. Gady (2015).
104. Minnick (2013).
105. Sharman (2015).
106. Schwartz, p. 38
107. Radyuhin (2013).
108. Klare (2013).
109. Singh (2015).
110. Yang (2014).
111. Rozman (2014).
112. Mankoff.
113. Christoffersen (2010).

Literature

An Baijie. 2017. China–Russia Relations Are Unshakable, Xi Says. *China Daily*, June 5. http://www.chinadaily.com.cn/interface/flipboard/158853/2017-07-05/cd_29993815.html.

Antonov, Anatoly. 2015. Deputy Defence Minister Anatoly Antonov Gave Speech in Singapore at the 14th Asia Security Summit "SHANGRI-LA DIALOGUE 2015". The IISS Shangri-La Dialogue, May 30, Ministry of Defence of the Russian Federation. http://eng.mil.ru/en/news_page/country/more.htm?id=12037863@egNews.

Apuzzo, Matt, Maggie Haberman, and Matthew Rosenberg. 2017. Trump Told Russians That Firing 'Nut Job' Comey Eased Pressure from Investigation. *New York Times*, May 19. https://www.nytimes.com/2017/05/19/us/politics/trump-russia-comey.html.

Barabanov, Mikhail. 2009. China's Military Modernization: The Russian Factor. Moscow Defense Brief, No. 4 (18), Centre for Analysis of Strategies and Technologies, Moscow.

BBC Monitoring. 2017. Russia Denies Changing Position on North Korea. June 27. www.mid.ru, retrieved from BBC Monitoring.

Blank, Stephen. 2011. *Toward a New Chinese Order in Asia: Russia's Failure*. NBR Special Report No. 26, National Bureau of Asian Research, March, 2011.

Blank, Stephen. 2012a. The End of Russian Power in Asia? *Orbis* 2012 (Spring): 249–266.

Blank, Stephen. 2012b. Russia's Ever Friendlier Ties to Vietnam—Are They a Signal to China? *Eurasia Daily Monitor*, November 30, The Jamestown Foundation. https://jamestown.org/program/russias-ever-friendlier-ties-to-vietnam-are-they-a-signal-to-china/.

Blank, Stephen. 2012c. Russia Plays Both Sides Against the Middle on Senkaku Islands. *Eurasia Daily Monitor* 9 (209), November 14, Jamestown Foundation. https://jamestown.org/program/russia-plays-both-sides-against-the-middle-on-senkaku-islands/.

Blank, Stephen. 2014a. What Effect Will Asian Sanctions Have Upon Russia? *Eurasia Daily Monitor*, The Jamestown Foundation, August 5. https://jamestown.org/program/what-effect-will-asian-sanctions-have-upon-russia/.

Blank, Stephen. 2014b. Russia and Japan: Can Two-Plus-Two Equal More Than Four? *Asia Pacific Bulletin*, No. 251, Washington, DC, East–West Center, March 6. Available at https://www.eastwestcenter.org/publications/russia-and-japan-can-two-plus-two-equal-more-four?utm_source=feedburner&utm_medium=feed&utm_campaign=Feed%3A+EWC_FeaturedPublications+(East-West+Center%3A+Featured+Publications).

Blank, Stephen. 2015a. Russo-Chinese Exercises in the Mediterranean. *Eurasia Daily Monitor*, The Jamestown Foundation, May 27. www.jamestown.org.

Blank, Stephen. 2015b. Russia and the Two Koreas in the Context of Moscow's Asian Policy. *Academic Paper Series*, Korean Economic Institute of America, Washington, DC, September.

Blank, Stephen. 2015c. Making Sense of the Russo-North Korean Rapprochement. *The Asan Forum*, January–February, III, No. 1.

Blank, Stephen. 2016. Russian Writers on the Decline of Russia in the Far East and the Rise of China. *The Jamestown Foundation*, Russia In Decline Project, September 13. http://www.jamestown.org/programs/edm/single/?tx_ttnews%5Btt_news%5D=45758&tx_ttnews%5BbackPid%5D=835&cHash=09b96170a161c826bcc56c8a28375229#.V97EF7WA360.

Blank, Stephen. 2017a. The Bloom Comes off the Arctic Rose. *Eurasia Daily Monitor*, The Jamestown Foundation, July 20. https://jamestown.org/program/the-bloom-comes-off-the-arctic-rose/.

Blank, Stephen. 2017b. Russo-Japanese Relations from a Regional Perspective. *International Journal of Korean Unification Studies* XXVI (1): 21–51.

Blinken, Antony J. 2015. An Enduring Vision for Central Asia. Brookings Institution, Washington, DC, March 31. http://www.state.gov/s/d/2015/240013.htm.

Bodner, Matthew. 2017. Russia's Defense Budget—Down, But Not Out. *The Moscow Times*, March 17. Available at https://themoscowtimes.com/articles/russias-defense-budget-down-but-not-out-57467.

Bond, Ian. 2016. Russia and China: Partners of Choice and Necessity. *Centre for European Reform Report*. Available at http://www.cer.eu/publications/archive/report/2016/russia-and-china-partners-choice-and-necessity.

Bordachev, Timofey. 2017. Russia–China: An Alliance for Peace or War? *Russia in Global Affairs*, June 20. Available at http://eng.globalaffairs.ru/book/Russia-China-An-Alliance-for-Peace-or-War-18783.

Bordachev, T., A. Kazakova, and A. Skirba. 2016. Institutions For a Peaceful Eurasia. *International Organizations Research Journal*, XI, No. 2.

Brown, James D.J. 2016. Japan's 'New Approach' to Russia. *The Diplomat*, June 18. https://thediplomat.com/2016/06/japans-new-approach-to-russia/.

Brown, James D.J. 2017. Abe, Putin Meet at G-20 as Disputed Northern Territories Recede Into Distance. *The Diplomat*, July 11. https://thediplomat.com/2017/07/abe-putin-meet-at-g-20-as-disputed-northern-territories-recede-into-distance/.

China Daily. 2010. China, Russia Call for Efforts in Asia-Pacific Security, September 28. Available at http://www.chinadaily.com.cn/china/2010-09/28/content_11361116.htm.

Christoffersen, Gaye. 2010. Russia's Breakthrough Into the Asia-Pacific: China's Role. *International Relations of the Asia-Pacific* X (1): 61–92.

Daily Sabah. 2017. Russia Expects China to Help Resolve Syrian Crisis. *Daily Sabah*, Istanbul, May 29, 2017. https://www.dailysabah.com/syrian-crisis/2017/05/29/russia-expects-china-to-help-resolve-syrian-crisis.

The Economist. 2015. The View from the Kremlin: Putin's War on the West. *The Economist Leader Opinion*, February 14. http://www.economist.com/news/leaders/21643189-ukraine-suffers-it-time-recognise-gravity-russian-threat-and-counter.

Einhorn, Bruce. 2016. Russia, China, and Japan Fill the Trump Trade Gap. *Bloomberg/Business Week*, December 1. https://www.bloomberg.com/news/articles/2016-12-01/russia-china-and-japan-fill-the-trump-trade-gap.

Fackler, Martin. 2014. Japan Imposes New Sanctions on Russia But Keep a Diplomatic Door Open. *New York Times*, August 6. https://www.nytimes.

com/2014/08/06/world/asia/japan-keeps-door-to-russia-open-while-imposing-sanctions.html?mtrref=www.google.no&gwh=A24C9E018D-4F032596AF7848EE809ADA&gwt=pay&assetType=nyt_now.

Fishman, Edward. 2017. The Senate Just Passes a Monumental New Russia Sanctions Bill,-Here's What's in it. *Atlantic Council*, June 14. http://www.atlanticcouncil.org/blogs/ukrainealert/the-senate-just-passed-a-monumental-new-russia-sanctions-bill-here-s-what-s-in-it.

Freidman, Thomas L. 2017. Trump Is China's Chump. *New York Times*, June 28. https://www.nytimes.com/2017/06/28/opinion/trump-china-asia-pacific-trade-tpp.html.

Gabuev, Alexander. 2015a. Eurasian Silk Road Union: Towards a Russia–China Consensus? *The Diplomat*, June 5. https://thediplomat.com/2015/06/eurasian-silk-road-union-towards-a-russia-china-consensus/.

Gabuev, Alexander. 2015b. The Silence of the Bear: Deciphering Russia's Showing at Shangri-La Dialogue. *Carnegie Moscow Center*, June 1. http://carnegie.ru/eurasiaoutlook/?fa=60263.

Gabuev, Alexander. 2016. A Pivot to Nowhere: The Realities of Russia's Asia Policy. Carnegie Moscow Center, April 22. http://carnegie.ru/commentary/63408.

Gady, Franz-Stefan. 2015. China to Receive Russia's S-400 Missile defense Systems in 12–18 Months. *The Diplomat*, November 17. https://thediplomat.com/2015/11/china-to-receive-russias-s-400-missile-defense-systems-in-12-18-months/.

Gravatt, Jon. 2010. Russia to Help Vietnam Build Naval Submarines. *Jane's Defense Weekly*, March 29, 2010. http://www4.janes.com.

Hagel, Chuck. 2013. The U.S. Approach to Regional Security. *The IISS Shangri-La Dialogue*, First Plenary Session, June 1. https://www.iiss.org/en/events/shangri-la-dialogue/archive/shangri-la-dialogue-2013-c890/first-plenary-session-ee9e.

Harder, Amy. 2017. Trump Follows Obama's Lead on Natural Gas Exports. *Axios*, May 12. https://www.axios.com/trump-follows-obamas-lead-on-natural-gas-exports-1513302242-feeb258a-5a9b-46c5-8146-aff20bfd1672.html.

Hoagland, Richard E. 2015. Central Asia: What's Next? Talk at Georgetown University, Washington, DC, March 30, 2015. http://www.state.gov/p/sca/rls/rmks/2015/240014.htm.

Hudson, John. 2017. The Trump Administration Has a New Plan for Dealing With Russia. *BuzzFeed News*, June 19. https://www.buzzfeed.com/john-hudson/this-is-the-trump-administrations-plan-for-dealing-with?utm_term=.uveqOJLJm#.ncl7Qe0e9.

Interfax. 2013. Interfax Information Services Group, Moscow, August 29. http://www.interfax.com/.

Interfax. 2014a. Interfax Information Services Group, Moscow, August 27. http://www.interfax.com/.

Interfax. 2014b. Interfax Information Services Group, Moscow, November 18. http://www.interfax.com/.

Interfax. 2014c. Moscow Withholds Comments On Japan Plan To Go Back on Constitutional Pacifism. Interfax Information Services Group, Moscow, July 27. http://www.interfax.com/.

Kaczmarski, Marcin. 2008. *An Asian Alternative? Russia's Chances of Making Asia an alternative to Relations With the West*. Centre for Eastern Studies, Warsaw, 35–36. https://www.osw.waw.pl/en/publikacje/policy-briefs/2008-06-15/asian-alternative-russias-chances-making-asia-alternative-to.

Kaczmarski, Marcin. 2012. Domestic Sources of Russia's China Policy. *Problems of Post-Communism* 59 (2) March/April: 3–17.

Kashin, Vasily. 2014. Interview to the Xinhua News Agency of China. *FBIS SOV*, August 27.

Kashin, Vasily. 2016. More Than Partnership: Political Expert Vasily Kashin on the Development of the Political and Economic Relations of Russia and China. *Vedomosti*, August 18.

Kawanami, Takeshi, and Issaku Harada. 2017. In Sharp Reversal, Sino–American Trade Relations Improve. *Nikkei Asian Review*, May 13. http://asia.nikkei.com/Politics-Economy/International-Relations/In-sharp-reversal-Sino-American-trade-relations-improve.

Keating, Joshua. 2013. Obama and Rouhani Agree: No More "Zero Sum."*Slate.com*, September 24, 2013. http://www.slate.com/blogs/the_world_/2013/09/24/iranian_president_hassan_rouhani_speaks_to_u_n_iran_poses_absolutely_no.html.

Kilina, Veronika. 2017. Pomoshchnik Putina priznalsya, chto nikto i predstavit' ne mog uroven' protivostoyaniya s SSHA pri Trampe [Putin's Assistant Admitted that no One Could Imagine the Level of Confrontation with the United States Under Trump], June 29. https://www.nakanune.ru/news/2017/6/29/22474635/.

Kireeva, Anna. 2017. The Positive Scenario. *The Asan Forum Alternative Scenarios*, June 17. http://www.theasanforum.org/category/alternative-scenarios/?post_id=8234&c_id=8375#content_wrap.

Klare, Michael. 2013. The Cold War Redux? *Asia Times Online*, June 3. www.atimes.com.

Lamothe, Dan. 2017. In Spending Bill, New Muscular Ways That the Pentagon Could Deter Russian Military Action. *Washington Post*, June 28. www.washingtonpost.com.

Landler, Mark. 2017. As Trump Bets On China's Help On North Korea, Aides Ask; Is It worth It? *New York Times*, June 15. https://www.nytimes.com/2017/06/15/

world/asia/china-xi-jinping-trump-north-korea.html?mtrref=www.google.no&gwh=CDAC3E2F155D6D00F641E23CF7FC70A2&gwt=pay.

Lavrov, Sergei. 2011. Russia–India: A Decade of Strategic Partnership. *International Affairs* 1: 3–5.

Lavrov, Sergei. 2016. Foreign Minister Sergei Lavrov's Remarks and Answers to Questions At the Meeting in Mongolia's Foreign Ministry, Ulan Bator, April 14, The Ministry of Foreign Affairs of the Russian Federation. http://www.mid.ru/en/press_service/minister_speeches/-/asset_publisher/7OvQR5KJWVmR/content/id/2233937.

Lee, Chung Min. 2015. *Fault Lines in a Rising Asia*. Washington, DC: Carnegie Endowment Press.

Lee, Renssalear, and Artyom Lukin. 2015. *Russia's Far East: New Dynamics in Asia Pacific and Beyond*. Boulder Colorado: Lynne Rienner Publishers.

Leichtova, Magda. 2014. *Misunderstanding Russia: Russian Foreign Policy and the West*. London and New York: Routledge.

Lo, Bobo. 2017. *A Wary Embrace: What the China–Russia Relationship Means for the World*, A Lowy Institute Paper: Penguin Special. https://www.lowyinstitute.org/publications/wary-embrace.

Lukashevich, Alexander. 2014. Reply by the official Representative of the Ministry of Foreign Affairs of Russia, Alexander Lukashevich, to the Question of the Mass Media Regarding the Decision of the Japanese Government to Refuse Self-Limitation in the Defence Area. Ministry of Foreign Affairs of the Russian Federations, July 7. http://www.mid.ru/en/foreign_policy/news/-/asset_publisher/cKNonkJE02Bw/content/id/678566.

Lukin, Alexander. 2017a. Russia Policy in Northeast Asia and the Prospects for Korean Unification. *International Journal of Korean Unification Studies* XXVI (1): 1–20.

Lukin, Artyom. 2017b. Soviet/Russian–Chinese Relationships: Coming Full Circle? In *Uneasy Partnerships: China's Engagement With Japan, the Two Koreas, and Russia in the Era Of Reform*, ed. Thomas J. Fingar. Stanford: Stanford University Press.

Lukonin, Sergei. 2017. Redefining Russia's Pivot and China's Peripheral Diplomacy. In *China–Russia Relations and Regional Dynamics: From Pivots to Peripheral Diplomacy*, March, ed. Lora Saalman. Stockholm: Stockholm International Peace Research Institute.

Luzyanin, Sergey, and Zhao Huasheng. 2017. *Russian–Chinese Dialogue; The 2017 Model*. Russian International Affairs Council, Moscow, May 28. http://russiancouncil.ru/en/activity/publications/russian-chinese-dialogue-the-2017-model/.

Makarov, I., and A. Sokolova. 2016. The Eurasian Economic Union and the Silk Road Economic Belt: Opportunities for Russia. *International Organizations Research Journal* 11 (2): 40–57.

Mankoff, Jeffrey. 2013. The Wary Chinese–Russian Partnership. *New York Times*, July 11. http://www.nytimes.com/2013/07/12/opinion/global/the-wary-chinese-russian-partnership.html.
Mehta, Aaron. 2015. Vietnamese Leader Predicts Closer US Military Ties. *Defense News*, July 8. https://www.defensenews.com/congress/budget/2015/07/08/vietnamese-leader-predicts-closer-us-military-ties/.
Ministry of Defense of the Russian Federation. 2014a. Open Source Center (in Russian), The Foreign Broadcast Information Service, Central Eurasia (FBIS SOV), November 18.
Ministry of Defense of the Russian Federation. 2014b. Nezavisimaya Gazeta Online (in Russian), Moscow, The Foreign Broadcast Information Service, Central Eurasia (FBIS SOV), November 20.
Ministry of Foreign Affairs of the People's Republic of China. 2008. Joint Statement of the People's Republic of China and the Russian Federation on the Current International Situation and Major International Issues, Beijing, May 23. Available at http://www.fmprc.gov.cn/mfa_eng/wjdt_665385/2649_665393/t465821.shtml.
Ministry of Foreign Affairs of the Russian Federation. 2015. Statement and Answers to Questions From the Media by Russian Foreign Minister S.V. Lavrov at the Press Conference on the Results of Russia's Chairmanship of the UN Security Council, New York, October 1, retrieved from BBC Monitoring.
Minnick, Wendell. 2013. Time Running Out for Taiwan if Russia Releases S-400 M. *Defense News*, May 25. Available at www.defensenews.com.
Mitchell, Andrea. 2014. Obama On Ukraine: This Is not a Zero-Sum Game. *MSNBC*, March 25. http://www.msnbc.com/andrea-mitchell-reports/watch/obama-on-ukraine-this-is-not-a-zero-sum-game-206208067816.
Mukhin, Vladimir. 2013. Preferable Tariffs for Navy Ships: Vietnam and Cuba Are Helping Russian Navy Solve Defense Missions in the World's Ocean, Moscow, *Nezavisimaya Gazeta* (in Russian), August 7.
Nguyen, Cuong T. 2015. The Dramatic Transformation in US–Vietnam Relations. *The Diplomat*, July 2. https://thediplomat.com/2015/07/the-dramatic-transformation-in-us-vietnam-relations/.
Nuland, Victoria. 2015. U.S. Policy After Russia's Escalation in Syria. Testimony Before the House Foreign Affairs Committee, Washington DC, November 4.
Oswald, Rachel. 2013. Russia Insists on Multilateral Nuclear Arms Control Talks. *Global Security Newswire*, May 28, 2013. http://www.nti.org/gsn/article/russia-insists-next-round-nuke-cuts-be-multilateral/.
Panda, Ankit. 2015. Russia Plans South China Sea Naval Exercise With China in 2016. *The Diplomat*, June 1. https://thediplomat.com/2015/06/russia-plans-south-china-sea-naval-exercise-with-china-in-2016/.

Panda, Ankit. 2017. Asian Publics Lose Confidence in the United States In the Trump Era. *The Diplomat*, June 28. https://thediplomat.com/2017/06/asian-publics-lose-confidence-in-the-united-states-in-the-trump-era/.

Putin, Vladimir. 2012. Russia and the Changing World. *Valdai Discussion Club*, February 27. http://valdaiclub.com/a/highlights/vladimir_putin_on_foreign_policy_russia_and_the_changing_world/?sphrase_id=251286.

Putin, Vladimir. 2014a. President Putin's Remarks to Security Council Meeting. Presidential Executive Office of Russia, July 22. http://eng.kremlin.ru/transcripts/22714.

Putin, Vladimir. 2014b. Conference of Russian Ambassadors and Permanent Representatives. Presidential Executive Office of Russia, July 1. http://eng.kremlin.ru/transcripts/22586.

Putin, Vladimir. 2015. Press Statements Following Russian–Chinese Talks. Presidential Executive Office of Russia, May 8. Available at http://en.kremlin.ru/events/president/transcripts/49433.

Putin, Vladimir. 2016a. Vladimir Putin's Annual News Conference. Presidential Executive Office of Russia, December 23. Available at http://kremlin.ru/events/president/news/53573.

Putin, Vladimir. 2016b. Interview to the Xinhua News Agency of China. Presidential Executive Office of Russia, June 23. Available at http://en.kremlin.ru/events/president/news/52204.

Putin, Vladimir. 2017. St Petersburg International Economic Forum Plenary Meeting. Presidential Executive Office of Russia, June 2. http://en.kremlin.ru/events/president/news/54667.

Radio Free Europe. 2014. Putin Says Moscow, Beijing Are Natural Allies. October 14. https://www.rferl.org/a/putin-says-moscow-beijing-natural-allies/26637208.html.

Radyuhin, Vladimir. 2010. Russia Renews Interest in Vietnam Base. *The Hindu*, October 8.

Radyuhin, Vladimir. 2013. The Dragon Gets a Bear Hug. *The Hindu,* March 8. www.thehindu.com/opinon/op–ed.

RIA Novosti. 2015. Russian Envoy, "Raised Focus on Relations With China Predates Western Sanctions, December 8. http://russialist.org/ria-novosti-russian-envoy-raised-focus-on-relations-with-china-predates-western-sanctions/.

RIA Novosti. 2014. Russia Seeks Several Military Bases Abroad—Defense Minister, February 26. http://en.ria.ru/military_news/20140226/187917901/Russia-Seeks-Several-Military-Bases-Abroad–Defense-Minister.html.

Rinna, Anthony V. 2016. China and Russia's North Korea Problem. *East Asia Forum,* July 16, 2016. http://www.eastasiaforum.org/2016/07/16/china-and-russias-north-korea-problem/.

Rozman, Gilbert. 2010. *Chinese Strategic Thought Toward Asia*. New York and London: Palgrave Macmillan.

Rozman, Gilbert. 2014. *The Sino-Russian Challenge to the World Order: National Identities, Bilateral Relations, and East Versus West in the 2010s*. Washington, DC: Woodrow Wilson Press.

Rozman, Gilbert (ed.). 2015. *On Korea, 2015*, 60–76. Washington, DC: Korean Economic Institute of America.

Saalman, Lora, ed. 2017. *China–Russia Relations and Regional Dynamics: From Pivots to Peripheral Diplomacy*, March. Stockholm: Stockholm International Peace Research Institute.

Schwartz, Paul. 2015. *Russia's Contribution to China's Surface Warfare Capabilities: Feeding the Dragon*. Washington, DC: Center for Strategic and International Studies.

Sharma, Shardul. 2017. Update: U.S. Allows LNG Exports to China. *Natural Gas World*, May 12. https://www.naturalgasworld.com/us-allows-lng-exports-to-china-37560.

Sharman, Christopher H. 2015. *China Moves Out: Stepping Stones Toward a New Maritime Strategy*. Center for the Study of Chinese Military Affairs: China Strategic Perspectives No. 9, Institute for National Strategic Studies, National Defense University, Fort McNair, Washington, DC, passim.

Shoigu, Sergei. 2017. Lecture at the Opening Ceremony of the II All-Russian Youth Forum in the Moscow State Institute of International Relations. Ministry of Defense of the Russian Federation, February 21. Available at http://eng.mil.ru/en/news_page/country/more.htm?id=12112529@egNews.

Silaev, Nikolai, and Andrey Sushentsov. 2017. Russia's Allies and the Geopolitical Frontier in Eurasia. *Valdai Papers*, No. 66, April.

Singh, Abhijit. 2015. The Emerging China–Russia Maritime Nexus in the Eurasian Commons. *The Diplomat*, September 17. https://thediplomat.com/2015/09/the-emerging-china-russia-maritime-nexus-in-the-eurasian-commons/.

The Straits Times. 2016. China, Russia Eye Closer Friendship Amid Tensions With West, June 26. http://www.straitstimes.com/asia/east-asia/china-russia-eye-closer-friendship-amid-tensions-with-west.

TASS. 2016. Free Trade Agreement between Eurasian Economic Union, Vietnam Comes into Force. *Russian News Agency*, October 5. http://tass.com/economy/904384.

TASS. 2017. Russia and US Beginning Strategic Stability Dialogue—Diplomat. *Russian News Agency*, July 20. http://tass.com/world/957005.

Tennis Maggie. 2017. Russia Suggests Revised Arms Talks. *Arms Control Today*, Arms Control Association, Washington, DC, May. https://www.armscontrol.org/act/2017-05/news/russia-suggests-revived-arms-talks.

Thayer, Carlyle A. 2012. The Russia–Vietnam Comprehensive Partnership. *East Asia Forum*, October 9. http://www.eastasiaforum.org/2012/10/09/the-russia-vietnam-comprehensive-partnership/.

Toloraya, Georgy and Vassily Gabetts. 2017. Solving the Korean Conundrum: Russia's Interaction With Major Actors in the Trump-Moon Era. *International Journal of Korean Unification Studies* XXVI (1): 109–150.

Tran, Rosa. 2016. Russia Supports China's Stance on South China Sea. *Sputnik International*, September 5. Retrieved from https://seasresearch.wordpress.com/2016/09/06/russia-supports-chinas-stance-on-south-china-sea/.

Trenin, Dmitri Trenin. 2016. National Interest, the Same Language of Beijing, Washington, and Moscow. Carnegie Moscow Center, December 29, http://carnegie.ru/2016/12/29/national-interest-same-language-of-beijing-washington-and-moscow-pub-67631.

Trenin, Dmitri. 2017. Russia's Evolving Grand Eurasia Strategy: Will It Work? Carnegie Moscow Center, Article, July 20. http://carnegie.ru/2017/07/20/russia-s-evolving-grand-eurasia-strategy-will-it-work-pub-71588.

Vietnam Net. 2013. Two Kilo Submarines to be Handed over to Vietnam this Sept. July 6, http://english.vietnamnet.vn/fms/government/78804/two-kilo-submarines-to-be-handed-over-to-vietnam-this-sept-.html.

Vorontsov, Alexander, and Georgy Toloraya. 2014. Military Alert on the Korean Peninsula: Time for Some Conclusions, Carnegie Moscow Center Paper, April 25. http://carnegie.ru/2014/04/25/military-alert-on-korean-peninsula-time-for-some-conclusions-pub-56010.

Wallander, Celeste. 2009. Russia Update: Is the Reset Working? *Council on Foreign Relations*, October 28. Available at https://www.cfr.org/event/russia-update-reset-working-0.

Wallander, Celeste. 2015. Interview by The German Marshall Fund of the United States, Warsaw, March 19. http://www.gmfus.org/videos/celeste-wallander-us-russian-strategy.

Weitz, Richard. (forthcoming). Russian Military Power and Policy in the Far East. In *The Russian Military in Strategic Perspective*, ed. Stephen J. Blank. Carlisle Barracks, PA: Strategic Studies Institute, US Army War College.

Wimbush, S. Enders, and Elizabeth M. Portale (eds.). 2017. *Russia in Decline*. Washington, DC: Jamestown Foundation.

Wishnick, Elizabeth. 2015. The New China–Russia–U.S. Triangle. *NBR Analysis Brief*. The National Bureau of Asian Research, December 16. Available at http://www.nbr.org/publications/nbranalysis/pdf/brief/121615_Wishnick_ChinaRussiaUS.pdf.

Wroughton, Leslie, and Matt Spetalnik. 2014. Russian Suspicions of U.S. Motives in Syria Make Cooperation Unlikely. *Reuters*, September 28, 2014. http://www.reuters.com/article/2014/09/28/us-syria-crisis-usa-russia-insight-idUSKCN0HN04T20140928.

Yahuda, Michael. 2017. Japan and the Sino-Russian Strategic Partnership. *Japan and the Sino-Russian Entente: The Future of Major-Power Relations in Northeast Asia*. Seattle: National Bureau of Research Asia, NBR Special Report No. 64, 2017.

Yang, Tommy. 2014. Why Russia–China Drills in the Baltic Sea a 'Political Signal To the East. *Sputnik International News*, July 21. https://sputniknews.com/military/201707191055682609-russia-china-naval-drills/.

Zezima, Katie. 2014. Obama Says Russia is a 'Regional' Power: Nuke in Manhattan a Bigger Threat. *Washington Post*, March 25. https://www.washingtonpost.com/news/post-politics/wp/2014/03/25/obama-russia-is-just-a-regional-power-nuke-in-manhattan-is-a-bigger-threat/?utm_term=.e8f90c4f284e.

Zhebin, Alexander. 2015. The Balance of Forces on the Korean Peninsula: Sanctions Against Pyongyang Have Not Always Been Calculated. *Nezavisimaya Gazeta Online* (in Russian), Moscow, April 1.

CHAPTER 11

The Japan–China–Russia Triangle and Security in North East Asia

Bjørn Elias Mikalsen Grønning

Japan, flanked by Russia to the north and China to the south, is particularly susceptible to their potential-coordinated political-military pressure. Japan, moreover, finds its strategic interests underpinned by the U.S.-led global order—an order that is at times challenged by China and Russia's concerted efforts. The geopolitical significance of Sino-Russian relations for Japan is further underscored by Tokyo's tense interaction with both of its great power neighbors. Historical animosity, mutual distrust, and competing territorial claims sour political and military relations and, occasionally, disrupt their economic interaction. These factors make Sino-Russian partnership a critical variable in Japan's strategic calculus. Indeed, they make a potential Sino-Russian military alliance a strategic worst-case scenario for Japan, short of abandonment by its U.S. superpower patron.[1]

Japan's geopolitical exposure to China and Russia makes an investigation into its take on the development of their alignment a particularly suitable case study of its broader implications. Accordingly, in this

B. E. M. Grønning (✉)
Norwegian Institute for Defence Studies, Oslo, Norway
e-mail: bjorn.gronning@ifs.mil.no

J. I. Bekkevold and B. Lo (eds.), *Sino-Russian Relations in the 21st Century*, https://doi.org/10.1007/978-3-319-92516-5_11

chapter, I examine the triangular dynamics between Japan and its two great power neighbors. I make two central arguments. First, Japan interprets recent developments in Sino-Russian relations as evidence of a tactical rather than strategic convergence, let alone an incipient Sino-Russian alliance. Second, the monumental security challenge that China's rise presents to Japan has altered Tokyo's strategic calculus vis-à-vis Russia. Japan cannot afford a two-front military posture, much less against two great powers, and so has increasingly pursued an autonomous strategic engagement with Moscow.

In order to understand Japan's contemporary approach to China and Russia, it is useful to consider the rather dramatic changes witnessed in the Japan–China–Russia triangle since the Cold War. Accordingly, I begin this chapter by breaking down Japan's role in and approach to triangular relations in the post-World War II (WWII) era into four distinct periods. In the first half of the Cold War, Japan as a U.S. ally played an important role containing communism in Asia. U.S. engagement of China in the early 1970s set the stage for a second phase featuring Japanese rapprochement with China. The end of the Cold War facilitated a third phase, characterized by Japanese economic engagement with China and Russia alike. Finally, in recent years, a fourth phase of triangular relations has emerged. Motivated by China's rise and enabled by the growing Sino-Russian power gap, Japan in the current phase pursues strategic engagement with Russia.

Cold War Trilateral Dynamics

In the immediate aftermath of WWII, the U.S. assigned Japan a pivotal role in containing communism in Asia. Over the next few years, Japan's importance to and prominence in the U.S. containment strategy grew in synch with the increasing Communist challenge. After emerging victorious from the Chinese Civil War in 1949, Mao Zedong travelled in 1950 to Moscow to align the two communist giants of Asia by signing the bilateral Treaty of Friendship, Alliance, and Mutual Assistance with the Soviet Union. Then, the East-West geopolitical divide was crystallized by the outbreak of the Korean War.

By the early 1960s, however, bilateral relations between China and Russia had deteriorated.[2] Coupled with the normalization of Sino-American relations in 1972,[3] this deterioration of Sino-Russian relations presented Japan with an opportunity to engage China. Japanese Prime

Minister Tanaka's visit to Beijing in September 1972 was the first visit by a Japanese Prime Minister to China since WWII. Normalizing relations with China was an important mechanism for managing its hostile relations with the Soviet Union.

Throughout the Cold War and well into the first post-Cold War decade, Japan's defense policy and posture focused on the perceived military threat emanating from the Russian Far East. Heavy and numerous ground forces were established to fight off a Soviet invasion from the north. A submarine-led naval force patrolled the strategic chokepoints connecting the Soviet Pacific Fleet's home waters in the Sea of Okhotsk to the open waters of the Pacific Ocean. Air bases hosted fighter jets scrambling to keep Russian aircraft out of Japanese airspace. At its height in the 1970s and 1980s, the Japan Ground Self-Defence Forces (JGSDF) marched 180 000 troops and 2 200 tanks and artillery units; the Japan Air Self-Defence Forces (JASDF) flew 430 combat aircraft; and the Japan Maritime Self-Defence Forces (JMSDF) sailed 60 destroyers and 16 submarines.[4]

Post-Cold War Trilateral Dynamics

The end of the Cold War altered the trilateral dynamics between Japan, Russia, and China. It became possible for Japan to engage both China and Russia, and Japan did so from a position of strength. In the 1980s and 1990s, Japan was an economic powerhouse. For instance, in 1995, Japan's GDP was eight times larger than that of China, and 16 times larger than Russia's GDP.[5] Nonetheless, the enormous power gap Japan enjoyed in the 1990s vis-à-vis China would gradually change, and so would the trilateral dynamics.

Japan–China Relations: Confrontation Ahead

From normalization in 1972 and over the next few decades, Japan made significant contributions to developing the Chinese economy by offering official development assistance (ODA), foreign direct investment (FDI), and eventually large trade volumes.[6] Friction over historical issues surfaced from time to time, but, overall, Tokyo and Beijing managed to build a solid relationship through the 1990s and early 2000s. China's extensive and remarkably rapid economic advances over the past few decades have enabled Beijing to boost its military expenditure and capabilities. Between 1990 and 2013, China's defense budget grew by an average of 10% annually, and it has been estimated that it will replace the United States as the world's leading defense spender within a few decades.[7] China's steady accumulation of wealth and power represents a major challenge to Tokyo. Most notably, it has put China in a position to contest American regional dominance in East Asia. In Japan's National Security Strategy (NSS), this power shift now tops the list of issues influencing the "security environment surrounding Japan and national security challenges."[8]

China's growing emphasis on naval power is of particular concern to Japan, as this sustained modernization effort is producing increasingly capable Chinese assets in a domain traditionally dominated by the American military.[9] Accentuated by China's forceful assertion of maritime claims,[10] this development is considerable concern to Japan as a country dependent on the U.S. security umbrella. China's advances raise the risks and costs of regional alliance commitments, challenge American naval dominance in the region, and undermine Japan's national security. While the NSS recognizes that the United States remains the world's largest power as a whole, it notes that the contemporary power shift "has substantially influenced the dynamics of international politics."[11]

Faced with past strategic challenges, notably neighboring a hostile Soviet superpower during the Cold War, Japan has responded primarily by investing in the U.S. alliance and its own military capabilities.[12] Japan's response to the China challenge is no exception. It is reallocating, modernizing, acquiring, and increasing overall inventories of air, naval, surveillance, and amphibious platforms for deployment in the East China Sea. It has altered its defense concept, twice, to strengthen deterrence in the altered security circumstances.[13] Japan has intensified military-operational, military-industrial, and defense policy cooperation with the United States. And Japan has supported the previous Obama administration's "rebalancing" toward Asia. In a quid pro quo for additional U.S. security assurances, Tokyo has extended its alliance commitments beyond the defense of Japan.[14] Japan, in sum, is reshaping its defense and alliance posture in an effort to counterbalance China's emerging military power.[15]

However, the China challenge has also incentivized Japan to broaden strategic cooperation beyond and as a supplement to the U.S. alliance and its indigenous defense posture[16]—involving not only US allies, such as Australia and the Philippines, but also India, Vietnam,[17] and, as will be discussed in greater detail below, Russia.

Unsurprisingly, Beijing has reacted negatively to Japan's rejuvenation in military and security affairs, which it interprets as wrongfully targeting China.[18] Moreover, Japan currently implements its controversial security and defense reforms against the backdrop of blatant nationalist gestures by Prime Minister Abe, adding insult to injury by directing Chinese attention to painful memories of Japanese wartime atrocities.

Even prior to Prime Minister Abe, neo-nationalist currents, challenged and fueled by China's power ascendancy, left their mark on domestic politics and bilateral relations. Administered by Japan, but claimed by China, maritime territory in the East China Sea has found itself a centerpiece of Sino-Japanese nationalist contentions. Reportedly breaking with a precedence of discretion, Japan in 2010 arrested and detained the captain of a Chinese fishing vessel operating in the disputed waters surrounding the islands, triggering a significant diplomatic crisis. Then, Japan in 2012 intervened in the islands' planned transfer of ownership from a private Japanese citizen to the outspokenly nationalist Governor of Tokyo. Japan's official rationale of minimizing negative impact on Sino-Japanese relations proved ineffective, as the frequency of Chinese vessels entering the islands' surrounding waters surged and caused bilateral tensions to rise.[19] As will be discussed below, this Sino-Japanese maritime confrontation has influenced Sino-Russian and Russo-Japanese relations alike, testifying to the triangular political dynamics in play between the three dominating actors indigenous to Northeast Asia.

Sino-Russian Relations: "Strategic Partners"

Sino-Russian relations have seen significant development in the post-Cold War. During the 1990s and early 2000s, military-industrial cooperation was a defining feature of Sino-Russian economic relations and a central component of their "strategic partnership". After a hiatus during 2006–2012, arms sales to China have experienced a major revival, with agreements to deliver 24 Su-35 fighter aircraft, four Lada-class submarines, and the S-400 multi-role air defense system.[20] The latter equips the People's Liberation Army (PLA) to reach well into Japanese airspace and enables, for the first time, a long-range land-based challenge to Japanese and U.S. air superiority in the East China Sea.[21] Likewise, the Su-35 challenges U.S. and Japanese air operations in the region. Japan's Ministry of Defence (MOD) recognizes the significance of this transfer, noting that the fighter is likely to strengthen China's air power, perhaps to the extent of impacting the regional security environment.[22]

Sino-Russian defense ties have also developed markedly in the area of joint military activity. In 2012, the two countries embarked on the "Maritime Cooperation" naval war games series, featuring anti-submarine warfare and live-fire exercises. Since then, the scope of their joint naval war games has expanded. In 2015, it incorporated amphibious assault training. By 2017, China and Russia had conducted naval exercises in the Sea of Japan, the East China Sea, the Mediterranean, and the Baltic Sea.[23]

By encouraging Russia to back its territorial claim, China has invited trilateral dynamics into the East China Sea dispute. Coinciding with the diplomatic turmoil caused by the 2010 fishing trawler incident, Russia and China in September 2010 committed via joint statements to support each other on sovereignty, unity, and territorial integrity. Since the statement was made shortly after the incident, it appeared to Japanese MOD analysts that China sought Russia's backing on its territorial claim vis-à-vis Japan.[24] It is argued that, while formally retaining its position of neutrality, Russia clearly favors China over Japan in their East China Sea island dispute.[25] As some media reports would have it, Russia blatantly waded in waist deep in support of China's claim by navigating three Pacific Fleet naval vessels near the islands in the summer of 2016.

Bilateral relations between China and Russia have recently developed most substantially in the economic realm, particularly in energy cooperation. In 2014, Moscow and Beijing signed two deals on Russian natural gas exports to China, boosting economic interaction while making energy cooperation one of the defining features of their "strategic partnership." For Russia, these agreements are important in order to diversify its energy exports, the vulnerability of which has been exposed by Western sanctions, and to support its ambitions to be a major Asia-Pacific power.[26] China is the key to Russia's energy goals in the Far East. But other prospective regional partners, not least of which Japan, are far from insignificant. In 2014, Japan ranked fifth in global energy consumption,[27] 91% reliant on imports, of which fossil fuels accounts for 93%, to meet its domestic demand following the 2011 Fukushima nuclear accident.[28] Coupled with geographic proximity between the Russian Far East and Japan, this makes for considerable geo-economic compatibility. Yet in 2014, Russia accounted for only 8 and 10% of Japan's oil and gas imports, respectively.[29]

Despite advances in Sino-Russian relations, Tokyo does not appear to be especially worried. For one, they see the contemporary Sino-Russian rapprochement not as an expression of strategic convergence, but rather primarily as promoted by Russian efforts to dull the negative effects of the diplomatic isolation imposed by the West. As Japanese MOD analysts note, "the Ukraine crisis has caused Russia to move increasingly to improve its relations with China."[30] Moreover, they perceive a Russian "fear" developing over an emerging economic overreliance on China. This, in their view, not only applies significant limitations to the contemporary Sino-Russian rapprochement, but moreover presents emerging opportunities for Japan.[31] Russia, they note, is "taking steps to avoid an over-reliance on China and to build a sustainable relationship with Japan."[32] Bilateral cooperation in extracting and trading Russian natural resources would serve both Russian and Japanese interests. For Moscow, it would enable it to diversify its energy revenues, at present heavily reliant on Europe and China. At present, 60% of Russia's crude oil exports are bound for European OECD-member states, while just 18% is exported to China. Russian reliance on Europe for gas exports is even more pronounced, as 75% is exported to European OECD-members.[33] For Tokyo, it would alleviate its dependence on imports from the Middle East and, relatedly, vulnerable sea-lanes.[34] Japan's 2013 National Security Strategy (NSS) explicitly identifies Russia's critical role in this respect, and emphasizes the importance of advancing energy cooperation with Moscow.[35]

The Japanese MOD notes, furthermore, the relatively low-powered nature of Sino-Russian military-industrial cooperation.[36] The expansion of Russo-Chinese joint naval exercises has in their view had insignificant impact on the strength of bilateral military cooperation and on their respective military capabilities.[37] They reduce these "joint maneuvers" to bilateral confidence building measures and to military-diplomatic signaling, with negligible practical military utility, aimed at the United States and its allies.[38] While recognizing that the recent resumption of high-tech military-industrial cooperation gives China access to sophisticated military assets,[39] these agreements have not attracted much public reaction from Japan and do not appear to have had any substantial impact on its defense planning. The limited number of assets involved in the deals and Japan's acquisition of F-35 fifth generation fighters and additional tactical submarines perhaps help to explain Tokyo's relatively relaxed response. Several entities within the MOD note that Sino-Russian arms deals were made possible by a convergence of tactical interests: China's need for state-of-the-art military technology, and Russia's attempts to alleviate Western geopolitical and economic pressure following its annexation of Crimea.[40]

They moreover see the increasing frequency and scope of Sino-Russian military exercises, not as evidence of an emerging alliance, but instead as a reflection of growing bilateral tensions arising from Russian concerns about Chinese military intentions and power.[41] Such exercises, they claim, are increasingly designed to enable Russia to assess China's military capabilities, and vice versa, and therefore, present no major cause for concern.[42] Finally, they find it unlikely for Russia to cooperate with China on such a sensitive issue as the East China Sea territorial dispute, reflecting a relaxed take by the Japanese MOD on the seemingly coordinated Russian and Chinese naval navigations near its contested territory.[43]

Overall, Japan recognizes that Russia is pursuing stronger working relations with China. However, it nuances this take at lengths. For one, the Japanese perceived it as strongly influenced by Russia's diplomatic isolation from the West rather than as a mere expression of strategic convergence between China and Russia. For another, they see no practical utility in the expansion of Sino-Russian war games. They, moreover, consider the contemporary Sino-Russian rapprochement significantly limited by Russian overreliance concerns. Finally and relatedly, they see opportunities to pursue and realize Japan's own strategic interests emerging in the wake of the contemporary Sino-Russian rapprochement. As previously addressed, and further detailed below, developments in Sino-Japanese relations incentivize Japan to improve relations with Russia. These developments further highlight the trilateral dynamics in play between the three leading powers of East Asia.

Japan–Russia Relations: Confronting a Legacy of Hostility

As the Soviet Union dissolved and the Cold War ended, Japan saw an overall reduction in the Russian Far East military threat against which its Self-Defense Forces had gained its strength over the preceding decades.[44] Reflecting the reduced threat environment, Japan's defense posture started to shift in the mid-1990s. Japan gradually retracted the military platforms established to deter and defend against Russia. By 2004, Japan Self-Defence Forces (JSDF) inventories had shrunk from 180.000 to 154.000 troops, from 2.200 to 800 tanks and artillery units, from 430 to 340 combat aircraft, and from 60 to 48 destroyers.[45]

Facilitated by the ensuing reduction in politico-military tensions, economic relations improved steadily as Japan and Russia began taking advantage of their geo-economic compatibility. Yet, the confrontational legacy of Cold War political-military relations persisted. Today, Russia's military posture in the Far East remains a source of bilateral friction. The frequency of JASDF intercepts of Russian aircraft approaching Japanese territory increased from 196 to 493 between 2006 and 2015.[46] Japanese defense analysts view such behavior as symptomatic of a hardline, hostile stance toward Japan.[47] Russia's occupation of the Northern Territories/South Kuriles, seized from Japan near the end of World War II, remains a major obstacle to better relations.[48] Following then President Medvedev's personal inspection of military installations in the disputed territories in 2010, the first ever visit to the islands by a Russian/Soviet head of state, the Japanese Foreign Ministry summoned the Russian ambassador to receive an official protest and temporarily recalled Japan's ambassador from Moscow. Prime Minister Kan denounced Medvedev's island visit as "an unforgivable outrage,"[49] igniting a diplomatic row that brought political-military relations to a post-Cold War low.[50] The sorry state of Russo-Japanese relation in early 2010 accentuates the coming of a fourth phase in Japan–China–Russia post-WWII triangular dynamics. In 2010, China's GDP surpassed that of Japan to become the world's second largest economy, and the collision between a Japanese coast guard vessel and a Chinese fishing vessel soon developed into a bilateral diplomatic crisis. A few months after the post-Cold War low point in Russo-Japanese relations, Japan's security diplomacy toward and relations with Russia would dramatically change character.

New Trilateral Dynamics: Japan's Strategic Outreach to Russia

In a summit with President Medvedev in November 2010, Japan's new Prime Minister Noda highlighted cooperation with Russia in the context of advancing "a foreign and security policy that could meet the needs of the times."[51] In June 2012, Noda agreed with President Putin to strengthen bilateral cooperation in security, defense, and maritime affairs, ambitions he reiterated later that year.[52]

Shinzo Abe's second term as Prime Minister from 2012 has reinforced this positive trend. Japan's fresh take on Russia features prominently in its NSS. "In order to ensure its security," it notes, "it is critical for Japan to advance cooperation in all areas, including security and energy."[53] In 2013, Japan and Russia established a "2+2" security dialogue between their respective Foreign and Defense ministers. The extension of this framework (previously limited to its closest allies, the United States and Australia) to Russia was a landmark in the bilateral relationship. After more than two decades, Russia had re-emerged as a central component of Tokyo's security strategy.

China's emergence as a great power challenging the regional status quo has compelled Tokyo not only to rethink but also reshuffle its priorities vis-à-vis Russia, emphasizing security and geopolitical interests over resolution of the territorial dispute. The magnitude of the China challenge has altered Japan's strategic calculus vis-à-vis Russia. Japan cannot afford a two-front military posture, much less against two great powers on opposing flanks. Efforts to bolster its defenses facing China have been hampered in the past by the need to devote substantial attention and resources to a potential threat from Russia. Tokyo has therefore sought to convert the Russian Far East into a safe "strategic rear." If successful, this would enable it to concentrate on China, while also reducing Moscow's geopolitical dependence on Beijing and the prospects of a deeper Sino-Russian strategic alignment. In short, the growing salience of the China threat in Japanese strategic thinking has brought about a major shift in attitudes and policies toward Russia. As a senior MOD official confirmed, "the Northern Territories issue has become less important than the China-factor in Japan's relations with Russia. Japan is trying to make friends with Russia to counterbalance China."[54]

As previously addressed, Tokyo's strategic engagement with Moscow corresponds with a broader trend in Japanese security policy. It is nonetheless striking and unique in two respects. The first is its military-strategic purpose, as opposed to the primarily normative purposes of the other notable cases.[55] The other is the unprecedented strategic autonomy it reveals on the part of Japan. Tokyo's pursuit of closer ties with other regional powers has been almost entirely under the auspices of the

U.S. alliance. Russia, however, is an altogether different case. At a time when Moscow's relations with Washington have deteriorated to their lowest point in decades,[56] Japan's outreach to Russia is a remarkably display of independence from, and even defiance of, the United States.

Constrained, yet Persistent Japanese Diplomacy

The crisis in Ukraine has, however, exposed the geopolitical limitations and hazards of Japan's strategic outreach to Russia on the one hand, and Tokyo's resolve to maintain it on the other. As direct Russian military involvement in Ukraine became increasingly apparent, Japan joined a U.S.-led effort to punish Moscow for its behavior.[57] Following Russia's formal annexation of Crimea in March 2014, Foreign Minister Kishida announced that Japan had halted discussions on easing visa restrictions, and frozen planned negotiations on three bilateral agreements.[58] Tokyo then answered President Obama's call to suspend Russia from the G8 by convening as the G7, starting with an emergency meeting to coordinate reciprocal action against Moscow.[59] The Hague G7 leaders' summit declaration condemned "Russia's illegal attempt to annex Crimea" and foreshadowed "coordinated sectoral sanctions."[60] In late April 2014, Kishida announced that Japan had issued visa denial orders for 23 individuals.[61] Following evidence of Russian complicity in the downing of the Malaysia Airlines flight MH17, a third round of sanctions was approved and implemented in early August, freezing the assets of 40 individuals and two organizations, and placing restrictions on imports from Crimea.[62] A fourth round of sanctions ensued in late September 2014, banning Russian financial institutions from issuing securities in Japan and restricting defense exports to Russia.[63] In December, Japan updated its list of subjects targeted by asset freeze measures, adding another 26 individuals and 14 organizations.[64]

This pattern highlighted the primary geopolitical limitation on Japan's strategic outreach to Russia, namely Tokyo's recognition that maintaining strong ties with Washington ultimately outranks the strategic objectives it pursues autonomously with Moscow. The Obama administration's policy of isolating the Putin regime placed high expectations on Tokyo, as U.S. State Department officials made clear.[65] The risk of upsetting its patron and undermining the strategically paramount Japan–U.S. alliance compelled a reluctant Tokyo to fall into line on sanctions against Russia. Other geopolitical factors reinforced this imperative.

Official Japanese statements repeatedly stressed opposition to changes in the territorial status quo by the threat or use of force or coercion.[66] Such statements implicitly juxtaposed Russia's annexation of Crimea to China's efforts to lay claim on the contested islands in the East China Sea. Finally, the international outcry at Russia's actions provided further impetus for Japanese sanctions. Projecting the appearance of a responsible state has become particularly important to Tokyo as it attempts to boost its international standing under the banner of "a proactive contribution to peace" by, amongst other, adopting a more muscular and international military posture.[67]

Nevertheless, although the Ukraine crisis has highlighted the geopolitical constraints on rapprochement with Russia, Japan has continued to pursue autonomous strategic objectives. Its sanctions against Russia were comparatively late and mild.[68] Statements on Russia's involvement in the Ukraine crisis have been notably softer than that of other G7 members. Indeed, Tokyo initially refrained from labeling sanctions by their proper name. It has consistently stressed G7 unity, signaling that its own sanctions have been implemented only under duress. It has emphasized the need to maintain dialogue with Moscow in order to obtain its cooperation in resolving the Ukraine conflict and other international crises, such as the civil war in Syria and North Korea's nuclear weapons and ballistic missile programs.

Contrasting U.S. attempts to isolate Russia, Tokyo has maintained its engagement with Moscow. Prime Minister Abe has continued his summitry with President Putin. They met four times between October 2014 and November 2015.[69] Abe sought to capitalize on Japan's 2016 G7 chairmanship, reiterating the importance of dialogue with Russia in the search for a solution to the conflict in Ukraine.[70] He also honored Putin by making an "unofficial" visit to Sochi in May 2016, followed by summits in Vladivostok in September and in Japan in December—all in the face of heavy American opposition.[71] Such developments not only highlight Tokyo's reluctant stance on sanctions but they also indicate that the Ukraine crisis has not fundamentally altered Japan's strategic calculus regarding Russia; its policy of strategic outreach remains very much alive. As a senior MOD official put it, "in the context of Russia' actions towards Ukraine, Japan *temporarily* has to set aside what it is trying to achieve in its relations with Russia [emphasis added]."[72] Japan's most recent Diplomatic Bluebook, outlining the Foreign Ministry's policies and activities for 2017, confirmed that "developing relations with Russia as Japan's appropriate partner in the region contributes to Japan's national interest and regional peace and prosperity."[73]

That said, Japan's pursuit of strategic interests vis-à-vis Russia has been hamstrung by its diplomatic commitments to the U.S. and the U.S. led sanctions regime. Despite recognizing the geopolitical pressure under which Japan has had to operate,[74] Russia has nevertheless taken measures that have exacerbated the difficulties in their bilateral relations. Following Japan's third round of sanctions in August 2014, Moscow imposed retaliatory sanctions, including blacklisting selected Japanese nationals from entering Russia.[75] The second "2+2" gathering of their respective foreign and defense ministers, scheduled to be held in Moscow in 2014, was postponed indefinitely. Russia has also intensified its military activity around Japan, with a sharp increase in incidents of JASDF fighter jets scrambling to intercept Russian aircraft approaching Japanese territory (see above). In 2014, Russian aircraft triggered JASDF fighters to scramble on 473 occasions, exceeding even the PLA (464).[76] Finally, Russia sharpened its rhetoric on the territorial issue, increased the number of official visits to the islands, and outlined plans to expand military infrastructure and installations there, including positioning anti-ship missile batteries and, potentially, building a supplementary naval base for its Pacific Fleet.[77]

While subordinate to the China-factor, Japan has not struck the territorial conflict off its political agenda with Russia. Japan has sought to negate negative developments in the territorial issue and stimulate overall bilateral rapprochement by leveraging its economy. Japan has taken a distinctly cooperative approach, pursuing progress via economic engagement. During President Putin's visit to Japan in December 2016, his first to Japan in more than a decade, Japan and Russia agreed to initiate economic cooperation in the disputed islands. Japan subsequently established an interdepartmental council on Japan–Russia joint economic activities in the disputed territories.[78] Japanese corporations then invested USD 16 billion into development projects in the Russian Far East, while Japan dispatched a delegation of public and private sector representatives on an inspection trip to the disputed islands to identify opportunities for further joint economic ventures.[79] While Moscow prepares warplane, missile defense, and naval deployments to the disputed islands,[80] recent engagement testifies to an increasingly pragmatic approach to the island issue on both sides.

Shifting Diplomatic Winds Under U.S. President Trump?

Notwithstanding its strong track record, Japanese Prime Minister's routinely remind the U.S. government of the paramount importance of the U.S.–Japan alliance. Upon the election of Donald Trump as President Obama's successor, it appeared more important than ever to project the pivotal role Japan and the alliance plays in U.S. foreign policy upon the incoming administration. However, already as President-elect Trump went China bashing, and given that he had called for an end to sanctions and the resumption of cooperation with Russia, Donald Trump's U.S. presidential election victory offered Japan some hope that the diplomatic headwinds were subsiding. Abe's first meeting with Trump in February 2017 indicated as much, Abe later stating that he had secured his backing to re-engage with Russia.[81] Soon after, Japan's foreign and defense ministers finally hosted their Russian counterparts for their long-postponed second "2+2" meeting.[82]

But these hopes proved premature. Trump's personal agenda notwithstanding, Washington remains in confrontation with Moscow over Ukraine, Syria, and, in particular, Russian interference in the U.S. presidential election. In July, the U.S. Congress voted overwhelmingly in favor of a bill to apply additional sanctions against Russia and prevent Trump from easing them without congressional approval. Faced with bipartisan consensus on the matter, Trump recognized that he would be unable to use his presidential veto and so signed the bill into law on 3 August. There then followed the mutual confiscation of diplomatic properties, the forced downsizing of the U.S. diplomatic presence in Russia,[83] and the closure of the Russian consulate in San Francisco.[84] For the foreseeable future, then, U.S. interests will continue to generate risks, constraints, and uncertainties for Japan's strategic engagement vis-à-vis Russia.

Conclusion

In this chapter, I have examined the triangular dynamics between Japan and its two great power neighbors in the context of recent developments in Sino-Russian relations and the rise of China. I find that Tokyo projects a wary but calm attitude towards China and Russia's recent collaborative efforts, largely due to its confidence that Moscow is sensitive to the growing power imbalance in the Sino-Russian relationship and dangers associated with becoming overly geopolitically dependent on Beijing.

In this connection, the Japanese government views the recent progress in the Sino-Russian partnership as reflecting a tactical rather than strategic convergence, let alone an alliance in the making. Moreover, it anticipates growing interest from Moscow in improved ties with Tokyo as a means of reducing Russia's overreliance on China and of maximizing its foreign policy flexibility. Tokyo welcomes this trend as it seeks to develop security enhancing mechanisms complementing its main pillar—American predominance in maritime East Asia—which is increasingly challenged by a rising China. Accordingly, Tokyo has recalibrated its strategic calculus: rapprochement with its former adversary to the north has emerged as a means to manage its emerging adversary to the south. Yet there is a long way to go before such a strategic shift can be consummated. Alignment with the U.S. remains Japan's primary threat management mechanism, ensuring its continued allegiance to Washington. While a strong U.S.-alliance inspires Japan's pursuit of an ambitious foreign policy agenda, the alliance also constrains Japan's ability to accomplish the agenda's autonomous objective vis-à-vis Russia.

Notes

1. Wishnick (2001), Weitz (2003), Nye (2015), Layne (2002).
2. Lühti (2008).
3. Dittmer (2004).
4. Ministry of Defense (1976), Patalano (2008).
5. IMF (2017).
6. Jerdén and Hagström (2012).
7. The Economist (2012).
8. National Security Council of Japan (2013).
9. Heginbotham et al. (2015), p. 21.
10. Grønning (2014).
11. National Security Council of Japan (2013).
12. See for instance Yamaguchi (2012), pp. 81, 84–85, Patalano (2008), pp. 865, 867, Samuels (2007), pp. 65, 104, 174, Hughes (2009), p. 311.
13. Grønning (2014), Bowers and Grønning (2017).
14. Cabinet of Japan (2014).
15. Grønning (2014), Bowers and Grønning (2017).
16. National Security Council of Japan (2013), p. 14, Ministry of Defense (2013b), p. 5.
17. Bowers and Grønning (2017).
18. South China Morning Post (2015).

19. Bowers and Grønning (2017).
20. South China Morning Post (2013), Pravda (2014).
21. For another analysis of the implications of the S-400 for Japan, see Mizokami (2015).
22. National Institute for Defense Studies (2016), p. 246.
23. China Military Online (2014), Tass (2015), Higgins (2017).
24. National Institute for Defense Studies (2011), p. 188.
25. Brown (2015).
26. Kremlin (2012).
27. Enerdata (2015).
28. U.S. Energy Information Administration (2015a).
29. Ibid.
30. National Institute for Defense Studies (2016), p. 209
31. Ibid., pp. 178, 218–219, National Institute for Defense Studies (2017), p. 186.
32. Ibid., p. 163.
33. Kim and Blank (2013), U.S. Energy Information Administration (2015b), pp. 137–140.
34. National Security Council of Japan (2013), pp. 8–9, 34.
35. Ibid., pp. 25–26.
36. The drop in Russian arms sales to China in the second half of the 2000s was due to Moscow's growing apprehensions about the widening imbalance of power between the two countries. More specifically, China's expanding indigenous arms productions became a source of friction. See National Institute for Defense Studies (2011), p. 203.
37. National Institute for Defense Studies (2016), pp. 209, 219.
38. Ibid., p. 222.
39. Ibid., p. 209.
40. Ibid., Ministry of Defense (2016), p. 84.
41. National Institute for Defense Studies (2012), pp. 187, 196, National Institute for Defense Studies (2013), p. 244, National Institute for Defense Studies (2014), pp. 222, 232–234.
42. National Institute for Defense Studies (2013), p. 293. National Institute for Defense Studies (2014), p. 232.
43. National Institute for Defense Studies (2017), p. 177.
44. National Institute for Defense Studies (1996).
45. Ministry of Defense (2010).
46. Ministry of Defense (2015).
47. Ministry of Defense (2013a), pp. 190–193.
48. For one Russian, one Japanese, and one Western example, see Amirov (2006), pp. 122–123, Hasegawa (1999), pp. 123, 125–126, Hornung (2012), p. 144.

49. The Telegraph (2011).
50. For more on the escalatory diplomatic exchange, see Brown (2014).
51. Ministry of Foreign Affairs (2011).
52. Ministry of Foreign Affairs (2012a), Ministry of Foreign Affairs (2012b).
53. National Security Council of Japan (2013), pp. 25–26.
54. Senior Official, Strategic Planning Office, Ministry of Defense, Personal Interview, 31 March, 2014.
55. Ibid.
56. Hahn (2013).
57. The White House (2014).
58. Ministry of Foreign Affairs (2014c).
59. Business Insider (2014).
60. European Commission (2014).
61. Ministry of Foreign Affairs (2014e).
62. Kantei (2014a), Ministry of Foreign Affairs (2014b).
63. Ministry of Foreign Affairs (2014d).
64. Ministry of Foreign Affairs (2014a).
65. Armstrong (2014).
66. Ministry of Foreign Affairs (2014c).
67. National Security Council of Japan (2013), p. 5.
68. Brown (2016), p. 4.
69. Ministry of Foreign Affairs (2015).
70. Barber and Harding (2016).
71. Meyer (2016), Ministry of Foreign Affairs (2016a, b).
72. Senior Official, Strategic Planning Office, Ministry of Defense, Personal Interview, 31 March, 2014.
73. Ministry of Foreign Affairs (2017a), p. 148.
74. Martin (2014), RT (2015), Sputnik International (2016).
75. Kantei (2014b).
76. Ministry of Defense (2015), Kelly (2014).
77. Agence France-Presse (2016).
78. Sputnik International (2017a).
79. Sputnik (2017b, c), Krasnoukhov (2017).
80. Osborn (2018).
81. Kyodo (2017).
82. Ministry of Foreign Affairs (2017b).
83. Rampton and Zengerle (2017).
84. State Department (2017).

Literature

Agence France-Presse. 2016. Russia To Deploy Missile Systems on Kuril Islands, Defense Minister Says. *Defense News*, March 25. http://www.defensenews.com/story/defense/international/asia-pacific/2016/03/25/russia-japan-kuril-islands/82261548/. Accessed 24 Apr 2016.

Amirov, V. 2006. Japan and the Asia-Pacific: A Russian Perspective. In *Russia, America, and Security in the Asia-Pacific*, ed. R. Azizian and B. Reznik, 112–123. Honolulu: Asia-Pacific Center for Security Studies.

Armstrong, R. 2014. U.S. Looks for Asian Cooperation on Sanctions Against Russia. *Reuters*, July 30. http://www.reuters.com/article/us-ukraine-crisis-asia-idUSKBN0FZ13720140730. Accessed 18 Apr 2016.

Barber, L., and R. Harding. 2016. Japan's Abe Calls for Putin to Be Brought in from the Cold. *Financial Times*, January 17. http://www.ft.com/cms/s/0/988d04c2-bcd3-11e5-846f-79b0e3d20eaf.html#axzz46C1jm0r4. Accessed 18 Apr 2016.

Bowers, I., and B.E.M. Grønning. 2017. Protecting the Status Quo: Japan's Response to the Rise of China. In *Strategic Adjustment and the Rise of China: Power and Politics in East Asia*, ed. Robert S. Ross and Øystein Tunsjø, 137–168. Ithaca, NY: Cornell University Press.

Brown, J.D.J. 2014. Hajime!—The Causes and Prospects of the New Start in Russian–Japanese Relations. *Asia Policy* 18: 81–110.

Brown, J.D.J. 2015. Towards an Anti-Japanese Territorial Front? Russia and the Senkaku/Diaoyu Dispute. *Europe-Asia Studies* 67 (6): 893–915.

Brown, J. 2016. Abe's 2016 Plan to Break the Deadlock in the Territorial Dispute with Russia. *The Asia-Pacific Journal* 14 (4): 1–26.

Business Insider. 2014. Obama Calls For Emergency G7 Meeting To Discuss Repercussions For Russia, March 24. http://www.businessinsider.com/obama-calls-for-emergency-g7-meeting-to-discuss-repercussions-for-russia-2014-3?IR=T. Accessed 17 Apr 2016.

Cabinet of Japan. 2014. Cabinet Decision on Development of Seamless Security Legislation to Ensure Japan's Survival and Protect Its People. http://www.mofa.go.jp/fp/nsp/page23e_000273.html. Accessed 25 May 2015.

China Military Online. 2014. Russian Naval Fleet Sets Off to China for Joint Exercise, May 14. http://eng.chinamil.com.cn/news-channels/china-military-news/2014-05/14/content_5903385.htm. Accessed 20 Feb 2015.

Dittmer L. 2004. Ghost of the Strategic Triange: The Sino-Russian Partnership. In *Chinese Foreign Policy: Pragmatism and Strategic Behavior*. Armonk and New York: M.E. Sharpe.

Enerdata. 2015. Global Energy Statistical Yearbook 2015. https://yearbook.enerdata.net/#energy-consumption-data.html. Accessed 22 Apr 2016.

European Commission. 2014. The Hague Declaration Following the G7 Meeting on March 24. 24 March. http://europa.eu/rapid/press-release_STATEMENT-14-82_en.htm. Accessed 16 Apr 2016.

Grønning, B.E.M. 2014. Japan's Shifting Military Priorities: Counterbalancing China's Rise. *Asian Security* 10 (1): 1–21.

Grønning, B.E.M. 2017. Japans's Security Cooperation with the Philippines and Vietnam. *Pacific Review*, pp. 1–20, https://doi.org/10.1080/09512748.2017.1397730.

Hahn, G.M. 2013. Russia in 2012: From 'Thaw' and 'Reset' to 'Freeze'. *Asian Survey* 53 (1): 214–223.

Hasegawa, T. 1999. The Northeast Asian Dimension. In *Japan and Russia in Northeast Asia: Partners in the 21st Century*, ed. V.I. Ivanov and K.S. Smith, 121–128. Westport, CT: Praeger.

Heginbotham, E., M. Nixon, F.E. Morgan, J. Hagen, J.L. Heim, J. Engstrom, S. Li, P. DeLuca, M.C. Libicki, and D.R. Frelinger. 2015. *The U.S.–China Military Scorecard: Forces, Geography, and the Evolving Balance of Power, 1996–2017*, RAND Corporation.

Higgins, A. 2017. China and Russia Hold First Joint Naval Drill in the Baltic Sea. *New York Times*, July 25. https://www.nytimes.com/2017/07/25/world/europe/china-russia-baltic-navy-exercises.html?mcubz=0. Accessed 10 Aug 2017.

Hornung, J.W. 2012. Japan and the Asia-Pacific. In *FROM APEC 2011 TO APEC 2012: American and Russian Perspectives on Asia-Pacific Security and Cooperation*, ed. R. Azizian and A. Lukin, 138–150. Honolulu and Vladivostok: Asia-Pacific Center for Security Studies and Far Eastern Federal University.

Hughes, C.W. 2009. 'Super-Sizing' the DPRK Threat: Japan's Evolving Military Posture and North Korea. *Asian Survey* 49 (2): 291–311.

International Monetary Fund. 2017. *IMF World Economic Outlook Database*, October. Available at https://www.imf.org/external/pubs/ft/weo/2017/02/weodata/.

Jerdén, B., and L. Hagström. 2012. Rethinking Japan's China Policy: Japan as an Accommodator in the Rise of China, 1978–2011. *Journal of East Asian Studies* 12: 215–250.

Kantei. 2014a. Press Conference by the Chief Cabinet Secretary (Excerpt), August 5. http://japan.kantei.go.jp/tyoukanpress/201408/5_a.html. Accessed 16 Apr 2016.

Kantei. 2014b. Press Conference by the Chief Cabinet Secretary (Excerpt), August 25. http://japan.kantei.go.jp/tyoukanpress/201408/25_a.html. Accessed 18 Apr 2016.

Kelly, T. 2014. Japan Jets Scrambling to Counter Rising Russian Incursions. *Reuters*, October 15. http://www.reuters.com/article/us-japan-russia-idUSKCN0I42NR20141015. Accessed 18 Apr 2016.

Kim, Y.K., and S. Blank. 2013. Rethinking Russo-Chinese Relations in Asia: Beyond Russia's Chinese Dilemma. *China: An International Journal* 11 (3): 136–147.

Krasnoukhov, Sergei. 2017. Japanese Business Delegation Visits Russia's Kuril Islands. *TASS Russian News Agency*, June 28. http://tass.com/politics/953604.

Kremlin. 2012. Address to the Federal Assembly, December 12. http://en.special.kremlin.ru/events/president/news/17118. Accessed 22 Apr 2016.

Kyodo. 2017. Abe Says Trump Encouraged Him to Boost Ties, Dialogue with Putin, February 14. https://www.japantimes.co.jp/news/2017/02/14/national/politics-diplomacy/abe-says-trump-encouraged-boost-ties-dialogue-putin/#.WaFJrm7-u71. Accessed 10 Aug 2017.

Layne, Chris. 2002. Offshore Balancing Revisited. *Washington Quarterly* 25 (2): 233–248.

Lühti, L. 2008. *The Sino-Soviet Split: Cold War in the Communist World*. Princeton, NJ: Princeton Univeristy Press.

Martin, A. 2014. Japan Announces Fresh Russia Sanctions. *Wall Street Journal*, September 24. http://www.wsj.com/articles/japan-announces-new-russia-sanctions-1411553420. Accessed 19 Apr 2016.

Meyer, H. 2016. Abe Eases Putin's Isolation With Talks on Territorial Dispute. *Bloomberg*, May 5. http://www.bloomberg.com/news/articles/2016-05-05/abe-breaks-putin-s-isolation-as-rare-g-7-leader-to-visit-russia. Accessed 9 May 2016.

Ministry of Defense. 1976. *National Defense Program Outline*.

Ministry of Defense. 2010. National Defense Program Guidelines for FY 2011 and Beyond.

Ministry of Defense. 2013a. *Defense of Japan 2013*.

Ministry of Defense. 2013b. National Defense Program Guidelines for FY 2014 and Beyond, December 17. http://www.mod.go.jp/j/approach/agenda/guideline/2014/pdf/20131217_e2.pdf. Accessed 19 Apr 2016.

Ministry of Defense. 2015. *Defense of Japan 2015*.

Ministry of Defense. 2016. *Defense of Japan 2016*.

Ministry of Foreign Affairs. 2011. Japan–Russia Summit Meeting (Overview), November 13. http://www.mofa.go.jp/region/europe/russia/meet1111.html. Accessed 16 Jan 2014.

Ministry of Foreign Affairs. 2012a. Japan–Russia Summit Meeting at the G20 Los Cabos Summit (Overview), June 19. http://www.mofa.go.jp/region/europe/russia/meeting1206_pm2.html. Accessed 16 Jan 2014.

Ministry of Foreign Affairs. 2012b. Japan–Russia Summit Meeting on the Occasion of APEC Leaders' Meeting in Vladivostok (Overview), September 8. http://www.mofa.go.jp/policy/economy/apec/2012/j_russia_sm.html. Accessed 9 Sep 2013.

Ministry of Foreign Affairs. 2014a. Additional Designation of Individuals and Entities Subject to the Measures to Freeze Assets of Those Who Are Considered to Be Directly Involved in "Annexation" of the Autonomous Republic of Crimea and the City of Sevastopol or Destabilization of Eastern Part of Ukraine, December 9. http://www.mofa.go.jp/press/release/press3e_000028.html. Accessed 20, 2016.

Ministry of Foreign Affairs. 2014b. Measures to Freeze Assets of Those Who Are Considered to Be Directly Involved in "Annexation" of the Autonomous Republic of Crimea and the City of Sevastopol or Destabilization of Eastern Part of Ukraine, August 5. http://www.mofa.go.jp/press/release/press4e_000387.html. Accessed 2 Oct 2014.

Ministry of Foreign Affairs. 2014c. Press Conference by Minister for Foreign Affairs Fumio Kishida, March 18. http://www.mofa.go.jp/press/kaiken/kaiken4e_000054.html. Accessed 15 June 2014.

Ministry of Foreign Affairs. 2014d. Press Conference by the Chief Cabinet Secretary (Excerpt), September 24. http://japan.kantei.go.jp/tyoukanpress/201409/24_p.html. Accessed 20 Apr 2014.

Ministry of Foreign Affairs. 2014e. Statement by the Minister for Foreign Affairs of Japan on the Sanctions Against Russia Over the Situation in Ukraine, April 29. http://www.mofa.go.jp/press/release/press4e_000281.html. Accessed 16 Apr 2016.

Ministry of Foreign Affairs. 2015. Japan–Russia Relations (Archives), November 15. http://www.mofa.go.jp/region/europe/russia/archives.html. Accessed 18 Apr 2016.

Ministry of Foreign Affairs. 2016a. Japan–Russia Summit Meeting on the Occasion of the 2nd Eastern Economic Forum, September 3. http://www.mofa.go.jp/erp/rss/page3e_000566.html. Accessed 10 Aug 2017.

Ministry of Foreign Affairs. 2016b. President of the Russian Federation to Visit Japan, December 18. http://www.mofa.go.jp/erp/rss/northern/page4e_000563.html. Accessed 10 Aug 2017.

Ministry of Foreign Affairs. 2017a. *Diplomatic Bluebook.*

Ministry of Foreign Affairs. 2017b. Japan–Russia Foreign and Defence Ministerial Consultation ("2+2" Ministerial Meeting), March 20. http://www.mofa.go.jp/erp/rss/northern/page4e_000593.html. Accessed 10 Aug 2017.

Mizokami, K. 2015. 5 Chinese Weapons of War Japan Should Fear. *The National Interest*, January 10. http://nationalinterest.org/feature/5-chinese-weapons-war-japan-should-fear-12009. Accessed 21 Mar 2015.

National Institute for Defense Studies. 1996. *East Asia Strategic Review 1996.*

National Institute for Defense Studies. 2011. *East Asian Strategic Review 2011*. Tokyo: The Japan Times Ltd.

National Institute for Defense Studies. 2012. *East Asian Strategic Review 2012*. Tokyo: The Japan Times Ltd.

National Institute for Defense Studies. 2013. *East Asian Strategic Review 2013*. Tokyo: The Japan Times Ltd.

National Institute for Defense Studies. 2014. *East Asian Strategic Review 2014*. Tokyo: The Japan Times Ltd.

National Institute for Defense Studies. 2016. *East Asian Strategic Review 2016*. Tokyo: The Japan Times Ltd.

National Institute for Defense Studies. 2017. *East Asian Strategic Review 2017*. Tokyo: The Japan Times Ltd.

National Security Council of Japan. 2013. National Security Strategy. December 17. http://japan.kantei.go.jp/96_abe/documents/2013/__icsFiles/afieldfile/2013/12/18/NSS.pdf. Accessed 19 Apr 2016.

Nye, J. 2015. A New Sino-Russian Alliance? January 12. http://www.project-syndicate.org/commentary/russia-china-alliance-by-joseph-s–nye-2015-01. Accessed 21 Mar 2015.

Osborn, Andrew. 2018. Russia Approves Warplane Deployment on Disputed Island Near Japan. *Reuters*, February 2. https://www.reuters.com/article/us-japan-russia-islands-military/russia-approves-warplane-deployment-on-disputed-island-near-japan-idUSKBN1FM169.

Patalano, Alessio. 2008. Shielding the 'Hot Gates': Submarine Warfare and Japanese Naval Strategy in the Cold War and Beyond (1976–2006). *Journal of Strategic Studies* 31 (6): 859–895.

Pravda. 2014. China to Receive Russian S-400 Systems in Exchange for Political Support, November 28. http://english.pravda.ru/world/asia/28-11-2014/129162-china_russia-0/. Accessed 19 Feb 2015.

Rampton, R., and P. Zengerle. 2017. Trump Signs Russia Sanctions Bill, Moscow Calls It 'Trade War'. *Reuters*. https://www.reuters.com/article/us-usa-trump-russia-idUSKBN1AI1Y4. Accessed 10 Aug 2017.

RT. 2015. Japan Admits US Pressure Behind Anti-Russian Sanctions—Duma Speaker, May 22. https://www.rt.com/politics/261113-naryshkin-japan-us-pressure/. Accessed 18 Apr 2016.

Samuels, R.J. 2007. *Securing Japan: Tokyo's Grand Strategy and the Future of East Asia*. Ithaca: Cornell University Press.

South China Morning Post. 2013. China to Buy Lada-Class Subs, Su-35 Fighters from Russia, March 25. http://www.scmp.com/news/china/article/1199448/china-buy-russian-fighters-submarines. Accessed 2 Mar 2015.

South China Morning Post. 2015. China Accuses Japan of Destabilising Regional Security After Tokyo Approves Security Bills, September 19. http://www.scmp.com/news/asia/east-asia/article/1859647/japan-parliament-passes-controversial-security-bills-amid. Accessed 20 Jan 2018.

Sputnik. 2016. US Pressure on Japan Restricts Moscow-Tokyo Dialogue, April 16. http://sputniknews.com/world/20160416/1038113380/us-russia-japan-cooperation.html. Accessed 18 Apr 2016.

Sputnik. 2017a. Japan Forms Interdepartmental Council on Cooperation with Russia on Kurils, February 7. https://sputniknews.com/politics/201702071050411717-japan-forms-russia-kurils-council/. Accessed 20 Jan 2018.

Sputnik. 2017b. Japan Investments in 21 Russian Far East Projects Amount to Over $16Bln, June 3. https://sputniknews.com/russia/201706031054268158-japan-invest-billions-russia-far-east/. Accessed 20 Jan 2018.

Sputnik. 2017c. Japan to Dispatch Expert Team to Russian Kurils to Look into New Mutual Projects, September 20. https://sputniknews.com/russia/201709201057540903-tokyo-japan-kuril-islands-cooperation/. Accessed 20 Jan 2018.

State Department. 2017. Senior Administration Official on Russia, August 31. https://www.state.gov/r/pa/prs/ps/2017/08/273751.htm. Accessed 2 Sept 2017.

Tass. 2015. Russia, China Set Up Headquarters Joint Mediterranean Sea Military Drills, May 7. http://tass.ru/en/russia/793463. Accessed 13 Apr 2016.

The Economist. 2012. The Dragon's New Teeth, April 7. http://www.economist.com/node/21552193. Accessed 31 Mar 2015.

The Telegraph. 2011. Japan Infuriated by Russia's Claim on Island Chain, February 8. http://www.telegraph.co.uk/news/worldnews/asia/japan/8310215/Japan-infuriated-by-Russias-claim-on-island-chain.html. Accessed 7 Jan 2014.

The White House. 2014. Statement of G-7 Leaders on Ukraine. https://www.whitehouse.gov/the-press-office/2014/03/12/statement-g-7-leaders-ukraine. Accessed 16 Apr 2016.

U.S. Energy Information Administration. 2015a. Japan, January 30. https://www.eia.gov/beta/international/analysis.cfm?iso=JPN. Accessed 22 Apr 2016.

U.S. Energy Information Administration. 2015b. Russia, July 28. https://www.eia.gov/beta/international/analysis.cfm?iso=RUS. Accessed 22 Apr 2016.

Weitz, R. 2003. Why Russia and China Have Not Formed an Anti-American Alliance. *Naval War College Review* 56 (4): 39–61.

Wishnick, E. 2001. Russia and China. *Asian Survey* 41 (5): 797–821.

Yamaguchi, N. 2012. Balance Threat Perceptions and Strategic Priorities. In *Maritime Strategy and National Security in Japan and Britain: From the First Alliance to Post-9/11*, ed. ALessio Patalano, 81–103. Brill.

CHAPTER 12

Whom to Call? In Search of a European Policy on Russia and China

Robin Allers

Introduction

In February 2017, one of the leading representatives of the European Union, Council President Donald Tusk, issued a warning to member states. In preparation of their next summit, he invited them to reflect on "three threats [to Europe], which have previously not occurred, at least not on such a scale."[1] As part of the first threat, "the geopolitical situation", Tusk singled out "an increasingly, let us call it, assertive China, especially on the seas, Russia's aggressive policy towards Ukraine and its neighbours" together with conflict and turmoil on Europe's southern periphery. More surprisingly, he also counted the United States under the newly elected president Donald Trump as a threat to European security:

> For the first time in our history, in an increasingly multipolar external world, so many are becoming openly anti-European, or Eurosceptic at best. Particularly the change in Washington puts the European Union in a difficult situation; with the new administration seeming to put into question the last 70 years of American foreign policy.

R. Allers (✉)
Norwegian Institute for Defence Studies, Oslo, Norway
e-mail: rallers@ifs.mil.no

J. I. Bekkevold and B. Lo (eds.), *Sino-Russian Relations in the 21st Century*, https://doi.org/10.1007/978-3-319-92516-5_12

Tusk furthermore emphasized that a disintegration of the European Union will not lead to the restoration of some mythical, full sovereignty of its member states, but to their real dependence on the great powers: the United States, Russia and China. His main argument was that only together could Europe be fully independent. The question left open by Tusk was whether Europe really should aim to be independent of the United States and if an independent role implied being a player in the concert of great powers.

Processes like the emergence of a coordinated European foreign policy, the rise of China, and Russia's resurgence after the demise of the Soviet Union are of a long-term structural nature. But these developments are also repeatedly propelled by "strategic shocks", events that require Europe to rethink, adapt, and reshape structures and policies. The end of bipolarity in 1989/90, the terrorist attacks of 9/11 and the financial crisis of 2008/9 count as such turning points in European and global history. In recent years, the crisis over Russia's illegal annexation of Crimea in 2014 has led to major changes in the West's relations with Russia and in the way Europe thinks about its security. Although it is too early to judge the long-term impact, the election of Donald Trump in 2016 may also qualify as a strategic shock in the sense that the new president's doctrine of America First forces Europe to rethink its role in the world.

The aim of this chapter is to examine Europe's policy on Russia and China. Europe—as the European Union and as a group of sovereign nation states—has a long tradition of pursuing economic and diplomatic relations with these powers. But Europe's policy on China and Russia has to be understood within the larger context of great power relations, and in particular in light of the United States' strategic choices. America's response to the dual development of China's economic and military rise and Russia's quest for great power influence presents Europe with a number of potential dilemmas. If the United States is rebalancing to Asia, what does this mean for transatlantic relations and Europe's role in global security? Can Europe still rely on the United States for its security or should it seek more strategic autonomy? Will Europe have to follow the United States in its turn towards Asia, or should Europe and the United States agree on a new transatlantic division of labour with Europe taking care of its own neighbourhood and Russia, and the United States engaging in balance of power politics in Asia? Do Europe and the United States share the same threat perceptions with regard to Russia and China? If not, how will this influence the future of transatlantic relations?

In the following pages, I will discuss to what extent Europeans see Russia and China as challenges of the same order and how they seek to meet these challenges by balancing deterrence and engagement. Next, I will analyze the importance of the transatlantic relationship for Europe's ties with Russia and China and discuss how Trump is threatening Western unity. In order to assess Europe's policies and thinking on Russia and China, however, we first need to analyze Europe's role, ambition and limitations as a player in international affairs.

Europe as a Foreign Policy and Security Actor

Henry Kissinger, former United States National Security Advisor and Secretary of State, is credited with two of the most scathing comments on European foreign policy. At the beginning of the 1970s, he famously wondered whom he should call if he wanted to speak with Europe. Whether he actually said it or not, the quote highlighted Europe's difficulties in speaking with one voice in international affairs.[2] Kissinger's other remark was even more unpalatable to European leaders. The United States, he claimed in a speech in 1973, "has global interests and responsibilities" whereas "our European allies have regional interests."[3] Both assessments were provocative given that the members of the newly enlarged European Community (EC, as it was called then) had just agreed to coordinate their foreign policies. Moreover, Britain, France and later West Germany attempted to engage China and the Soviet Union economically and diplomatically.[4] In fact, Kissinger's statements need to be understood in light of growing tensions between the United States and an increasingly independent Europe.[5] It is true, nevertheless, that neither national initiatives for détente and ostpolitik nor multilateral processes like the Conference for Security and Cooperation in Europe (CSCE) were possible without the participation of the superpowers. Ultimately, the United States and the Soviet Union claimed control over all contacts between the blocs and Nixon's visit to Beijing in 1972 became the pivotal moment in the West's relations with China.[6] The EC played a minor part in the geopolitical dimension of the Cold War. Relations between the EC and the Soviet Union remained mainly at the bilateral level and were not formalized before the end of the 1980s. In fact, Moscow never fully accepted the EC as a partner, regarding it "with disdain, as a capitalist cartel".[7] By contrast, the Community's relations with China contributed substantially to extending Europe's geographical reach as an external actor. In 1975, the EC and China established diplomatic relations—four years before the United States—and in 1978 they signed their first trade agreement. In 1988, the European Commission opened a delegation in Beijing.[8] A workshop on Sino-European relations during the Cold War concluded that "China, unlike the Soviet Union, was a strong supporter of European political and economic integration because it believed it would be useful in forging a multi-polar world."[9]

Four decades after Kissinger's assessment of Europe as an incoherent actor with regional interests, much has changed. Since the beginning of the 1990s, the European Union has had a Common Foreign and Security Policy (CFSP) and in the 2000s, it also officially became a security actor with a Common Security and Defence Policy (CSDP). Today, the EU is a global player with diplomatic missions in every country and membership or associate status in hundreds of global, regional and sub-regional forums and dialogues. For many countries—including Russia and China—the EU is the biggest trading partner, and in many regions of the world, it wields considerable influence as the largest provider of humanitarian assistance and long-term development aid.[10] However, as in Kissinger's time, Europe as an international actor continues to confuse. According to then Commission president Juan Manuel Barroso, the Lisbon Treaty of 2009 had solved the "so-called Kissinger question" by strengthening the role of the High Representative for Foreign Affairs and Security Policy together with a set of other measures.[11] Faced with four presidents (Council, Commission, Parliament, rotating presidency), a High Representative and other commissioners with external responsibilities plus national leaders like the German Chancellor or the French President, outsiders and insiders nevertheless continue to wonder whom to call and where to look if they want to know the European standpoint.[12]

Is Europe's influence limited to soft power and geographically restricted to its neighbourhood? In answering this question, we have to take into account that over the past decade, great power rivalry has again become the centre of attention in world politics.[13] In a realist view that sees international relations as a balance of powers, Europe does not count as an equal. Scholars and commentators often discuss the great power dimension of ongoing and potential conflicts in the Middle East and Asia as if Europe were not a key player. This omission or at least negligence may be due to Europe being a multidimensional foreign policy and security actor, composed of nation states and common structures, simultaneously operating in the framework of the EU, NATO and other formats. Furthermore, the European Union is a global economic and financial power, but lacks the will and the capacity to back up diplomacy and soft power with military force.

Arguably, the most pointed description of Europe as a foreign policy and security actor is by Robert Kagan, who juxtaposed the United States as Mars with Europe as Venus. Under the influence of the Iraq war of 2002/2003, Kagan compared America's willingness to project military power with Europe's reluctance to do so.[14] This characterization builds on Francois Dûchene's understanding of Europe as a "civilian power". Developed in the 1970s, this concept remained at the centre of debates on Europe's role as an actor in international relations until today.[15] Although the EU has developed a common security policy and nurtures ambitions of strategic autonomy, it maintains a preference for civilian measures. However, according to its High Representative, there is no contradiction here:

> The European Union has always prided itself on its soft power – and it will keep doing so, because we are the best in this field. However, the idea that Europe is an exclusively 'civilian power' does not do justice to an evolving reality. For instance, the European Union currently deploys seventeen military and civilian operations, with thousands of men and women serving under the European flag for peace and security – our own security, and our partners'. For Europe, soft and hard power go hand in hand.[16]

The image of a weak and predominantly civilian foreign and security actor changes if one analyses Europe's influence in a more holistic way. One does not need to agree with Andrew Moravcsik that Europe is "the 'invisible superpower' in contemporary world politics",[17] but when aggregated the continent's economic, diplomatic and military resources make it a global actor with considerable influence. Critical voices remark that the EU, despite having all available instruments, is unwilling to become a comprehensive power. But Europe is certainly no soft or civilian power when the western (or transatlantic) and national dimensions are considered. All European countries maintain armed forces for the purpose of national defence and they contribute troops and capabilities to multinational operations in the framework of NATO and the EU, and through contributions to the United Nations and the OSCE. The EU strives for strategic autonomy, member states defend their sovereignty, and NATO wants to be the principal security framework for collective defence. But these frameworks depend on each other, cooperate and constitute Europe's security and defence in a division of labour.[18] When Europe's assets are aggregated, as Moravcsik recommends, the "oft-repeated phrase that 'Americans are from Mars and Europeans are from Venus' is a great sound bite but a misleading policy analysis."[19]

Relations with Russia and China illustrate how the Western, the European and the national dimensions of European security cooperation interact. Europeans know that they stand stronger together and they are committed to common policies and jointly agreed principles. Nevertheless, member states continue to pursue national policies and accept, in some degree, that this may undermine their common position. German Chancellors frequently visit China with large business delegations and hold joint cabinet meetings to strengthen bilateral ties.[20] They also defend projects such as the Nord Stream 2 pipeline through the Baltic Sea against complaints from American and European allies, and resist interventions from the European Commission.[21] EU members like Hungary and Greece accept support from Russia and have become increasingly receptive to Chinese investments as part of the Belt and Road Initiative (BRI).[22] The United Kingdom and France, for their part, maintain a comparatively large military presence in the Asia-Pacific region supporting their self-perception as security actors whose influence and interests are global.[23]

In each case, member states have to weigh the advantages of engaging bilaterally against the danger of undermining a position of common strength and standing alone in face of a great power. The challenge is to maintain cohesion—of Europe and of the West. Concluding his letter to member states, Tusk asked European leaders to remind themselves and their American colleagues of the United States' own motto, "*united we stand, divided we fall*". Europe's influence as an external actor and its ability to deal with external challenges to its security and prosperity depend on unity and a strong transatlantic relationship. Europe is a great power in international relations only if the Western, the European and the national dimensions work together. This is why the prospect of a weakened transatlantic relationship and the potential erosion of European unity are seen as the biggest threats to Western security.

Russia as a Threat, China as a Challenge?

At the beginning of the 2000s, Europe had quite similar ambitions for its relations with Russia and China. The EU's first security strategy published in 2003 called for "closer relations with Russia" and hoped that "respect for common values will reinforce progress towards a strategic partnership." The same document put China in the same category as India and Canada, as a country with which the EU intended to establish a strategic partnership.[24] Over the past decade, however, perceptions and relations have developed in very differently. Today, European security strategies like the EU Global Strategy or national white papers and defence reviews present Russia as a resurgent and revisionist power, aggressive and a potential threat. In their rare references to China, by contrast, the same documents note its rising global influence and regional assertiveness but do not identify it as a direct security challenge or threat.[25] A key reason for this difference is the Ukraine crisis of 2014, but there are also more structural factors.

One such factor is geography. Russia is Europe's immediate neighbour and although few Europeans fear Russian invasion they are concerned about its increased military presence from the Arctic and the Baltic Sea down to the Black Sea. Moreover, the fact that Russia's "sphere of influence" overlaps with countries which wish to be under the EU's and NATO's security umbrella is a source of tension and potential conflict. By contrast, as Ian Bond observes, "most Europeans (including policy-makers) tend to take an 'out of sight, out of mind' approach to all but the most serious problems in Asia".[26] To be sure, Tusk and other European decision makers acknowledge China's maritime assertiveness. But unlike Russian military exercises and strategies of hybrid or unconventional warfare, China's destabilising activities in its neighbourhood are not perceived as a threat to Europe's territorial integrity. Nor are Europeans agreed on the prospect of closer security cooperation between the great powers. In the aftermath of the Ukraine crisis, some observers saw a new and "frightening" alliance emerging between Moscow and Beijing. They feared that Western sanctions would drive Russia closer towards China and that both countries might develop economic and financial structures independent from the West and immune to its pressure. After all, Russia had the oil that China needed and both could profit from extended defence cooperation. Others cautioned, however, that such an alliance would be unequal, with China in the driver's seat, and that earlier attempts at closer cooperation had failed because of rival interests in Central Asia. Moreover, while both countries have an interest in countering America's geopolitical dominance, China in particular is wary about endangering its economic relations with Europe.[27] The Chinese navy's participation in a Russian exercise in the Baltic Sea in 2017 made headlines in Europe and was interpreted by some as an expression of China's strategy of maritime expansion and even as a provocation.[28] However, concerns about the exercise, which was part of a longer circumnavigation with several joint drills and port visits, seem to have been limited. According to a study by the European Council of Foreign Relations points out, "[China's] move is interesting as it seems to show that global power projection and reciprocal support with Russia are mixed with regional diplomacy."[29]

History also plays a role. The Cold War divided Europe into an eastern and western bloc. Now, countries that had been part of the Warsaw Pact and of the Soviet Union have become EU and NATO members. Others, like Georgia, Ukraine and some countries in South-Eastern Europe lie in a sort of grey zone. Europe's economic prosperity and political stability is attractive to them, but they still have strong historical ties to Russia, which sees them as part of its zone of influence. The end of the Cold War also left a map where NATO members like the Baltic States are home to significant Russian-speaking minorities. Perhaps even more important is Putin's view of the collapse of the Soviet Union as "the greatest geopolitical catastrophe" of the 20th century, one exacerbated by the eastward enlargement of the EU and NATO.[30] Seen from Moscow, the West has continued to provoke it by seeking to incorporate countries such Georgia and Ukraine, and by refusing to include Russia in a reformed Euro-Atlantic security structure. As one commentator has put it, the Ukraine crisis of 2013–2014 demonstrated "that the European Union is a hostile competitor, poaching on its security periphery."[31] Europe–China relations are not darkened by similar shadows from the past. Europe's troubled colonial history in the Asia-Pacific region may still shape attitudes and perceptions, but this does not stand in the way of economic and political engagement.[32]

Finally, the way Russia and China act on the international scene differs significantly. Vladimir Putin's method of restoring Russia's great power status is built on militarisation, an aggressively anti-Western discourse, and the intimidation of neighbours. Until 2014, this approach worried Europeans but did not destroy hopes of peaceful co-existence and even strategic partnership with Russia. With the annexation of Crimea and destabilisation of Ukraine, this has fundamentally changed. Russia might insist on the defensive character of its actions, but the combination of militarisation and aggressive rhetoric is perceived as threatening to Europe's security. As mentioned above, China has traditionally been more willing to accept Europe and the EU as a partner. And China's interest in both goes far beyond trade. From contributions to the European Financial Stability Fund (ESFF) to the use of surpluses to buy European debt and invest in European companies (often including crucial technology transfers), China is an increasingly important economic partner.[33] As with its engagement in other parts of the world, Beijing pursues a pro-active diplomacy in the form of various regional dialogue formats,[34] and offers participation in ambitious infrastructure and investment projects like the BRI. After a long period of hesitation, 18 European countries have joined the Asian Infrastructure and Investment Bank (AIIB).[35] According to Eberhard Sandschneider, one of Germany's foremost experts on China, "Russia thinks in spheres of influence, Europe thinks in cooperations, China thinks in investments."[36] Despite differences and a great deal of suspicion with regard to Chinese motives, the latter two strategies are obviously more in accord.[37] As *The Economist* remarked, "unlike Vladimir Putin ... Xi is not a global troublemaker who seeks to subvert democracy and destabilize the West."[38] The Chinese regime's rhetoric of global responsibility and endorsement of multilateral diplomacy make it much easier for Europe to ignore the Communist party's authoritarian rule and downplay the PLA's regional assertiveness.[39]

The Primacy of Détente and Multilateralism

Notwithstanding the differences in their relations with Europe, Russia and China are both great powers that strive for supremacy in their neighbourhood and for influence in global affairs. Regardless of whether Europeans see these powers as a direct threat to their security, they must acknowledge that Moscow and Beijing do not share their interest in a liberal rules-based world order. They also need to be aware that Russia and China are willing and able to pursue their interests in much more sophisticated ways than in the past. Aggressive economic activities and espionage have always been part of the game. In recent years, however, cyber-attacks and information campaigns have become more widespread. In its threat assessment for 2017, the Norwegian Intelligence Service highlighted that "the most serious cyber threats to Norwegian systems will continue to originate from Russia and China". As both countries put considerable efforts in developing cyber capabilities, intelligence gathering, sabotage and manipulation with digital means are expected to become more systematic and aggressive, but also "better managed and more technically advanced."[40] Other European countries make similar assessments. A German report notes that "[the] consequences for our country range from weakened negotiating positions to high material costs and economic damage all the way to impairment of national sovereignty".[41] Europeans can scarcely overlook, too, that Russia and China reject criticisms of their human rights record, which they deem as interference in their domestic affairs. As Martin Kettle from *The Guardian* points out, China's Xi may be a reformer who speaks warmly about globalism and the fight against climate change but he

> has no interest in western or any other kind of democracy, let alone any sympathy for street protests or strikes, and he certainly has no time for separate systems in Taiwan, Hong Kong or Tibet; nor is he in any way a pacifist or a nuclear disarmer.[42]

Despite these challenges, however, there are several reasons why Europe continues to give priority to engagement, dialogue, and cooperation. First, there are major economic incentives. The benefits of engaging with China—the world's second largest economy and the largest contributor to world growth over last ten years—are obvious. For the EU as a group and for many individual member states, notably Germany, China has become the largest trading partner.[43] The benefits of trading with Russia are perhaps less evident. Nevertheless, the EU is Russia's main trading and investment partner and while Russia is only the EU's fourth biggest trade partner, it is the largest supplier of energy products, including oil, gas, uranium and coal.[44] There are concerns that economic engagement with a great power can lead to dependency, and that individual national interests and vulnerabilities may undermine a common approach.[45] Restrictive measures like the sanctions against Russia or the arms embargo against China, imposed in response to the repression of the Tiananmen protests in 1989, are under constant pressure from political and economic interest groups.[46] However, the fact that Europe has managed to maintain these restrictive measures over several years suggests that member states ultimately appreciate the security of unity.

Another reason for engagement is fear of conflict. The debate over sanctions is not just economic, but also political; critics see them as an obstacle to dialogue and cooperation or, worse still, as a step towards escalation.[47] In response to Russia's military buildup and aggressive behavior, Europeans have settled on a broad set of measures to improve NATO's military preparedness. Although not all member states see Russia as a threat, they understand the need to reassure their Eastern European allies. At the same time, Europeans have been careful not to escalate any confrontation and to maintain dialogue. Compromises found at the NATO summits in Wales (2014) and Warsaw (2016) ensured that the deployment of multinational forces to the Baltics and Poland did not violate existing agreements with Russia.[48] NATO has also reinstated the NATO-Russia council and although no normalisation of relations is in sight, alliance officials argue for increased political dialogue and better military lines of communication[49] With regard to China, Europeans do not see it as posing a territorial threat, but fear that great power rivalry could embroil them in military confrontation. For example, when North Korea threatened to attack the US base in Guam, it triggered a debate about whether this would automatically activate the alliance's mutual defence clause. While Guam is outside the geographic area defined by the North Atlantic Treaty's Article 6, it is highly unlikely that European allies would refuse assistance in the case of an attack on their American ally.[50]

Finally, Europeans know that in a multipolar and increasingly complex world, they need Russia and China to help deal with regional conflicts and global challenges. The war in Syria cannot be resolved without Russia, and crisis management in the Asia-Pacific region depends on China. Beyond regional conflicts, Russia and China are key players in addressing climate change, nuclear proliferation, international terrorism and transnational crime. Commenting on President Macron's first strategic review, the French Defence minister refused to classify China as an existential threat. She also stated that Russia was "not a threat in itself" and that it could play a critical role in resolving problems "in certain regions." Consequently, it was "necessary to ... develop further frameworks of dialogue".[51]

Ever since the days of détente and ostpolitik, efforts to engage Russia and China have been controversial among allies and partners. While Europeans may agree that the best way to bring authoritarian great powers on board is by engaging them in multilateral structures, they disagree about how far cooperation should go, and how much to expect from it. In the past, European efforts to engage could count on the active or at least tacit support of the United States. However, with the latter rebalancing to Asia, and the arrival of an anti-multilateralist in the White House, the prospect of a unified Western approach towards Russia and China has become more uncertain.

The Transatlantic Challenge

Major shifts in US grand strategy have often led Europeans to reconsider the transatlantic relationship. Initiatives to strengthen Europe's ability to act more independently sometimes came as a result of disagreement with the United States but also in response to concerns about US retrenchment, i.e. a lack of interest in Europe or isolationist tendencies more generally. Differences were particularly evident during the administration of George W. Bush, culminating in open disagreement over the invasion of Iraq in 2002–2003. While Europeans felt a greater like-mindedness with President Barack Obama's approach of strategic patience and engagement towards Russia, Iran and North Korea, they were concerned about his emphasis on Asia. Early in his presidency, in November 2009, Obama declared that he would be the first Pacific president, and during the following months the administration sustained its focus on the region through military and diplomatic engagement, bilaterally and in multilateral forums. Soon there was talk of a "pivot to Asia".[52] In an article in *Foreign Policy* in November 2011 titled "America's Pacific Century", Secretary of State Hillary Clinton underlined the rationale behind the United States' rebalancing—namely, the need to adapt to the realities of a new international order.[53] The same month, Obama elaborated further on this policy in an address to the Australian Parliament,[54] before heading off to Bali to become the first American president to attend the East Asia Summit. Both the EU and their American partners were eager to emphasize that the transatlantic relationship remained the cornerstone of Western security. It was clear, however, that the future relationship between the world's only superpower, the United States, and its main challenger China would have a major bearing on Europe's role in world politics. The "pivot" led to a debate in Europe about transatlantic relations, and about what kind of role Europe should play in Asian security affairs.

Some saw America's rebalancing to the Asia-Pacific as an argument for more European security involvement in the region. Former Australian

Prime Minister Kevin Rudd warned in 2012 that an introspective Europe was missing the opportunity to shape the global order in Asia and was instead running "the risk of talking itself into an early economic and therefore globally political grave".[55] "The same year, a report by the Atlantic Council suggested that America should "pivot" to Asia with Europe, emphasising the value of a strong Western partnership in a changing world order.[56] By 2017, as China's influence became even more evident, analysts were warning that "Europe can no longer simply leave Asian security problems for the US to sort out, as it has for the last 70 years".[57] On the other hand, others argued that Europe should stay out of great power rivalry in distant regions and concentrate on its neighbourhood. Echoing Kissinger's notion of the United States as a global and Europe as a regional actor, this view suggested a division of labour whereby Europe would leave security issues in the Asia-Pacific to the United States, and shoulder more responsibility for security in its own neighbourhood.[58]

The real picture is, of course, much more complex. European nations may have little or no appetite for balancing China's military power.[59] This does not mean, though, that they can ignore the security dimension of the West's relations with Asia. China's growing influence and the geopolitical rivalries arising from it affect the security of vital sea lines of communication and the free access to ports on which Europe depends. Moreover, such rivalries can escalate into a major confrontation. Military conflict involving the United States and its regional allies in the South China Sea, in the Indian Ocean, or in the Pacific would necessarily raise the question of European assistance. Europeans would see it as their prime responsibility to mediate and work for a political solution. In the case of an attack, however, the question would rather be how than if Europe would assist its ally.

Few would disagree that the geopolitical implications of China's economic and military rise will remain a major challenge for the West. However, although the debate about the consequences of US rebalancing is important, confrontation and tensions in other regions represent a much more immediate security threat to Western interests. The Middle East and North Africa as well as the Baltic Sea and the Black Sea region are hotspots where regional conflicts and great power rivalry go hand in hand and which neither Europe nor the United States can afford to ignore. Thus, the Ukraine crisis eventually forced European allies to invest more in collective security, but it also pushed the United States to reconfirm its military engagement in Europe. In response to the Islamic State's (IS) terror regime in Iraq and Syria, Washington formed a global coalition to which all European states made military contributions. When it comes to deterring Russia and combating terrorism in the Middle East and North Africa, Europe and the United States cooperate on the basis of broadly similar threat perceptions and in the framework of a well-established but highly flexible security architecture. It is the prospect of a weakened security community that brings Europeans like Tusk to regard Trump's foreign policy as a threat on the same level as a more assertive China and a resurgent Russia.

The Trump Challenge

It is still too early to assess the implications of the Trump presidency for international relations and European security. There are concerns, however, that a combination of isolationism and escalatory behaviour will put the transatlantic alliance under severe stress. To be sure, the results of Obama's foreign policy were mixed at best and many allies in Europe, Asia and the Middle East were left disappointed. With Trump it is unclear to what extent he follows any strategy at all and how much his foreign policy will be determined by flattery and animosity. So far, Trump's approach towards China has shifted between the confrontational stance proposed by some advisers and the positive dynamic of his personal encounters with Xi Jinping. During the election campaign and as president-elect, Trump attacked Beijing for its trade policies, suggested a review of the One-China policy, and threatened to reconsider America's engagement in Asia (worrying allies like South Korean and Japan).[60] In the White House he lauded Xi for his leadership before attacking him again for not doing enough to stop North Korea's nuclear programme. During his first tour of Asia in November 2017, Trump indicated a more structured approach first outlined by Secretary of State Rex Tillerson. The "Indo-Pacific strategy" is a rebranding of the Obama "pivot", but fails to specify how efforts to commit Beijing to a coalition against North Korea can be squared with countering China's geopolitical influence.[61] There are serious doubts that Trump's transactional approach and leader-to-leader diplomacy can compensate for the lack of multilateral engagement he has demonstrated by withdrawing from the Trans-Pacific Partnership (TPP) Agreement. The end-result may be a weakening of America's position, allowing China to become ever more dominant. Trump's attempts to revive relations with Russia have scarcely fared any better.[62] First, allegations about improper contacts between some of his advisers and Russian intelligence agencies have undercut his ability to initiate a rapprochement. Then Congress imposed new sanctions to punish the Kremlin for interfering with the US presidential election. Trump keeps insisting that a good relationship with Putin's Russia is possible, but given the structural divergences between the two powers, mutual disappointment and suspicion might just as easily lead to another crisis. As a forum of US–China experts concluded in May 2017, "uncertainty is the watchword for U.S.-China relations"[63] and much the same can be said about US–Russia interaction.

For Europe, this means that the fundamental dilemmas connected to America's global outlook remain in place. Yet Trump's volatile approach and isolationism bring new challenges as well. On the one hand, the president's unpredictability in international affairs combined with doubts over his administration's decision-making have heightened concerns about the consequences of unintended and uncontrolled great power rivalry. Faced with the potential threat of escalation, Europeans have stepped up their role in global diplomacy. German Chancellor Angela Merkel has offered to mediate in the crisis with North Korea.[64] Similar to their handling of the Ukraine crisis, Europeans seek to combine national initiatives with multilateral approaches. They also look to supplement formal channels with smaller, more operative formats. In the Ukraine crisis, the Normandy Four—Russia, Ukraine, Germany and France—has become the principal mechanism of conflict management. With regard to East Asia, a German government spokesman noted that "the six-party format used in the Iran nuclear talks - Britain, China, France, Germany, Russia and the United States - might someday prove useful in tackling the North Korea conflict."[65] In the Iran negotiations, the P5+1 (the permanent members of the UN Security Council plus Germany and the EU) grouping, also called the E3+3, has indeed established itself as a format in which Europe's influence is considerable.[66]

On the other hand, Trump's scepticism towards multilateralism calls into question the very foundation of European security. Trump has called NATO obsolete and queried the existence of the EU. To be sure, he has since softened his criticisms of both, and his most senior cabinet members—the "adults" or "grown-ups" in the administration[67]—have reassured allies and partners of America's continuing commitment to

European security. There is reason to believe, however, that the president's anti-multilateralism is genuine and deep-rooted. According to two of his advisers, Trump "embarked on his first foreign trip with a clear-eyed outlook that the world is not a 'global community' but an arena where nations, nongovernmental actors and businesses engage and compete for advantage."[68]

By withdrawing from multilateral agreements and questioning the relevance of international organisations, Trump undermines the post-war liberal order on which Europe, with the support of the United States, has built its success and influence. Europeans have responded in two ways to this challenge. At home, they have invested in security and defence to an unprecedented degree. The combined impact of the Ukraine crisis and Britain's decision to leave the EU has led to the most comprehensive restructuring of European defence in decades. NATO is investing again in collective defence and readiness and the EU has revitalized plans for closer defence cooperation within the framework of the CSDP. Trump's blunt insistence on burden-sharing combined with his lack of interest in multilateralism has pushed these plans even further. Merkel's conclusion from their meeting at the Hamburg G 20 summit in April 2017 was "that we Europeans must really take our fate into our own hands".[69] With the election of an explicitly pro-European president in France, chances for closer cooperation are better than in a long time. In December 2017, 25 EU member states signed an agreement to go ahead with Permanent Structured Cooperation (PESCO), a concept that allows "those member states willing and able to jointly develop defence capabilities, invest in shared projects, or enhance the operational readiness and contribution of their armed forces". To support these projects and to "foster defence cooperation from research to the development phase of capabilities", the EU vowed to establish a European Defence Fund (EDF) and a Coordinated Annual Review on Defence (CARD).[70] At the global level, Europe has responded to Trump's withdrawal from international agreements and multilateral diplomacy by encouraging powers like China to take more responsibility. Merkel's meetings with Xi in Hamburg inspired officials and journalists to speak of an "an informal alliance" to take up the leadership baton dropped by the United States.[71] Separately, Xi spoke of deepening German–Chinese relations into a strategic partnership. This has raised concerns that Beijing prefers dealing with Berlin instead of the more complicated EU, but such worries appear groundless. Despite its more active involvement in the Asia-Pacific region, Berlin knows better than to abandon the strength provided by a bloc of 28 (27) nations.[72] Other member states, too, see the EU as an instrument for intensifying relations with China.[73]

In sum, Trump's ambivalent approach towards Russia and China and his scepticism towards multilateralism, risk undermining the transatlantic relationship. In observing a growing divergence between the United States and Europe, analysts warn that "US bashing" does not help as Europe continues to depend on Washington and lacks the political will to develop into a truly autonomous actor.[74] However, this is hardly what Europeans want. As Tusk pointed out in February 2017, a weakening of the transatlantic relationship cannot be in Europe's interest. While they are alienated by Trump's zero-sum approach to diplomacy and disconcerted over his threats of trade war, Europeans do not intend to balance the United States in ways that endanger the transatlantic alliance. Striving for more strategic autonomy does not preclude them from maintaining close relations with the United States and preserving NATO as their main security framework. This is why many European leaders have been careful to qualify their criticisms of Trump, and have emphasized the importance of engaging with Washington.[75]

Conclusion

Great powers like Russia, China and the United States, but also many foreign policy analysts and scholars, struggle to understand Europe as an actor in international relations. European governance is complex, multi-layered and constantly struggling for cohesion. Internationally, Europeans act as part of NATO, in the framework of the EU and as nation states. There might never emerge just one number to call if one wants to know the European position.[76] However, as Moravcsik has pointed out, formal and informal policy coordination "permits European governments to act as a unit to influence the outside world."[77]

Faced with two great powers that aggressively seek to extend their regional dominance and global influence, and with an ally that pursues a transactional approach to trade and security partnership, Europeans have to perform a delicate balancing act. They know that only by standing together can they wield influence in the concert of great powers. Yet they must also defend their right to act as sovereign states and seek individual national dividends from the global economy. Europeans are principled defenders of a liberal rules-based international order, but realize that the rise of great powers with a different understanding of the world forces them to compromise. There are many reasons why Europe needs to develop into a more autonomous international actor, but there are equally many reasons why the transatlantic relationship should remain a priority.

Better relations with China and Russia do not necessarily have to undermine Western cohesion. While there is undoubtedly a strong desire in Germany and other European countries to engage China (and ultimately Russia) in the liberal multilateral order, there is little chance that either Moscow or Beijing will be able to exploit transatlantic disagreements to divide the West. In the Ukraine crisis, Germany has successfully played a dual role in forging consensus on sanctions and leading mediation and dialogue with Russia, all the time anchoring its decisions at the EU level and coordinating its moves with Washington. For economic, cultural and above all security reasons, Europe's commitment to the transatlantic alliance remains strong.[78] Fundamental differences in approaches to human rights and the rule of law make it impossible for European leaders to advance relations with China and Russia beyond a certain point. Consequently, EU–China relations are not, as some suggest, "forging ahead without the United States".[79] At the same time, Europe is self-confident enough and has a powerful basket of carrots (aid, trade agreements) and sticks (sanctions) that enables it to play a more independent role in international affairs. In fact, Europe has an important role to play in the concert of great powers that goes beyond securitizing its neighbourhood and pursuing trade interests. As Michael Mazarr and Hal Brands point out,

> however "normal" it may be, great-power conflict is nonetheless disconcerting and dangerous. It raises the chance of a major, "systemic" war that could have cataclysmic consequences and it undermines the functioning of international institutions. It complicates international efforts to address a range of pressing problems that are inherently transnational in nature and thus require a broad, multilateral response.[80]

In times when the United States turns away from multilateralism, Europe's most important task is to use its soft power to defend and advance a liberal rules-based international order.

Notes

1. European Council (2017).
2. As Kissinger himself later said, if he actually made the remark or not doesn't matter—it is a great line that depicts the problem and has motivated Europeans ever since to speak with one voice… See Rachman (2009) and EuroNews (2007).
3. Kissinger (1973).
4. The United Kingdom recognized the People's Republic of China already in 1950, while the United States supported Chiang Kai-shek's Taiwan, and De Gaulle recognized China in January 1964, playing on the Sino-Soviet rift that had occurred a few years earlier. On the global dimension of Germany's ostpolitik, see Fink and Schaefer (2009).
5. Winand (2010).
6. Tudda (2012).
7. Liebich (2016).
8. For an overview see the European External Action Service's timeline, EEAS (2015).
9. Fardella et al. (2015), p. iii.
10. For an overview see the EEAS homepage. https://eeas.europa.eu/headquarters/headquarters-homepage_en.
11. Brunnstrom (2009).
12. As German chancellor Angela Merkel became the continent's leading political figure, some concluded that "Henry Kissinger will no longer need to ask for Europe's telephone number", see Augstein (2015).
13. Pillai (2014), Bew (2015).
14. Kagan (2003).
15. Orbie (2006).
16. Mogherini (2016).
17. Moravcsik (2017).
18. Whitman (2004).
19. Moravscik (2017).
20. Kudnani and Parello-Plesner (2012).
21. Reuters (2017), Butler (2017).
22. Dunai (2017), Lai (2017), Horowitz and Alderman (2017).
23. In addition to participation in EU or UN missions and rescue operations, France also "regularly exercises its right of maritime and air navigation in the area. The behaviour of its naval and air assets reflects its commitment to the lawful, free and unhampered use of all oceans and their above airspaces, in accordance with the United Nations Convention on the Law of the Sea. Such behaviour likewise shows the firm opposition of France to the use of measures of intimidation, of

coercion or force." For details see Directorate General for International Relations and Strategy (2016). Britain has also stated its intention to be "back east of Suez" reversing its exit from the region in the 1970s. In light of Brexit and the idea of "global Britain" the government plans to reopen naval bases and to dispatch aircraft carriers (yet to be built) to keep open sea lanes. The idea behind this is to be taken seriously as a great power and to underwrite commercial interests rather than to confront China, Vasagar (2016).

24. European Union (2003).
25. See European Union (2016), German Federal Government (2016), Ministère des Armeés (2013), and Ministère des Armeés (2017). See also Kirchner et al. (2016), p. 1.
26. Bond (2017), p. 2.
27. Gabuev (2016).
28. Higgins (2017), Borchert (2017).
29. Godement and Vasselier (2017).
30. BBC (2005).
31. Liebich (2016), Wilhelmsen and Godzimierski (2017).
32. Although, as Gideon Rachman points out, post-brexit plans for a new "global Britain" strategy largely ignore that "countries once colonized or defeated by Britain [...] harbour decidedly ambivalent feelings about the UK.", Rachman (2017a).
33. Godement (2011), Alderman and Barboza (2011).
34. The best-known initiative is the 16+1 format involving countries from central Europe, in and outside the EU. But China also looks further north. See Valášek (2017), Institute for Security and Development Policy (2016), Sverdrup Thygeson et al. (2018).
35. Stanzel (2016).
36. Heilmann und Sandschneider (2015), author's translation.
37. And they are both in disaccord with the US strategy which, according to Sandschneider, has a "geo-military and geostrategic orientation".
38. The Economist (2017a).
39. In his speeches at the World Economic Forum in Davos and in connection with the G20 summit in Hamburg, Xi presented China as the defender of globalization, see Fidler (2017).
40. Norwegian Intelligence Service (2017), pp. 30–36.
41. Quoted in Shalal (2017).
42. Kettle (2017).
43. Wagner and Nienaber (2017).
44. See Delegation of the European Union to Russia homepage https://eeas.europa.eu/delegations/russia/35939/european-union-and-russian-federation_en.

45. Bond (2017).
46. Recently, Britain's decision to leave the EU has re-opened the discussion whether to keep the arms embargo in place. See Godement (2016), Harding (2016).
47. Fischer (2015).
48. Allers (2017).
49. Frears et al. (2016), Sanders (2017).
50. Barnes (2017). While Article 5 commits allies to mutual assistance in case of an attack—one for all, all for one, Article 6 limits the area of NATO operations to North of the Tropic of Cancer. According to NATO, there have never been doubts, however, that the alliance could operate longer to the south if necessary. NATO, Collective defence—Article 5, https://www.nato.int/cps/ic/natohq/topics_110496.htm.
51. Parly (2017), author's translation.
52. Allen (2009), Lieberthal (2011).
53. Clinton (2011).
54. The White House (2012).
55. Rudd (2012).
56. Burns et al. (2012), p. 12.
57. Bond (2017).
58. Tunsjø (2013), p. 9.
59. Beckley (2017).
60. Hadar (2017), Haas (2017).
61. Ayres (2017), Parameswaran (2017), Sevastopulo (2017).
62. Legvold (2017). Apparently the Kremlin believed, a real reset was possible, see Hudson (2017).
63. This was the conclusion of a forum by US–China experts in May 2017, Rovner (2017).
64. Quoted in Shalal and Rinke (2017). See also Gutschker (2017). According to a diplomat working in the Federal Chancellery, China trusts German diplomacy, German Ministry of Defence (2017).
65. Quoted in Shalal and Rinke (2017).
66. Illustrating her involvement in the Iran talks, the EU's High representative Federica Mogherini was even considered a candidate for the Nobel Peace prize together with former US Secretary of State John Kerry.
67. The Economist (2017b), Mann (2017).
68. McMaster and Cohn (2017). See also article by same authors in New York Times. https://www.nytimes.com/2017/07/13/opinion/the-trump-vision-for-america-abroad.html.
69. Reuters (2017b).
70. EEAS (2018).
71. Champion et al. (2017).

72. Mohan (2017), Masala et al. (2015).
73. Casarini (2017).
74. Dempsey (2017), Rachman (2017b).
75. The Economist (2017c).
76. In fact, as an adviser to Federica Mogherini's points out, there will never be one European phone number and there isn't one in most of today's democracies. Mogherini herself ironized that she was not sure anymore whom to call in Trump's Washington D.C., See Tocci (2018).
77. Moravcsik (2017).
78. For a list of arguments to invest in a strong transatlantic partnership, see the op-ed by a group of German experts published in Die Zeit and the New York Times, Group of German experts (2017).
79. Casarini (2017).
80. Mazarr and Brands (2017).

References

Alderman, Liz, and David Barboza. 2011. Europe Tries to Lure Chinese Cash to Back Rescue of Euro. *New York Times*, October 28. http://www.nytimes.com/2011/10/29/world/asia/europe-seeks-chinese-investment-in-euro-rescue.html?pagewanted=all.

Allen, Mike. 2009. America's First Pacific President. *Politico*, November 13. http://www.politico.com/news/stories/1109/29511.html.

Allers, Robin. 2017. Modern Deterrence? NATO's Enhanced Forward Presence on the Eastern Flank. In *NATO and Collective Defence in the 21st Century*, ed. Karsten Friis. Routledge.

Augstein, Franziska. 2015. How Angela Merkel Became Europe's Undisputed Leader. *The Guardian*, February 15. https://www.theguardian.com/commentisfree/2015/feb/15/angela-merkel-germany-ukraine-putin-obama.

Ayres, Alyssa. 2017. Tillerson on India: Partners in a "Free and Open Indo-Pacific". Council on Foreign Relations, October 18. https://www.cfr.org/blog/tillerson-india-partners-free-and-open-indo-pacific.

Barnes, Julian. 2017. If North Korea Attacks Guam, U.S. Holds Open Option for NATO Mutual Defense. *Wall Street Journal*, September 22. https://www.wsj.com/articles/if-north-korea-attacks-guam-u-s-may-push-for-nato-mutual-defense-1506093433.

BBC. 2005. Putin Deplores Collapse of USSR. *BBC News*, April 25. http://news.bbc.co.uk/2/hi/4480745.stm.

Beckley, Michael. 2017. Balancing China: How the United States and its Partners Can Check Chinese Naval Expansion. War on the Rocks, University of Texas, November 15. https://warontherocks.com/2017/11/balancing-china-united-states-partners-can-check-chinese-naval-expansion/.

Bew, John. 2015. The Syrian War and the Return of Great Power Politics. *New Statesman*, December 15. https://www.newstatesman.com/world/middle-east/2015/12/syrian-war-and-return-great-power-politics.

Bond, Ian. 2017. European Policy in Asia: Getting Past Mercatorism and Mercantilism. *Centre for European Reform Insight*, September 7, available at http://www.cer.eu/sites/default/files/insight_IB_7.9.17.pdf.

Borchert, Thomas. 2017. Russisch-chinesische Provokation im Baltikum. *Frankfurter Rundschau*, July 26. http://www.fr.de/politik/militaermanoever-russisch-chinesische-provokation-im-baltikum-a-1320086.

Brunnstrom, David. 2009. EU Says It Has Solved the Kissinger Question. *Reuters*, November 20. https://www.reuters.com/article/us-eu-president-kissinger/eu-says-it-has-solved-the-kissinger-question-idUSTRE5AJ00B20091120. Accessed 22 Oct 2017.

Burns, Nicholas R., et al. 2012. Anchoring the Alliance. *Atlantic Council*, May, Washington, DC. http://www.atlanticcouncil.org/images/files/publication_pdfs/403/051412_ACUS_Burns_AnchoringAlliance.pdf.

Butler, Nick. 2017. Nord Stream 2. A Test of German Power. *Financial Times*, July 3. https://www.ft.com/content/4875c9ff-0868-3798-8f66-4efa667eb5ba.

Casarini, Nicola. 2017. A New Era for EU–China Relations? How They Are Forging Ahead Without the United States. *Foreign Affairs*, June 6. https://www.foreignaffairs.com/articles/china/2017-06-06/new-era-eu-china-relations.

Champion, Marc, Peter Martin, and Brian Parkin. 2017. China, Germany Step up as U.S. Retires From World Leadership, *Bloomberg*, July 4. https://www.bloomberg.com/news/articles/2017-07-03/as-u-s-retires-from-world-leadership-china-and-germany-step-up.

Clinton, Hillary. 2011. America's Pacific Century. *Foreign Policy*, November. http://www.foreignpolicy.com/articles/2011/10/11/americas_pacific_century?page=full.

Dempsey, Judy. 2017. Europe's Illusionaries. *Strategic Europe*, October 17, available at http://carnegieeurope.eu/strategiceurope/?fa=73440&utm_source=rssemail&utm_medium=email&mkt_tok=eyJpIjoiWlRBNFpXUX-lZamc1T0dabSIsInQiOiI2eUtNN2FMTzBQK1BsaEZCTU9kVWlidWJFM-kFIZVFhVHorXC9rdVFrNTZOWkJYTE9XeEQ0U0FjSW5Kd1wvRUx0bU-J0OVV6cTkxRVlkVCtcL2ZRVDlTY1FjOG1nZ3JqaEZtSFVqUFNJakpR-bElXU1ZcL3NIZ25GaDNHcHpWeFpGK0FLNjcifQ%3D%3D.

Directorate General for International Relations and Strategy. 2016. France and Security in the Asia-Pacific. http://www.defense.gouv.fr/content/download/475376/7615622/file/201606-PlaquetteAsiePacifiqueEN.comp.pdf.

Dunai, Marton. 2017. Hungary Tests EU Nerves Frayed by Russia as Putin Visits Budapest. *Reuters*, February 1. https://www.reuters.com/article/us-russia-hungary/hungary-tests-eu-nerves-frayed-by-russia-as-putin-visits-budapest-idUSKBN15G4XW.

EEAS. 2015. European External Action Service's Timeline, updated 5 February, available at https://eeas.europa.eu/headquarters/headquarters-homepage_en/15872/EU-China%20relations%20Timeline.

EEAS. 2018. European External Action Service, Factsheet, Permanent Structured Cooperation, March 5. https://eeas.europa.eu/sites/eeas/files/eu_factsheet_pesco_permanent_structured_cooperation_en_0.pdf.

EuroNews. 2007. Kissinger Speaks on Iran, European–Russian Relations and EU's Political Future. March 31, available at http://www.euronews.com/2007/03/31/kissinger-speaks-on-iran-european-russian-relations-and-eu-s-political-future.

European Council. 2017. "United We Stand, Divided We Fall", Letter by President Donald Tusk to the 27 EU Heads of State or Government on the Future of the EU Before the Malta Summit, Brussels, January 31, available at http://www.consilium.europa.eu/en/press/press-releases/2017/01/31/tusk-letter-future-europe/pdf.

European Union. 2003. *A Secure Europe in a Better World*, European Security Strategy, Brussels, December 12, available at https://europa.eu/globalstrategy/en/european-security-strategy-secure-europe-better-world.

European Union. 2016. Shared Vision, Common Action: A Stronger Europe. A Global Strategy for the European Union's Foreign and Security Policy, European Union, June. http://eeas.europa.eu/archives/docs/top_stories/pdf/eugs_review_web.pdf.

Fardella, Enrico, Christian F. Ostermann, and Charles Kraus (eds.). 2015. *Sino-European Relations During the Cold War and the Rise of a Multipolar World. A Critical Oral History*. Washington, DC: Wilson Center. https://www.wilsoncenter.org/sites/default/files/Sino_European_Relations_during_Cold_War_Rise_of_Multipolar_World_%282015%29.pdf.

Fidler. 2017. China's Xi Jinping Speech Seen as Move to Fill Global Leadership Role. *Wall Street Journal*, January 17. https://www.wsj.com/articles/chinas-xi-jinping-speech-seen-as-move-to-fill-global-leadership-role-1484660546.

Fink, Carole, and Bernd Schaefer. 2009. *Ostpolitik, 1969–1974: European and Global Responses*. Cambridge: Cambridge University Press.

Fischer, Sabine. 2015. European Union Sanctions Against Russia. Objectives, Impact and Next Steps. *SWP Comments*, March, https://www.swp-berlin.org/fileadmin/contents/products/comments/2015C17_fhs.pdf.

Frears, Thomas, Lukasz Kulesa, and Denitsa Raynova. 2016. Managing Hazardous Incidents in the Euro-Atlantic Area: A New Plan of Action, European Leadership Network, Policy, Policy Brief, November 2. https://www.europeanleadershipnetwork.org/commentary/russia-west-incidents-on-the-rise/?mc_cid=fc44423228&mc_eid=b166b184b6.

Gabuev, Alexander. 2016. Friends with Benefits? Russian–Chinese Relations After the Ukraine Crisis. Carnegie Moscow Center, June 29, http://carnegie.ru/2016/06/29/friends-with-benefits-russian-chinese-relations-after-ukraine-crisis-pub-63953.

German Federal Government. 2016. *The White Paper on German Security Policy and the Future of the Bundeswehr*, Berlin, available at https://www.bundeswehr.de/resource/resource/.

German Ministry of Defence. 2017. China vertraut deutscher Diplomatie im Nord-Korea Konflikt. BMVG.de, October 4. https://www.bmvg.de/de/aktuelles/china-vertraut-deutscher-diplomatie-im-nordkorea-konflikt-18584.

Godement, Francois. 2016. China and Brexit: What's in It for Us? *European Council on Foreign Relations Special Issue*, September. http://www.ecfr.eu/page/-/CA_MES_2016.pdf.

Godement, Francois, and Abigael Vasselier. 2017. China at the Gates: A New Power Audit of EU–China Relations. *European Council on Foreign Relations*, December 1. http://www.ecfr.eu/publications/summary/china_eu_power_audit7242.

Godement, Francois, et al. 2011. The Scramble for Europe. *European Council on Foreign Relations*, July. http://www.ecfr.eu/content/entry/chinas_scramble_for_europe.

Group of German Experts. 2017. In Spite of It All, America. *New York Times*, October 11. https://www.nytimes.com/2017/10/11/world/europe/germany-united-states-trump-manifesto.html.

Gutschker, Thomas. 2017. « Merkel: Deutschland kann im Nordkorea-Konflikt vermitteln », *Frankfurter Allgemeine Sonntagszeitung*, September 10. http://m.faz.net/aktuell/politik/kanzlerin-im-f-a-s-gespraech-merkel-deutschland-kann-im-nordkorea-konflikt-vermitteln-15191111.amp.html.

Haas, Benjamin. 2017. Steve Bannon Compares China to 1930s Germany and Says US Must Confront Beijing. *Guardian*, September 11. https://amp.theguardian.com/us-news/2017/sep/11/steve-bannon-compares-china-to-1930s-germany-and-says-us-must-confront-beijing.

Hadar, Leon. 2017. The Limits of Trump's Transactional Foreign Policy. *The National Interest*, January 2. http://nationalinterest.org/feature/the-limits-trumps-transactional-foreign-policy-18898.

Harding, Robin. 2016. Japan Fears Brexit Blow to EU Arms Embargo on China. *Financial Times*, July 4. https://www.ft.com/content/219af680-41c6-11e6-b22f-79eb4891c97d.

Heilmann, Sebastian, und Eberhard Sandschneider. 2015. „Das ist eine Bombe". Scheitert China?, im Gespräch, *Internationale Politik*, July 1. https://zeitschrift-ip.dgap.org/de/ip-die-zeitschrift/ip-laenderportraet/ip-laenderportraet-archiv/laenderportraet-china-2-2015/das-ist.

Higgins, Andrew. 2017. China and Russia Hold First Joint Naval Drill in the Baltic Sea. *New York Times*, July 25. https://www.nytimes.com/2017/07/25/world/europe/china-russia-baltic-navy-exercises.html.

Horowitz, Jason, and Liz Alderman. 2017. Chastised by E.U., a Resentful Greece Embraces China's Cash and Interests. *New York Times*, August 26. https://www.nytimes.com/2017/08/26/world/europe/greece-china-piraeus-alexis-tsipras.html.

Hudson, John. 2017. Russia Sought a Broad Reset with Trump, Secret Document Shows. *Buzz Feed News*, September 13. https://www.buzzfeed.com/johnhudson/russia-sought-a-broad-reset-with-trump-secret-document-shows?utm_term=.geLr7RM00#.hyaQr6Vaa; https://www.buzzfeed.com/amphtml/johnhudson/putin-spokesman-confirms-russia-reached-out-to-trump.

Institute for Security and Development Policy. 2016. Sino-Nordic Relations: Opportunities and the Way Ahead, Stockholm. http://isdp.eu/content/uploads/2016/11/2016-Sino-Nordic-Relations-Opportunities-and-the-Way-Ahead.pdf.

Kagan, Robert. 2003. *Of Paradise and Power. America and Europe in the New World Order*. New York: Alfred A. Knopf.

Kettle, Martin. 2017. We are Obsessed with Brexit and Trump: We Should Be Thinking About China. *The Guardian*, October 20. https://amp.theguardian.com/commentisfree/2017/oct/20/trump-xi-world-leader-chinese-communist-party-congress-speech.

Kirchner, Emil J., Thomas Christiansen, and Han Dorussen (eds.). 2016. *Security Relations Between China and the European Union: From Convergence to Cooperation?* Cambridge University Press.

Kissinger, Henry A. 1973. Address Given by Henry A. Kissinger, New York, April 23. https://www.cvce.eu/content/publication/2002/9/30/dec472e3-9dff-4c06-ad8d-d3fab7e13f9f/publishable_en.pdf.

Kudnani, Hans, and Jonas Parello-Plessner. 2012. China and Germany: Why the Emerging Special Relationship Matters for Europe. *ECFR Policy Brief*, European Council on Foreign Relations, May, London. https://www.files.ethz.ch/isn/173460/ECFR55_CHINA_GERMANY_BRIEF_AW.pdf.

Lai Suetyi. 2017. Understanding Europe's Interest in China's Belt and Road Initiative. Carnegie, May 10. http://carnegieendowment.org/2017/05/10/understanding-europe-s-interest-in-china-s-belt-and-road-initiative-pub-69920.

Legvold, Robert. 2017. U.S.–Russian Relations in the Trump Era, *ISSF POLICY Series*, America and the World—2017 and Beyond. The International Security 'Studies Forum, September 6. https://issforum.org/roundtables/policy/1-5ax-russia.

Lieberthal, Kenneth. 2011. The American Pivot to Asia. *Foreign Policy*, December 21. http://www.foreignpolicy.com/articles/2011/12/21/the_american_pivot_to_asia.

Liebich, Andrew. 2016. *Ressentiment: Understanding Russia's Attitude to the EU*. Graduate Institute Geneva, April 6. http://graduateinstitute.ch/home/relations-publiques/news-at-the-institute/news-archives.html/_/news/corporate/2016/ressentiment-understanding-russi.

Mann, James. 2017. The Adults in the Room. *New York Review of Books*, October 26. http://www.nybooks.com/articles/2017/10/26/trump-adult-supervision/.

Masala, Carlo, et al. 2015. Maritime Sicherheit im Indischen Ozean. Mehr deutsches Engagement im Ozean des 21. Jahrhunderts. *KAS Analysen und Argumente*, Juni, http://www.kas.de/wf/doc/kas_41590-544-1-30.pdf?150904102712.

Mazarr, Michael, and Hal Brands. 2017. Navigating Great Power Rivalry in the 21st Century. War on the Rocks, April 5. https://warontherocks.com/2017/04/navigating-great-power-rivalry-in-the-21st-century/.

McMaster, H.R., and Gary D. Cohn. 2017. America First Doesn't Mean America Alone. *Wall Street Journal*, May 30. https://www.wsj.com/articles/america-first-doesnt-mean-america-alone-1496187426.

Ministère des Armeés. 2013. *Livre Blanc sur la Defense*. Paris, available at https://www.defense.gouv.fr/.

Ministère des Armeés. 2017. *Strategic Review of Defence and National Security*. Paris, October. http://www.defense.gouv.fr/english/content/download/514659/8664385/Strategic%20review%20of%20defense%20and%20national%20security%202017%20%E2%80%93%20Key%20points.pdf.

Mogherini, Federica. 2016. Foreword. *Shared Vision, Common Action: A Stronger Europe. A Global Strategy for the European Union's Foreign and Security Policy, European Union*, June. http://eeas.europa.eu/archives/docs/top_stories/pdf/eugs_review_web.pdf.

Mohan, Garima. 2017. Engaging with the Indian Ocean. Opportunities and Challenges for Germany. GPPI, November 2017. http://www.gppi.net/fileadmin/user_upload/media/pub/2017/Mohan_2017_Engaging_with_the_Indian_Ocean.pdf.

Moravcsik, Andrew. 2017. Europe is Still a Superpower. *Foreign Policy*, April 13. http://foreignpolicy.com/2017/04/13/europe-is-still-a-superpower/.

Norwegian Intelligence Service. 2017. *Annual Report Focus 2017*, available at https://forsvaret.no/en/ForsvaretDocuments/Fokus2017_2002_ENGELSK_v2.pdf.

Orbie, Jan. 2006. Civilian Power Europe. Review of the Original and Current Debates. *Cooperation and Conflict* 41 (1): 123–128.

Parameswaran, Prashanth. 2017. Trump's Indo-Pacific Strategy Challenge. *The Diplomat*, October 27. https://thediplomat.com/2017/10/trumps-indo-pacific-strategy-challenge/.

Parly, Florence. 2017. « La France veut conserver une autonomie stratégique ». *Le Monde*, October 13. http://www.lemonde.fr/international/article/2017/10/13/florence-parly-la-france-veut-conserver-une-autonomie-strategique_5200442_3210.html#GA5jDR0stlA5t0Tb.99.

Pillai, Chad. 2014. The Return of Great Power Politics—Re-Examining the Nixon-Doctrine. War on the Rocks, March 27, University of Texas, https://warontherocks.com/2014/03/the-return-of-great-power-politics-re-examining-the-nixon-doctrine/.

Rachman, Gideon. 2009. Kissinger Never Wanted to Dial Europe. *Financial Times*, July 22. https://www.ft.com/content/c4c1e0cd-f34a-3b49-985f-e708b247eb55.

Rachman, Gideon. 2017a. Brexit Reinforces Britain's Imperial Amnesia. *Financial Times*, March 27. https://www.ft.com/content/e3e32b38-0fc8-11e7-a88c-50ba212dce4d.

Rachman, Gideon. 2017b. Angela Merkel's Blunder, Donald Trump and the End of the West. *Financial Times*, May 29. https://www.ft.com/content/dc911cb8-4449-11e7-8519-9f94ee97d996.

Reuters. 2017a. No Need for EU Mandate to Negotiate Nord Stream 2-Merkel. June 15. https://www.reuters.com/article/germany-estonia-nordstream/no-need-for-eu-mandate-to-negotiate-nord-stream-2-merkel-idUSB4N1G002D.

Reuters. 2017b. «After Summits with Trump, Merkel Says Europe Must Take Fate into Own Hands». May 28. https://www.reuters.com/article/us-germany-politics-merkel/after-summits-with-trump-merkel-says-europe-must-take-fate-into-own-hands-idUSKBN18O0JK.

Rovner, Joshua, et al. 2017. Policy Roundtable 1-9 on U.S.–China Relations and the Trump Administration. ISSF, May 13. https://issforum.org/roundtables/policy/1-9-us-china.

Rudd, Kevin. 2012. Speech at the 48th Munich Security Conference. http://www.securityconference.de/Kevin-Rudd.837+M544261a91d7.0.html.

Sanders, Lewis. 2017. NATO Chief Predicts Increased Dialogue with Russia in 2018. Deutsche Welle, December 29. http://www.dw.com/en/nato-chief-predicts-increased-dialogue-with-russia-in-2018/a-41966005.

Sevastopulo, Demetri. 2017. Trump Gives Glimpse of 'Indo-Pacific' Strategy to Counter China. *Financial Times*, November 13. https://www.ft.com/content/e6d17fd6-c623-11e7-a1d2-6786f39ef675.

Shalal, Andrea. 2017. Germany Big Target of Cyber Espionage and Attacks: Government Report. *Reuters*, July 4. https://www.reuters.com/article/us-germany-espionage/germany-big-target-of-cyber-espionage-and-attacks-government-report-idUSKBN19P0UC.

Shalal, Andrea, and Andreas Rinke. 2017. Germany Tries to Defuse N. Korea Tensions, Praises China. *Reuters*, August 16. https://www.reuters.com/article/us-northkorea-missiles-germany/germany-tries-to-defuse-n-korea-tensions-praises-china-idUSKCN1AW1GM.

Stanzel, Angela. 2016. A German View of the Asian Infrastructure Investment Bank. *European Council on Foreign Relations*, April 21. http://www.ecfr.eu/article/commentary_a_german_view_of_the_aiib_7275.

Sverdrup Thygeson, Bjørnar, Wrenn Yennie Lindgren, and Marc Lanteigne (eds.). 2018. *China and Nordic Diplomacy*. Routledge Focus.

The Economist. 2017a. Xi Jinping has More Clout than Donald Trump. The World Should Be Wary. October 14. https://www.economist.com/news/leaders/21730144-do-not-expect-mr-xi-change-china-or-world-better-xi-jinping-has-more-clout.

The Economist. 2017b. Counsel of Warriors: Donald Trump's Generals Cannot Control Him. November 9. https://www.economist.com/news/briefing/21731112-americas-president-loves-men-uniform-and-they-often-give-him-sound-advice-it-mr.

The Economist. 2017c. Germany is Not the New Leader of the Free World. *The Economist*, July 8. https://www.economist.com/news/europe/21724832-angela-merkel-may-sound-tough-donald-trump-her-country-still-depends-america-germany.

The White House. 2012. Remarks by President Obama to the Australian Parliament. November 17. http://www.whitehouse.gov/the-press-office/2011/11/17/remarks-president-obama-australian-parliament.

Tocci, Nathalie. 2019. Who Do I Call If I Want to Call the US? *Politico*, March 14. https://www.politico.eu/article/who-do-i-call-if-i-want-to-call-the-us/.

Tudda, Chris. 2012. *A Cold War Turning Point: Nixon and China, 1969–1972*. Baton Rouge: Louisiana State University Press.

Tunsjø, Øystein. 2013. Europe's Favourable Isolation. *Survival*, 55/5.

Valášek, Tomáš. 2017. China and Central Europe: Don't Believe the Hype. Carnegie Europe, November 28. http://carnegieeurope.eu/strategiceurope/74844.

Vasagar, Jeevan. 2016. Britain Revives Military Engagement East of Suez. *Financial Times*, December 23. https://www.ft.com/content/3477fe5a-c809-11e6-8f29-9445cac8966f.

Wagner, Rene, and Michael Nienaber. 2017 China Steams Past U.S., France to be Germany's Biggest Trading Partner. *Reuters*, February 24. https://www.reuters.com/article/us-germany-economy-trade/china-steams-past-u-s-france-to-be-germanys-biggest-trading-partner-idUSKBN1622SO.

Whitman, Richard G. 2004. NATO, the EU and ESDP: An Emerging Division of Labour? *Contemporary Security Policy* 25 (3): 430–451.

Wilhelmsen, Julie, and Jakub Godzimierski. 2017. Spiral of Distrust. In *NATO and Collective Defence in the 21st Century*, ed. Karsten Friis. Routledge.

Winand, Pascaline. 2010. Kissinger's Year of Europe and the Europeans. In *We Are on the Right Path. Willy Brandt and European Unification*, ed. Andreas Wilkens. The Hague, The Netherlands: Dietz Verlag.

PART IV

The Future of Sino-Russian 'Strategic Partnership'

CHAPTER 13

Conclusion: Sino-Russian Relations in the 21st Century

Jo Inge Bekkevold

In this volume, we have examined converging and diverging trends in Sino-Russian relations over the past decade, and how the Sino-Russian dynamic shapes international affairs. The contributors subscribe to two overarching assessments. First, the Sino-Russian partnership has expanded considerably, and is stronger than it has ever been. Russia has moved closer to China, a turn in Russian policy that China has embraced. This shift in Russian policy became evident in the immediate aftermath of the global financial crisis, and has been further consolidated as a result of Moscow's annexation of Crimea and Western sanctions. Second, the growing power gap between China and Russia is changing the nature of their relationship, with China emerging as the dominant partner. This growing asymmetry creates new challenges. China's rise provides Moscow with an alternative economic and strategic partner, one that is able and willing to resist Western pressure. However, moving closer to an increasingly powerful China reduces Moscow's room for maneuver, not only in its relationship with Beijing but also in its wider foreign policy in the Asia-Pacific and Central Asia. Moreover, as China

J. I. Bekkevold (✉)
Norwegian Institute for Defence Studies, Oslo, Norway
e-mail: jib@ifs.mil.no

J. I. Bekkevold and B. Lo (eds.), *Sino-Russian Relations in the 21st Century*, https://doi.org/10.1007/978-3-319-92516-5_13

grows stronger, Beijing's grand strategy and role in international affairs may evolve in a different direction from Moscow's. In this concluding chapter, I highlight some of the key themes in the Sino-Russian partnership, consider its implications for the world, and suggest some scenarios of how it might develop over the next decade and beyond.

A Strengthened Partnership

During the 1990s and early 2000s, normalization of the bilateral relationship and skepticism towards American hegemony were the two dominant drivers of Sino-Russian relations. By the time the border between the two states was completely demarcated in 2008, the relationship had also been fully normalized. The United States continues to be an important common denominator in the Sino-Russian relationship. Moreover, cooperation between Beijing and Moscow has since become more multifaceted, and is today based on several key drivers: expanding economic ties; growing energy partnership; deepened policy coordination; and renewed military cooperation.

Intensified Strategic Rivalry with the United States

For much of the post-Cold War era, China's and Russia's respective relationships with the United States have ebbed and flowed. China built a close economic relationship with the United States, and Russia during the early years of the Putin presidency reached out to the United States and supported the War on Terror. Yet, strategic rivalry remained a permanent feature in their relationships with Washington, and in recent years this has intensified. US–Russia relations are currently at their lowest point since the end of the Cold War, while strategic rivalry between China and the United States has risen to unprecedented levels, despite growing economic relations.

The latest US National Security Strategy from December 2017 states that "China and Russia want to shape a world antithetical to U.S. values and interests. China seeks to displace the United States in the Indo-Pacific region, expand the reaches of its state-driven economic model, and reorder the region in its favor. Russia seeks to restore its great power status and establish spheres of influence near its borders."[1] In this new era of great power rivalry, the United States looms large in Moscow and Beijing and continues to play a critical role in reinforcing the Sino-Russian partnership.

Expanding Economic Cooperation

The rapid growth of trade and other forms of economic engagement has strengthened the bilateral partnership. At the same time, this has become increasingly asymmetrical. China plays a far more important role in the Russian economy than the other way around, and for both countries the volume of trade with the West is significantly greater than with each other.[2] Alexander Gabuev notes in his chapter that it was only after the global financial crisis that Russia started to view China more seriously as an economic partner. As the business communities in these two countries get to know each other, we can expect bilateral trade to expand. However, it is unlikely that China will replace Europe as trading partner to Russia. Moreover, Chinese corporations do not necessarily give Russian companies any beneficial treatment compared to business partners from any other country.

Russia surpassed Saudi Arabia as China's top crude oil supplier in 2015, and booming energy cooperation is one of the most important developments in the Sino-Russian relationship. Yet Russia's increased economic dependency on the Chinese energy market also represents a source of vulnerability. China has several alternatives beside Russia for oil and gas imports; global oil prices are unlikely to rebound to previous levels; and international climate change policies may further strengthen Beijing's position vis-à-vis a Russia heavily dependent on energy exports.

Political Synergies and Policy Coordination

The personal affinity between Vladimir Putin and Xi Jinping has further strengthened the bilateral relationship. When Putin returned as President in 2012, he prioritized close partnership with China, while Xi, like his predecessors, chose Russia as the destination for his very first presidential visit. In March 2018, Putin was re-elected as President for another six years, and the Chinese Communist Party's removal of the two-term limit on the presidency opens for the possibility of Xi Jinping staying in power beyond 2022/23. The "special relationship" between Putin and Xi will, therefore, remain a critical element in the larger relationship. However, the enhanced political partnership goes well beyond mere personal affinity. It builds on close institutional ties that have grown over the years, characterized by the number of high-level bilateral meetings as well as multilateral cooperation mechanisms. The formal political dialogue has been extended to include regular meetings between Chinese and Russian authorities at nearly all levels of government, from central authorities in the respective capitals down to local officials.

In addition, the expansion of cooperation in sectors such as education, culture, sports, tourism, and youth means that a traditionally top-down driven relationship is now being complemented by more bottom-up initiatives. This latter development bodes well for cross-border integration between the Russian Far East and China's North East. Sinophobia in Russia has given way to a more optimistic outlook and the realization that Chinese investments in this region are positive and even necessary.

The growing authoritarianism in Russia and China has reinforced political synergies. Both countries reacted strongly against Western support for the color revolutions in Georgia (2003), Ukraine (2004), and Kyrgyzstan (2005), and have strengthened their control over the activities of domestic and foreign non-governmental organizations.

Renewed Military Cooperation

Military cooperation between Moscow and Beijing has expanded significantly, as exemplified by the growing number, scope, and complexity of joint military exercises. Although these exercises remain relatively narrow in scope and duration with limited emphasis on interoperability, both sides see them as very useful, both in terms of political signalling, and as a means of gaining operational experience.

Meanwhile, Moscow and Beijing have signed several large arms sales contracts transferring some of Russia's most advanced weapons platforms into Chinese hands. Although there are still uncertainties about the long-term sustainability of these sales, they nevertheless highlight a major shift in Russian thinking. The weapon platforms Russia is now providing to the PLA are based on the premise that China is much more likely to engage in a maritime conflict with the United States than it is to embark on a land campaign against Russia. In fact, the biggest potential threat to the Sino-Russian arms relationship is commercial, not security. China is fast closing the technology gap on Russia, thereby reducing the need for imports. In a few years' time, Russia could find itself competing directly with China in the international arms market.

The Growing Power Imbalance and Its Consequences

The second notable change in the Sino-Russian relationship is the growing power imbalance in Beijing's favor. In 1997, when Russia and China signed their "Joint Declaration on a Multipolar World", China's GDP of USD 965 billion was only twice as large as Russia's.[3] By 2016, it was almost ten times larger. Indeed, China's military expenditure of 225 billion USD that year amounted to 20% of Russia's GDP.

This widening power gap changes the bilateral relationship and how the two countries view each other. Beijing and Moscow need time to adjust to the reality that China has moved from being junior partner to senior partner in the relationship. So far, however, they appear to be adapting relatively well. Relations between them have become closer and more trusting.

This can partly be explained by a shift in strategic thinking in Moscow. Reviewing its China strategy in the aftermath of the Ukraine Crisis, the Russian leadership came to the conclusion that its earlier "China threat" perception had been exaggerated. Beijing's military build-up was not directed at Russia, but towards the Western Pacific where it was building up its sea power and engaging in a strategic rivalry with the United States. Russia also knows that it can still rely on its non-strategic nuclear weapons to deter Chinese aggression. Finally, Moscow's diminished threat perception vis-à-vis China owes much to Beijing's policy of reassurance since the 1990s.[4] China has been careful to respect Russia as a great power and give Putin face on the international stage. China's ability to keep Russia onboard despite the growing power gap is one of the greatest success stories of Chinese diplomacy. While its growing power represents a challenge to Moscow, the Russian leadership believes that engaging with China is safer and more profitable than attempting to counterbalance or contain it.

To grasp the full meaning and consequences of the growing power gap between China and Russia, we need to view this asymmetry in the larger context of great power politics and the shifting balance of power in the international system. Today, China's GDP is larger than the combined GDP of Japan, India, and Russia, and its defence expenditure is also larger than the total defence expenditures of the same three countries. According to IMF estimates, by 2022 China's GDP will account for as much as 78% of the US GDP. In terms of purchasing power parity (PPP), China's GDP has already surpassed that of the United

States. This means that China has not only outgrown Russia, but is also emerging as a peer-competitor to the United States—a shift that has fundamentally altered how Beijing sees its role in the world.

The idea of a G-2 made up of the United States and China caught a lot of winds in its sails among observers and pundits during the financial crisis in 2008–2009, but neither the United States nor China really subscribed to the idea at the time.[5] Until relatively recently, China still adhered to Deng Xiaoping's dictum "keep a low profile, hide your capabilities" as the guiding principle of its foreign policy. While Russia has been both eager and clever to inflate its influence and standing in international affairs, and especially so under Putin, China has often tried to play down its importance. No longer. Xi Jinping's promotion of "a new type of Great Power relations" during the US–China summit at Sunnylands, California in 2013 was an invitation for a reset in relations after a few bumpy years, but it also indicated that China now wanted to be seen as a great power at the same level as the United States.[6] This core principle was enshrined at the 19th Party Congress in Beijing in October 2017 when "Xi Jinping Thought on Socialism with Chinese Characteristics for a New Era" was written into the Party Constitution. With China ready to take the center stage in international affairs together with the United States, its relationship with Russia has moved backstage, irrespective of whether Sino-US relations will be characterized by cooperation or competition.

In the "Joint Declaration on a Multipolar World" signed by Russia and China 20 years ago, the two countries stated that "The cold war is over. The bipolar system has vanished. A positive trend towards a multipolar world is gaining momentum".[7] Russia still wants to see itself as a great power in an increasingly multipolar world of declining Western power, but the international system seems more likely to move into a new bipolar system revolving around the United States and China.[8] In such a system, Russia would be a secondary player at best.

Of course, it will still be an important partner to China. A cordial relationship with Moscow is one of the pillars enabling Beijing to take on Washington, and it remains sensitive to Russian concerns about China's rise. Nevertheless, as China grows stronger, and its role and ambitions in world politics change, it might find it increasingly challenging to adhere to a policy of reassurance towards Russia.

Indeed, several of the contributors to this volume argue that the effects of the growing asymmetry between China and Russia are already evident in their interaction in various regions, notably the Asia-Pacific and Central Asia. And it is likely to have a growing influence in the Middle East, the Arctic, and Europe. The growing power gap in China's favor means that it is no longer sufficient to look at converging or diverging interests between Beijing and Moscow to assess their partnership. With increased Russian dependency on China, Moscow has to take into consideration Chinese concerns despite diverging interests.

Regional Developments

Asia-Pacific

Although Russia has raised its profile as a foreign policy player and security actor in East Asia, taking part in all the important regional mechanisms, exporting arms, executing port visits, and joining China in a growing number of joint military exercises, Russia's position as an Asia-Pacific country has never been weaker than it is today. Notwithstanding the overall modernization of its armed forces, Russia's military presence in the region remains modest. Its defence posture continues to be primarily targeted towards NATO on its European flank, not towards the Asia-Pacific. More crucially, Russia has declined economically relative to the three Northeast Asian countries of China, Japan, and South Korea. In 2016, its GDP accounted to only 10% of China's and 25% of Japan's, and was less than South Korea's.

China has encouraged and supported Russia in its quest for great power status in the Asia-Pacific region. However, this is mainly about giving Putin and Russia face. Russia's growing dependence upon China raises important questions about its future role in the region. Nurturing the relationship with Beijing on the one hand and building bilateral relations with other capitals in the region on the other hand will become an increasingly difficult balancing act for Moscow. It is telling, for example, that Russia has largely failed to develop a true energy pivot to Asia, and instead is increasingly beholden to the Chinese energy market.

Another example is the development on the Korean Peninsula. Putin hopes to position Russia as a power broker with regard to North Korea, but this is scarcely feasible without Beijing's consent. Moreover, Pyongyang's interest in engaging directly with Washington limits both Moscow's and Beijing's leverage with regard to North Korea. It is too early to tell if the ongoing talks with Pyongyang will lead to substantial changes, but in a future "open-door" policy, the Pyongyang regime would certainly want to diversify its trade and political relations beyond both China and Russia.

Arguably, the two most important indicators of how the Sino-Russian partnership will unfold in the Asia-Pacific over the next few years are Vietnam and Japan. Moscow has been able to build on its Cold War legacy and still enjoys a close relationship with Hanoi. Until recently, Beijing has not objected to Russian arms sales to Vietnam, despite Hanoi reaching out to the United States, Japan, and India in addition to Russia in an effort to improve its strategic autonomy vis-a-vis China. Stephen Blank argues, however, in this volume that Beijing is changing its position on this issue. Russia and Vietnam continue their high-level defense dialogue, with Russian Defense Minister Sergei Shoygu visiting Hanoi in January 2018, followed by a visit to Moscow by Vietnam's Defense Minister Xuan Lich to Moscow in April, but the future development of Russian arms sales to Vietnam will inform us about Russia's room for maneuver within the more asymmetric Sino-Russian partnership. Moreover, Russian arm sales to Vietnam are not only under pressure from Beijing, but also from Vietnam's growing partnership with India.

Much is said about the Putin-Xi axis, but Putin also has a very close working relationship with the Japanese Prime Minister Abe. Japan, more than any Western country, is engaging with Russia post-Ukraine. If Moscow is sincere in its efforts improving Russo-Japanese ties as a means of reducing its dependence on China, as Grønning observes in this volume, it is proof that Moscow is not willing to fully "kowtow" to Beijing's agenda. It furthermore tells us that Japan will have an important position in Russian foreign policy in the coming years. It will be difficult for Moscow to achieve a genuine rapprochement with Tokyo in the face of their territorial dispute and the US–Japan alliance, but they currently have a dialogue discussing pragmatic solutions to the dispute about the Northern Territories. If they achieve a breakthrough on this issue, it will be a huge step forward in Russo-Japanese relations. Improved relations with Tokyo will increase Moscow's leverage vis-à-vis Beijing.

Central Asia

Russia's limited leverage in the Asia-Pacific means that the increasingly dominant position of China most likely will not lead to tension in the bilateral relationship in this region. Central Asia is different, because here China is step by step encroaching upon a historically Russian sphere of influence. In the wake of the global financial crisis, it has surpassed Russia as the main trading partner of Central Asia, and become the main investor and creditor in the region. Moscow has tried to adapt to this new reality by claiming a de facto "division of labor" in which it plays the role of security provider, while Beijing is the engine for economic growth. But the realization of this vision faces major obstacles.

The number of new Chinese regional organizations and funding vehicles related to its Belt and Road Initiative suggest that Beijing is also broadening its institutional engagement in the region. Stability in Central Asia is fundamental if China wants to succeed with the land-based leg of its Belt and Road Initiative. As China expands its footprint in Central Asia, it is likely to take on a larger role in security affairs to protect its interests. Protecting overseas interests was in 2013 included as one of the core tasks of the PLA, and it might very well be called into action in the volatile region of Central Asia.

Whether a larger Chinese security presence in Central Asia will take place as a unilateral Chinese effort, or within the multilateral framework of the Shanghai Cooperation organization (SCO) remains to be seen. However, with India and Pakistan joining the SCO in 2017, and now also talks about Iranian as well as Turkish membership, it seems very unlikely that the SCO will develop into a regional high security organization.

Russia is probably not able to resist the growing Chinese interests in Central Asia, but if Beijing deviates too far from its reassurance policy towards Russia and stops being sensitive towards Russian concerns in this region, this will lead to friction in their relationship.

South Asia

South Asia is emerging as a new region to assess Sino-Russian relations, due to China's growing footprint in the region and Moscow's traditional friendship with New Delhi. India is Russia's closest partner in Asia, after China. Many Russians and Indians would tell you that Russia has a deeper relationship with India than with China.

Beijing and India, on the other hand, have not settled their border, and in addition to its long-term friendship with Pakistan, China is developing closer ties with several countries in South Asia, as well as increasing its presence in the Indian Ocean. China's rise and increased footprint in India's neighborhood have set in motion notable changes in India's defense and security policy with potential negative repercussions for Moscow's ties with New Delhi. Above all, in order to offset India's growing power gap to China, New Delhi is building closer ties to the United States, including buying American weapon platforms.

India is concerned about a strong Sino-Russian footprint in Central Asia, as this would seriously reduce its own leverage in the region. Nevertheless, in consideration of the strained relationship between Russia and the US, it will be increasingly challenging for New Delhi to maintain close ties with Moscow as it leans closer towards Washington. Furthermore, as India is buying arms from the United States, and upgrading its own defense industry, Russia's position in the Indian arms market will diminish. In fact, the Indian Air Force (IAF) reportedly wants to discontinue work on one of the most ambitious joint Indo-Russian defense programs to date- the co-development and production of a fifth generation fighter aircraft.[9] If New Delhi decides to close the door to Moscow, it would be a huge blow to Russia's position in Asia and its leverage vis-à-vis China. The role of India and the China-Russia-India triangle will largely be shaped by the new Indo-Pacific strategic theatre, as I will revert to later.

The Middle East

China's rise has made it more challenging for Russia to influence developments in the Far East and even in Eurasia. In the Middle East, on the other hand, Russia has considerable leverage and acts as a bona fide great power. In fact, reduced Russian leverage in the Asia-Pacific and Central Asia has made it even more important for Moscow to act as a great power in the Middle East.

China, too, is rapidly increasing its economic and strategic presence. With the erosion of American hegemony, a new great power triangle is emerging in the Middle East between the United States, Russia, and China. Moscow and Beijing share many views on the Middle East, but we should not expect them to agree on every issue.

China's policy in the Middle East has so far mainly been driven by geo-economic concerns. China could be tempted to act as a power-broker in the region, in similar terms as Russia does through the Astana talks. In such a scenario, Beijing and Moscow will take each other concerns and viewpoints into careful consideration.

However, if China increases its security presence in the Middle East, there is no guarantee that Moscow will accommodate Chinese encroachment on yet another Russian sphere of influence. Nonetheless, a Chinese security engagement in the Middle East—beyond UN peacekeeping or anti-piracy operations—belongs to the future. This would be a totally new "modus operandi" for the PLA, and it requires an increased Chinese naval presence in the Indian Ocean Region.

The Arctic

The development of Sino-Russian relations in the Arctic confirms the larger picture of a flourishing partnership. Russia has endorsed China's observer status in the Arctic Council; the two sides are engaged in large-scale energy cooperation through the Yamal LNG project; and the Northern Sea Route has been written into China's Belt and Road Initiative. Moscow has the role of gatekeeper or door-opener for Chinese engagement in the Arctic. An increased Chinese footprint in the Arctic is hardly feasible without Russian consent. However, for Russia to develop for instance the Northern Sea Route into a commercial sustainable alternative gateway between Asia and Europe, it would need to reach out beyond China, and engage with authorities and business communities in a number of countries in both Europe and Asia.

Although some in Moscow regard the increased Chinese interest in the Arctic with suspicion, Beijing is sensitive to Russian concerns and the key role the Arctic plays in Russia's national security thinking. Moreover, the Arctic is rather low on the list of priorities in Beijing, and China will not seek a leading role in the region. For instance, a joint Sino-Russian naval exercise in the Arctic Ocean, like the ones undertaken in the Baltic Sea or in the Mediterranean, should not be ruled out, but this would not make China an Arctic great power, and the geopolitical implications of it should not be exaggerated.

Europe

Geography makes the impact of Sino-Russian relations different on the European flank of the Eurasian continent than on the Asia-Pacific flank. No European country has to worry about the geographic proximity of both China and Russia the same way as Japan does. Nonetheless, in an international system increasingly shaped by great power rivalry, the Europe–China–Russia triangle has become critically important. NATO has responded to Russia's aggressive behavior by reinforcing its Eastern European members, but for Washington it is China's rise that represents the greater challenge to its global interests. This divergence of view presents the transatlantic relationship with a number of challenges.

One such challenge is that as the United States deploys more military capabilities into the Asia-Pacific, Europe will need to take greater responsibility for its own security. Conversely, Tokyo worries that instability in Europe will force the United States to relocate military resources from Asia to its European flank, thereby exposing Japan to China's military ambitions.[10]

A related challenge comes from differing threat perceptions in Europe and the United States. Whereas there is broad agreement about the threat posed by Russia, European policy-makers have a more positive view of China than does Washington. It said that, it is unlikely that Moscow and/or Beijing will be able to exploit such disagreements to divide the West.

Allers notes in his contribution to this volume that Europeans have to acknowledge that the regimes in Moscow and Beijing do not share all their interest in a liberal rules-based world order. While Europe's policy on Russia largely will be determined by Moscow's neighborhood policies and military posture, Europe's approach to China will mainly be driven by Beijing's agenda towards global governance and international order.

China, Russia, and International Order

The balance of power and consent towards the United States as the liberal leviathan, two of the building blocks in what John Ikenberry calls the "liberal hegemonic order," are shifting.[11] But although the building blocks in the international system are changing, this does not necessarily mean that the system as such is unravelling, only that there is greater uncertainty. Great powers still cooperate, but despite growing economic interdependency and deepened institutional links, the overall trend is towards great power competition and rivalry. It has been argued that although there is a crisis of authority—meaning that American leadership is in decline—the world order is not in a crisis because emerging powers largely agree to the fundamental and deep principles of the current order.[12]

Indeed, China and Russia have in different ways responded to the existing international system and its institutions, building extensive ties with the Western-led liberal order. But now that the latter is suffering from a crisis of authority, will they look to change their approach? The answer will be contingent not just on political will, but also economic capabilities and strategic capacity.

Russia can undermine the international order, but Russia is not in a position to reshape it. Having developed within the economic opportunities afforded by the liberal order, China does not share Russia's fundamental counterhegemonic disposition towards the West, and with its global economic interests, China has a larger stake in the international order in some form. Nonetheless, as it becomes stronger it will be tempted to reconstruct international order in ways that directly favor its interests. Already Beijing is reconfiguring a grand strategy more in line with its new, more assertive, and globalist position in international affairs.[13] It is building institutions and financial instruments like the Asian Infrastructure Investment Bank (AIIB) and the New Silk Route Fund, which are not only about increasing inter-connectivity, but are also part of a strategy of developing a community of neighboring states that will be sensitive to Beijing's interests and priorities.

At the same time, there has been a significant shift on the question of the so-called "China model." Whereas previously the Chinese authorities were careful to avoid any suggestion of "exporting" this model to others, Xi's recent statements point to a new level of ambition, whereby China assumes a global leadership role on norms and values. Moscow's response to this shift will depend on the degree of Russian dependence on China.

The Danger of Nationalism and Imperial Overstretch

The influence of Russia and China in the international system will ultimately depend on their domestic fortunes. There is a danger that great power ambitions in Moscow and Beijing will exceed their military and especially economic capacities, and lead to what Paul Kennedy termed "imperial overstretch."[14]

Russia has in later years used a higher percentage of its GDP on defense than most other countries,[15] and the securitization of Russian politics could hamper the country's economic development. The economic forecast for future growth of between 1–2% over the next

3–5 years in Russia is equivalent to the forecast of G-7 countries,[16] but from a much lower base. According to estimates from the International Monetary Fund, Russia's GDP in 2022 will be the same size as Australia's, it will be smaller than Canada's GDP, and account for only 40% of that of Germany. In 2022, Russia will possess a GDP slightly larger than Spain, Mexico, and Indonesia.[17] These economic statistics are hardly those of a great power.

China's prospects look more promising, but its economy also has its challenges, with a fast increasing debt-to-GDP ratio. Xi believes that stronger top-down governance will make for more effective policy implementation. Combating vested interests to achieve economic rebalancing was one of the reasons why he was given such a strong mandate when he became party leader in 2012. But Xi also risks strangling the very idea and goal that the he set out to achieve, by constraining market forces through excessive state interventionism.

Internationally, China is pursuing a continental as well as a maritime strategy building sea power simultaneously—an extraordinarily ambitious and difficult undertaking. It risks overstretching itself, and provoking a long-term strategic confrontation with the United States and its allies and partners in the Indo-Pacific theatre.

China and Russia are indispensable partners in the solution of a number of global and transnational problems. However, the nationalist sentiments driving the great power ambitions in these two countries could also turn, and lead to more inward-looking authoritarian societies with a mercantilist approach to international affairs. Even China, more deeply engaged in globalization than Russia, still often continues to brood on the injustices of the past instead of celebrating the success of economic reforms.[18]

The brewing trade war between the United States and China, or an outright US containment strategy towards China, could of course be the spark leading to a more mercantilist Chinese economic policy. Nevertheless, for the time being, it seems more likely that China will try to position itself in the driving seat for continued globalization, albeit one with more Chinese characteristics. During the tough negotiations with the United States in the late 1990s over WTO membership as well as during the global financial crisis in 2008–2009, critical voices within China raised questions about Beijing's strategy of market reforms and deeper integration with the international economy. However, on both occasions, China continued on the path of globalization. Xi Jinping's speech at the Boao Forum in April 2018, in the midst of US President Trump's threats of a trade war, also pointed in the same direction, that China is willing to further open its market.[19]

China and Russia: An Alliance in the Making?

In this final part, I will discuss some scenarios for how the Sino-Russian partnership might evolve over the next decade. Most of all, with China embracing Russia's eastward turn, it is legitimate to ask if we see a Sino-Russian alliance in the making. However, for the time being, there is actually little to suggest that China and Russia will enter into a formal military alliance.

Although both Moscow and Beijing view the United States as the biggest threat to their security, the two dominant countries in this triangle, the United States and China, continue to mix cooperation and confrontation in their bilateral relationship. As alluded to earlier, the strategic rivalry between China and the United States has been intensified, but the two countries also maintain close economic relations. The existing "strategic partnership" with Russia already allows China to maintain a reduced presence on the Russian border, and to channel resources into the maritime theatre confronting the United States in the Pacific. A formal alliance with Russia would add little to the current arrangement, and indeed could turn out to be thoroughly counterproductive—damaging China's hugely important economic ties with the United States.

Nonetheless, although a formal Sino-Russian alliance seems unlikely today, things could change. First of all, the United States could change its China policy. The United States has since the early 1990s pursued a mixed policy of engagement and containment, also called congagement,[20] in its policy vis-à-vis China. With China emerging as the peer-competitor to the United States in the international system, the United States might shift towards more containment, and some argue that this shift in policy is already taking place.[21] Such a shift in US policy could increase China's incentive for entering a formal military alliance with Russia, but not necessarily. The likelihood of a formal Sino-Russian military alliance also depends on the balance of power in the international system.

Since the end of the Cold War, the international system has been characterized by US primacy, also called the 'unipolar moment' because of the dominant position of the United States. It is argued that it is futile for second ranked great powers like China and Russia to balance in a unipolar system, meaning against US primacy.[22] However, with the balance of power in the international system now changing, second ranked powers might be more tempted to counterbalance the United States. If US primacy is replaced by a new multipolar system, with several great powers, the importance of alliances will increase. However, if the post-Cold War, US-led order gives way to a new bipolar system, alliances will become less relevant, since the second-ranked great powers will scarcely be able to tilt the balance of power between the two poles (or superpowers) one way or the other.[23]

Although Moscow and Beijing have called for a multipolar world order in place of US hegemony, China has grown so much more powerful than Russia that a new Sino-American bipolarity seems much more probable.[24] In a new Sino-American bipolar world structure, entering into an alliance with Russia will not add much to China's power vis-à-vis the United States.

Even with a more clear-cut US containment strategy towards China, a formal alliance would add little to the current arrangement of 'strategic partnership', and could possibly embroil China in Russia's military adventures in Europe and the Middle East. Similarly, Russia would be wary of supporting assertive Chinese behavior towards Vietnam, India, and even Japan, or become entangled in a maritime dispute in the Pacific.

Yet if the idea of an alliance appears anachronistic, some form of strategic alignment with another second ranked great power could still be useful in a bipolar system. The obvious historical precedent is the United States playing the 'China card' against the Soviet Union in the 1970s and 1980s. When China tilted closer to the United States, the Soviet Union had to balance two flanks, which proved to be a costly undertaking.

In fact, the existing 'strategic partnership' between Russia and China is a form of alignment, enabling both Moscow and Beijing to keep their common rear safe and to channel resources into more pressing theatres, the European flank for Russia and the maritime theatre in the case of China, without any collective defense obligations.

One indicator of further Sino-Russian alignment will be their response to the deployment of US ballistic missile defense systems in Asia and Europe, and the possible unraveling—or evolution—of the Intermediate-Range Nuclear Forces (INF) Treaty.[25] In April 2017, Admiral Harry

Harris, commander of US Pacific Command, recommended that the United States renegotiate the treaty because it limited its ability "to counter Chinese and other countries' cruise missiles and land-based missiles".[26] It has been suggested that the treaty could be modified to permit the deployment of missiles in Asia while prohibiting them in Europe.[27] However, Moscow would scarcely accede to an arrangement that would be viewed as entirely hostile in Beijing.

One more long-term scenario that might consolidate Sino-Russian alignment is if the emerging Indo-Pacific strategic theatre turns into two confronting blocs, between the United States, Japan, India and Australia on the one hand and China and Russia on the other. Gurpreet S. Khurana, who first coined the "Indo-Pacific" term in 2007, wrote a piece in *The Washington Post* observing how his original intention with the concept—describing how Asian nations from the Indian Ocean to the Pacific are linked together through cooperation—is now turning into a new geopolitical framework that divides Asia into friends and enemies, with the growth of the quadrilateral security dialogue between the United States, Japan, India and Australia.[28]

As for now, this quadrilateral security dialogue is only the first signs of a possible American containment strategy towards China. Furthermore, the United States, Japan, India and Australia are currently all among China's larger trading partners. Nonetheless, it should not be ruled out that the dynamic between China and this new quadrilateral develops into two blocs with a maritime based axis of democracies of the United States and allies on one side, facing the two continental based more authoritarian powers China and Russia on the other side. In such a situation, China would look to strengthen its relationship with Russia, depending on the balance of power between China and the United States. If the United States fails to contain the maritime rise of China, Beijing would not necessarily need to further strengthen its relationship with Moscow.[29] Due to Russia's relative weakness in Asia, China can really not hope for anything more from Russia than keeping its rear safe, and Europe preoccupied.

Another possible change in the Sino-Russian relationship is of course if Moscow turns, and suddenly decides that China is a bigger threat to its security than the United States and NATO. Moscow has moved closer to Beijing in recent years despite the growing power gap in China's favor. Hence, a shift in Russian policy will probably not be triggered by China's continued rise, but rather by a fundamental change in China's

Russia policy from reassurance towards a more assertive approach. A more assertive Russia policy could either be the result of failed diplomacy in Beijing, based on Chinese over-confidence, or the result of a calculated shift in China's Russia policy based on the assumption that Russia's relative decline gives Beijing expanded room for maneuver across Eurasia.

If Moscow decides to tilt closer to the West, would the United States make use of this opportunity to play the 'Russia card' against China? In principle, Washington could do this, but there are at least two reasons for why this might not work.

First of all, as Schwartz and others have pointed to in this volume, because of Russia's relative weakness in Asia it will not be able to counter-balance China the same way as China could contribute to balance Soviet during the last part of the Cold War. Second, despite improved relations with the United States/NATO, Moscow would most likely still want to keep a solid defense posture facing Europe, and it has not forgotten the history of imperial overstretch during the Cold War resulting from the Soviet Union defending two flanks simultaneously.

The Sino-Russian relationship is changing. How this relationship develops further is increasingly determined by the policies of the senior partner in the relationship, China, and the strategic rivalry between China and the United States.

Notes

1. White House (2017), p. 25.
2. China became Russia's largest trading partner in 2010, and in 2016 trade with China accounted for 14% of Russia's total trade turnover. The same year, as much as 21% of Russia's import originated in China. For China, on the other hand, trade with the European Union, the United States and Japan dwarf its trade with Russia. The European Union as a bloc is also Russia's by far largest trading partner, accounting for more than 40% of Russia's trade. See European Commission (2018) and Ernst & Young (2017).
3. IMF (2017).
4. This observation is shared by several of the contributors to this volume. For an in-depth study of Chinese reassurance policies towards Russia, see Christopher Weidacher Hsiung (2018) *China's reassurance strategy toward Russia in the post-cold war period*, PhD dissertation, Department of Political Science, University of Oslo.

5. The concept of G-2 was originally launched by C. Fred Bergsten with the Peterson Institute back in 2005. See Bergsten (2009) and Bush (2011).
6. Zeng and Breslin (2016).
7. Russian–Chinese Joint Declaration on a Multipolar World and the Establishment of a New International Order, accessed November 15, 2017 at http://www.un.org/documents/ga/docs/52/plenary/a52-153.htm.
8. For the most comprehensive analysis of an emerging bipolar world structure, see Tunsjø (2018).
9. Gady (2017).
10. For a good discussion of Tokyo's concerns, see Hyodo (2017).
11. Ikenberry (2011).
12. Ikenberry (2016).
13. Bekkevold (2018), Tunsjø (2018).
14. Kennedy (1987).
15. In the 2010–2016 period, Russia on average spent 4.3 percentage of its GDP on defence, in comparison to 3.9 percentage for the United States, and only 1.9 percentage for China. In comparison, most European NATO members are not fulfilling the goal of spending two percent of GDP on defence, SIPRI (2018).
16. IMF (2017).
17. Ibid.
18. Fewsmith (2016), p. 93.
19. *China Daily* (2018).
20. See for instance Harner (2015).
21. For example, Aron Friedberg asked already in 2012 if the US policy of congagement towards China had outlived its usefulness; See Friedberg (2012), p. 90. A Council on Foreign Relations report from 2015 advises the US to shift to a strategy of balancing China, see Blackwill and Tellis (2015). Øystein Tunsjø argues that both the United States and China are shifting their respective policies from hedging (mixing cooperation and confrontation) towards more confrontation and balancing, see Tunsjø (2017), pp. 41–68.
22. For an introduction to the debate on unipolarity in international politics, see Layne (2006), Wohlforth (1999), and Brooks and Wohlforth (2005).
23. For a discussion on polarity and alliances, see Waltz (1979).
24. Tunsjø (2018).
25. Panda (2018).
26. Harris (2017).
27. Montgomery (2014).
28. Khurana (2017).
29. See for instance Robert Ross for the larger maritime contest between the US and China in the Indo-Pacific, Ross (2018).

Literature

Bekkevold, Jo Inge. 2018. China's Grand Strategy in a New Era. *IAPS Dialogue*, University of Nottingham. https://iapsdialogue.org/2018/02/12/chinas-grand-strategy-in-a-new-era/. Accessed 10 Mar 2018.

Bergsten, C. Fred. 2009. "Two's Company", Letter. September/October Issue, *Foreign Affairs*. https://www.foreignaffairs.com/articles/americas/2009-09-01/twos-company. Accessed 15 Nov 2017.

Blackwill, Robert D., and Ashley J. Tellis. 2015. Revising U.S. Grand Strategy Toward China. Council Special Report No. 72, March, *Council on Foreign Relations*, New York.

Brooks, Stephen G., and William C. Wohlforth. 2005. Hard Times for Soft Balancing. *International Security* 30 (1), Summer: 72–108.

Bush, Richard C. 2011. The United States and China: A G-2 in the Making? *Brookings*, October 11. https://www.brookings.edu/articles/the-united-states-and-china-a-g-2-in-the-making/. Accessed 15 Nov 2017.

China Daily. 2018. Highlights of Xi's Keynote Speech at Boao Forum, April 10. http://www.chinadaily.com.cn/a/201804/10/WS5acc15a6a3105cdcf6517259_2.html. Accessed 11 Apr 2018.

Ernst & Young. 2017. China and Russia in 2017: An Intricate Path of Growth, April. http://www.ey.com/Publication/vwLUAssets/EY-china-and-russia-2017-eng/$FILE/EY-china-and-russia-2017-eng.pdf. Accessed 2 Mar 2018.

European Commission. 2018. Directorate-General for Trade. http://trade.ec.europa.eu/doclib/docs/2006/september/tradoc_113440.pdf. Accessed 2 Mar 2018.

Fewsmith, Joseph. 2016. The Challenges of Stability and Legitimacy. In *China in the Era of Xi Jingping: Domestic and Foreign Policy Challenges*, ed. Robert S. Ross and Jo Inge Bekkevold. Washington, DC: Georgetown University Press.

Friedberg, Aron L. 2012. *A Contest for Supremacy: China, America and the Struggle for Mastery in Asia*. New York: W. W. Norton.

Gady, Franz-Stefan. 2017. India Wants Out of 5th Generation Fighter Jet Program with Russia. *The Diplomat*, October 23. https://thediplomat.com/2017/10/india-wants-out-of-5th-generation-fighter-jet-program-with-russia/. Accessed 18 Nov 2017.

Harner, Stephen. 2015. Council on Foreign Relations' Revising U.S. Grand Strategy Toward China Threatens a New Cold War. *China–US Focus*, April 22. https://www.chinausfocus.com/foreign-policy/council-on-foreign-relations-revising-u-s-grand-strategy-toward-china-threatens-a-new-cold-war. Accessed 12 Apr 2018.

Harris, Harry B. 2017. Statement of Admiral Harry B. Harris Jr., U.S. Navy Commander, U.S. Pacific Command Before the House Armed Service

Committee on U.S. Pacific Command Posture, 26 April. http://docs.house.gov/meetings/AS/AS00/20170426/105870/HHRG-115-AS00-Wstate-HarrisH-20170426.PDF. Accessed 8 Mar 2018.

Hyodo, Shinji (ed.). 2017. *East Asian Strategic Review 2017*. Tokyo: National Institute for Defence Studies.

Ikenberry, G. John. 2011. *Liberal Leviathan: The Origins, Crisis, and Transformation of the American World Order*. Princeton: Princeton University Press.

Ikenberry, G. John. 2016. American Leadership May Be in Crisis, but the World Order is Not. *Washington Post*, January 27. https://www.washingtonpost.com/news/in-theory/wp/2016/01/27/american-leadership-is-in-crisis-but-the-world-order-is-not/?utm_term=.dd5d2d34b784. Accessed 9 Mar 2018.

IMF. 2017. *World Economic Outlook Database*. International Monetary Fund, October 2017. https://www.imf.org/external/pubs/ft/weo/2017/02/. Accessed 15 Nov 2017.

Kennedy, Paul. 1987. *The Rise and Fall of the Great Powers*. New York: Random House.

Khurana, Gurpreet S. 2017. Trump's New Cold War Alliance in Asia is Dangerous. *Washington Post*, November 14. https://www.washingtonpost.com/news/theworldpost/wp/2017/11/14/trump-asia-trip/?utm_term=.49064ace19f0. Accessed 8 Mar 2018.

Layne, Christopher. 2006. The Unipolar Illusion Revisited: The Coming End of the United States' Unipolar Moment. *International Security* 31 (2), Fall: 7–41.

Montgomery, Evan Braden. 2014. China's Missile Forces Are Growing: Is it Time to Modify the INF Treaty? *National Interest*, July 2. http://nationalinterest.org/feature/chinas-missile-forces-are-growing-it-time-modify-the-inf-10791. Accessed 7 Mar 2018.

Panda, Ankit. 2018. The Uncertain Future of the INF Treaty. *Council on Foreign Relations*, February 21. https://www.cfr.org/backgrounder/uncertain-future-inf-treaty. Accessed 8 Mar 2018.

Ross, Robert S. 2018. Troubled Waters. *The National Interest* 155, May/June: 53–61.

SIPRI. 2018. Military Expenditure Database. https://www.sipri.org/sites/default/files/Milex-share-of-GDP.pdf. Accessed 9 Mar 2018.

Tunsjø, Øystein. 2017. U.S.–China Relations: From Unipolar Hedging Toward Bipolar Balancing. In *Strategic Adjustment and the Rise of China: Power and Politics in East Asia*, ed. Robert S. Ross and Øystein Tunsjø. Ithaca and London: Cornell University Press.

Tunsjø, Øystein. 2018. *The Return of Bipolarity in World Politics: China, the United States, and Geostructural Realism*. New York: Columbia University Press.

Waltz, Kenneth N. 1979. *Theory of International Politics.* Long Grove: Waveland Press.

White House. 2017. *National Security Strategy of the United States*, Washington, DC, December. https://www.whitehouse.gov/wp-content/uploads/2017/12/NSS-Final-12-18-2017-0905.pdf.

Wohlforth, William C. 1999. The Stability of a Unipolar World. *International Security* 24 (1), Summer: 5–41.

Zeng, Jinghan, and Shaun Breslin. 2016. China's 'New Type of Great Power Relations': A G2 with Chinese Characteristics? *International Affairs* 92 (4), July: 773–794.

Index

J. I. Bekkevold and B. Lo (eds.), *Sino-Russian Relations in the 21st Century*, https://doi.org/10.1007/978-3-319-92516-5

T

CPSIA information can be obtained
at www.ICGtesting.com
Printed in the USA
LVHW07*1234300718
585364LV00008B/296/P

9 783319 925158